MW01199463

Lecture Notes in State and Local Public Finance

(Parts I and II)

World Scientific Lecture Notes in Economics and Policy

ISSN: 2630-4872

Series Editor: Ariel Dinar *(University of California, Riverside, USA)*

The World Scientific Lecture Notes in Economics and Policy series is aimed to produce lecture note texts for a wide range of economics disciplines, both theoretical and applied at the undergraduate and graduate levels. Contributors to the series are highly ranked and experienced professors of economics who see in publication of their lectures a mission to disseminate the teaching of economics in an affordable manner to students and other readers interested in enriching their knowledge of economic topics. The series was formerly titled World Scientific Lecture Notes in Economics.

Published:

Forthcoming:

For the complete list of volumes in this series, please visit
www.worldscientific.com/series/wslnep

World Scientific Lecture Notes in Economics and Policy – Vol. 8

Lecture Notes in State and Local Public Finance

(Parts I and II)

John Yinger
Syracuse University, USA

World Scientific

EW JERSEY • LONDON • SINGAPORE • BEIJING • SHANGHAI • HONG KONG • TAIPEI • CHENNAI • TOKYO

Published by

World Scientific Publishing Co. Pte. Ltd.

5 Toh Tuck Link, Singapore 596224

USA office: 27 Warren Street, Suite 401-402, Hackensack, NJ 07601

UK office: 57 Shelton Street, Covent Garden, London WC2H 9HE

Library of Congress Cataloging-in-Publication Data
Names: Yinger, John, 1947–   author.
Title: Lecture notes in state and local public finance : (Parts I and II) /
    by John Yinger (Syracuse University, USA).
Description: New Jersey : World Scientific, [2019] | Series: World scientific lecture notes in
    economics and policy ; Volume 8 | Includes indexes.
Identifiers: LCCN 2019003538| ISBN 9789811200908 (hc : alk. paper) |
    ISBN 9789811202070 (pbk : alk. paper)
Subjects: LCSH: Finance, Public--United States. | Local finance--United States.
Classification: LCC HJ275 .Y56 2019 | DDC 336/.01373--dc23
LC record available at https://lccn.loc.gov/2019003538

British Library Cataloguing-in-Publication Data
A catalogue record for this book is available from the British Library.

For any available supplementary material, please visit
https://www.worldscientific.com/worldscibooks/10.1142/11296#t=suppl

Desk Editors: Herbert Moses/Sylvia Koh

Typeset by Stallion Press
Email: enquiries@stallionpress.com

About the Author

 **John Yinger** is Trustee Professor of Economics and Public Administration at the Maxwell School, Syracuse University and Director of the Education Finance and Accountability Program in Maxwell's Center for Policy Research. He has published journal articles on many topics in state and local public finance and three of his books fall into this field, as well. These books are *Property Taxes and House Values* (1988; co-authored), *America's Ailing Cities* (1991; co-authored), and *Helping Children Left Behind* (2004; editor). In 2017, Professor Yinger won the Steven D. Gold Award, which is given jointly by the Association for Public Policy Analysis and Management, the National Tax Association, and the National Conference of State Legislatures to "someone who has made a significant contribution to public financial management in the field of intergovernmental relations and state and local finance." Professor Yinger also has taught at Harvard University, the University of Michigan, and the University of Wisconsin; served as a Senior Staff Economist at the President's Council of Economic Advisers; and co-directed several state-level tax or aid studies. He received his Ph.D. in Economics from Princeton University in 1975.

Contents

Part II: State and Local Public Finance for Master's Degree Students   **313**

Introduction

The lecture notes in this book cover two classes I have been teaching at the Maxwell School of Syracuse University for many years: a Ph.D. level seminar in public finance with a state and local focus and a master's level class in state and local public finance. Both classes are offered in the Department of Public Administration and International Affairs.

These notes address issues of state and local finance that arise in the United States, which has a decentralized federal system relative to rest of the world. These notes are most likely to be helpful, therefore, to professors and students in classes covering state and local public finance in the U.S. Nevertheless, questions concerning intergovernmental aid, the assignment of taxes and public services to different levels of government, and many other aspects of public finance in a federal system of government are relevant in most other countries. As a result, the concepts and public finance principles covered in these notes have wide applicability.

Part 1 of this book contains lecture notes for a Ph.D. level class designed to help students become public finance scholars, with a focus on state and local governments. Consequently, the notes go beyond the description of institutions and policies to consider the formulation and testing of hypotheses. These notes assume that the students are familiar with intermediate microeconomics and econometrics. Although the notes are not highly technical, they sometimes contain algebraic derivations and/or discussions of the econometric procedures used by various studies. A few lectures discuss policy issues that are closely linked to the research questions on a topic, but the focus is always on the requirements for good research, not policy design. The notes draw on public finance research in both public administration and economics.

The selected topics covered in these notes include the supply of local public services (including production functions, cost functions, and efficiency), the demand for local public services (including local responses to state aid, household choice of a community, and the impact of local public services on house values), state and local revenues, state and local economic development, and state and local bonds. Most of the notes are designed for a single eighty-minute class session, although a few of them require twice as much time. About half of the topics in this book are also covered in Yinger (2020), which is a collection of published articles on education finance. In many cases, therefore, the chapters in Yinger (2020) provide readings to accompany the lecture notes in this book.

Part 2 contains notes for a master's class in state and local public finance. This class is designed for master's degree students in public administration or public policy, but the notes may be suitable for advanced undergraduates, as well.[1] Almost all of the students who take this class at the Maxwell School find jobs in the public sector or in private firms, both for-profit and nonprofit, that interact with government. To best serve these students, this class has a strong policy focus. It also describes important institutions and describes

---

[1]This class has a long history. In 1976, I was hired as an assistant professor by the Department of City and Regional Planning in Harvard University's Graduate School of Design. Helen "Sunny" Ladd and Howard Bloom were hired at the same time. The three of us prepared a class in state and local public finance, which we all ended up teaching at various times. We all left Harvard in 1986, but Sunny then ended up teaching the class at Duke University, Howard taught it at New York University, and I started teaching it at the Maxwell School. In fact, I taught it every year from 1986–1987 to 2016–2017. This 31 year streak was broken in 2018 when I went on a research leave. The course notes have obviously changed a great deal over the years, thanks largely to the great questions asked by my students, but the basic organization of the class and many of the public finance principles are holdovers from the class the three of us designed so many years ago.

key research results, but the objective in presenting this material is to provide background for policy decisions.

These lecture notes cover the following topics: state and local government expenditures, state and local government revenues, financing state and local capital projects, fiscal aspects of state and local economic development, and intergovernmental fiscal relations.[2] In my experience, case studies and student projects provide valuable complements to this lecture material.[3] A fourteen-week semester has twenty-eight class sessions, so Part 1 and 2 in this book allow for nine non-lecture classes. In a typical semester, I reserve five classes for case studies and four for student presentations of their own projects.

The public finance issues that arise in a federal system are important and intellectually challenging. My hope is that these lecture notes will be helpful for professors and students who are studying these issues, either as scholars or as practitioners.

---

[2]These topics are all covered in the textbook by Fisher (2015). Although my perspective on several issues differs from Fisher's, I think his textbook is excellent.
[3]Several case studies are available at my website: https://joyinger.expressions. syr.edu/.

Part I

PUBLIC FINANCE SEMINAR
FOR PH.D. STUDENTS

Lecture 1

The Property Tax

- **Class Outline**
  1. **The U.S. Federal System**
  2. **The Design of the Local Property Tax**
  3. **Property Tax Relief Provisions**

1. The U.S. Federal System

- **The Federal System in the U.S.**
  - Broad outlines defined by *constitutions*
  - Details determined by politics
- **Units Defined by U.S. Constitutions**
  - The Federal Government
  - State Government
- **Units Defined by State Constitutions**
  - The State Government
  - Counties and (usually) Townships
  - Municipalities (Cities and Villages)
  - School Districts
  - Special Districts
    - No townships in the South and West.
    - No counties in Connecticut, Rhode Island, and the District of Columbia.

County   Township   Municipality   School District

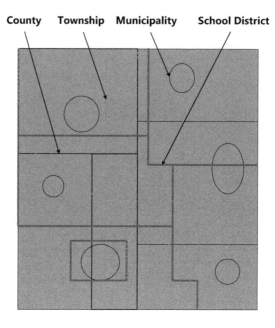

- DC, Maryland, North Carolina, Alaska, and Hawaii have no independent school districts. Hawaii has one state district.
- Sixteen states have dependent and independent school districts.

  □ Virginia has one independent and 135 dependent school systems.

  □ Louisiana has 69 independent school districts and one dependent school system.

- The U.S. has lots of **special districts**: 38,266 in 2012.
- Eight states have over 1,000 special districts (Illinois, California, Colorado, Missouri, Kansas, Washington, Nebraska, and Oregon).
- Special districts vary greatly by state; the most common are:

  □ Fire Protection Districts (5,865)

  □ Water Supply Districts (3,522)

  □ Housing and Community Development Districts (3,438)

  □ Drainage and Flood Control Districts (3,248)

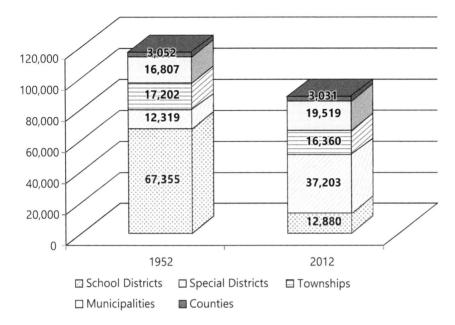

Number of Governments, by Type of Government, 1952 and 2012.
Source: Census of Governments (2012).

Variation Across States, 2012.

State	Total	County	Town	Muni.	School	Special
Alaska	177	14	0	148	*0	15
California	4,350	57	0	482	*1,025	2,786
Hawaii	21	3	0	1	*0	17
Illinois	6,968	102	1,431	2,729	905	3,232
Mass.	852	5	298	53	*84	412
Nebraska	2,581	93	419	530	272	1,267
New York	3,454	57	929	617	*679	1,172
Penn.	4,905	66	1,546	1,015	514	1,764
Texas	4,856	254	0	1,214	*1,079	2,309
Virginia	497	95	0	229	*1	172

Source: Census of Governments (2012).
*An asterisk indicates that the state has additional school districts that are dependent on another local government or, in the case of Hawaii, on the state government.

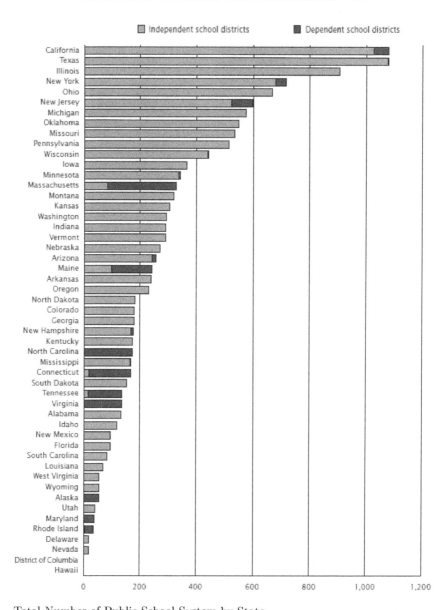

Total Number of Public School System by State.
Sources: U.S. Census Bureau, 2012 Census of Governments: Organization Component. Hogue (2013).

- **State and Local Revenue**
  - States receive about one-third of their revenue from the federal government, mainly for TANF and Medicaid.
  - Local governments receive about one-third of their revenue from their state, mainly for education.
  - Local own-source revenue comes mainly from the property tax.
  - The following numbers come from the U.S. Bureau of the Census:

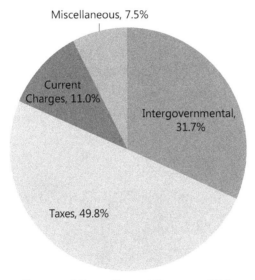

Sources of State General Revenue, 2015.

State Taxes, 2015.

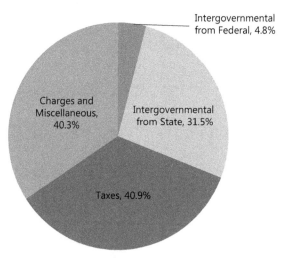

Sources of Local General Revenue, 2014.

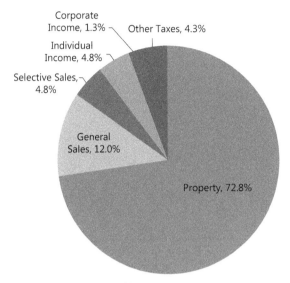

Local Taxes, 2014.

- **State and Local Expenditure**
  - State and local governments divide responsibility for education, highways, welfare.
  - About 30% of their spending is for education, often split about 50–50.
  - Highways are a surprisingly low 6% of spending.

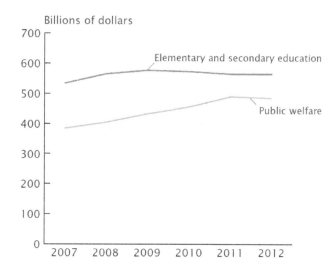

State and Local Governments Select Expenditures: 2007–2012.
Source: U.S. Census Bureau, 2007 and 2012 Census of Governments: Finance—
Surveys of State and Local Governments Finances and Intercensal Estimates from
the Annual Surveys of State and Local Government Finances.

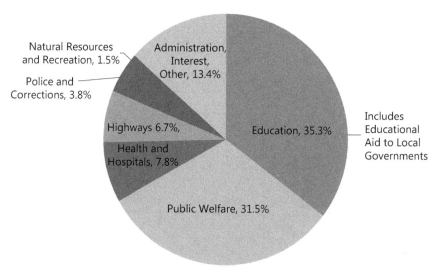

State General Spending, 2014.

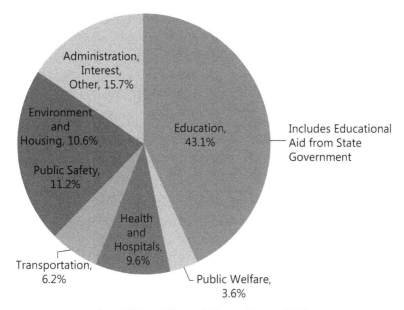

Local Direct General Expenditure, 2014.

2. The Design of the Local Property Tax

A property tax is levied on all private properties in a jurisdiction, with the exception of properties owned by non-profit organizations, such as churches and universities.

The tax payment, T, on the ith parcel equals the jurisdiction's nominal tax rate, m, multiplied by the parcel's assessed value, A; i.e.

$$T_i = mA_i$$

2.1. *The Nominal Tax Rate*

The **nominal tax rate** is often called a **mill rate** (hence the symbol m) because it is often expressed in terms of mills.

- In the dictionary, a "mill" is defined as one-tenth of a cent or one-thousandth of a dollar, so a "mill rate" is the dollars of tax per $1,000 of assessed value.

o A tax rate of 20 mills, for example, indicates that a house assessed for $100,000 must pay an annual tax of (20) ($100) = $2,000.

o A 20 mill tax rate corresponds to a 2% tax rate, so one can also say that a mill equals one-tenth of a percent.

• The mill rate is usually set by **local elected officials**, such as the school board or the mayor and the city council.

o In some cases, particularly in school districts, it must be ratified directly by the voters.

o As discussed below, many states place some limits on property tax rates and may entirely eliminate local control.

2.2. *Assessment*

• The base of a property tax is property wealth, or at least property wealth in the form of real estate.

• The market value of property (V, the amount the property could command in a competitive market) is an objective measure of this wealth.

• The administrative problem is that V is not observed unless the property is sold in a competitive market, which is not true for most properties in most years.

• This problem is solved through a **tax assessor**, who must estimate the market value of every property in every year. This estimate is called assessed value, A.

• In a few states, the property tax also applies to some types of personal property or to business inventories and equipment.

2.2.1. *Assessing method*

An assessor has three principal methods for estimating the market value of a property.

• The **market data method** has three steps:

o collect information on houses that sold along with information on property and neighborhood characteristics for all houses;

o run a regression analysis of sales price on property and neighborhood characteristics for houses that sold; and

o predict the sales prices of houses that did not sell on the basis of their property and neighborhood characteristics and the estimated impact of those characteristics on sales price.

This approach works best when many sales can be observed, as for residential property in a large suburb; sometimes simple comparisons replace regression analysis.

- The **income method** estimates the market value of a property based on the income it generates.

  o The market value of any asset, which is what a willing buyer would pay for it, is the present value of the sum of net benefits from owing it.

  o Information on the flow of net benefits and on the discount rate can therefore be used to calculate a market value.

  o This tool is particularly useful for rental property, such as an apartment building, because this type of property rarely sells but generates a clear stream of rental benefits.

  o We will explore algebra behind this type of calculation when we study property tax capitalization later in the class.

- The **cost method** estimates the market value of property based on the average cost per square foot of building a comparable building.

  o With this tool, the cost of land must be added separately, and adjustments must be made for depreciation and obsolescence.

  o The conceptual foundation for this approach comes from a basic result in microeconomics, namely, that in a competitive market, the long-run equilibrium price of a product is the minimum point on its long-run average cost curve.

  o This approach is best suited for properties, such as factories, that do not sell very often and that do not have easily predicted flows of net benefits. In some cases, however, this approach produces surprisingly accurate results even for residential property.

2.2.2. *The effective property tax rate*

Regardless of method or assessor qualifications, however, assessment quality still varies from one jurisdiction to the next.

- Moreover, it often varies within a jurisdiction.
- As result,
  - o the mill rate in one jurisdiction is not necessarily comparable to the mill rate in another jurisdiction,
  - o and the fact that two houses in the same jurisdiction pay the same mill rate does not imply that they face the same tax burden.
- To facilitate comparisons across properties, both within and across jurisdictions, we need another concept, namely the **effective property tax rate**.
- The effective property tax rate, t, is defined to be the tax payment, T, as a share of the market value of a property, V. For the ith parcel,

$$t_i \equiv \frac{T_i}{V_i}$$

- Remember that assessed value, A, is only an estimate of V, so A may not equal V, and

$$t_i \equiv \frac{T_i}{V_i} = \frac{mA_i}{V_i} = m\left(\frac{A_i}{V_i}\right)$$

- Now consider two jurisdictions with the same mill rate, one which sets assessments at 50% of market value and the other which sets assessments at 100% of market value.

  - o Clearly the real burden of the property tax, t, is only half as large in the first jurisdiction, because, in effect, only half of the market value of each property is being taxed.

- Similarly, even within a jurisdiction where all the properties face the same mill rate, unequal assessment practices can lead to higher effective tax rates on some properties than on others.

- This equation provides a general way to correct for assessment practices when comparing effective tax rates both across two jurisdictions and between any two properties in the same jurisdiction.

2.3. *Assessing Quality*

Although assessors are elected officials in some places, the level of professionalism in assessing has increased steadily overtime.

As a result, the quality of assessing, in terms of its accuracy in predicting market values, has also increased.

This trend is the result of pressure from voters for more fair and accurate assessments, of policies in some states that encourage or require assessment enhancements, and of improved assessing methods.

- Assessing practices affect variation in the A/V ratio within a jurisdiction.
- This variation can cause horizontal inequity (unequal treatment of taxpayers with the same house value) and vertical inequity (higher tax rates for taxpayers with lower house values).

Vertical inequity can arise, for example, when A is held fixed over time due to a lack of reassessment, but V increases more rapidly in rich neighborhoods than in poor neighborhoods.

- As a result, the assessing profession and many states set standards for assessment accuracy.
- The quality of assessments within a jurisdiction is determined by the extent to which the A/V ratio is **uniform**.

Assessments can be fair if all houses are assessed at 10% of their market value or at 100% of their market value, but they are not fair if some houses are assessed at 10% while others are assessed at 100%.

- The most widely used measure of assessment uniformity is the **coefficient of dispersion or COD**, which is defined by

$$\text{COD} = \frac{100}{M} \left(\frac{\sum_i \left| \frac{A_i}{V_i} - M \right|}{N} \right)$$

where A_i/V_i is the A/V ratio for the ith parcel, M is the median A/V ratio, and N is the number of parcels.

- Many states impose requirements on local assessing, such as a mandated A/V ratio.
- As shown earlier, t is unaffected by lowering the A/V ratio and raising m by the same percentage.

It is perhaps not surprising, therefore, that many states do not require 100% assessment.

Tae Ho Eom (*Pub. Budgeting & Fin.*, 2008; based on his Maxwell dissertation) reports that about 44% of the states call for 100% assessment, whereas other states call for A/V ratios from 4.5% (North Dakota) to 70% (Connecticut).

- As we will see, however, deviations from 100% assessment some-times do have behavioral consequences.
- Eom (2008) reports that actual average A/V ratios often fall below the target set by the state.
- Perhaps the most important determinant of the deviation between the target and actual ratio — and of assessment accuracy — is the state's requirement for the frequency of **reassessment**, also called **revaluation**, which is a comprehensive updating of the assessed values in a jurisdiction.

Thirteen states require annual reassessment, 26 states require reassessment at a longer interval, and nine states leave reassessment up to the local taxing jurisdiction. (The other two states did not respond to this survey.)

- When reassessment does not take place for many years, the numerator of the A/V ratio stays fixed while the denominator rises.

As a result, states that allow along time between reassessments tend to have average A/V ratios well below the target set by the state.

- One troubling twist to this issue arises in states with assessment caps, which set a maximum percentage increase in a property owner's assessed value.

    Proposition 13 in California limits assessment increases to 2% per year starting in 1975, but re-sets assessed values to market values upon resale.

- With a 2% assessment limit, people who have remained in the same house for 40 years have seen their assessments rise by $[(1.02)^{40}-1] = 120.8\%$, whereas people who move into a house after 40 years of 10% annual housing appreciation (this is California!) face an assessment (equal to market price) that has increased $[(1.10)^{40} - 1] = 4,425.9\%$.

    If these two houses had the same A and V to begin with, then the owner of the second house faces a property tax payment (and an effective property tax rate), that is $4,425.9/120.8 = 36.6$ times as high as that of the first house!

- The U.S. Supreme Court has ruled that this type of tax variation based on length of residency is legal. For more details, see Sexton, Sheffrin & O'Sullivan (NTJ, 1999).
- New York has a weakly enforced requirement for re-assessment every 4 years and does not require a particular A/V ratio.
- In New York in 1999, only 50% of assessing jurisdictions had revalued within the previous 5 years and 18% of these jurisdictions had not revalued in the previous 20 years (Eom, 2008).
- Nevertheless, even in New York the accuracy or assessments and the frequency of reassessments has been going up over time. See: https://www.tax.ny.gov/research/property/reports/cod/201 3mvs/index.htm.

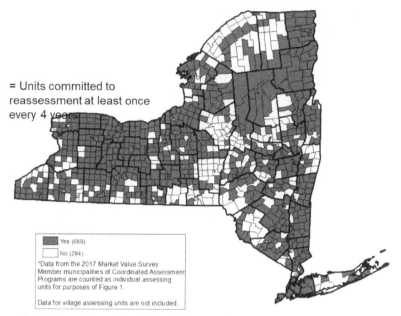

New York State Assessing Units Meeting State Guidelines for All-Property Assessment Uniformity.

Source: https://www.tax.ny.gov/research/property/reports/cod/2017mvs/index. htm.

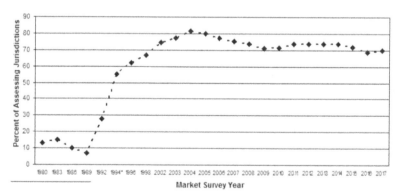

* In measuring assessment equity for 1994 and subsequent survey years, acceptable levels of the coefficient of dispersion (COD) statistic were increased for the more rural assessing units. Recent reassessment programs that were reviewed and verified for the 1996 and subsequent surveys were deemed uniform.

Percent of County, City and Town Assessing Jurisdictions with Assessment Uniformly, 1980–2017.

Source: https://www.tax.ny.gov/research/property/reports/cod/2017mvs/index. htm.

○ The resulting average A/V ratios in New York State (same source as above) are:

Level of Assessment, as Measured by 2013 State Equalization Rate.

Level of Assessment	Number of Assessing Units*
0.00–10.00	56 (5.7%)
10.01–25.00	33 (3.4%)
25.01–50.00	48 (4.9%)
50.01–75.00	143 (14.6%)
75.01–100.00	667 (68.0%)
Greater than 100.00	34 (3.4%)
Total	981 (100%)

*Data for the individual municipalities within a Coordinated Assessment Program (CAP) are reported. Data for special assessing units of Nassau County and New York City are excluded.

2.4. *Variation in Property Tax Design*

• In virtually every state, the basic design of a property tax is altered in one way or another.
• One state, Minnesota, uses a progressive rate structure; many states use.
• Classification.
• Tax relief measures.
• Tax limitations.
• Property tax alternatives for non-profit property, see: http://data toolkits.lincolninst.edu/subcenters/significant-features-property-tax/state-by-state-property-tax-at-a-glance.

2.4.1. *Classification*

- Some states allow local jurisdictions to impose different tax rates on different types of property, a policy known as **property tax classification.**
- In most cases, classification leads to a higher tax rate on business than on residential property; this possibility links to the discussion of local economic development in later classes.
- Classification can be implemented either by allowing different A/V ratios or, more commonly, different ms for different types of property.
  - These two methods are equivalent: A 20% higher effective tax rate (t) for business, for example, ca be implemented either by multiplying m by 1.2 or by multiplying (A/V) by 1.2.
- Poor assessment practices often lead to a higher t on business than on residential property, even without classification.
  - In the case of poor assessments, however, businesses can appeal their relatively high assessments and often receive large settlements from the taxing jurisdiction.

3. Property Tax Relief Provisions

Most states provide property tax relief to aid certain taxpayers, such as veterans or the elderly, or to make the tax more progressive.

- Key relief measures, to be explored in a later class, are:
  - Circuit breakers, which give a rebate when property taxes exceed a certain percentage in a taxpayer's income.
  - Homestead exemptions, which exempt the first $X of assessed value from the tax.

3.1. *Property Tax Limitations*

Many states also have some type of limitation on property tax rates, property tax revenue, the change in property tax revenue, the change in spending, or the change in assessments.

We will explore some of these provisions in later classes.

A former Maxwell colleague, Sharon Kioko (now at the University of Washington), is an experton this topic. See Kioko (2011).

3.2. *Treatment of Non-Profit Property*

All states exempt property owned by non-profit organizations from the property tax, so long as this property is used for non-profit purposes.

Moreover, some cities have a great deal of tax-exempt property, in the form of university buildings, places of worship, or non-profit organizations.

• The figure, "Estimated value of exempt property owned by non-profits as a percent of total property value", gives some examples:

The presence of tax-exempt property is a challenge for cities because many non-profit organizations use public services, such as streets, trash collection, and police and fire protection.

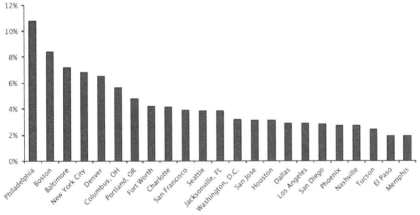

Estimated Value of Exempt Property Owned by Nonprofits as a Percent of Total Property Value (2006).

Notes: These statistics should be viewed as rough estimates. Policymakers should exercise caution when drawing conclusions from these data, because the quality of assessments of exempt property is wide-ranging and often unreliable.

Source: Lipman (2006).

As a result, many cities make other arrangements, such as:

- Special property tax assessments for certain services (e.g. sewer hook-ups).
- Fees for services.
- Negotiated payments in lieu of taxes (PILOTs), or
- Negotiated services in lieu of taxes.

For more on this topic, see the report by Kenyon and Langley (2010) at: https://www.lincolninst.edu/publications/policy-focus-reports/payments-lieu-taxes.

3.3. *The Determinants of Assessment Quality*

- Now we get to research.
- Eom (2008) provides a detailed analysis of the determinants of assessment uniformity, as measured by the COD.
- Using data for assessment districts in New York State in 1992, he regresses the residential COD on
  - the number of years since the last reassessment in the district,
  - whether any reassessment took place in the district during the sample period,
  - the average A/V ratio in the district,
  - the (log of) the number of residential properties,
  - the (log of) the assessor's salary,
  - whether the assessor is elected (instead of appointed), and
  - an extensive list of other explanatory variables, which are not considered here.

Eom treats the following variables as endogenous:

- The number of years since the last reassessment in the district.
- Whether any reassessment took place in the district during the sample period.
- The average A/V ratio in the district.
- The (log of) the assessor's salary.

His instruments are as follows:

- County average reassessment lag.
- Share of no-revaluation assessing units in the county.
- County average equalization rate.
- County population.
- Log of county average manufacturing wage.
- Log of county average wage in all occupations.

3.3.1. *A methodological aside: Selecting instruments*

We will often encounter endogenous variables (and instrumental variable fixes) in this class.

We can evaluate instruments with four tests, which will be developed more fully in later classes.

- Test 1. The instrument(s) must make conceptual sense.
- Test 2. The instrument(s) must help explain the endogenous variable.
- Test 3. The instrument(s) must not have a direct impact on the dependent variable.
- Test 4. The instrument(s) must not be "weak".

Determinants of Residential Assessment Uniformity (New York Assessing Units, 1992).

S. No.	Variables	Coefficients (*t*-statistics)	β-coefficients
	Reassessment lag[a]	**−0.016** [2.147]**	−0.312
1	Dummy for no revaluation[a]	**−0.260** [1.861]*	−0.230
2	Equalization rates[a]	**0.219** [1.740]*	0.166
3	Log of number of residential properties	**0.058** [2.375]**	0.125
4	Dummy for units contracting assessment	**−0.193** [3.477]***	−0.096
	Median house value as a share of median income	0.044 [2.360]**	0.115
	Median tax share	**0.201** [4.854]***	0.303
	Share of adults with college or higher eduction	**1.489** [4.418]***	0.169
	Share of commercial and industrial property	−0.147 [1.039]	−0.033
	Log of interaction between income and tax share	−0.160 [2.376]**	−0.191
5	Log of operating assessment budget per parcel[a]	**0.109** [2.909]***	0.122
	Dummy for elected assessor (I = yes)	0.019 [0.537]	0.015
	Share of vacant houses	**−0.322** [2.042]**	−0.103
	Share of houses in urbanized area	0.142 [2.196]**	0.091

Header spanning: **Dependent Variable: Residential Assessment Uniformity (−ln(COD))**

[a]Treated as endogenous variables. Significance level: * = 10%, ** = 5%, *** = 1%.

3.3.2. *Eom's instruments*

Eom's instruments seem to pass the first two tests.

- They make conceptual sense.
- They are significant in the first-stage regression.

They do not appear to directly impact assessment quality, so they seem to pass the third test.

This claim cannot be formally tested. Various tests can determine if an instrument (or set of instruments) is exogenous under the assumption that another instrument is exogenous, but there is no general test.

They may or may not pass the fourth test.

The weak instrument issue is fairly new. Scholars used to use as many instruments as possible, but this can cause serious bias. Weak instrument tests are now available.

- Eom's principal results are:
  - Assessment uniformity declines with the time since the last revaluation.
  - Assessment uniformity is lower in districts that did not revalue in the sample period than in districts that did (10%).
    - More frequent reassessment leads to more assessment uniformity!
  - Assessment uniformity increases with the average A/V ratio (10%).
    - Lower A/V ratios facilitate deviations from uniform assessments, perhaps because the link between A and V is much easier to observe when the A/V ratio is close to 100%.
  - The technology of assessing is characterized by large economies of scale.
    - The greater the number of parcels, the greater the assessment uniformity, all else equal.
    - States should consolidate assessing districts!

- These economies of scale have also been found by other studies, including Sjoquist and Walker (*NTJ*, 1999).
- ○ Assessment uniformity increases with the salary of the assessor.
  - Because salary is treated as an endogenous variable, this result suggests that districts with exogenous traits that make them willing to pay more to attract a higher-skilled assessor are rewarded with more uniform assessments.

3.4. *Property Tax Limitations*

Another big topic in the property tax literature is property tax limitations, or TELs (for tax and expenditure limitations).

Most states have some kind of limitation.

- These limitations can apply to:
  - ○ Property taxes for a certain type of jurisdiction.
  - ○ Combined property taxes for all local jurisdictions.
  - ○ Property tax increases.
  - ○ Spending increases.
- See Kioko (*Pub. Budget. & Finance*, 2011).

3.5. *Property Tax Limitations and Special Districts*

- TELs usually do not apply to special districts, such as an industrial development agency or an airport authority.
- Special districts are created by local governments; they can levy property taxes.
- This leads to the question: Do TELs encourage local governments to set up special districts?
- This is the question addressed an article by Pengju Zhang's (*Economics of Governance*, 2018; based on PAIA Dissertation).

3.6. *Zhang*

- Zhang assembles a county level data set for 1972 to 2012.
- He regresses the number of special districts on a variable indicating the presence of TELs in the county, with many control variables.
- He uses several different measures of TELs to capture variation in their stringency.

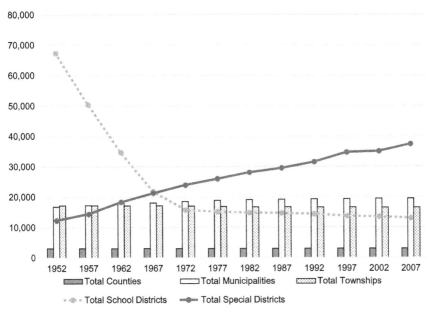

The Number of Local Governments, 1952–2007.

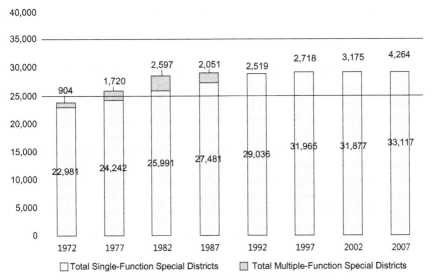

The Growth of Special Districts, 1972–2007.

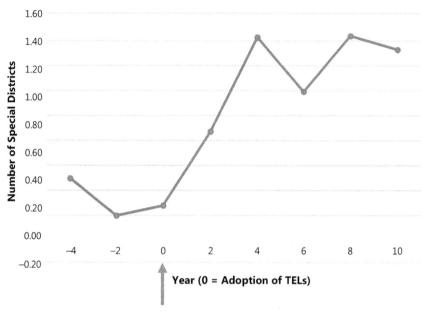

The Creation of Special Districts in Event Time.

The Structure of Four TEL Indicators.

	1 Overall Property Tax Rate Limits	2 Specific Property Tax Rate Limits	3 Property Tax Levy Limits	4 Property Assessment Limits	5 General Revenue Limits	6 General Expenditure Limits
TEL Indicator			1 or 2 or 3 or 4 or 5 or 6			
Binding Property Tax TEL Indicator			1&4 or 2&4 or 3			
General Revenue TEL Indicator			5			
General Expenditure TEL Indicator			6			

Note: This table is heavily based on discussion in Mullins and Wallin (*PB&F*, 2004).

Regression Results.

Variables	Model 1	Model 2	Model 3	Model 4	Model 5
TEL Indicator	0.567***				
	(0.167)				
Binding Property Tax TEL Indicator		0.770***			
		(0.148)			
General Revenue TEL Indicator			1.805***		
			(0.627)		
General Expenditure TEL Indicator				0.777	
				(0.676)	
TEL Index					0.0366**
					(0.0164)
Population (log)	3.475***	3.458***	3.387***	3.387***	3.362***
	(0.916)	(0.910)	(0.905)	(0.912)	(0.905)

Note: Dependent variable = number of special districts in the county; regression includes county fixed effects and many controls. Significance level: ** = 5%, *** = 1%.

3.7. *Robustness Checks*

- Add political taste variables.
- Add state-specific time trends.
- See if special districts were added before TELs were adopted.
- Add 5 year lagged state aid to account for possible link between state-level pressure that affects both TELs and special districts.
- Use IVs (interaction between the indicator of the first-wave of TELs and the relative conservativeness; the difference between the citizen and state government ideology indexes).
- The main results do not change with any of these checks.
- Like any good research, this study leads to more questions:

  ○ Whether TELs are appropriate to the extent that they effectively lower the cost and improve government efficiency.
  ○ Whether special districts are desirable to local residents as byproducts of TELs.

Lecture 2

Public Production Functions

- **Class Outline**
  1. **Why Production Functions?**
  2. **Education Production Functions**
  3. **Stiefel, Schwartz, Ellen**

1. Why Production Functions?

- Scholars and policy makers often want to understand the *technology of public production.*
- The basic idea of a production function is simple, but it turns out that production functions raise an astonishingly large number of methodological issues.
- Different scholars make different decisions about what is important.
- I hope to give you a sense of some key trade-offs today, with a focus on education production functions.

1.1. *Definition*

- A production function translates inputs, say K and L, into an output, say Q.
- A simple form (Cobb–Douglas):

$$Q = AK^a L^b \quad \text{or}$$
$$\ln\{Q\} = \ln\{A\} + a \ln\{K\} + b \ln\{L\}$$

If $a + b = 1$, the function has constant returns to scale (as measured by Q, not population).

1.2. *Duncombe and Yinger*

- Bill and I took a look at production functions for fire services in New York (*J. Public Economics*, 1993).
- We measure output by fire losses as a share of property value.
- We identify two key measures of scale:
  - Service quality (i.e. level of output).
  - The number of people served.
- We find:
  - Increasing returns to *quality scale* (cost per unit of quality goes down as quality goes up).
  - Constant returns to *population scale* (cost per capita is constant as population changes).

2. Education Production Functions

$$Y_{ijT} = \alpha X_{ijT} + \sum_{t=1}^{t=T-1} \lambda^{T-t}(\alpha X_{ijt}) + \mu_i + \delta_{jT} + \gamma_T + \varepsilon_{ijT},$$

where

Y = student test score,
i = student; j = school; t = year; T = current year,
X = inputs (= student, school, teacher traits),
μ = student fixed effect (FE),
δ = school, grade/school, or teacher FE,
γ = year FE,
λ = parameter to measure degrading of skills,
ε = random error.

2.1. *Education Production Function Notes*

- Note that the fixed effects (FEs) are designed to capture unobservable factors.

- Different FEs require different data structures.

  o Student FE's cannot be estimated with a single year of data because there would only be one observation for each student.
  o School or teacher or grade/school FE's can be estimated with a single year of data.
  o They are also compatible with student FE's because students change schools and teachers.

- As we will see, the key is to be clear about the question you want to ask and then to use the most general approach that is possible with your data.

2.2. *Production Function Form*

$$Y_{ijT} = \alpha X_{ijT} + \sum_{t=1}^{t=T-1} \lambda^{T-t}(\alpha X_{ijt}) + \mu_i + \delta_{jT} + \gamma_T + \varepsilon_{ijT}$$

- This *linear form* is the starting point in most studies.
- This form is not consistent with production theory, but works well and is easy to estimate.
- Expressing X and Y in logs (rarely done) is the same as the Cobb–Douglas form given earlier.
- However, even the assumptions behind a Cobb–Douglas form can be rejected.

  o See David Figlio, "Functional Form and the Estimated Effects of School Resources," *Economics of Education Review*, April 1999, pp. 241–252.

- Using a general form (trans-log) changes the answer!
- Figlio finds that a general form, unlike a linear form, leads to significant (but not large) impacts of school resources on student outcomes.
- But linear forms still dominate because they are simple to estimate and do not require such large sample sizes.
- These are the kind of trade-offs you will have to make in your own research!

2.3. *Estimation Strategy 1, No FEs*

- Assume $\mu = \delta = 0$ (= no FE's!).
- Subtract equation for $\lambda Y_{ij(T-1)}$ to eliminate summation.
- Lagged Y should be considered endogenous because it is correlated with ε_{ijT-1}, but some studies ignore this.

  ○ Requires two years of data for Y (and a lagged instrument).

$$Y_{ijT} = \alpha X_{ijT} + \lambda Y_{ijT-1} + (\gamma_T - \lambda\gamma_{T-1}) + (\varepsilon_{ijT} - \lambda\varepsilon_{ijT-1})$$

- The big problem with this strategy, of course, is that it assumes away student FEs (or else changes their meaning to be something that fades over time at rate λ).

  ○ Traits such as motivation cannot be observed, but they both influence performance and are correlated with included explanatory variables.

  ○ This strategy is more credible if a study has a large number of control variables for student traits.

2.3.1. *Estimation strategy 1A*

- Add school, school/grade, or teacher FE's to Strategy 1.

  ○ One must be able to link students to schools or school and grade or (rarely possible) teachers.

- This gets away from the assumption that $\delta = 0$,

  ○ But still does not estimate student FEs.

  ○ With a longer panel, one could use school-by-year FEs (or school/grade by year).

2.3.2. *Estimation strategy 1B?*

- The literature assumes that λ is the same for all students.

  ○ But this does not appear to be the case:

    ■ higher-income students go to math and music camp!

  ○ This issue could be introduced with interactions between $Y_{ij(T-1)}$ and various student traits.

- There may be a study that does this, but I have not come across it (= research opportunity!).

2.3.3. *Variation in learning*

- A related point is that the coefficient of interest, α, may also depend on student traits, including traits picked up by the FEs.

  - Addressing this problem is beyond the scope of these notes.
  - I also do not consider systematic measurement error in Y, which is addressed in some articles.

2.4. *Strategy 2, Complete Degrading*

- Assume $\lambda = 0$ (complete skill degrading).

  - Specify equation in difference form.

- Student (μ) FE's drop out (= are accounted for).
- School FE's may drop out, but not school/grade or teacher FE's (not included in equation below).

  - Requires two years of data for X and Y.
  - The γ term is the constant.

$$Y_{ijT} - Y_{ijT-1} = \alpha(X_{ijT} - X_{ijT-1}) + (\gamma_T - \gamma_{T-1})$$
$$+ \, (\varepsilon_{ijT} - \varepsilon_{ijT-1})$$

- Note that the student FE's account for all student unobservables and X's before year $T - 1$.

  - The problem comes in year $T - 1$.

    - The form of the X variables for period $T-1$ in the estimating equation is based on the assumption that $\lambda = 0$.
    - So these explanatory variables are mis-specified if there is not complete skill degrading.

- Also, with student FE's, the coefficients are estimated based solely on variation over time, which may be limited, especially with only two years of data.

2.4.1. *Strategy 2A*

- Add school, school/grade, or teacher FEs.
- Requires better data.
- Still assumes no degrading of skills.

2.4.2. *An aside on "value-added"*

- The change in a student's test score from one year to the next is called the "value-added."

  ○ But the term is not used consistently.

- Some people (e.g. one study discussed below) say they are estimating a "value-added" model when they introduce a lagged test score (Strategy 1).
- Other say a "value-added" model is equivalent to differencing test scores (Strategy 2).

  ○ Whatever terminology you prefer, make sure your assumptions about degrading are clear!

2.4.3. *Differencing vs. FEs*

- With a two year panel, first-differencing and the use of student FEs are equivalent techniques.
- With a longer panel, they are not quite equivalent.

  ○ A FEs model has a clearer interpretation and is generally preferred in the education literature.
  ○ There are some technical issues regarding standard errors, which I am not going to cover.

- So when I say "difference," I really mean "FEs" when the panel is longer than 2 years.

2.5. *Strategy 3, No Degrading*

- Assume $\lambda = 1$ (no degrading — ever!!).

  ○ Specify the equation in difference form.

- Student (μ) and perhaps school (δ) FE's cancel out; school/grade or teacher FE's do not (omitted here).

  o Requires 2 years of data for Y.

$$Y_{ijT} - Y_{ij(T-1)} = \alpha X_{ijT} + \sum_{t=1}^{t=T-1} (\alpha X_{ijt}) + \mu_i + \delta_j + \gamma_T + \varepsilon_{ijT}$$

$$- \alpha X_{ij(T-1)} + \sum_{t=1}^{t=T-2} (\alpha X_{ijt}) + \mu_i + \delta_j + \gamma_{T-1}$$

$$+ \varepsilon_{ij(T-1)})$$

$$= \alpha X_{ijT} - \alpha X_{ij(T-1)} + \alpha X_{ij(T-1)} + (\gamma_T - \gamma_{T-1})$$

$$+ (\varepsilon_{ijT} - \varepsilon_{ijT-1})$$

$$= \alpha X_{ijT} + (\gamma_T - \gamma_{T-1}) + (\varepsilon_{ijT} - \varepsilon_{ijT-1})$$

- The problem with this strategy is similar to the problem with Strategy 2 — it mis-specifies the X variables unless its assumption of $\lambda = 1$ is correct.
- The student FE's account for all time-invariant student traits and all X variables before year $T - 1$.

  o However, without the no-degrading assumption, the X variables for the year $T - 1$ belong in the equation.

2.5.1. *Reinterpretation of strategy 3*

- Some people interpret this set-up as regressing value-added on current student and school traits.
- Hence unobserved student, school, and teacher traits are interpreted as part of current factors.

  o Under this interpretation student FE's do not cancel, and panel data are needed.
  o Teacher FE's obviously still are relevant.

o This approach also completely flips the assumption of skill degrading because it ignores past X's, which is equivalent to assuming that $\lambda = 0$.

2.6. *Strategy 4, Great Data!*

- Estimate a differenced value-added model.
  - o Accounts both for degrading and student FE's.
- Requires 3 years of data (including two for instrument).

$$Y_{ijT} - Y_{ij(T-1)} = \alpha X_{ijT} + \sum_{t=1}^{t=T-1} \lambda^{T-t}(\alpha X_{ijt}) + \mu_i + \delta_j + \gamma_T + \varepsilon_{ijT}$$

$$- \alpha X_{ij(T-1)} + \sum_{t=1}^{t=T-2} \lambda^{(T-1)-t}(\alpha X_{ijt}) + \mu_i$$

$$+ \delta_j + \gamma_{T-1} + \varepsilon_{ij(T-1)}$$

$$= \alpha X_{ijT} - \alpha X_{ij(T-1)} + \lambda \alpha X_{ij(T-1)}$$

$$+ (\lambda - 1) \sum_{t=1}^{t=T-2} \lambda^{(T-1)-t}(\alpha X_{ijt}) + (\gamma_T - \gamma_{T-1})$$

$$+ (\varepsilon_{ijT} - \varepsilon_{ijT-1})$$

$$\Delta Y_{ijT} = \alpha \Delta X_{ijT} + \lambda \Delta Y_{ijT-1}$$

$$+ ((\gamma_T - \gamma_{T-1}) - \lambda(\gamma_{T-1} - \gamma_{T-2}))$$

$$+ ((\varepsilon_{ijT} - \varepsilon_{ij(T-1)}) - \lambda(\varepsilon_{ijT-1} - \varepsilon_{ij(T-2)}))$$

3. Stiefel, Schwartz, Ellen

- Production Function Study of the Black–White Test Score Gap (*JPAM*, 2007).

$$\text{Test}_{ij} = \beta_0 + \beta_1 \text{ Black}_i + \beta_2 \text{ Hispanic}_i + \beta_3 \text{ Asian}_i + \beta_4 \text{ SES}_{ij}$$

$$+ \beta_5 \text{ Ed}_{ij} + u_j + \varepsilon_{ij} \tag{2.1}$$

- Great NYC Data (70,000 students!).
  - Estimation **Strategy 1A** ($\lambda = 0.6$).
- Several endogenous variables.
- Uses FE at school and classroom level.
- Preferred models add lagged Test$_{ij}$ to right side.

3.1. *Stiefel, Schwartz, Ellen, Results*

- A large share of the black–white and Hispanic-white gaps in test scores is explained by the control variables.
  - But a significant gap remains.
  - Their Table "New York City racial test score gaps, difference from mean white student test score, based on uncontrolled regressions, 2000–2001" is just raw differences.
  - Their Table "Regression results for reading test scores, New York City public school students, 2000–2001, value-added models"

New York City Racial Test Score Gaps, Difference from Mean White Student Test Score, Based on Uncontrolled Regressions, 2000–2001.

	5th Grade Reading	5th Grade Math	8th Grade Reading	8th Grade Math
Black	−0.726***	−0.805***	−0.776***	−0.844***
	(0.011)	(0.011)	(0.012)	(0.011)
Hispanic	−0.712***	−0.724***	−0.785***	−0.747***
	(0.011)	(0.010)	(0.012)	(0.011)
Asian	−0.091***	0.179***	−0.054***	0.203***
	(0.013)	(0.015)	(0.017)	(0.016)
Constant (White	0.535***	0.542***	0.554***	0.537***
mean)	(0.009)	(0.009)	(0.010)	(0.009)
Observations	70,638	72,004	55,921	57,787
R^2	0.09	0.14	0.12	0.16

Notes: Constant term represents mean white student test score. The other coefficients capture difference from mean white student test score. Robust standard errors in parentheses. *significant at 10%; **significant at 5%; ***significant at 1%.

Regression Results for Reading Test Scores, New York City Public School Students, 2000–2001, Value-Added Models.

	5th Grade			8th Grade	
	(1)	(2)	(3)	(4)	(5)
Prior test score	0.616*** (0.004)	0.608*** (0.004)	0.540*** (0.005)	0.656*** (0.005)	0.622*** (0.005)
Socioeconomic Characteristics					
Black	−0.191*** (0.009)	−0.106*** (0.012)	−0.099*** (0.012)	−0.250*** (0.009)	−0.201*** (0.011)
Hispanic	−0.104*** (0.009)	−0.044*** (0.011)	−0.044*** (0.011)	−0.227*** (0.009)	−0.165*** (0.010)
Asian	0.004 (0.011)	0.016 (0.012)	0.011 (0.011)	−0.007 (0.012)	0.040*** (0.012)
Free lunch	−0.149*** (0.008)	−0.100*** (0.009)	−0.076*** (0.009)	−0.202*** (0.010)	−0.151*** (0.010)
Reduced-price lunch	−0.072*** (0.011)	−0.051*** (0.011)	−0.042*** (0.011)	−0.098*** (0.013)	−0.075*** (0.012)
Age	−0.029*** (0.006)	−0.028*** (0.006)	−0.032*** (0.006)	−0.080*** (0.005)	−0.079*** (0.005)
Female	0.012** (0.005)	0.012** (0.005)	0.011** (0.005)	0.206*** (0.005)	0.200*** (0.005)
Other than English at home	0.009 (0.007)	0.009 (0.008)	0.013* (0.008)	0.033*** (0.007)	0.011 (0.007)
Foreign-born	0.054*** (0.009)	0.057*** (0.009)	0.064*** (0.009)	0.006 (0.008)	0.021*** (0.007)
Individual Schooling Characteristics					
Took LAB	−1.223*** (0.074)	−1.171*** (0.073)	−1.175*** (0.073)	−0.856*** (0.067)	−0.827*** (0.066)
LAB <= 40th percentile	0.398*** (0.049)	0.394*** (0.048)	0.408*** (0.049)	0.274*** (0.051)	0.249*** (0.051)
LAB percentile	0.020*** (0.001)	0.019*** (0.001)	0.020*** (0.001)	0.013*** (0.001)	0.013*** (0.001)

(Continued)

(*Continued*)

Part-time special education	−0.156*** (0.012)	−0.177*** (0.012)	−0.145*** (0.012)	−0.275*** (0.009)	−0.297*** (0.009)
Same school as last year	0.017* (0.009)	−0.045*** (0.011)	−0.049*** (0.011)	0.081*** (0.010)	0.055*** (0.010)
Attendance	0.007** (0.001)	0.006*** (0.001)	0.005*** (0.001)	0.011*** (0.000)	0.010*** (0.000)
Constant	−0.619*** (0.091)	−0.530*** (0.092)	−0.319*** (0.092)	−0.285*** (0.089)	−0.237*** (0.088)
School fixed effects	No	Yes	No	No	Yes
Classroom fixed effects	No	No	Yes	No	No
Number of fixed effects		667	2,892		278
Number of students	70,638	70,638	70,076	55,921	55,921
R^2	0.50	0.52	0.56	0.60	0.63

Notes: Column 3 includes classrooms with at least five students, reducing the number of students by 562 and the number of schools by four. Robust standard errors in parentheses. *significant at 10%; **significant at 5%; ***significant at 1%. Models include dummy variables to indicate whether free lunch, reduced price lunch, and prior test score are non-missing.

uses Strategy 1 (columns 1 and 4) or Strategy 1A (columns 2, 3, and 5).

○ Columns 2 and 5 use school FE; column 3 uses classroom FE.
○ So adding student characteristics and lagged test score makes a large difference.
○ The black–white gap, for example, goes from a z-score difference of 0.776 in 8th grade reading to a difference of 0.250.
○ School or classroom FEs do not alter this result very much.

○ The black–white gap goes from 0.250 to 0.201.
○ Student-level FEs (not estimated) might also matter.
○ No endogeneity correction, which might also matter.

3.2. Grade Span

• Other papers with a similar methodology, the same data, and some overlap in authors are:

○ Amy Ellen Schwartz, Leanna Stiefel, Ross Rubenstein, and Jeffrey Zabel. (2011). "The Path Not Taken: How Does School Organization Affect Eighth-Grade Achievement?" *Educational Evaluation and Policy Analysis*, 33 (3) (September): 293–317.
○ Amy Ellen Schwartz, Leanna Stiefel, and Michah W. Rothbart. (2016). "Do Top Dogs Rule in Middle School? Evidence on Bullying, Safety, and Belonging." *American Educational Research Journal*, 53 (5) (October): 450–1484.

• Students do better, it turns out, in schools with longer grade spans.

3.3. Rivkin, Hanushek, and Kain

• An influential production function study:

○ S. G. Rivkin, E. A. Hanushek, and J. F. Kain. (2005). "Teachers, Schools, and Academic Achievement." *Econometrica*, 73(2) (March): 417–458.

• Great data for Texas;
• >1 million observations.
• Students linked to grades and schools.
• *Strategy 3A.*
• School-by-year and school-by-class FE.
• Assumes no degrading.
• Their initial set-up is:

$$\Delta A_{ijgs}^c = \gamma_i + \theta_j + \delta_s + v_{ijgs}^c \qquad (2.2)$$

"Test score gain in grade g is written as an additive function of student (γ), teacher (θ), and school (δ) fixed effects along with a random error (v) that is a composite of time-varying components. The fixed student component captures the myriad family influences including parental education and permanent income that affect the rate of learning; the fixed school factor incorporates the effects of stable school characteristics including resources, peers, curriculum. etc. Finally, the teacher component captures the average quality of teacher j over time. Of course families, schools, and teachers all change from year to year, and such changes receive considerable attention in the analysis below."

- Their final estimating equation is:

"Equation (2.3) describes the value-added empirical model that forms the basis of our examination of school resource effects on achievement. This is a modified version of equation (2.2) that adds a vector of school resource characteristics (SCH) measured at the grade level and a set of observable, time varying family characteristics (X):"

$$\Delta A^c_{ijgs} = \text{SCH}^c_{gs}\lambda + X^c_{ig}\beta + \underbrace{\gamma_i + \delta_{sy} + \omega_{gs} + v^c_{ijgs}}_{\text{Composite error}} \qquad (2.3)$$

"The family characteristics include indicator variables for students who switch schools and students who are eligible to receive a free or reduced price lunch. Teacher and school characteristics are computed separately for each grade and subject, and they include the average class size in regular classrooms, the proportion of teachers with a master's degree, and the proportion of teachers who fall into four experience categories: zero years, one year, two years, and three or four years (with the omitted category being five years and above). The composite error terms should be reinterpreted as the unobserved components of students and schools. Note that we have added two additional error terms: school-by-year fixed effects (δ_{sy}) and school-by-grade fixed effects (ω_{gs}). These absorb the school fixed effects previously considered."

- This paper finds significant, but small impacts of class size and teacher traits on value-added.
  - o It is famous because it uses FEs to isolate the impact of unobserved within school variation (= teacher quality) on student performance — and shows that it has a large impact.
- Other studies have matched students to teachers and replicate this result with teacher FE.
  - o J. E. Rockoff. (2004). "The Impact of Individual Teachers on Student Achievement: Evidence from Panel Data," *American Economic Review*, (May): 247–252, uses **Strategy 2A**.

3.4. *Teacher Fixed Effects*

- This literature on teacher FEs led to a revolution in education policy.
- Teacher FEs were estimated in many states and the results used to reward or sanction teachers.
- It seems to me that policy got ahead of research. Some studies showed that teachers with higher FEs generate higher student performance, but there was no clear evidence that a system to reward such teachers made led to student performance gains.
- The federal government weakened its requirements and many states, including NY, have now backed away from evaluating teachers based on their FEs.
- The literature on teacher FEs is beyond the scope of this class, but here are a couple issues to investigate if you are interested in this topic:
  - o Teacher FEs have to be estimated. Methods and available data differ. Is it possible to estimate reliable teacher FEs with data available in most states?
  - o Teacher FEs can be included in an accountability scheme in many different ways. Should they be used for tenure decisions? Should they affect annual raises? Can they lead to equitable treatment across teachers with different types of teaching assignments?

- A couple of citations on the topic:
  - Douglas N. Harris, Tim R. Sass. (2014). "Skills, Productivity and the Evaluation of Teacher performance." *Economics of Education Review*, 40: 183–204.
  - Tim R. Sass, Anastasia Semykina, Douglas N. Harris. (2014). "Value-added models and the measurement of teacher productivity." *Economics of Education Review*, 38: 9–23.
  - The latest evidence indicates that basing teacher rewards on test-score gains will not boost student achievement: https://www.rand.org/pubs/research_reports/RR2242.html.

Lecture 3

Program Evaluation

1. Why Program Evaluation?

- Public finance is the study of government spending and taxation and related issues.
- A key question in the study of government spending is whether various programs have the desired impacts.
- Today we will take a first look at the evaluation of these impacts, building on the foundation of a public production function.

1.1. *What is a Treatment Effect?*

- In the standard case, we want to know what was **caused** by a given government program — the "**treatment**."
- Another way to put it: We want to know how the world is different **with** the program than **without** it.

1.2. *The Challenge*

- The trouble is that we cannot observe the same set of people at the same time both receiving the program (the "with" world) and not receiving the program ("without").

47

○ Thus, the people who receive the program might be different than the people who do not receive it (or circumstances might be different when recipients are in the program and when they are not).

• As a result, comparisons between "treatment" and "control" samples are plagued by:

○ The effects of **unobserved** factors, such as student motivation.
○ The effects of **observed** factors that are not adequately taken into account.

• Every day in the paper you can see how easy it is to be confused about this.

○ "We should implement charter schools because the kids in Charter School X have higher test scores than other kids."
○ Not so fast. The kids in this school (or their parents) may be more highly motivated, than other kids, for example.

1.3. *Random Assignment*

• At a conceptual level, the best way to address these issues in most cases is by *randomly assigning* people to treatment.
• If assignment is random, individual traits (observed or not) are not correlated with treatment and do not cause bias.

○ Observable factors also do not differ systematically between the treatment and control groups. We'll see why this matters shortly.
○ So many studies are based on an "experiment" in which people are randomly assigned to treatment and control.

• Or in which there is a lottery (i.e. a random selection mechanism) for participation in a program.
• Or some other quasi-random mechanism.
• Random assignment is not possible or appropriate in all cases, however.

○ It is often expensive or difficult to manage or focused on a secondary issue.
○ It may be politically infeasible, as when there is a disagreement about which school districts should get a certain "treatment."

- ○ It may be undermined by perfectly legal behavior, such as teachers leaving a school because a certain new program is implemented.
- One example of a potential problem is that some people randomly selected to receive a treatment may decide not to participate or to drop out after a while.
- Hence, the people who receive the full treatment are not randomly selected any more.
  - ○ Some studies deal with this by looking at the effect of the **"intent to treat,"** that is, by comparing the entire sample of people who were selected for treatment with the control sample.
  - ○ Other studies may try to estimate the impact of the **"treatment on the treated,"** perhaps with a selection correction.
- Another problem can arise if the results of a study based on random assignment are pushed too far.
  - ○ A class size experiment (discussed below) with random assignment found higher performance from lower class sizes. When California implemented financial incentive to lower class sizes in elementary grades, school districts ended up hiring less-qualified teachers, and student performance went down. Some districts also found ways to receive the incentives by mixing grades — and lowering achievement. See Chingos (*JPAM*, 2013).
  - ○ Charter schools are usually studied based on the random assignment created by an admissions lottery. These results only apply to the set of children whose parents are willing to apply to the charter school and may not generalize to all children. Moreover, this method cannot be applied to schools that are not oversubscribed, i.e. the less desirable schools. In addition, any expansion of charter schools may run into the same teacher-shortage problem as the California class size experiment.

1.4. *Regression Method*

- If you do not have data based on random assignment (and you probably won't), you need to think about the biases from both unobserved and observed variables.

- o If you are interested in public finance, take classes in program evaluation and econometrics!
- In the case of **unobservables** you can:
  - o Use fixed effects when possible.
  - o Use an IV procedure if you have an instrument.
  - o Collect more data if you can.

1.5. *Matching*

- Matching problems have to do with differences in the **observable** characteristics of the treatment and control samples.
- The most important issue is that a comparison of these two samples can yield biased results *when the impact of the treatment depends on an observable variable.*
- Suppose you want to estimate

$$Y = a + bX + e$$

where X is the treatment, and suppose

$$b = \alpha + \beta Z$$

- Thus, the impact of the program, b, depends on some observable trait, Z.
- The impact of a pre-K program, for example, might be higher for students from low-income families.
- In this case, it is pretty clear that the estimated impact of the program depends on the distributions of Z in the treatment and control samples; if these distributions are different, the estimate of b will be biased.
  - o Matching methods address this problem by ensuring that the treatment and control samples are "matched," which means that they have the same distribution of observable traits.
- This is a complex topic, but the most basic approach, **propensity score matching**, is straightforward.

- Identify variables that predict whether an individual (or other unit of observation) received the treatment.
- Run a probit regression with the probability of treatment as the dependent variable.
- Calculate a **propensity score** (= predicted probability of treatment) for each observation.
- For each treatment observation, select the control observation with the closest propensity score.
  - Check to see that the treatment and control samples are "balanced," i.e. that they have the same distribution of explanatory variables.
  - The program impact is the average outcome (Y) for the treatment sample minus the average outcome for this "nearest neighbor" sample.
- There are many variations on this theme, e.g.
  - Fancier methods for selecting the matching sample without throwing out so much information.
  - Complex balancing tests.
  - Combining propensity scores and regression methods.

2. Knowledge is Power Program (KIPP)

- The Knowledge is Power Program (KIPP) is the nation's largest charter school provider.
  - KIPP schools feature a long school day, an extended school year, selective teacher hiring, strict behavior norms, and a focus on math and reading.
  - Overall 99 KIPP schools serve 27,000 students, mainly low-income, minority students.

2.1. *Angrist et al. (JPAM, 2012)*

- Angrist *et al.* study the KIPP Academy Lynn, founded in 2004 in Lynn, Mass.

Angrist *et al.* samples.

Lottery cohort (1)	Calendar years observed (2)	Grades observed (3)	Number of applicants (4)	Number of applicants in lottery sample (5)	Percent offered (6)	Percent attended (7)	Average years at KAL (winners) (8)
2005 to 2006	2006 to 2009	5 to 8	138	106	0.925	0.670	2.56
2006 to 2007	2007 to 2009	5 to 7	117	86	0.674	0.535	2.29
2007 to 2008	2008 to 2009	5 to 6	167	118	0.627	0.534	1.68
2008 to 2009	2009	5	207	136	0.537	0.397	0.70
All cohorts	2006 to 2009	5 to 8	629	446	0.679	0.525	1.85

Notes: This table reports characteristics of the four lotteries conducted at KIPP Academy Lynn from 2005 to 2008. Column (2) reports the calendar years (spring) in which test scores are observed for applicants in each lottery cohort, and column (3) reports the corresponding outcome grades. Column (4) gives the total number of applicants in each year, and column (5) gives the number of applicants in the lottery sample, which excludes sibling applicants, late applicants, repeat applicants, applicants without baseline demographics, applicants who could not be matched to the MCAS data, and applicants who had completed 6th or 7th grade prior to the lottery. Columns (6) to (8) give summary statistics for the lottery sample.

- Mass. law requires a lottery to select students.
- Angrist *et al.* make use of this lottery to study the impact of this KIPP school.

  ○ They match about 95% of KIPP applicants with state data on a student's scores and demographics.

- They end up with 466 applicants observed in different lottery years for different numbers of years before and after entering shown in the Table "Angrist *et al.* samples."

2.1.1. *2SLS Strategy*

"We model the causal effect of KIPP Lynn attendance on test scores as a function of time spent attending KIPP Lynn, using the following equation:

$$y_{igt} = \alpha_t + \beta_g + \sum_j \delta_j d_{ij} + \gamma' X_i + \rho s_{igt} + \epsilon_{igt} \qquad (3.1)$$

Here, y_{igt} denotes the scores of student i tested in year t in grade g. The variable s_{igt} records calendar years spent at KIPP Lynn as of the test date, where partial years at KIPP are coded as full years. This conservative coding reduces the magnitude of the resulting 2SLS estimates. The (average) causal effect of interest is ρ. The terms α_t and K_g are year-of-test and grade-of-test effects, while X_i is a vector of demographic controls with coefficient γ, and ϵ_{igt} is an error term that captures random fluctuation in test scores. The dummies d_{ij} indicate three of the four KIPP Lynn application cohorts, indexed by j. Note that application cohort is an important control variable because the probability of winning a seat at KIPP varies from year to year."

"We use randomly assigned lottery offers as an instrument for s_{igt}. Lottery offers affect the amount of time spent at KIPP and are likely to be unrelated to unobserved factors that influence test scores." The first-stage equation can be written as

$$s_{igt} = \lambda_t + K_g + \sum_j \mu_j d_{ij} + \Gamma' X_i + \pi Z_i + \eta_{igt} \qquad (3.2)$$

"where λ_t and K_g are year-of-test and grade effects. The excluded instrument is the lottery-offer dummy Z_i, with first-stage effect π. Specifically, Z_i indicates students offered a seat at KIPP Lynn sometime between the lottery date for the relevant application cohort (usually in March) and the start of the following school year. These offers were determined by randomly assigned lottery-sequence numbers. The reduced form generated by this two-equation system comes from substituting (2) for s_{igt} in (1). The reduced-form effect is the coefficient on Z_i in a regression of y_{igt} on Z_i with the same controls and data structure as in equations (1) and (2). Because the model is just identified, 2SLS estimates of ρ are given by the ratio of reduced-form to first-stage coefficients."

- They find that each year in this KIPP school boosts reading scores by 0.12 s.d. and math scores by 0.3 to 0.4 s.d. — big effects!

  o The effects are larger for special education students and students with limited English proficiency.
  o The effects are larger for students who start out behind their peers.
  o They carefully qualify their results.

- KIPP might "have little impact on middle-class children or those with college-educated parents."
- The effects of KIPP "may also differ for students whose parents are reluctant to apply to a charter school ... with KIPP's strict behavioral standards."
- A substantial KIPP expansion might not work so well due to limits in "the supply of principals and teachers who can execute the KIPP model."

3. Class Size

- It seems plausible that students will do better in a smaller class where they get more attention.
- The magnitude of this possible impact is crucial, because lowering class size is very expensive.

3.1. *Does Money Matter*

- Class size also intersects with a key debate in education: Does money matter?
- In a couple widely cited reviews (*JHR*, 1979; *JEL*, 1986) Eric Hanushek argues that money does not matter; his own work (e.g. the study cited in the last class) finds small but significant impacts for class size.
- If smaller class sizes raise performance, money clearly does matter.

3.2. *Boozer/Rouse (JUE, July 2001)*

- This paper follows through on a simple insight:
  ○ If school officials believe class size matters, they may assign the hardest-to-educate students to smaller classes.
- This behavior introduces a positive correlation between class size and performance that reflects student assignment, not the impact of class size.
  ○ The studies reviewed by Hanushek do not find that class size matters because they confound student assignment with class size effects.

- Notice the irony: Class size appears to be unimportant because school officials think it is important!

- Formally, class size is correlated with unobserved factors that influence performance, so it is endogenous.

- Boozer and Rouse have data from the National Educational Longitudinal Study of 1988 (NELS), a national random sample of 8th graders, followed to 12th grade.

  - They lost students who do not stay in the panel or who have missing information, such as race.
  - They end up with 11,726 kids from 756 schools for an 8th and 10th grade panel and 7,959 kids from 827 schools for 8th, 10th, and 12th grades.

- They find much smaller sizes for special needs and remedial classes (about 10) than for regular and gifted (about 22).

- They treat class size as endogenous and use a differenced, value-added approach.

  - Using the statewide student-teacher ratio as an instrument, they find a strong negative relationship between class-size and student performance.
  - OLS indicates that the relationship is positive and significant.

- Boozer and Rouse also find that black and Hispanic students are in much larger classes than non-Hispanic white students, all else equal.

  - Eliminating this difference this would close roughly one-third of the gap in test score gains between blacks and whites!

3.3. *Krueger (QJE, May 1999)*

- This article is a study of the Tennessee Student/Teacher Achievement Ratio experiment, also known as Project STAR.

  - In 1985–1986 kindergarten students and their teachers were randomly assigned to one of three groups: small classes (13–17), regular-size classes (22–25), and regular-size classes with a full-time teacher's aide.

- ■ Students were then supposed to stay in the same size class for four years. Each year the students took a battery of tests.
- ■ Over 6,000 students were involved each year. The final sample is 11,600 students from 80 schools over 4 years.

- Some complexities:
  - Students in the last two categories were re-randomized in response to parent complaints, which means there is less continuity of classmates in these two categories.
  - About 10% of students switched between small and regular classes between grades, usually in response to parental complaints.
  - Class sizes were hard to control because some students moved during the year. So the small classes were 11–20 and the regular classes were 15–30.
  - There was attrition from the sample.

- Krueger estimates an education production function with test score as the dependent variable and with school-level fixed effects.
  - He includes a variable for SMALL class type.

- Randomization buys a lot: There is no correlation between SMALL and unobservables, unless it is due to departures from the randomization procedure.
- The impact of SMALL is significant and positive in K, 1, 2, and 3.
- He also estimates a 2SLS model.
  - The first stage predicts class size based on assignment to SMALL and other things.
  - The impact of (predicted) class size is negative and significant for every grade.

- Other results:
  - Pooling across grades does not alter the results.
  - A value-added version (only possible for some grades) yields the same results.
  - The impacts are very significant economically, with benefits at least equal to costs.

3.4. *Krueger and Whitmore (EJ, January 2001)*

- Krueger and Whitmore (2000) find class-size effects (based on STAR) that decline over time but persist through 8th grade.
- Small classes also raise the probability of taking a college entrance exam (SAT or ACT) and raise the score on the test.
- They also find that despite the short duration of the experiment, it has benefits that exceed its costs.

3.5. *Tennessee STAR*

- The Tennessee STAR data have been used for other studies.
- For example, Dee (*ReStat*, 2004) takes advantage of the random teacher assignments to show that black kids do better when they have black teachers.

3.6. *Review Article*

- For much more, see the following review article (cited earlier) on class size:

  Matthew M. Chingo. (2013). "Class Size and Student Outcomes: Research and Policy Implications," *JPAM*, Spring.

Lecture 4

Public Cost Functions

- **Class Outline**
  1. **Cost Functions**
  2. **B/M/O Framework**
  3. **Issues in Estimating Cost Functions**
  4. **Examples**

1. Cost Functions

- Production functions lead to cost functions.
- Production functions indicate the maximum output at a given level of inputs.
- Cost functions indicate the minimum spending required to produce a given output at given input prices.
- Both assume maximizing behavior.

1.1. *Which is the Best Approach?*

- Although they both shed light on the technology of public production, cost functions and production functions have different strengths and weaknesses for empirical analysis.
- You have to figure out the best approach given the question you want to answer and the data that are available to you.

1.2. Cost Functions in Education

- Cost functions are ideal at the school district level, where spending and output are observed.
- A cost function, unlike a production function, can include many outputs.
- Many public policies, such as state aid, are linked to the district-level, so district-level cost studies link directly to policy.
- Cost functions do not work well for other scales, however.
- It is not possible to estimate cost functions at the individual or classroom level because the dependent variable, spending, is unavailable (and even hard to define).
- Studies of school-level cost functions run into serious endogeneity problems without obvious instruments.

1.3. District Production Functions in Education

- As we have seen, production functions work well with student-level data.
- Several studies use classroom data.
- They do not work well at the school or district-level, however, because many inputs (e.g. counseling) cannot be observed.
  - ○ Hanushek has argued (in presentations at AEFP and, with co-authors, in the *Peabody Journal of Education* (2008)) that one can estimate production functions with "spending" as the input.
- Using this approach, he finds that spending does not affect performance.
- I disagree.
- The assumption that spending is the input, implies that any equal-cost combination of inputs yields the same performance.
- Spending includes inefficiency, so this approach has a huge errors-in-variables problem.
- See Duncombe/Yinger in the *Peabody Journal* in 2011.

2. B/M/O Framework

- Research on public cost functions builds on a framework first proposed in a famous 1969 *NTJ* article by Bradford, Malt, and Oates.

  ○ They model government production in two stages and argue that "environmental" conditions, defined below, play a big role.

- They show that these conditions need to be considered in any cost function estimation.

- B/M/O start with a 1st-stage production function for intermediate outputs (their direct or D-outputs):

$$G = g\{K, L\}$$

- Then G goes into a 2nd-stage production function for final outputs (their consumed or C-outputs).

$$S = s\{G, N\}$$

- The first stage is similar to private production. Police patrol hours (G) as a function of police officers (L) and police cars (K), for example.

- But what people really care about is the final output (S), such as protection from crime.

- The key insight is that the production of S depends on the environment (N) in which it is produced.

  ○ Examples of "Environment"

  - **Police**: Poor people are more likely to be victims of crime and to be desperate enough to turn to crime.
  - **Fire**: Old houses catch fire more often and burn faster; fire spreads faster when housing is closely packed.
  - **Education**: Children from poor families are more likely to bring health or behavioral problems to school, and less likely to have lessons reinforced at home.

- Adding input prices (P) and a random error (ε) leads to the 1st-stage cost function where E stands for spending:

$$E = f\{G, P, \varepsilon\}$$

  o Now insert the inverted 2nd-stage production functions:

$$G = s^{-1}\{S, N\}$$

  o To get the 2nd-stage cost function:

$$E = c'\{s^{-1}\{S, N\}, P, \varepsilon\} = c\{S, N, P, \varepsilon\}$$

3. Issues in Estimating Cost Functions

- Cost-function studies should address five key questions (See Duncombe/Nguyen-Hoang/Yinger in AEFP Handbook).
  o What is the output?
  o What is the best way to account for inefficiency?
  o What student traits should be included?
  o How should the endogeneity of output and wages be handled?
  o What is the best functional form?

3.1. *Picking the Output*

- Public services are often complex and output measures (S) are often difficult to find.
- Some studies use determinants of voter demand for the output, such income, instead of measuring output directly.
- Starting with Downes and Pogue (*NTJ*, 1994) education cost function studies now use output measures.
- So what are good output measures?

  o Fire: Probability of fire and loss from a fire.
  o Education: Test scores (what grade? what test?), graduation rate (based on what cohort?).
  o Assessment: COD.

3.2. *Accounting for Efficiency*

- Cost is defined as **minimum possible spending** or spending using best practices.
- We only observe **actual spending**, which also reflects deviations from best practices = deviations from efficiency ($e = 1$).
- Thus, a more accurate formulation is

$$E = \frac{c\{S, N, P\}}{e}$$

- Some perspective:
- e depends on S.

  - There is no such thing as efficiency in general — only in efficiency in producing a specified S.

- If S is defined as math and English scores, a school district that provides extensive science, social studies, art, and music may be judged to be efficient.
- If S is defined as music contest victories, school districts with great math and English scores may be judged inefficient.
- A wasteful district may be judged inefficient in everything, but waste is only a subset of inefficiency.
- The problem:

  - e cannot be directly observed.

- Several methods are available.
- Include variables that determine e (examples below).
- Use data envelopment analysis (e.g. D/Y, *NTJ*, June 1998).
- Use stochastic frontiers analysis (e.g. Gronberg, Janson, and Taylor, *PJE*, 2011).
- Use district fixed effects (Downes and Pogue, *NTJ*, 1994).
- Key assumptions:

  - 1st Approach: Can identify variables that influence e.
  - 2nd Approach: The functional form restrictions in DEA are correct.

- o 3rd Approach: e is not correlated with observable factors in the cost regression.
- o 4th Approach: Ignores efficiency factors that vary over time.

3.3. Student Traits

- Many student traits might affect costs, including:
  - o Coming from a family below the poverty line.
  - o Speaking English as a second language.
  - o Being an immigrant.
  - o Having special needs.
- Enrollment also matters; most studies find a U-shaped link between enrollment and costs.

3.4. Cost Indexes and Pupil Weights

- In some applications (including the demand models considered in a later class), it is helpful to have a cost index for each district.
- Cost indexes are equivalent (exactly in some cases) to pupil weights plus a teacher-cost adjustment.
- This is our next topic.

3.5. Functional Form

- Most studies use a multiplicative cost function for spending per pupil:

$$E = S^{\alpha} N^{\beta} P^{\gamma} \varepsilon^{\delta}$$
$$\ln\{E\} = \alpha\ln\{S\} + \beta\ln\{N\} + \gamma\ln\{P\} + \delta\ln\{\varepsilon\}$$

- But a few studies use trans-log or some other more general method; these methods require larger sample sizes than are generally available.

3.6. Endogeneity

- Performance is endogenous because it is a product of the same set of decisions (and unobserved district traits) as is spending.

- Teacher wages are endogenous because they may reflect unobserved district traits that affect both bargaining and spending.
- Instruments for performance are difficult to come by.

  ○ Bill Duncombe and I draw on the "copy-cat" or "yardstick" theory, which is that districts are influenced by the decisions of similar districts.

- Our instruments are exogenous characteristics of comparison districts.
- We do not use choices by comparison districts because the copy-cat theory says causation runs in both directions!!!
- We do not use traits of neighboring districts, because these traits might reflect household sorting across districts in response to performance.
- Some other scholars use the number of districts or the presence of private schools as indicators of competition.
- Instruments for wages are not so difficult to find.
- First, make the wage variable comparable across districts by controlling for teacher experience.

  ○ Use starting wages or wages at a certain level of experience.

- Then use some measure of private sector wages as an instrument.

  ○ Private sector wages in a particular sector or occupation roughly comparable to teaching.
  ○ Metropolitan area population, which clearly affects wages.

4. Examples

4.1. *Duncombe/Yinger, ITPF, 2011*

- A study of school districts in California.
- Data for 2003–2004 and 2004–2005 are pooled; year fixed effects.

  ○ District fixed effects are not included because there is not enough over-time variation to estimate the model's coefficients.

- The instruments for S come from the copy-cat (or yardstick competition) theory.

Expenditure Equation Estimates for California School Districts (2003–2004 and 2004–2005).

Variables	OLS		2SLS		Fuller L1ML ($\alpha = 1$)	
	Coefficient	t-statistic	Coefficient	t-statistic	Coefficient	t-statistic
Intercept	2.0997*	1.73	−17.8712**	−3.52	−18.6749**	−4.67
Academic Performance Index	0.2992**	1.98	2.6294**	3.78	2.7390**	5.05
Cost variables						
Predicted minimum teacher salaries	0.3079**	5.79	0.9055**	2.14	0.9193**	2.76
Share of free lunch students	−0.0004	−0.87	0.0052**	2.95	0.0054**	3.89
Share of limited English language students	0.0041**	6.98	0.0052**	4.76	0.0052**	6.17
Share of disabled students out of classroom 80% of the time	0.0052	0.67	0.0197**	2.17	0.0204**	2.84
Enrollment	−0.1756**	−7.50	−0.1813**	−5.00	−0.1811**	−6.11
Enrollment squared	0.0087**	5.78	0.0083**	3.57	0.0083**	4.40
Percent 3-year enrollment change if positive	−0.0952**	−4.34	−0.0872**	−3.54	−0.0868**	−3.91
Percent 3-year enrollment change if negative	−0.3417**	−4.21	−0.3688**	−3.23	−0.3699**	−3.96
Elementary district (1 = yes)	−0.0719**	−4.42	−0.2014**	−5.33	−0.2071**	−7.15
High school district (1 = yes)	0.0028	0.10	0.1576	2.34	0.1655**	3.18
Variables Associated with Voters' Incentives						
Median earnings (2000)	0.1832**	5.44	−0.0030	−0.05	−0.0105	−0.21
Revenue limit components of adjusted income	1.0179**	7.54	1.0871**	6.45	1.0900**	8.28
Categorical aid component of adjusted income	−0.4152**	−2.61	−0.4701*	−1.90	−0.4703**	−2.10
Federal aid component of adjusted income	0.8167**	4.42	0.6781**	2.56	0.6717**	3.05

(Continued)

(Continued)

	OLS		2SLS		Fuller L1ML ($\alpha = 1$)	
Variables	Coefficient	*t*-statistic	Coefficient	*t*-statistic	Coefficient	*t*-statistic
Parcels per pupil (inverse of tax price)	0.0486**	4.44	0.0377**	2.43	0.0373**	3.06
Population migration rate (2000)	0.0022**	3.55	0.0016*	1.83	0.0015**	2.27
Variables Associated with School Officials' Incentives						
Categorical aid as percent of total operating revenue	0.4455**	3.08	0.6779**	3.03	0.6862**	3.80
Other Variables						
Year = 2004 (1 = yes)	0.0010	0.15	0.0803**	3.87	0.0837**	4.49

Significance level: * = 10%, ** = 5%.

- ○ The comparison-district characteristics we include are the share of students in poverty, the share of the student who are African–American, and median house value.
- ○ Comparison districts are districts in the same labor market area = MSA.
  - ■ "Our instrument for teacher salaries is the log of estimated comparable private wages in the same labor market area."
- Tests for weak instruments and instrument exogeneity.

4.2. *Nguyen-Hoang/Yinder, JEF, 2014*

- A study of school districts in Massachusetts.
- Data for 2001–2006; 296 districts.
- District and year fixed effects are included.
- "We designate all of the other districts in the same county as comparison jurisdictions; this approach ensures that the comparison jurisdictions are close enough to be visible but are not limited to neighboring jurisdictions, which might share a district's unobservable traits."

Expenditure Equation Regression Results (2001–2006) Dependent Variable: Log of Total Operating Expenditures Per Pupil.

Variables	Base (1)	Without Logged Non-School Costs C_M (2)	Interacted with Regional Dummy (RD) (3)
Cost variables			
Log of student performance	2.519 (3.55)***	2.641 (3.59)***	2.687 (3.59)***
Log of average teacher salary	0.703 (2.67)***	0.642 (2.49)**	0.571 (1.97)**
Log of enrollment	−0.235 (−2.84)***	−0.218 (−2.59)***	−0.210 (−2.75)***
Squared log of enrollment	0.01 (2.63)***	0.01 (2.37)**	0.01 (2.32)**
Percentage of ELL students	0.008 (1.50)	0.008 (1.58)	0.008 (1.51)
Percentage of special education students	0.007 (2.70)***	0.007 (2.80)***	0.008 (2.91)***
Percentage of low-income students	0.011 (3.14)***	0.012 (3.23)***	0.011 (2.96)***
Dummy variable (= 1 for grade 6–12 districts, = 0 otherwise)	0.033 (0.74)	0.042 (0.92)	0.025 (0.55)
Dummy variable (= 1 for K–12 districts, = 0 otherwise)	0.169 (3.30)***	0.177 (3.43)***	0.151 (2.89)***
Efficiency variables			
Chapter 70 aid component of adjusted income	1.650 (2.66)***	1.839 (2.90)***	1.626 (2.50)**
Log of median income	−0.001 (−0.01)	−0.005 (−0.06)	−0.005 (−0.06)
Log of tax share	−0.173 (−4.80)***	−0.190 (−5.42)***	−0.168 (−4.40)***
Percentage of owner-occupied housing units	0.002 (1.94)*	0.002 (1.91)*	0.002 (1.32)
Percentage of families with school-age children	−0.002 (−0.73)	−0.002 (−0.69)	−0.001 (−0.58)
Regional districts (RD) (= 1 for RD and = 0 otherwise)	−0.078 (−1.97)**	−0.007 (−0.32)	−0.074 (−1.98)**

(Continued)

(*Continued*)

	Base	Without Logged Non-School Costs C_M	Interacted with Regional Dummy (RD)
	(1)	(2)	(3)
Other variables			
Log of non-school costs (logged C_M)	0.084 $(2.20)^{**}$		0.222 $(2.99)^{***}$
Logged C_M × RD			−0.185 $(-2.30)^{**}$
Number of observations	1,776	1,776	1,776

Significance level: $^* = 10\%$, $^{**} = 5\%$, $^{***} = 1\%$.

- o "The yardstick competition theory indicates that a jurisdiction responds to the performance of jurisdictions in its comparison group. Therefore, we use as IVs exogenous traits of comparison jurisdictions that influence their performance."
- o "More specifically, the IVs are the average percentages of low-income and special education students in comparison school districts."

- Our two IVs for W[teacher wages] are the log of the annual average wage in comparable private sector jobs and the average share of African–American population in comparison-districts.

  - o The yardstick competition discussed previously justifies the use of the second IV, as several studies show that teacher mobility — and thus salaries to attract and retain them — varies significantly, depending on the district demographics.

- Tests for weak instruments and instrument exogeneity.

4.3. *Eom, Duncombe, Nguyen-Hoang, Yinger, EF&P, 2014*

- A study of school districts in New York.
- Data for 1999–2011; about 610 districts.
- District and year fixed effects are included.

Structural Cost Function Results (1999–2011) (Dependent Variable: Logged Education Expenditures Per Pupil).

Variables	Current Expenditures		Operating Expenditures	
	Performance Index 1 (1)	Performance Index 2 (2)	Performance Index 1 (3)	Performance Index 2 (4)
Performance measure	0.38 $(2.49)^{**}$	0.62 $(2.56)^{**}$	0.34 $(2.27)^{**}$	0.55 $(2.31)^{**}$
Cost-related variables				
Teacher salary	0.20 $(4.32)^{***}$	0.21 $(4.35)^{***}$	0.20 $(4.40)^{***}$	0.21 $(4.42)^{***}$
% of free lunch students	0.014 $(2.90)^{***}$	0.016 $(2.95)^{***}$	0.013 $(2.72)^{***}$	0.015 $(2.76)^{***}$
% of LEP students	−0.0020 (-1.02)	−0.0014 (-0.70)	−0.0020 (-1.03)	−0.0015 (-0.75)
% of students with severe disabilities	0.010 $(2.56)^{**}$	0.011 $(2.57)^{**}$	0.0098 $(2.46)^{**}$	0.010 $(2.44)^{**}$
Enrollment	−0.58 $(-2.78)^{***}$	−0.53 $(-2.46)^{***}$	−0.66 $(-3.20)^{***}$	−0.62 $(-2.90)^{***}$
Enrollment squared	0.0078 (0.56)	0.0044 (0.31)	0.013 (0.95)	0.010 (0.70)
% three-year log enrollment change if positive	−0.035 $(-8.281)^{***}$	−0.035 $(-8.25)^{***}$	−0.034 $(-8.24)^{***}$	−0.035 $(-8.20)^{***}$
% three-year log enrollment change if negative	−0.026 $(-5.21)^{***}$	−0.027 $(-5.30)^{***}$	−0.025 $(-5.06)^{***}$	−0.026 $(-5.12)^{***}$
Efficiency-Related Variables				
STAR tax share $(1 - X/V)$	−0.11 $(-2.11)^{**}$	−0.10 $(-1.97)^{**}$	−0.12 $(-2.28)^{**}$	−0.11 $(-2.15)^{**}$
Adjusted aid ratio $[(A/Y)(V/\bar{V})$ $(1 - X/V)]$	2.06 $(5.62)^{***}$	2.00 $(5.76)^{***}$	2.02 $(5.50)^{***}$	1.97 $(5.61)^{***}$
Local tax share	−0.041 $(-2.21)^{**}$	−0.040 $(-2.15)^{**}$	−0.042 $(-2.27)^{**}$	−0.041 $(-2.21)^{**}$
Income per pupil	0.036 $(2.31)^{**}$	0.031 $(1.96)^{**}$	0.037 $(2.39)^{**}$	0.033 $(2.07)^{**}$
% of college graduates	0.00039 (0.35)	0.00054 (0.50)	0.00054 (0.49)	0.00070 (0.65)
% of youths	0.0034 $(1.65)^{*}$	0.0042 $(1.93)^{*}$	0.0031 (1.49)	0.0038 $(1.73)^{**}$

Significance level: $^{*} = 10\%$, $^{**} = 5\%$, $^{***} = 1\%$.

- Instruments for student performance:
  - Average percent of high cost students in the rest of the county.
  - Average percent of LEP students in the rest of the county.
- Instrument for teacher wage:
  - Annual county average salary of manufacturing jobs.
- Tests for weak instruments and instrument exogeneity.

- Results
  - The performance coefficient (instrumented) shows that money matters!!!
  - Costs rise with teacher salaries (instrumented).
  - It costs about 140% more for a poor kid than for a non-poor kid to reach the same performance.
  - Kids with severe disabilities raise costs for other kids.
  - Costs are a U-shaped function of enrollment (although 2nd-term is not significant).
  - In the short run, an increase in enrollment decreases costs per pupil (by raising class size), and a decrease in enrollment raises costs (by shrinking class size).
  - Efficiency controls work as expected.

4.4. *Other Examples*

- Downes and Pogue (*NTJ*, 1994).
- Imazeki/Reschovsky (*NTJ*, 2004).
- Imazeki (*EF&P*, 2008).
- Review by Golebiewski (*PJE*, 2011).

Lecture 5

Cost Indexes and Pupil Weights

- **Class Outline**
  1. **Costs and Policy**
  2. **The Cost Function**
  3. **Pupil Weights**

1. Costs and Policy

- Many state aid programs, primarily in education, are designed to give all jurisdictions the money they need to meet some performance objective.
- Because some places must pay more to get the same performance, aid programs of this type require estimates of cost differences across jurisdictions.
- Key Concepts:
  - ○ Expenditure need (EN) = the amount a jurisdiction must spend to meet a given set of performance objectives.
  - ○ Cost index = an index of expenditure need relative to a baseline.
  - ○ Pupil weight = a component of cost associated with a particular type of student.

2. The Cost Function

$$S_j = \alpha_0 T_j^{\alpha_T} Z_j^{\alpha_Z} P_j^{\alpha_P} \exp\left\{ \sum_i \beta_i C_j^i \right\}$$

where

S = spending per pupil;

T = performance measures;

Z = controls for efficiency, etc.;

P = input prices;

C = share of students in a category.

- EN is the spending required to meet a performance target if non-cost factors are set at the state-wide average and cost factors are allowed to vary across districts.
- Endogenous cost factors (wages) must be predicted.

  ○ Let a tilde ($\sim$) indicate a target, a bar (-) indicate an average, and a hat ($\wedge$) indicate a predicted value (from 2SLS). Then....

- EN for district j is

$$\hat{S}_j = a_0 \widetilde{T}^{a_T} \bar{Z}^{a_Z} \hat{P}_j^{a_P} \exp\left\{\sum_i b_i C_j^i\right\}$$

- EN for the average district is

$$\hat{S}_{j*} = a_0 \widetilde{T}^{a_T} \bar{Z}^{a_Z} \bar{\hat{P}}^{a_P} \exp\left\{\sum_i b_i \bar{C}^i\right\}$$

2.1. Cost Index

- The cost index for district j is its own EN divided by EN in the average district, or

$$I_j = \frac{\hat{S}_j}{\hat{S}_{j*}} = \frac{(\hat{P}_j)^{a_P} \exp\left\{\sum_i b_i C_j^i\right\}}{(\bar{\hat{P}})^{a_P} \exp\left\{\sum_i b_i \bar{C}^i\right\}}$$

- With these forms, EN does not depend on the target performance.

2.1.1. *Cost index results from Duncombe/Yinger, EER, 2005*

Cost Index Results.

	Standard Cost Function	
	Without Special Education	With Special Education
Using census poverty and LEP		
Large cities		
New York City	170.2	172.0
Yonkers	159.2	166.3
Upstate big three	135.5	143.6
Small cities		
Downstate	140.3	141.7
Upstate	110.8	113.9
Suburbs		
Downstate	114.8	115.1
Upstate	93.8	93.9
Rural		
Upstate	93.6	93.0

3. Pupil Weights

- EN with no disadvantaged students.
- Impact of disadvantaged students

$$\Delta \hat{S}_j^i = a_0 \tilde{T}^{a_T} \bar{Z}^{a_Z} \hat{P}_j^{a_P} \exp\{b_i C_j^i\} - a_0 \tilde{T}^{a_T} \bar{Z}^{a_Z} \hat{P}_j^{a_P}$$
$$= \hat{S}_j^0 (\exp\{b_i C_j^i\} - 1).$$

- Weight = Extra Cost/Pupil as a share of no disadvantaged student spending

$$W_j^i = \frac{\Delta \hat{S}_j^i}{\hat{S}_j^0 C_j^i} = \frac{(\exp\{b_i C_j^i\} - 1)}{C_j^i}.$$

3.1. *Cost Indexes vs. Weights*

- The D/Y article shows that a district's measure of expenditure need is approximately the same regardless of whether it is based on a cost index or pupil weights.

  o With only one measure of student disadvantage, the two approaches yield exactly the same result.

3.1.1. *Direct estimation of weights*

- An alternative, nonlinear approach is to estimate

$$S_j = (e^{\gamma 0} T_j^{\gamma T} Z_j^{\gamma Z} P_j^{\gamma P}) \left(1 + \sum_i \omega_i C_j^i \right).$$

- This yields the weights directly and gives similar results.

3.1.2. *D/Y, pupil weight results*

- These weights have an enormous impact on the cost of education.

  o The 2011 census poverty rate is 43.4% for Syracuse and 46.1% for Rochester.
  o Just from this factor, costs are as much as $43.4 \times 1.667 = 72.9\%$ higher in Syracuse than in a district with no poverty.

Estimated Pupil Weights.

	Simple Average	Pupil-Weighted Average	Directly Estimated
Without Special Education			
Child Poverty	1.415	1.491	1.667
LEP	1.007	1.030	1.308
With Special Education			
Child Poverty	1.224	1.281	1.592
LEP	1.009	1.033	1.424
Special Education	2.049	2.081	2.644

- In a typical state, however, the weight in the state aid formula is 10–20%, not 167%.

3.1.3. *Other approaches*

- Successful Schools.
- Professional Judgment:
  - Panels,
  - Computer-based.
- Evidence-based.

3.2. *Teacher Cost Indexes*

- Teacher cost indexes are difficult to estimate.
- The most intuitively plausible method is straightforward:
  - Regress teacher wages on teacher quality, the district classroom environment (e.g. the poverty rate), and characteristics of the local labor market.
  - Predict wages that each district must pay to attract teachers of a given quality in a given labor market (both held constant) and its own environment (allowed to vary).
- The trouble is that teacher quality is difficult to measure and variables indicating classroom environment (e.g. the poverty rate) are correlated with unmeasured components of teacher quality.
  - The result is that environmental variables often have the wrong sign and the teacher wage index makes no sense.
- Another possibility is to use a measure of teacher value-added, but this approach difficult (as discussed in an earlier class) and may not be meaningful at the school district level.
- Other approaches include:
  - An index of private wages in occupations with similar educational requirements.
  - Measures of the cost of living or housing costs in the area, or even of population in the area (which is correlated with the cost of living).

3.3. Expenditure Need in Cities

- EN is a general concept that does not apply just to education.
- Another step in the analysis is to add spending responsibilities.
  - Some cities, for example, have to provide ports, airports, hospitals, or higher education, whereas others do not.
- In *America's Ailing Cities*, Ladd and Yinger calculate expenditure need indexes for the 70 largest cities in the U.S., using a cost index and a service responsibility index.
- This gives a comprehensive measure of what a city would have to spend to provide a given quality or public services based on factors outside its control.
- The results for EN per capita
  - Average: $571
  - Minimum: $162
  - Washington, D.C: $3,189
  - Next highest: $2,251
- The five cities with population over 1 million had an EN of $879 compared to $509 for the cities with population under 100,000.
- The lowest income cities had an EN of $890 compared to $409 for the richest cities.

Lecture 6

School District Consolidation

- **Class Outline**
    1. **History of Consolidation**
    2. **Are There Economies of Size?**
    3. **Methodological Challenges**
    4. **Conclusions and Policy Implications**
    5. **Other Consolidation Research**
    6. **Supplemental Material for O/Y**

Note: This lecture presents Duncombe and Yinger (*EF&P*, 2007).

1. History of Consolidation

- **Consolidation has eliminated over 100,000 school districts since 1938.**

    ○ This is a drop of almost 90%.

    ○ Consolidation continues today, but at a slow pace.

- **Consolidation is a big issue in state aid programs.**

    ○ Several states have aid programs to encourage district "reorganization," typically in the form of consolidation.

    ○ Other states encourage consolidation through building or transportation aid.

    ○ About one-third of the states compensate school districts for sparsity or small scale — thereby discouraging consolidation.

New York School Districts Consolidating Between 1987 and 1995.

District Pair	Year of Consolidation	Enrollment	District Pair	Year of Consolidation	Enrollment
Bolivar	1995	690	Dannemora	1989	250
Richburg		380	Saranac		1,360
Bolivar-Richburg		1,070	Saranac-Dannemora		1,610
Cobleskill	1994	1,860	Broadalbin	1988	970
Richmondville		390	Perth		620
Cobleskill-Richmondville		2,250	Broadalbin-Perth		1,590
Cohocton	1994	250	Cherry Valley	1988	480
Wayland		1,640	Springfield		250
Wayland-Cohocton		1,890	Cherry Valley-Springfield		730
Savona	1993	420	Jasper	1988	490
Campbell		710	Troupsburg		250
Campbell-Savona		1,130	Jasper-Troupsburg		740
Cuba	1992	1,010	Draper	1987	1,990
Rushford		310	Mohonasen		920
Cuba-Rushford		1,320	Mohonasen-Draper		2,910
Mount Upton	1991	270	Edwards	1987	290
Gilbertsville		260	Knox Memorial		420
Gilbertsville-Mount Upton		530	Edwards-Knox		710

1.1. *Economies of Size and Consolidation*

- Economies of size exist if education cost/pupil declines with enrollment.

  ○ Consolidation lowers cost/pupil if there are economies of size.

- Previous studies estimate cross-section cost functions.

  ○ Most find a U-shaped relationship between cost/pupil and size.
  ○ No previous statistical study looks at consolidation directly.

- This study estimates economies of size using panel data for New York State.

○ The data include all rural school districts, including 12 pairs that consolidated.

○ The sample period is 1985 to 1997.

○ We estimate economies of size (and other cost effects of consolidation) with panel methods.

2. Are There Economies of Size?

● Potential Sources of Economies of Size:

○ Indivisibilities (i.e. Publicness);

○ Increased Dimension (i.e. Efficient Use of Capital);

○ Specialization;

○ Price Benefits of Scale;

○ Learning and Innovation.

● Potential Sources of Diseconomies of Size:

○ Higher Transportation Costs;

○ Labor Relations Effects;

○ Lower Staff Motivation and Effort;

○ Lower Student Motivation and Effort;

○ Lower Parental Involvement.

2.1. *The Cost Model in Duncombe/Yinger*

$$E = E\{S, P, N, M, C, Z\}$$

E = spending per pupil (total or in a subcategory); S = school performance (test scores, dropout rate); P = input prices (teacher wage); N = enrollment; M = student characteristics; C = consolidation; Z = variables that influence school-district efficiency. Data for 212 districts over 13 years.

3. Methodological Challenges

3.1. *Challenge #1*

- **Consolidation might be endogenous.**
- **Responses:**
  - Use district-specific fixed effects.
  - Use district-specific time trends.
  - Control for change in superintendent.
  - Standard simultaneous-equations procedure not feasible; use a control function as final check.

Structure of D/Y Fixed Effects.

District	Year	Fixed Effect for District A	Fixed Effect for District B	Post-Consolidation Fixed Effect for Pair
A	1	1	0	0
A	2	1	0	0
A	3	1	0	0
A	**Consolidation: 4**	0.33	0.67	1
A	5	0.33	0.67	1
A	6	0.33	0.67	1
B	1	0	1	0
B	2	0	1	0
B	3	0	1	0
B	**Consolidation: 4**	0.33	0.67	1
B	5	0.33	0.67	1
B	6	0.33	0.67	1

Notes: The dependent variable for district i is expenditure per pupil in district i (before consolidation) or in the combined district of which district i is a part (after consolidation); in this example, district A has 33% of the total enrollment in the two districts the year before consolidation (3 year).

- Implications of Fixed Effects and Time Trends.
  - Because consolidation is a long process, not an event, we believe this approach is adequate protection against endogeneity.
  - This approach highlights the impact of enrollment change.
  - This price is that we cannot estimate the coefficients of other variables with precision.

3.2. Challenge #2

- Consolidation may have non-enrollment effects that change over time.
- Responses:
  - Include post-consolidation fixed effect for each pair.
  - Include post-consolidation time trend for each pair.

3.3. Challenge #3

- Performance, teacher salaries, and state aid are endogenous.
- Responses:
  - Use two-stage least squares.
  - Select instruments from exogenous characteristics of comparable districts (e.g. income and aid in neighboring districts, manufacturing wage).
  - Conduct over-identification test.
  - Conduct weak-instrument test.

3.4. Challenge #4

- Capital spending and associated state aid are lumpy.
- Responses:
  - Use 4 year averages in capital spending regression (for spending, enrollment, aid, property value).
  - Adjust fixed effects and time trends.
  - Adjust post-consolidation fixed effects.

Cost Regression Results for Rural School Districts in New York, 1985–1997.

Variable	Operating		Capital	
	Coefficient	*t*-statistic	Coefficient	*t*-statistic
Intercept	10.9811	5.27	−24.56679	−2.21
Log of enrollment	**−1.6307**	**−3.28**		
Square of log of enrollment	0.0587	1.79		
Consolidation intercept change (average)	**0.5157**	**8.75**		
Consolidation time trend change (average)	**−0.0142**	**−4.54**	**0.08190**	**2.15**
Outcomes				
Percent of students below minimum competency on PEP tests (3rd and 6th grades)	−0.0076	−0.69	−0.12227	−1.32
Percent of graduates receiving Regents diploma	0.0009	0.57	−0.02922	−1.27
Log of teacher salaries (1–5 years)	0.7293	2.60	0.76713	0.34
Other cost factors				
Percent secondary students	0.00007	0.04	−0.69998	−0.24
Percent receiving subsidized lunch	0.00004	0.07	−0.00338	−0.67
Efficiency factors				
State aid ratio	−0.2241	−0.72	1.46611	0.12
Log of property values	0.0227	0.67	−1.212E-03	−0.08
Log of average income	−0.1459	−2.16	0.12930	0.44
Superintendent change in last two years (1 = yes)	0.0062	1.37	−0.03288	−0.56
Sample size	2,734		2,721	

Coefficients of Enrollment Variables and Implied Economies of Size, New York School Rural Districts, 1985–1997.

	Regression Coefficients		Economies of Size		
Expenditure Category	ln (Enrollment)	[ln (Enrollment)]^2	From 300 Pupils to 600 Pupils	From 900 Pupils to 1,800 Pupils	From 1,500 Pupils to 3,000 Pupils
Spending by object					
Operating (all but capital)	−1.6307	0.0587	−61.7%	−53.5%	−49.6%
(*t*-statistic)	(−3.28)	(−1.79)			
Capital spending	—	—	0.0%	0.0%	0.0%
(*t*-statistic)					
Spending by function					
Instructional	−0.8368		−44.0%	−44.0%	−44.0%
(*t*-statistic)	(−4.22)				
Teaching	−0.8445		−44.3%	−44.3%	−44.3%
(*t*-statistic)	(−4.11)				
Noninstructional					
Central administration	−1.1202		−54.0%	−54.0%	−54.0%
(*t*-statistic)	(−3.38)				
Transportation	−0.4678		−27.7%	−27.7%	−27.7%
(*t*-statistic)	(−1.26)				

Non-Enrollment Cost Effects of Consolidation, New York Rural School Districts.

	Regression Coefficients		Non-Enrollment Cost Effects	
	Average Intercept (*t*-statistic)	Average Trend (*t*-statistic)	Ten-Year Horizon	Thirty-Year Horizon
Spending by object				
Total	n/a	n/a	55.93%	28.17%
Operating spending	0.5157	−0.0142	55.91%	28.08%
(*t*-statistic)	(8.75)	(−4.54)		
Capital spending	—	0.082	56.07%	28.17%
(*t*-statistic)		(2.15)		
Spending by function				
Instructional	0.5092	−0.0136	55.33%	27.79%
(*t*-statistic)	(5.93)	(−3.41)		
Teaching	0.4969	−0.0094	56.73%	28.49%
(*t*-statistic)	(5.58)	(−2.32)		
Noninstructional				
Central administration	0.5196	−0.0526	30.07%	15.11%
(*t*-statistic)	(4.09)	(7.92)		
Transportation	0.3887	−0.0379	22.29%	11.20%
(*t*-statistic)	(2.66)	(−4.26)		

4. Conclusions and Policy Implications

- Operating Costs
  - Thanks to economies of size, consolidation cuts operating costs for rural school districts in New York by up to one-third over 10 years.
  - Adjustment costs exist, but they phase out quickly over time — except in transportation.
  - The cost savings are largest when consolidation combines two very small districts; two 1,500 pupil districts can only save 14% per pupil.
- Capital Costs
  - There are no economies of size in capital spending.
  - The state aid that accompanies consolidation raises inefficiency so that no capital cost savings result.

Net Cost Changes from Consolidation, New York School Rural Districts, 1985–1997.

	Type of Consolidation		
	From 300 Pupils to 600 Pupils	From 900 Pupils to 1,800 Pupils	From 1,500 Pupils to 3,000 Pupils
Total Spending			
Enrollment effects only	−56.04%	−48.60%	−45.07%
Enrollment plus non-enrollment Cost effects of consolidation			
Ten-year horizon	−31.45%	−19.84%	−14.35%
Thirty-year horizon	−43.69%	−34.15%	−29.64%
Operating Spending			
Enrollment effects only	−61.72%	−53.52%	−49.64%
Enrollment plus non-enrollment Cost effects of consolidation			
Ten-year horizon	−40.31%	−27.53%	−21.48%
Thirty-year horizon	−50.97%	−40.47%	−35.50%
Capital Spending			
Enrollment effects only	0.00%	0.00%	0.00%
Enrollment plus non-enrollment Cost effects of consolidation			
Ten-year horizon	56.07%	56.07%	56.07%
Thirty-year horizon	28.17%	28.17%	28.17%

o This short-run inefficiency increase may be partially offset by long-run increases in student performance.

4.1. *Policy Implications*

• Encourage Consolidation

o New York, and probably many other states can lower education costs by encouraging school districts to consolidate.

- Focus on Small, Rural Districts
  - Consolidation incentives should concentrate on small districts; the benefits of consolidation disappear for consolidated districts above about 4,000 pupils.
- Be Careful to Monitor Capital Spending and to Minimize Aid Changes After Consolidation
  - State policy makers should not encourage (or even allow) wasteful capital spending in recently consolidated districts.

4.2. *Other Possible Consequences of Consolidation*

- Cost equations cannot measure
  - Losses of consumer surplus.
  - Higher transportation costs for students and parents.
  - Changes in dimensions of school performance other than test scores and drop-out rates.
- Consolidation is a choice
  - Net benefits must be positive.
  - But they need not equal cost savings.
  - Property value impacts provide one measure.

5. Other Consolidation Research

5.1. *Hu and Yinger (NTJ, 2008)*

- Regress Change in House Value (Tract Level) on Consolidation (Plus Controls)
  - Interact with enrollment to pick up scale economies.
  - Control for change in state aid to pick up other effects.
  - Treat consolidation as endogenous, using consolidations in 1960s and number of districts, both at county level, as instruments.
- Results
  - Consolidation raises value in small-enrollment districts.

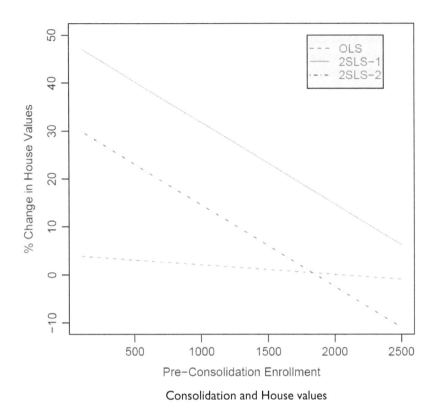

Consolidation and House values

○ Net benefits run out at about 3,000 pupils.
○ After controlling for state aid increases associated with consolidation, net benefits run out at about 2,000 pupils.
○ Even in small districts, net benefits are negative in high-wealth
  tracts.

5.2. *Duncombe, Yinger, and Zhang* (*PFQ, 2016*)

• This article is based on house sales in upstate New York State from
  2000 to 2012.
• Double sales are used to difference out time-invariant unobservables.
• Consolidation occurred in three sets of districts.

2SLS Results for the Sales Market after First Differencing.

	(1)	(2)	(3)	(4)
Consolidation during the 1990s	0.231	0.488	0.316	0.841
	(0.154)	(0.285)	(0.208)	(0.358)
Consolidation*Enrollment90			−0.017	−0.017	−0.018
			(0.007)	(0.007)	(0.007)
Change in Aid				0.289	0.293
				(0.120)	(0.122)
Consolidation*Ratio of tract to district property				−0.535
value per pupil				(0.273)
Housing structures	Yes	Yes	Yes	Yes
Neighborhood characteristics	Yes	Yes	Yes	Yes
Instrument variables:				
Number of consolidations in each county in the 60s	Yes	Yes	Yes	Yes
Number of neighboring districts	Yes	Yes	Yes	Yes
Number of consolidations in each county in the 60s*			Yes	Yes
Aid90				
N	1425	1418	1415	1415

- Propensity score matching (PSM) is used to make sure the with- and without-consolidation observations are comparable.
- The key intuition for PSM:
  - The impact of a program or event may depend on other variables.
  - So if the with- and without-program samples have different values for other variables, estimates of program effect may be biased.
  - PSM is a technique to ensure that the two samples have the same distribution of other variables, so this bias disappears.
  - PSM does not account for unobservables.

- **Findings**
  - Except in one large district, consolidation has a negative impact on house values during the years right after it occurs.
  - This effect then fades away and is eventually reversed.

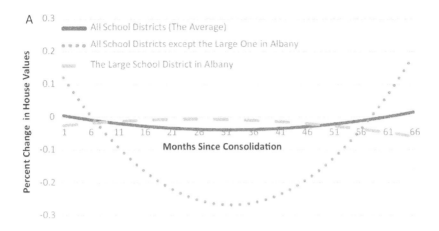

o This pattern suggests that it takes time either for the advantages of consolidation to be apparent or for the people who prefer consolidated districts to move in.

o As in previous studies, the long-run impacts of consolidation on house values are positive in census tracts that initially have low incomes.

o But negative in high-income census tracts, where parents may have a relatively large willingness to retain the non-budgetary advantages of small districts.

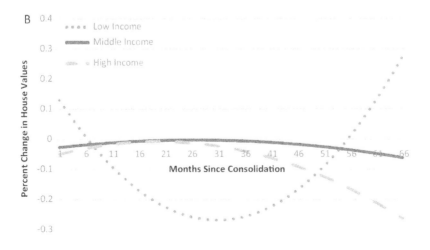

6. Supplemental Material for O/Y

6.1. *D/Y's Instruments for 2SLS (Performance and Teacher Wage are Endogenous)*

For the operating cost models, the final set of instruments includes the log of average values of per pupil income and per pupil operating aid in adjacent districts and the log of average private sector wages, the log of average manufacturing wages, the unemployment rate, and the ratio of employment to students in the district's county.

6.2. *D/Y's Control Function Estimation (For Potential Endogeneity of Consolidation Decision)*

[O]ur logit model estimates the probability of consolidation in a given year as a function of the number of years since the previous consolidation in the same county, the preceding three-year change in the district's enrollment, the total state aid ratio in districts with similar enrollment, and the instruments identified for our cost regression.

6.3. *D/Y's Cost Function Estimates*

Estimated using linear 2SLS regression with district fixed effects and trend variables. Student outcomes, state aid, and teacher salaries are treated as endogenous. The dependent variable for the operating cost model is the log of real per pupil spending. The dependent variable for the capital cost model is the four-year average of the log of real per pupil capital spending adjusted for depreciation using a 2% annual rate.

State aid for the operating cost model is real per pupil operating aid (without supplements for consolidation) divided by average income. For the capital cost model, the four-year average of total real state aid per pupil is divided by average income in that year.

Lecture 7

Demand for Public Services: The Median Voter and Other Approaches

- **Class Outline**
  1. **The Starting Point**
  2. **Household Demand for Public Services**
  3. **Estimating Household Demand Using Surveys**
  4. **The Median Voter Theorem**
  5. **Estimating Household Demand Using Community Data**
  6. **Examples**
  7. **Three Challenges**

1. The Starting Point

- An household's demand for local public services, like its demand for private goods, depends on its *income*, the *price* of the *services*, the price of *alternatives*, and its *preferences*.

  o But with two **big twists**:

    ▪ There is no market price.
    ▪ The demand for public services can be expressed in several different ways as explained in the following sections.

1.1. *Lack of a Market Price*

- Most public services are funded by taxes, not prices.
  - o Hence, the "price" is defined as the cost of an additional unit of service.
- And this price depends on the tax system.
  - o **Tax Price** = How much would the individual pay if taxes were raised enough to provide one more unit of the service to everyone in the jurisdiction.
  - o A more formal definition will be derived later.

1.2. *How is Demand Revealed?*

- The demand for services can be expressed:
  - o Through voting (today's class).
  - o Through bidding for housing and choice of a community (the subject of later classes).
  - o Through the purchase of private substitutes, such as private schools, security guards, or access to a gated community (not covered in any class, but worth studying!).

2. Household Demand for Public Services

- A Household's Budget Constraint.
  - o Income (Y) must be spent on housing (H) with price (P), property taxes $(tV = tPH/r)$ and other stuff $(Z$ with price 1):

$$Y = Z + PH + tV$$
$$= Z + PH + t\frac{PH}{r}$$
$$= Z + PH\left(1 + \frac{t}{r}\right)$$

2.1. *The Community Budget Constraint*

- In a community, sending *per household* (E) to achieve the desired service level (S) must equal property tax revenue per household

(t multiplied by average V) and state aid (A).

$$E\{S\} = t\bar{V} + A$$

- Other local revenue sources are not considered here; state aid is considered in more detail in later classes.

2.2. *Solving for Tax Price*

- Solve the community budget constraint for t:

$$t = \frac{E\{S\} - A}{\bar{V}}$$

- Substitute into the household budget constraint:

$$Y = Z + \mathrm{PH} + (E\{S\} - A)\left(\frac{V}{\bar{V}}\right)$$

- Tax price is the cost of one more unit of S, i.e. the derivative of the household budget constraint with respect to S, or,

$$\text{Tax Price} = \mathrm{TP} = \left(\frac{\partial E}{\partial S}\right)\left(\frac{V}{\bar{V}}\right) = \mathrm{MC}\left(\frac{V}{\bar{V}}\right)$$

where MC is the resource cost of another unit of S, and the ratio of V to average V is the *tax share*.

Note: If E is total spending, the tax share is V divided by total V— a true share.

3. Estimating Household Demand Using Surveys

- With TP defined, we can write down a household demand function:

$$S = S\{Y, \mathrm{TP}, \text{ Other Prices, Preference Variables}\}$$

- The problem: How to estimate this function?
  - One answer: Through surveys.

3.1. *Survey Studies of Household Demand*

- Approach 1: Surveys of voting on a referendum.
  - ○ The demand function defines a latent variable, which can be studied with a discrete-choice model, with Y and TP as explanatory variables.
  - ○ This approach also can be applied to a survey of preferences for increasing, decreasing, or not changing spending.
- Approach 2: Surveys of spending preferences: "How much would you like to spend?"
  - ○ Use a multiplicative form with desired spending $(= (S)(AC))$ as the dependent variable (assuming AC $=$ MC):

$$S = AY^{\theta}TP^{\mu} = AY^{\theta}MC^{\mu}\left(\frac{V}{\overline{V}}\right)^{\mu}$$

$$E = (S)(AC) = AY^{\theta}MC^{\mu+1}\left(\frac{V}{\overline{V}}\right)^{\mu}$$

4. The Median Voter Theorem

- Although household voting is not observed, the outcomes of voting in a community are easy to observe — on referenda or in the form of spending or service levels.
- The median voter model provides a way to estimate a demand model at the community level — where the data are!

4.1. *Bergstrom and Goodman*

- This famous paper (*AER*, 1973) starts with an obvious point: the voter in the middle of the demand distribution is always on the winning side.
- It then adds assumptions about the structure of demand and taxes (that demand depends on Y and TP, that there is a property tax, and that the demand for housing, H, is a function of Y).
- And shows that the voting outcome in a community is determined by the voter with the median Y and median TP.

- In symbols:

$$S = S\{Y_{Median},\ \text{TP}_{Median},\ X\}$$

$$= S\left\{Y_{Median},\ \text{MC}\left(\frac{V_{Median}}{\bar{V}}\right), X\right\}$$

- This was revolutionary because it specified the demand for S using data just on median Y and median TP, which are readily observed.
  - Scholars can proceed "as if" voting outcomes depend only on the demand of this abstract median voter.

4.2. *Problems with Median Voter Models*

- Logical problems:
  - If demand is not one-dimensional and preferences do not take certain forms, the public choice mechanism may not be well defined. This is *Arrow's Impossibility Theorem:* it is impossible to write down a general model of public choice for complex decisions.
  - Example: Private schools. Some people with a high demand for public services under some circumstances (no private alternative) may have a low demand under others (a good private school nearby).
- Institutional problems:
  - The median voter model says institutions are neutral. Politicians and bureaucrats have no impact on observed spending or service quality (except perhaps through inefficiency — more later). Also, results are assumed not to be skewed by non-participation. This may not be true.
    - Example: Renters. The tax price idea applies to owners, but its application to renters is unclear. Are public service benefits to renters cancelled by rent increases? It is also hard to find a significant renter variable in a median voter model.
- Tiebout bias:
  - More on this later.

○ Basically, this is a form of selection bias in which people with low incomes but high demand for services based on unobserved factors end up in jurisdictions with high-quality services.

5. Estimating Household Demand Using Community Data

5.1. *The Budget Constraints*

- The median voter's constraint:

$$Y = Z + PH + tV = Z + PH\left(1 + \frac{t}{r}\right)$$

○ The community budget constraint (now with efficiency):

$$E \equiv \frac{C\{S\}}{e} = t\bar{V} + A$$

○ The combined constraint:

$$Y + A\left(\frac{V}{\bar{V}}\right) = Z + PH + \frac{C\{S\}}{e}\left(\frac{V}{\bar{V}}\right)$$

5.2. *Components*

- Tax Price:

$$\text{TP} \equiv \frac{\partial \text{Spending}}{\partial S} = \frac{dC}{dS}e^{-1}\left(\frac{V}{\bar{V}}\right) = (\text{MC})e^{-1}\left(\frac{V}{\bar{V}}\right)$$

- Augmented Income:

$$Y^A \equiv Y + A\left(\frac{V}{\bar{V}}\right)$$

- Because these terms come from the budget constraint, they appear in any demand function.
- The augmented income term contains both voter income and state aid weighted by tax share.

○ The Bradford/Oates equivalence theorem (*AER*, 1971) says these two components should have the same impact on voter demand for public services.

- But a large empirical literature (especially in education) says that intergovernmental aid has a much bigger impact on voter demand for the public service than does voter income.
- This is called the "flypaper effect," labeled f, and we will consider it at length in the next class.

5.3. *Tiebout Bias*

- As discussed at length in later classes, household must compete for entry into desirable communities — a literature that began with a famous article by Tiebout (*JPE*, 1956).

  - The people who win this competition are the ones with a higher demand for public services, which depends on their observed and unobserved demand traits.
  - As pointed out by Goldstein and Pauley (*JPubE*, 1981), these unobserved traits may create a correlation between the error term and the measure of service quality, and hence lead to biased estimates of income and price elasticities = Tiebout bias.
  - Jurisdiction fixed effects and/or good data on jurisdiction traits are needed to minimize this bias.

5.4. *Constant Elasticity Demand*

- General Form:

$$S = K \left(Y + (1+f)A \left(\frac{V}{\overline{V}} \right) \right)^\theta \left((\text{MC}) e^{-1} \left(\frac{V}{\overline{V}} \right) \right)^\mu$$

- Linear Form to Estimate:

$$\ln\{S\} = K^* + \theta \ln \left\{ Y + (1+f)A \left(\frac{V}{\overline{V}} \right) \right\}$$

$$+ \mu \ln \left\{ (\text{MC}) e^{-1} \left(\frac{V}{\overline{V}} \right) \right\}$$

$$= K^* + \theta \ln \left\{ Y \left(1 + (1+f) \left(\frac{A}{Y} \right) \left(\frac{V}{\overline{V}} \right) \right) \right\}$$

$$+ \mu \ln \left\{ (\text{MC}) e^{-1} \left(\frac{V}{\overline{V}} \right) \right\}$$

$$= K^* + \theta \ln \{Y\} + \theta \ln \left\{ 1 + (1+f) \left(\frac{A}{Y} \right) \left(\frac{V}{\overline{V}} \right) \right\}$$

$$+ \mu \ln \left\{ (\text{MC}) \, e^{-1} \left(\frac{V}{\overline{V}} \right) \right\}$$

$$\cong K^* + \theta \ln \{Y\} + \theta(1+f) \left(\frac{A}{Y} \right) \left(\frac{V}{\overline{V}} \right)$$

$$+ \mu_1 \ln \{\text{MC}\} - \mu_2 \ln \{e\} + \mu_3 \ln \left\{ \frac{V}{\overline{V}} \right\}$$

- Notes:
  - The last line uses the approximation that $\ln\{1 + a\} \approx a$.
  - This formulation differs slightly from Eom *et al.* (*EF&P*, 2014), which has f alone instead of $(1 + f)$ in the augmented income term.
  - The version here has a flypaper effect of zero if the Bradford/Oates equivalence theorem holds; more on this in a later class.

5.5. *The Big Problem: Endogeneity*

- Note that this equation includes MC, which depends on the level of S, except in the unlikely event that there are constant returns to quality scale (i.e. the same marginal cost for all units of S).
- It also includes e, which may depend on MC as well as on key explanatory variables, such as Y and tax share.
- A solution: Model MC and e.
- Most studies ignore these problems!

5.5.1. *The cost function*

- A multiplicative form:

$$\overset{\text{Enrollment}}{\underset{\underset{\underset{\text{Teacher} \quad \text{Student}}{\text{Salaries} \quad \text{Traits}}}{}}{C\{S\} = \kappa S^\sigma W^\alpha N^\beta P^\lambda}}$$

- Implies that

$$\text{MC} \equiv \frac{\partial C\{S\}}{\partial S} = \sigma \kappa S^{\sigma-1} W^\alpha N^\beta P^\lambda$$

5.5.2. *Efficiency*

- Assume demand for services other than S and monitoring incentives depend on augmented income, TP, and other factors, M:

$$e = k\, M^\rho \left(Y + (1+f)A \left(\frac{V}{\bar{V}} \right) \right)^\gamma (\text{MC})^{\delta_X} \left(\frac{V}{\bar{V}} \right)^\delta$$

Note that $\text{MC} = \text{MC}fSg$ but e refers to other, unspecified outputs, so δ_X is a cross-price elasticity.

5.5.3. *The full expenditure function*

- Also recall that $E = C\{S\}/e$. Substitute MC and e into this expression to obtain

$$E = k^* \, (S^{\sigma - \delta_X(\sigma-1)})(W^\alpha N^\beta P^\lambda)^{1-\delta_X}$$
$$\times \left(M^{-\rho} \left(Y + (1+f)A \left(\frac{V}{\bar{V}} \right) \right)^{-\gamma} \left(\frac{V}{\bar{V}} \right)^{-\delta} \right)$$

which can be estimated in log form using the approximation discussed earlier.

5.5.4. *The demand function*

- Now substitute MC and e into the demand function and solve for S to get an estimating equation:

$$S = K^* \left(Y + (1+f)A \left(\frac{V}{\bar{V}} \right) \right)^{\theta*} \left((C^*)\, (e^*)^{-1} \left(\frac{V}{\bar{V}} \right) \right)^{\mu*}$$

where the expressions with asterisks can all be identified with the expenditure results; C^* and e^* only include determinants of C and e other than S.
- Note that the simultaneity problem is solved with algebra, not econometrics.

5.5.5. *Common error*

- Most studies ignore e.
- But if e is a function of augmented income and TP, then the coefficients of these variables in a demand function reflect efficiency effects as well as demand effects.
- They do not just give demand elasticities!

6. Examples

6.1. *Massachusetts (Nguyen–Hoang/Yinger (JEF, 2014))*

- MA has property tax limits with overrides.
- MA has no independent school districts, so voter demand for education may depend on costs of other services.
- We observe 296 districts over 6 years.
- We use year dummies, but no district fixed effects.
- Service quality is measured with a state-defined Student Performance Index.

6.2. *California Estimates (D/Y, 2011)*

- About 900 school districts in 2 years (2003–2004 and 2004–2005).
- Service is measured by an index (API) of several tests in several grades developed for the California school accountability system.
- No fixed effects, but clustered errors.

6.2.1. *Tax Price with Parcel Tax*

- The budget constraints

$$Y = Z + tV + P$$

Parcel Tax Amount

$$E \equiv \frac{C\{S\}}{e} = t\bar{V} + A + NP$$

Number of Households

- Solve for P and substitute:

$$Y + \frac{t\bar{V} + A}{N} = Z + tV + \frac{C\{S\}}{eN}$$

$$\text{TP} \equiv \frac{\partial \text{ Spending}}{\partial S} = \frac{dC}{dS}\frac{1}{eN} = \frac{\text{MC}}{eN}$$

6.2.2. *Instruments*

- The copy-cat variables are instruments in the cost equation.

Demand Estimation Regression Results (2001–2006) for Massachusetts. Dependent Variable: Log of Student Performance Index.

	Base	Without Logged Non-school Costs (CC_{MM})	(CC_{MM}) Interacted with regional dummy (RD)
Income and price variables	(1)	(2)	(3)
Chapter 70 aid component of adjusted income	1.576	1.871	1.917
	(2.47)**	(2.57)**	(2.58)**
Log of median income	0.082	0.076	0.075
	(2.09)**	(1.96)*	(2.01)**
Log of tax share	−0.265	−0.288	−0.287
	(−4.05)***	(−3.87)***	(−3.75)***
Log of cost index	−0.472	−0.513	−0.504
	(−6.38)***	(−6.33)***	(−6.08)***
Log of efficiency index	1.548	1.547	1.705
	(4.01)***	(3.87)***	(3.67)***
Log of non-school costs	−0.020		−0.034
	(−1.82)*		(−1.92)*
Other variables			
Regional districts (RD) (= 1 for RD and = 0 otherwise)	−0.068	0.009	−0.079
	(−1.98)**	(1.02)	(−2.03)**
$CC_{MM} \times RD$			−0.249
			(−2.48)**
Percent of college graduates	0.003	0.004	0.003
	(3.63)***	(3.60)***	(3.75)***
Percent of senior citizens	0.000	0.000	0.000
	(0.02)	(0.07)	(0.18)
Percent of low-income students in comparison districts	−0.001	−0.001	−0.001
	(−2.33)**	(−2.30)**	(−2.13)**
Percent of special ed students in comparison districts	0.008	0.007	0.007
	(1.48)	(1.37)	(1.22)
Year dummies (2002, 2003, 2004, 2005, 2006)	Yes	Yes	Yes
Constant	Yes	Yes	Yes
Number of observations	1776	1776	1776

Note: *t*-statistics are in parentheses. The significance levels are * = 10%, ** = 5%, and *** = 1%.

Demand Equation Estimates, California School Districts (2003–2004 and 2004–2005).

Variables	OLS		2SLS		Fuller LIML (α=1)	
	Coefficient	t-statistic	Coefficient	t-statistic	Coefficient	t-statistic
Intercept	3.4281**	8.96	3.4978**	8.51	3.4964**	10.37
Augmented Income Variables						
33rd percentile of income distribution	0.1454**	10.72	0.1441**	9.44	0.1442**	11.29
Revenue limit component of adjusted income	0.2860**	2.96	0.2771**	2.63	0.2775**	3.33
Revenue limit component of adjusted income with tax share	0.0984	1.18	0.0986	1.17	0.0986	1.54
Categorical aid component of adjusted income	−0.0501	−0.99	−0.0558	−1.00	−0.0556	−1.16
Federal aid component of adjusted income	0.0755	0.77	0.0554	0.43	0.0562	0.56
Contributions component of adjusted income	0.6396**	2.98	1.3818	0.67	1.3576	0.87
Tax Price Variables						
Tax share (= inverse of parcels per pupil)	−0.0143**	−2.09	−0.0135*	−1.81	−0.0136**	−2.27
Tax share in majority renter districts	0.0031	1.20	0.0034	1.24	0.0034	1.62
Cost index	−0.1578**	−7.60	−0.1575**	−7.44	−0.1575**	−7.88
Efficiency index	0.0861	1.23	0.0856	1.16	0.0858	1.38
Preference Variables						
Percent of population 5 to 17 years old	−0.0031**	−4.30	−0.0029**	−2.93	−0.0029**	−3.70
Percent of population above age 65	0.0017**	3.16	0.0017**	3.03	0.0017**	3.86

(Continued)

(*Continued*)

Variables	OLS		2SLS		Fuller LIML (α=1)	
	Coefficient	*t*-statistic	Coefficient	*t*-statistic	Coefficient	*t*-statistic
Percent of population that is African American	−0.2064**	−4.19	−0.2045**	−4.10	−0.2045**	−5.62
Elementary district (1 = yes)	0.0158**	3.39	0.0155**	2.82	0.0155**	3.68
High school district (1 = yes)	−0.0364**	−4.56	−0.0352**	−4.12	−0.0352**	−5.22
Copy-Cat Variables (for Comparison Districts)						
Share of free lunch students	−0.0005*	−1.72	−0.0004	−1.36	−0.0004*	−1.70
Percent of population that is African American	−0.0024**	−2.89	−0.0023**	−2.60	−0.0023**	−3.47
Median house value	−0.0227**	−2.66	−0.0229**	−2.74	−0.0229**	−3.30

Note: The dependent variable is the log of API; the contributions and efficiency variables are treated as endogenous in the second and third models; sample size is 1821; robust standard errors are reported (controlling for clustering at district level in the 2SLS model); a* (**) indicates significance at the two-tailed 10(5)% level.

7. Three Challenges

- Units are not clear; performance is at student level, but voting is at household level; different studies use different adjustment methods (or none!).
- The role of renters is not clear; no study finds strong renter effect; perhaps renters don't care about the service level because better services mean higher rents.
- The role of Tiebout bias is not clear; income distribution variables do not seem to help, but jurisdiction fixed effects probably do.

Lecture 8

State Aid

1. The U.S. Education Finance System

- State elected officials make the rules for elementary and secondary education.
- State elected officials also design the education finance system:
  - State aid ($\approx$47% of total in average state).
  - Property taxes and perhaps other local taxes ($\approx$45%).
  - Compensation for homestead exemptions.
- The federal government provides a little funding ($\approx$8%), tax breaks for property taxes, and some incentives (through NCLB).

1.1. *Data Note*

- It is hard to pin down the sources of education spending.
  - The aggregate Census data only includes *independent* school districts.
  - Many districts, including Syracuse, are dependent, that is, they are departments in a city government.

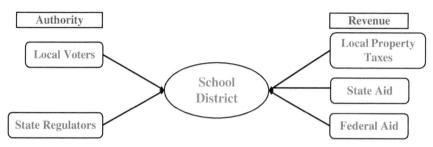

Education Finance in the U.S.

- One effort to account for this (McGuire, Papke, and Reschovsky in the *Handbook of Education Finance and Policy*, 2nd Edition) finds that in 2010–2011:

  - Local sources provided 43.1% of school K-12 school revenue.
  - Local property taxes supplied 82.1% of this local revenue.
  - States provided 44.1%.
  - The federal government provided 12.5%.

1.2. The Education Finance System

- The broad rules are laid out in a *state constitution*, which has phrases such as "a system of free public schools' or "a sound, basic education."

  - **Elected officials** design a system that meets their objectives, which usually (but not always!) do not involve much re-distribution.
  - People in low-performing districts bring suits into the **state courts**, and the state courts rule on the constitutionality of the system designed by elected officials.

    - "The education of children is a fundamental value of the people of the State of Florida. It is, therefore, a paramount duty of the state to make adequate provision for the education of all children residing within its borders. Adequate provision shall be made by law for a uniform, efficient, safe, secure, and high quality system of free public schools that allows students to obtain a high quality education and for the establishment, maintenance, and operation of institutions of higher learning and other public education programs that the needs of the people may require." Fla. Const. art. IX, § 1(a).

- As a result of the 2002 amendments, Florida's constitution also requires the legislature to make adequate provision for reduced class sizes, and provides that every four-year-old child in the state have access to a "high quality pre-kindergarten learning opportunity." Fla. Const. art. IX, § 1(b).
- Prior to 1998, the constitution simply required the state to make "[a]dequate provision ... for a uniform system of free public schools."

1.3. *The Role of the Courts*

- 1971: *Serrano* decision by California Supreme Court rejected California's education finance system based on U.S. and California Constitutions.

  o It is unfair, the court said, for a child's education to depend on the *wealth* of his school district.

- 1972: *Rodriquez* decision by the U.S. Supreme Court ruled out education claims based on U.S. Constitution.
- Since 1971:

  o *Forty three* state courts have heard *challenges* to their state's education finance system.

  o *Twenty* more education finance systems have been *declared unconstitutional* by a state supreme court.

  o Court decisions have led to *major education finance reforms* in many states, including California, Kentucky, New Hampshire, New Jersey, Texas, Vermont.

  o Several states have implemented *major reforms without a court mandate*, including Kansas, Maryland, and Michigan.

    - One careful accounting of all the court cases can be found in:

      □ S.P. Corcoran and W. N. Evans, "Equity, Adequacy, and the Evolving State Role in Education Finance," *Handbook of Research in Education Finance and Policy*, 2015.

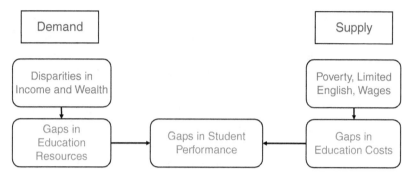

Sources of Student Performance Gaps.

1.4. *Educational Disparities*

- What the courts are responding to are enormous *disparities in both resources and student performance* across school districts within a state.
- This disparities arise because districts vary widely in both *available resources and educational costs.*
- Large cities, which often contain many poor families, have particularly low student performance.

1.4.1. *Educational disparities, examples*

- The 17 cities in the table "NAEP 4th Grade Math, 2015" are the ones that volunteered to participate in the NAEP (National Educational Assessment Program) tests in 2015. (Three counties and Washington, D.C. also participated.)
- Many disadvantaged cities (e.g. Buffalo, Rochester, Syracuse, Milwaukee, Newark) are not included.
  - ○ The state averages include the cities; if the city is a large share of state population, the score for "rest of state" could be very different from the score for the state as a whole.
    - ■ In the case of NYC, e.g. which has 39.3% of New York State's students, the city proficiency rate is only 63.7% of the rate in the rest of the state.
- Similar disparities exist for 8th grade math and for 4th and 8th grade reading.

NAEP 4th Grade Math, 2015.

| City | Percent Proficient | | |
	City	State	City/State (%)
Albuquerque	28	27	**103.7**
Atlanta	26	35	74.3
Austin	47	44	**106.8**
Baltimore	12	40	**30.0**
Boston	33	54	61.1
Charlotte	51	44	**115.9**
Chicago	30	37	81.1
Cleveland	13	45	**28.9**
Dallas	34	44	77.3
Detroit	5	34	**14.7**
Fresno	14	29	**48.3**
Houston	36	44	81.8
Los Angeles	22	29	75.9
Miami	41	42	97.6
NYC	26	35	74.3
Philadelphia	15	45	**33.3**
San Diego	31	29	**106.9**

Source: U.S. Department of Education.

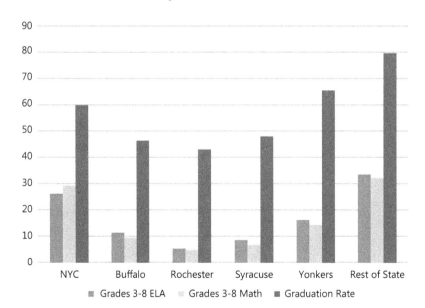

Proficiency and Graduation Rates in New York, 2013.
Source: New York State Education Department.

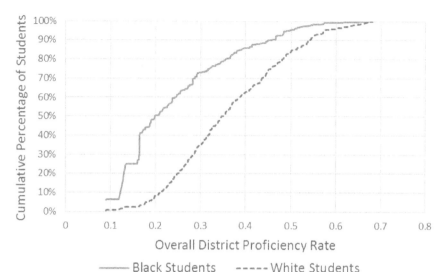

Distribution of Students by Overall District Proficiency Rate, New York State Excluding NYC, 2014.

Source: Yinger, J. "Unequal Access to Good Schools in New York State." http:// cpr.maxwell.syr.edu/efap/about_efap/ie/April_2015.pdf.

2. Key Questions in Education Finance Reform

- What is the best way to measure the education provided by a school district?

  ○ What do we want schools to provide?

- What is the appropriate equity standard?

  ○ How would we recognize a fair outcome if we saw it?

2.1. *Measuring Education*

- Spending per pupil is a poor measure of education:

  ○ Easy to measure, but hard to interpret.
  ○ Rejected by most courts.

- Spending ignores variation in the cost of education due to
  - ○ Concentrated disadvantage among students.
  - ○ The high cost of attracting teachers to some districts.
- Pupil performance, such as test scores and drop-out rates, provides a better measure of education
  - ○ It corresponds with what parents want.
  - ○ It is consistent with the trend toward setting higher **standards**.
  - ○ It is consistent with **accountability** programs (discussed next class).
- An education cost index provides a bridge between performance and spending
  - ○ An equivalent approach is using higher "weights" for disadvantaged students.

2.2. *Educational Adequacy*

- **Adequacy** is the equity standard emphasized in most recent court decisions and by most policy makers:
  - ○ Every student should be in a school that delivers an adequate average student performance.
- An adequacy standard does not eliminate all disparities:
  - ○ Districts are allowed to provide above-adequate educations if they can.
- Adequacy is achieved by a **foundation aid** program (discussed below).

2.3. *Other Equity Standards*

- Access Equality:
  - ○ The education provided by a district should depend only on its property tax rate.
  - ○ Refers to fairness for *taxpayers*, not students.
  - ○ Is achieved by power-equalizing aid (discussed below).
  - ○ Was the main issue in *Serrano*.

- Wealth Neutrality:
  - Educational outcomes should not be correlated with school district wealth.
  - Difficult to achieve.
- Equality:
  - All school districts should provide the same level of education.
  - May require state provision, as in Hawaii.

3. Types of State Aid

3.1. *The Foundation Aid Formula*

- Forty states use a **foundation aid formula**, designed to achieve educational **adequacy**.
- The foundation aid formula is

$$A_j = E^* - t^* V_j$$

$A_j =$ **aid per pupil** to school district j.

$E^* =$ **foundation spending** per pupil (state-selected; the same in every district).

$t^* =$ **minimum required property tax rate** (state-selected; the same in every district).

$V_j =$ actual **property tax base** per pupil in district j.

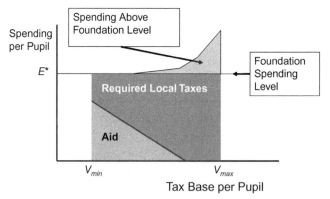

The Foundation Aid Formula.

- A foundation aid formula can easily be adjusted for educational costs (that is, focused on performance):

$$A_j = S^* C_j - t^* V_j$$

S^* = foundation spending level per pupil **in a district with average costs**

C_j = **educational cost index** for district j.

- Pupil weights can also be used.
- This formula is equivalent to offsetting fiscal disparities across schools.
- A foundation formula must address four issues:

  ○ How much spending is "adequate"?
  ○ Should the foundation level be adjusted for variation in education costs across districts?
  ○ Should a minimum local property tax rate be required?
  ○ How should burden of funding an adequate education be distributed?

3.1.1. *What spending is adequate?*

- ***Rose* decision in Kentucky:**

  ○ "sufficient oral and written communication skills to enable students to function in a complex and rapidly changing civilization"
  ○ "sufficient understanding of governmental processes to enable the student to understand the issues that affect his or her community, state, and nation"
  ○ "sufficient levels of academic or vocational skills to enable public school students to compete favorably with their counterparts in surrounding states, in academics or in the job market"

- ***CFE* decision in NY:**

  ○ "meaningful high school education, one which prepares them to function productively as civic participants"

3.1.2. *Adjust for costs?*

- Districts with higher costs must spend more to achieve any given performance level.
- So a cost adjustment is needed to combine a *performance* definition of education with an *adequacy* standard.
- According to Verstegen and Knoeppel (*J. Ed. Fin.*, 2012), 36 states adjust aid for student poverty and 42 states adjust for English language learners.
  - But no state does a comprehensive, estimated cost adjustment.
  - Full cost adjustment leads to extensive re-distribution, which is politically difficult, and requires statistical procedures.

3.1.3. *Require minimum tax rate?*

- To reach foundation spending, E^*, a district must levy at least the selected tax rate, t^*.
- But when a school district receives state aid, it only spends some of the money on education — the rest goes to relief from local taxes.
- Thus, the foundation level of spending will not be achieved unless a minimum rate of t^* is required!

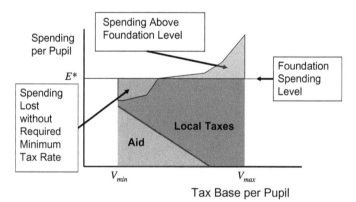

Foundation Aid without Minimum Tax Rate Requirement.

3.2. *Power-equalizing Aid*

- **Power-equalizing** (or **guaranteed tax base**, GTB) aid, is the main program in three states and a supplementary program in 10 others.
  - ○ The idea behind GTB aid is that a district's spending should depend on tax effort, not tax base:

$$E_j = t_j V,$$

  where V^* is a policy parameter set by the state.
- To determine the associated aid formula, note that

$$E_j = A_j + t_j V_j = t_j V^* \text{ or } A_j = t_j(V^* - V_j)$$

- Combining this with the GTB formula leads to:

$$A_j = E_j \left(1 - \frac{V_j}{V^*} \right)$$

- GTB is matching aid; the state share of spending decreases with V_j.
- If $V^* <$ maximum V_j, then matching rates are negative in rich districts.
  - ○ This is called **recapture**.
  - ○ Vermont is an example.
- Raising V^* raises the cost of GTB aid.
  - ○ To offset this effect, set matching rates at a fraction of the value in the above formula.
  - ○ That is, flatten the line in the following picture.
- GTB aid can be adjusted for costs (but rarely is):

$$A_j = E_j \left(\frac{S^* C_j}{S^* \bar{C}} - \frac{V_j}{V^*} \right) = E_j \left(C_j - \frac{V_j}{V^*} \right)$$

- Using GTB as a supplement to foundation aid is misguided:
  - ○ Foundation aid already requires poor districts to set tax rates above their desired level.
  - ○ Adding GTB aid will not induce any further tax rate increases.

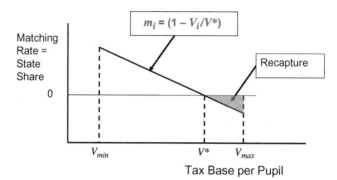

Power-Equalizing Aid.

3.3. Comparing Foundation and GTB Aid

- GTB aid is often thought to be more equalizing than foundation aid.
- In fact, however, price elasticities are small, so the response to GTB aid is small, even for poor districts (see D/Y, *NTJ*, 1998).
- So:
  - Foundation aid is much more equalizing at the bottom of the property value distribution (and is the only way to ensure adequacy).
  - GTB aid is more equalizing at the top of the property value distribution — at least if it includes recapture.

3.4. Wealth Neutrality

- Wealth neutrality is defined as a zero correlation between property wealth and performance outcomes.
  - This is the same as a flat regression line for performance as a function of wealth.
- When it was first proposed, many people thought GTB aid would lead to wealth neutrality.
- But a famous paper by Feldstein (*AER* 1975) shows that this would be true only by coincidence because outcomes depend on the behavioral responses to the matching rates.

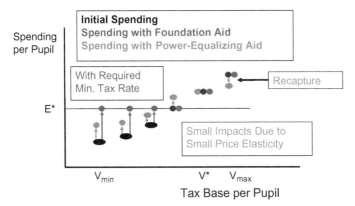

Comparing Foundation and GTB Aid.

○ A low response by low-wealth districts (which seems to be the case) would lead an upward sloping line.

○ A high response by low-wealth districts would lead to a downward sloping line.

4. Research on State Aid

• Bradford/Oates Equivalence Theorem;
• The Flypaper Effect;
• Matching Aid;
• Aid and Efficiency.

4.1. *The Bradford/Oates Equivalence Theorem*

• Recall from the last class that augmented income is:

$$Y^A \equiv Y + A\left(\frac{V}{\overline{V}}\right)$$

where A is lump-sum aid per pupil.

• The B/O theorem says that one should not compare aid and income, but should instead compare tax-share weighted aid and income (*AER*, 1971).

○ This approach accounts for the fact that the value of aid to a voter depends on the voter's tax share.

o If her tax share is 0.5, she only pays $0.50 for a $1.00 increase in property taxes; equivalently, $1 of aid only saves her $0.50.

4.1.1. *This set-up leads to two key points*

- First, the expression for augmented income in the budget constraint (and hence in the demand function) is inherently nonlinear.
- A specification with $\ln\{Y\}$ and $\ln\{A\}$ (let alone Y and A) makes no sense!
- But a close approximation is available to make the term linear.

4.1.2. *The approximation*

$$\theta \ln\{Y^A\} \equiv \theta \ln \left\{ Y + A\left(\frac{V}{\overline{V}}\right)\right\}$$

$$\equiv \theta \ln\{Y\} + \ln\left\{1 + \theta\left(\frac{A}{Y}\right)\left(\frac{V}{\overline{V}}\right)\right\}$$

$$\approx \theta \ln\{Y\} + \theta\left(\frac{A}{Y}\right)\left(\frac{V}{\overline{V}}\right)$$

4.2. The Flypaper Effect

- Second, even after the Bradford/Oates correction, income and aid do not have the same impact on education demand.
- This is the flypaper effect, f.
- The income term with f is:

$$\theta \ln\{Y\} + \theta(1+f)\left(\frac{A}{Y}\right)\left(\frac{V}{\overline{V}}\right)$$

4.2.1. *Estimates of the flypaper effect*

- This specification is by no means universal.
- Studies that use it or something equivalent usually find a value of f in the 10–15 range.
- Eom *et al.* (2014) claim to find much larger flypaper effects with this specification.

- o But Nguyen-Hoang and Yinger (2018a) show that Eom *et al.* make a scaling error in their aid term.
- o When this error is corrected, their approach leads to flypaper effects in the same range.
- The estimates in N-H/Y (2018a) are between 12 and 14.

4.2.2. *Interpreting the flypaper effect*

- The value of f is the dollars of voter income that are needed to have the same impact on education spending (or performance in some models) as a dollar of state aid with the B/O weights.
- Another approach is to calculate how much of each dollar of aid is spent and how much is turned into tax relief.

  - o Nguyen-Hoang/Yinger find that $0.04 of every dollar of voter income is spent on education.
  - o They also find that, on average, $0.30 of every $1 of state aid is spent on education; the rest goes to property tax relief.
  - o The spending share is higher when voters' tax share is higher.
  - o The comparable average spending share for federal aid is $0.73.

4.3. *Matching Aid*

- With matching aid, the community budget constraint is

$$\left(\frac{C\{S\}}{e} - A \right)(1 - m) = t\bar{V}$$

- So the household budget constraint

$$Y + A \left(\frac{V}{\bar{V}} \right)(1 - m) = Z + PH + \left(\frac{C\{S\}}{e} \right)\left(\frac{V}{\bar{V}} \right)(1 - m)$$

- And tax price is

$$\text{TP} = \text{MC}\frac{V}{\bar{V}}(1 - m)$$

- The matching rate:
  - Note that in this formulation, the matching rate is the state share

  $$m = \frac{S}{S + L}$$

  - Some studies use the state match per dollar of local or

  $$m^* = \frac{S}{L}$$

  - This leads to:

  $$\left(\frac{C\{S\} - A}{e}\right)\left(\frac{1}{1 + m^*}\right) = t\bar{V}$$

- Matching vs. lump-sum aid:
  - There is a well-known theorem that matching aid has a more stimulative effect than equal-cost lump-sum aid.
  - This is an application of the classic microeconomic theorem that price subsidies have larger effects (per dollar) than cash grants.
  - The relevant graph follows:

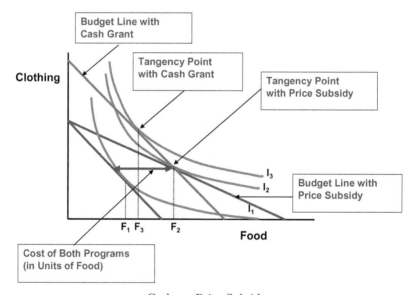

Cash vs. Price Subsidy.

- This theorem fails to consider two key elements of the demand for public services:
  - According to the Bradford/Oates equivalence theorem, matching aid alters the value of existing lump-sum aid (and, to be specific, makes it less stimulative).
  - Both matching and lump-sum aid may alter efficiency, but these effects are not well understood.
- With matching and lump-sum aid the household budget constraint is

$$Y + (1+f)A \left(\frac{V}{\bar{V}}\right)(1-m)$$

$$= Z + PH + \left(\frac{C\{S\}}{e}\right)\left(\frac{V}{\bar{V}}\right)(1-m)$$

- Matching aid affects the value people place on lump-sum aid (because it alters their tax price).
- This effect could reverse the standard theorem because it lowers the stimulative impact of matching aid.

4.4. *Aid and Efficiency*

- Both matching and lump-sum aid appear in augmented income, which affects efficiency.
- Moreover, matching aid appears directly in tax price, which also affects efficiency.
- Hence both type of aid may alter efficiency, but in different ways; these effects might reverse the standard theorem.

4.5. *Tax Exemptions as Aid*

- The New York STAR property tax exemption is like matching aid.
  - With STAR, $T = t(V - X) = tV(1 - X/V)$; the matching rate is X/V. Hence

$$Y + (1+f)A \left(\frac{V}{\bar{V}}\right)\left(1 - \frac{X}{V}\right) = Z + PH + \left(\frac{C\{S\}}{e}\right)\left(\frac{V}{\bar{V}}\right)\left(1 - \frac{X}{V}\right)$$

○ That's what we estimate in the STAR paper (Eom *et al.*, *EF&P*, 2014). The price elasticity on the STAR term is −0.6.

4.5.1. *Salience and STAR*

- Inspired by an experiment by Chetty *et al.* (*AER*, 2009), many scholars not look for the impact of salience or visibility.
- Large changes are more salient than small changes.
- Highly publicized tax changes are more salient than others.
- STAR (equivalent to matching aid) was highly publicized in its early years.
- STAR was phased in, with 3 years of large changes, followed by many years of small adjustments.
- So the STAR price elasticities should be largest at the beginning, which is what Nguyen-Hoang and Yinger find in a 2018 working paper on STAR price elasticities (2018b; a follow-up to Eom *et al.*, 2014).

4.5.2. *What causes the flypaper effect?*

- Many hypotheses have been offered to explain the flypaper effect.
- Hines and Thaler (*JEP*, 1995) argue that it arises from the behavioral economics concept of framing.

  ○ Money that flows into a government's budget is framed by households as support for public services, whereas money that flows into a household budget is framed as support for general consumption.

- The working paper by Nguyen-Hoang and Yinger on the flypaper effect (2018a) finds empirical support for this hypothesis.

  ○ STAR exemptions appear on a homeowner's tax bill, so it is reasonable to think that they are framed as part of their "local public education" budget, with a primary impact on education demand decisions.
  ○ In 2007–2009, STAR exemptions were supplemented by STAR rebate checks which were 30% of STAR exemption savings in

2007 (with adjustments base on income in 2008 and 2009); these checks arrived in the mail.

   ○ It is reasonable to suppose that these rebate checks are unlabeled income, and hence appear in a household's general budget, with minimal impact on the demand for school quality.

- Although this framing hypothesis is reasonable, the STAR rebates are formulated as an adjustment to the STAR tax share; in effect they increase the STAR exemption amount by 30% (with some variation in 2008 and 2009).

   ○ Another possibility, therefore, is that voters view the rebates as an adjustment to their tax share — not as an addition to unlabeled income.

- The main tests in N-H/Y compare an econometric specification in which rebates are treated as part of the STAR tax share and a specification in which the tax savings from the rebates are treated as income.

   ○ Let t be the school district's tax rate and τ be the rebate percentage. Then in the rebate years.

   ○ Specification 1 (STAR tax share with rebates):

$$\text{STAR Tax Share} = \left(1 - \frac{X}{V} - \frac{\tau X}{V}\right) \equiv \left(1 - \frac{X(1+\tau)}{V}\right)$$

   ○ Specification 2 (Income plus STAR tax savings):

$$Y^* = Y + t\tau X$$

- N-H/Y conduct specification tests for these two specifications.

   ○ The specification consistent with framing (with the tax savings from rebates in income) dominates the other specification.

   ○ N-H/Y also have some additional evidence supporting framing; check out the paper if you are interested.

- The N-H/Y working paper also goes over many other theories about the causes of the flypaper effects.

   ○ In the case of state aid to education, the available evidence does not support any of these other theories.

Bidding and Sorting

- **Class Outline**
  1. **Bidding**
  2. **Sorting**
  3. **Is a Federal System Efficient?**

Class Overview

- This class provides an intuitive overview of the concepts of bidding and sorting and the use of these concepts in understanding a system of local governments.
- A more formal treatment can be found in Ross and Yinger, *Handbook of Regional and Urban Economics*, Vol. 3, 1999.

Three Related Questions

- How do households select a community in which to live? (= *The subject of this class*)
- How do communities select the levels of local public services and the property tax rate? (= *Demand!*)
- Under what conditions is the community-choice process compatible with the local voting process? (= *General Equilibrium*)

Tiebout

- Charles Tiebout argued in a famous 1956, *JPE* article that people shop for a community, just as they shop for other things.

o This process came to be known as "shopping with one's feet."
o The Tiebout model became very influential both because it identified an important type of behavior to be studied and because it concluded that the community-choice process is **efficient**.
o Although Tiebout's model has neither a housing market nor a property tax, many people (not including me) still accept his efficiency claim, at least to a first approximation.

The Consensus Post-Tiebout Model, Assumptions

• Households care about housing, public services, and other goods.
• Households fall into distinct income/taste classes.
• Households are mobile (i.e. can move costless across jurisdictions).

o So an equilibrium cannot exist unless all people in a given income/taste class achieve the same level of satisfaction.

• All households who live in a jurisdiction receive the same level of public services.
• Residence in a jurisdiction is a precondition for the receipt of public services there (an assumption undermined by some education choice programs).
• Public services are financed through a local property tax.
• An urban area has many local jurisdictions, which have fixed boundaries and vary in their local public service quality and property tax rates.
• Households are homeowners (or else they are renters and the property tax is shifted fully onto them through rents).

1. Bidding

• These assumptions describe a housing market in which households compete for access to the most desirable locations, i.e. those with the best combinations of public services and property tax rates.

- This competition takes the form of housing *bids*, with different bids for different types of household.
- An analysis of bidding is based on four concepts:
  - Housing is measured in units of *housing services*, H, which can be thought of as quality-adjusted square feet.
  - The associated *housing price*, labeled P, is what a household bids *per unit of H* per year.
  - The *rent* for a housing unit, R, equals PH. If the unit is an apartment, $R = PH$ is equivalent to the annual rent.
  - If the unit is owner-occupied, R is not observed but is implicit. The *value* of a housing unit, V, is the amount someone would pay to own that unit; it equals the present value of the flow of net rental services associated with ownership or $V = PH/r = R/r$.

1.1. *The Bid Function*

- P is the amount a household is willing to pay per unit of H in a jurisdiction with service quality S and property tax rate t: $P = P\{S, t\}$.
- A bid function is defined for all values of S and t, regardless of whether or not these values are the ones a household actually experiences.
- We will have to do some more work to figure out market prices.
- This logic is expressed in the following two figures:
  - Figure "Housing Bids as a Function of Public Service Quality (Holding the Property Tax Rate Constant)" shows how bids (P) change as S changes (holding t constant).
  - Figure "Housing Bids as a Function of the Property Tax Rate (Holding Public Service Quality Constant)" shows how bids change as t changes (holding S constant).
- These curves hint at the idea that housing prices reflect S and t but we are not quite there yet.

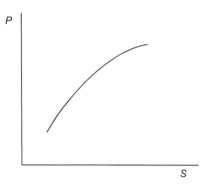

Housing Bids as a Function of Public Service Quality (Holding the Property Tax Rate Constant).

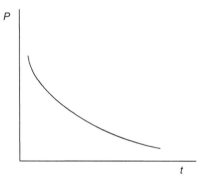

Housing Bids as a Function of the Property Tax Rate (Holding Public Service Quality Constant).

2. Sorting

- If all household are alike, then Figures "Housing Bids as a Function of Public Service Quality (Holding the Property Tax Rate Constant)" and "Housing Bids as a Function of the Property Tax Rate (Holding Public Service Quality Constant)" describe market outcomes; in equilibrium housing prices will adjust to exactly compensate households who end up in low-S or high-t jurisdictions.

  ○ This compensation idea is a key to the intuition.

- But obviously households are not all alike, and different types of households must *sort* across jurisdictions.

2.1. *Sorting and Slopes*

- The key idea in the consensus model is that households sort according to the steepness of their bid functions.
  - ○ The slope is $\partial P/\partial S$; a steeper slope corresponds to a greater willingness to pay (WTP) for an *increment* in S.
- Housing sellers prefer to sell to the highest bidder, so a steeper slope wins where S is higher.
- Note that in the long run sellers prefer the highest P, not the highest PH.
- H can be adjusted by adding on to a housing unit or dividing it into smaller units.
- The seller wants the highest return per unit of H, which is given by P.

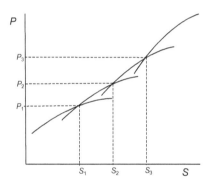

Consensus Bidding and Sorting.

2.2. *The Price Envelope*

- In Figure "Consensus Bidding and Sorting", the observed market price function is the *envelope* of the underlying bid functions, say P^E. In other words, the price function is the set of winning bids. This function shows how S and t show up in housing prices.
  - ○ This phenomenon is known as *capitalization*, because it has to do with the impact of annual flows (S and t) on the value of a capital asset (a house).
  - ○ As we will see, many studies estimate capitalization!

2.3. *Sorting and Bid-Function Heights*

- One subtle point in Figure "Consensus Bidding and Sorting" is that the *heights* of the bid functions adjust so that each type of household has enough room.

  ○ To get the logic right, start with a point at which the bid functions of two groups intersect — i.e. their heights are the same.

- From this starting point, it is obvious that the group with the steeper bid function bids more where S is higher.
- It is impossible to shift the heights around so that (a) both groups live somewhere and (b) the group with the flatter slope lives where S is higher.

2.4. *The Single-Crossing Condition*

- It is logically possible for household type **A** to have a steeper bid function than household type **B** at one value of S and for a household type **B** to have a steeper bid function at a different value of S.

  ○ In this case it may be impossible to find an equilibrium.
  ○ Almost all scholars rule out this case with the so called single-crossing condition, which is that if household type A has a steeper bid function than household type B at one value of S, it also has a steeper bid function at any other value of S.
  ○ This assumption is equivalent to a regularity condition on the underlying utility functions.

2.5. *Sorting and Empirical Research*

- Figure "Consensus Bidding and Sorting" has two key implications for empirical work.
- First, any estimate of the impact of S on P (or on R or V) blends WTP (movement along a bid function) and sorting (shifting across bid functions).

- ○ In Figure "Consensus Bidding and Sorting", for example, $(P_3 - P_1)$ does not measure any group's WTP for S_3 vs. S_1.
- ○ It is very difficult to untangle these two effects!
- Second, the market relationship between S and P, that is, the envelope, is very unlikely to be linear (or even log-linear).
  - ○ Because sorting is based on bid-function slopes, the slope of the winning bidder (the one we observe) goes up as the level of S increases.
  - ○ Figure "A Nonlinear Envelope with Linear Bid Functions" gives a simple example with linear bid functions (which correspond to a constant MWTP, which is equivalent to a horizontal demand curve).
  - ○ But Figure "A Nonlinear Envelope with Nonlinear Bid Functions." shows that the envelope may still have a declining slope.

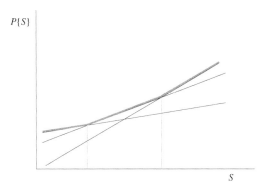

A Nonlinear Envelope with Linear Bid Functions.

2.6. *Normal Sorting*

- Under normal circumstances, higher-income households will pay more for an increment in S. See Figure "The Demand for Local Public Services", where MB = MWTP (and a subscript 2 indicates high-income).
- So high-income households will normally win the competition in high-S jurisdictions.

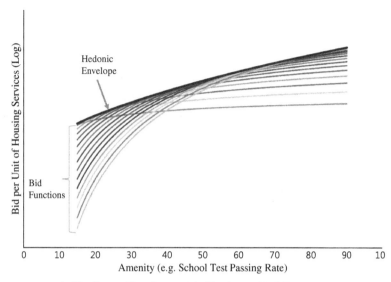

A Nonlinear Envelope with Nonlinear Bid Functions.

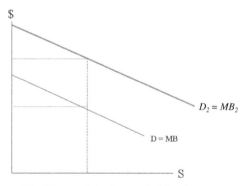

The Demand for Local Public Services.

- Low-income households win the competition in low-S jurisdictions because they are willing to accept low H, e.g. by doubling up, and hence can bid a lot per unit of H.
- The formal condition for normal sorting is that the ratio of the income and elasticities of demand for S must exceed the income elasticity of demand for H.

$$-\frac{\theta}{\mu} > \alpha$$

- Note that α matters because a household's WTP for S (and hence its bid) is spread out over the number of units of H it buys.

2.7. Sorting and Inequality

- Sorting results in a system of local governments in which some jurisdictions are much wealthier than others.
- Moreover, as discussed earlier in the class, the cost of public services is often linked to poverty.
  - The overall result is a federal system in which both resources and costs are unevenly distributed — and in which higher-income people receive higher levels of S.
- The key normative tradeoff: community choice vs. equality of opportunity.
- One way to show the link between sorting and inequality is to obtain a measure of what people bid for all neighborhood attributes put together and then determine whether this measure is linked to income.
- Some evidence of this type comes from the neighborhood measure in my 2015, *JUE* article (more later on the estimating method). Figure "Income and Neighborhood Quality" shows that this link is very strong!

2.8. Heterogeneity within a Jurisdiction

- Sorting implies a tendency for jurisdictions to be homogeneous by income.
- But this homogeneity is not complete:
  - Other factors influence demand.
  - Heterogeneous communities arise where bid functions cross as shown in Figure "Heterogeneity with Consensus Bidding and Sorting" which is the revised version of Figure "Consensus Bidding and Sorting". Many household types could live in a large jurisdiction.

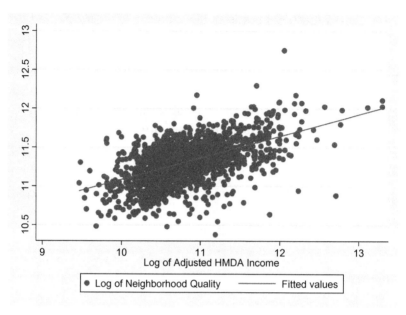

Income and Neighborhood Quality.

Note: In this figure, income is the income of households receiving mortgages; the Home Mortgage Disclosure Act (HMDA) data is the source of this variable.

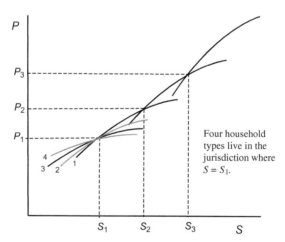

Heterogeneity with Consensus Bidding and Sorting.

2.9. *Sorting and Tax Rates*

- Figures "Consensus Bidding and Sorting" and "Heterogeneity with Consensus Bidding and Sorting" holds t constant.
- In fact, t does not affect sorting.

  ○ Any household is willing to pay \$1 to avoid \$1 of property taxes (or to bid 1% more in a location where t is 1% lower).
  ○ Sorting only involves S.

- Nevertheless, sorting is sometimes shown with net bids that reflect both S and t. See Figure "Consensus Bidding and Sorting Net of Taxes".

  ○ Eventually these net bid functions turn town as the marginal benefit from S falls short of the tax cost.

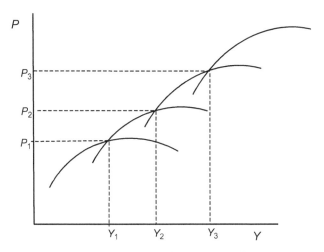

Consensus Bidding and Sorting Net of Taxes.

2.10. *The Hamilton Approach*

- Bruce Hamilton (*Urban Studies*, 1975) developed a Tiebout-like model with housing and a property tax based on three crucial assumptions:

o Housing supply is elastic (presumably by movement in jurisdiction's boundaries).

o Zoning is set at exactly the optimal level of housing for the residents of a jurisdiction.

o Government services are produced at a constant cost per household.

- The striking implication of the Hamilton assumptions is that capitalization disappears. See Figure "Hamilton Bidding and Sorting".

- Everyone ends up in their most-preferred jurisdiction, so nobody bids up the price in any other jurisdiction.

- This prediction (no capitalization) is rejected by all the evidence (to be covered in future classes).

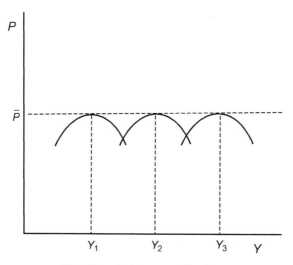

Hamilton Bidding and Sorting.

3. Is a Federal System Efficient?

- Tiebout (with no housing or property tax) said picking a community is like shopping for a shirt and is therefore efficient (in the allocative sense).

- This result is replicated with a housing market and a property tax under the Hamilton assumptions.
  - These assumptions are extreme and the model is rejected by the evidence.

3.1. *Sources of Inefficiency*

- Heterogeneity:
  - Heterogeneity leads to inefficient levels of local public services.
  - Outcomes are determined by the median voter; voters with different preferences experience "dead-weight losses" compared with having their own jurisdiction.
  - See Figure "Inefficiency Due to Heterogeneity".

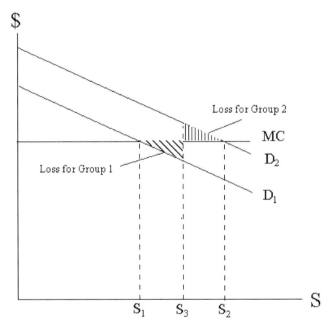

Inefficiency Due to Heterogeneity.

3.2. *Heterogeneity in Services?*

- The consensus model assumes that all households in a jurisdiction receive the same services.

- o This is not true; higher-income neighborhoods have better police protection and probably better elementary schools, for example.
- o This eliminates some of the inefficiency in Figure "Income and Neighborhood Quality" — but adds to inequality.
- This topic is poorly understood; research is needed!

3.3. *Sources of Inefficiency*

- The Property Tax:
  - o Producers of housing base their decisions on P, whereas buyers respond to $P(1 + t/r)$, (which, as we will see, is constant across jurisdictions).
  - o This introduces a so-called "tax wedge" between producer and consumer decisions, which leads to under-consumption of housing.

3.4. *Hamilton and Inefficiency*

- These two sources of inefficiency disappear in Hamilton's model:
  - o Boundaries adjust so that all jurisdictions are homogeneous (despite extensive evidence that boundaries do not change for this reason).
  - o Zoning is set so that housing consumption is optimal (despite the incentives of residents to set zoning above their housing level so new residents pay more).

3.5. *Conclusions on Efficiency*

- The Hamilton model shows how extreme the assumptions must be to generate an efficient outcome.
- Nevertheless, many scholars defend our federal system as efficient.
- Instead of identifying policies, such as intergovernmental aid programs, to improve its efficiency.

Property Tax Capitalization

1. Introduction

- The basic bidding model implies that the price of housing services will be higher in jurisdictions with lower property taxes.

  ○ This is called *property tax capitalization.*

- Although he was not the first to estimate property tax capitalization, *Wallace Oates* (my public finance professor) brought new attention to the topic with his famous 1969 *JPE* paper on the *Tiebout hypothesis.*

  ○ Oates used data for suburbs in NJ and found evidence of tax and service capitalization (more later).

1.1. *What is Property Tax Capitalization?*

- It is just the impact of the present value of expected annual property tax payments on the value of a property.
- It can be derived from an asset pricing model or from the household maximization problem in bidding models.

1.1.1. *Asset value*

- The value of an asset equals the *present value* of the net benefits from owning it.
- Without property taxes, the amount someone is willing to pay for a house is the present value of the *rental benefits*, or

$$V = \sum_{y=1}^{L} \frac{\hat{P}H}{(1+r)^y} = \frac{\hat{P}H}{(1+r)} + \frac{\hat{P}H}{(1+r)^2} + \cdots + \frac{\hat{P}H}{(1+r)^L}$$

where $\hat{P}$ is the pre-tax price of housing services, H is housing services, r is the real *discount rate*, and L is the *expected lifetime* of a house.

1.1.2. *The magic of algebra*

$$V(1+r) = \hat{P}H + \frac{\hat{P}H}{(1+r)} + \frac{\hat{P}H}{(1+r)^2} + \cdots + \frac{\hat{P}H}{(1+r)^{L-1}}$$

and

$$V - V(1+r) = -\hat{P}H + \frac{\hat{P}H}{(1+r)^L}$$

or

$$V[1 - (1+r)] = \hat{P}H[(1+r)^{-L} - 1]$$

or

$$V = \hat{P}H \left(\frac{1 - (1+r)^{-L}}{r} \right) = \frac{\hat{P}H}{r'}$$

where

$$r' = \frac{r}{1 - (1+r)^{-L}}$$

1.1.3. *House value simplified*

- If the real value of rental services is constant over time and L is large, this equation reduces to:

$$V = \frac{\hat{P}H}{r}$$

- *The value of a house equals its annual rental value divided by a discount rate.*
- Because housing lasts a long time, this is a reasonable — and obviously helpful — simplification.

1.1.4. *Adding property taxes*

- The *property tax payment*, T, is the product of a *nominal tax rate*, m, and an *assessed value*, A.
- It is also the product of an *effective tax rate*, t, and a *market value*, V.
- In symbols

$$T = mA = tV$$

- Annual property taxes represent an *expense* for a homeowner.
- *With this new expense*, the house value equation becomes:

$$V = \sum_{y=1}^{L} \frac{\hat{P}H}{(1+r)^y} - \sum_{y=1}^{L} \frac{tV}{(1+r)^y}$$
$$= \frac{\hat{P}H}{r} - \frac{tV}{r}$$

- Note that property taxes are added as a *flow* because they must be paid every year — a flow that is "capitalized."
- This equation assumes that property taxes are *fully capitalized*.

- As we will see, this might not be the case, so a more general form is:

$$V = \sum_{y=1}^{L} \frac{\hat{P}H}{(1+r)^y} - \sum_{y=1}^{L} \frac{\beta t V}{(1+r)^y}$$

$$= \frac{\hat{P}H}{r} - \frac{\beta t V}{r}$$

where β is the "*degree of property tax capitalization;*" i.e. the impact of a \$1 increase in the present value of property taxes on the value of a house.

1.2. *The Degree of Property Tax Capitalization*

- A value of β equal to 1.0 corresponds to *full capitalization.*
- A value of β equal to 0.0 corresponds to *no capitalization.*
- If β equals to 0.5 a \$1 increase in the present value of property taxes leads to a \$0.50 decrease in the value of a house.
- *The value of β need not be the same under all circumstances.*

1.2.1. *The capitalization equation*

- Solving the above for V yields the well-known form for the *capitalization equation*:

$$V = \frac{\hat{P}H}{r + \beta t}$$

- Thus, *houses facing higher effective property tax rates (t) will have lower values (V).*
- The strength of this relationship depends on β.

1.3. *How Does Tax Capitalization Arise?*

- *Real estate brokers* indicate anticipated property tax payments so buyers can make comparisons across houses.
- *Lenders* require mortgage plus tax payments to equal a fixed percentage of an applicant's income.

○ An increase in T must be *offset* by a drop in the mortgage, and hence a drop in how much the applicant can pay for the house, V.

1.3.1. *Expectations*

- Another issue is that the expected lifetime of current tax rates might be $N < L$. In this case, we need to use r', not r:
- This leads to:

$$V = \sum_{y=1}^{L} \frac{\hat{P}H}{(1+r)^y} - \sum_{y=1}^{N} \frac{\beta t V}{(1+r)^y}$$

$$= \frac{\hat{P}H}{r} - \frac{\beta' t V}{r'}$$

where β' is the "degree of property tax capitalization" *after accounting for differences in expectations.*

- Now when we solve for V we get:

$$V \left(1 + \frac{\beta' t}{r'}\right) = \frac{\hat{P}H}{r}$$

or

$$V = \frac{\hat{P}H}{r\left(1 + \frac{\beta' t}{r'}\right)} = \frac{\hat{P}H}{r + \left(\frac{r}{r'}\beta'\right)t} = \frac{\hat{P}H}{r + \beta'[1 - (1+r)^{-N}]t}$$

$$= \frac{\hat{P}H}{r + \beta t} = \frac{\hat{P}H}{r\left(1 + \frac{\beta}{r}t\right)}$$

where

$$\beta = \left(\frac{r}{r'}\right)\beta'$$

- The coefficient to be estimated, β, is the expression in front of t, so it includes both β' and the impact of different expectations about the lifetime of a house and of property taxes.
- This explains why we need both β and β'; the first is what we estimate but the second is the underlying degree of capitalization.
- It is still not obvious why we need to consider expectations — hold on.

1.3.2. *Inter- and intra-jurisdiction variation*

- These equations apply *within a community.*
  - Recall that

$$t = m\left(\frac{A}{V}\right)$$

  - *Poor assessments* result in higher assessment–sales ratios, and hence higher effective tax rates, for some houses than for others.
- These equations also apply *across communities*, which may have very different effective tax rates.

1.3.3. *Property tax changes*

- Here is a *change form* of the equation:

$$V_1 = \frac{\hat{P}H}{r + \beta t_1} \quad \text{and} \quad V_2 = \frac{\hat{P}H}{r + \beta t_2}$$

so

$$V_2 - V_1 \equiv \Delta V = \frac{\hat{P}H}{r + \beta t_2} - \frac{\hat{P}H}{r + \beta t_1} = \hat{P}H\left(\frac{1}{r + \beta t_2} - \frac{1}{r + \beta t_1}\right)$$

$$= \hat{P}H\left(\frac{-\beta(t_2 - t_1)}{(r + \beta t_1)(r + \beta t_2)}\right) = \left(\frac{\hat{P}H}{r + \beta t_1}\right)\left(\frac{-\beta \Delta t}{r + \beta t_2}\right)$$

$$= V_1\left(\frac{-\beta \Delta t}{r + \beta t_2}\right)$$

so

$$\frac{\Delta V}{V_1} = \left(\frac{-\beta \Delta t}{r + \beta t_2}\right)$$

1.3.4. *The strategy in PTHV*

- In Yinger *et al.* (*Property Taxes and House Values, PTHV*, 1988) this equation is used to study *intra-jurisdictional* capitalization, that is, the capitalization of effective property tax rate differences within a community.

- To remove the impact of inter-jurisdictional tax differences/ changes, and of other factors that vary over time, the dependent variable is *deflated* using a housing price index.
- This removes from V the impact of any change in the average effective tax rate (among other things) and leaves just the impact of the change in the deviation from the average tax rate.
  - Now express the effective tax rate as $t = \bar{t} + (t - \bar{t})$ and put an "*" on V to indicate deflation.

$$\frac{\Delta V^*}{V_1^*} = \left(\frac{-\beta \Delta t}{r + \beta t_2}\right) = \frac{-\beta \left((\bar{t}_2 - \bar{t}_1) + [(t_2 - \bar{t}_2) - (t_1 - \bar{t}_1)]\right)}{r + \beta[\bar{t}_1 + (\bar{t}_2 - \bar{t}_1) + (t_2 - \bar{t}_2)]}$$

- Deflation implies that

$$(\bar{t}_2 - \bar{t}_1) = 0$$

- Accurate revaluation implies that

$$(t_2 - \bar{t}_2) = 0$$

  - Hence:

$$\frac{\Delta V^*}{V_1^*} = \frac{-\beta \left((t_2 - \bar{t}_2) - (t_1 - \bar{t}_1)\right)}{r + \beta \bar{t}_1} = \frac{-\beta \Delta t^*}{r + \beta \bar{t}_1} = b \Delta t^*$$

where

$$b = \frac{-\beta}{r + \beta \bar{t}_1}$$

and

$$\beta = \frac{br}{1 - b\bar{t}_1}$$

Thus, with data on $\bar{t}_1$, an estimate of b, and an assumption about r, one can obtain an estimate of β.

1.3.5. *Error in PTHV*

- These equations correct an error in PTHV.
- The algebra in that book mistakenly ignores the denominator of the previous equation.

○ As we will see below, this mistake implies that the book understates the value of β by about 30%.

1.3.6. *Research issues in estimating β*

- *First,* this estimation involves a nonlinear relationship between t and V, even after taking logarithms, so it cannot be estimated with linear regression methods.
- After taking logs, the basic equation is:

$$\ln(V) = \ln(\hat{P}) + \ln(H) - \ln(r) - \ln\left(1 + \frac{\beta}{r}t\right)$$

1.3.6.1. Research Issue 1

- One can use the approximation $\ln\{1 + a\} \approx a$, but it may not be very good in this case, because $(\beta/r)t$ may not be close to zero.

  ○ A change form of the equation may work better. It can be estimated with NL2SLS.
  ○ With reassessment, it can be estimated in linear form under the assumption that assessments are accurate, i.e. that

$$(t_2 - \bar{t}_2) = 0$$

- Note that it is impossible to separate β and r in the estimation.
- One can only estimate their ratio.

  ○ This leads to the next issue. . . .

1.3.6.2. Research Issue 2

- *Second,* the value of the discount rate, r, is not observed, and it is impossible to estimate r and β separately.
- Most studies follow Oates by estimating a value of β/r, assuming a value for r, and then calculating the implied value of β.
- The trouble with this approach is that the value of β depends on an untested assumption that varies across studies.

  ○ In fact, the most extreme estimates of β in the literature, in either direction, are driven largely by extreme assumptions about r.

- ■ Moreover, scholars are amazingly careless about r, often using a nominal interest rate, when the theory clearly shows that a real rate, say 2 to 5%, is needed.
- ■ A real rate equals the nominal or market rate minus anticipated inflation.

- o PTHV takes a long-run, low-risk nominal rate (as for an investment in housing) and subtracts anticipated inflation based on a study of the factors that determine inflation expectations. This leads to a three percent rate.

1.3.6.3. Research Issue 3

- *Third*, the asset-pricing logic behind tax capitalization requires assumptions about house buyers' *expectations*.
- To be specific, this logic predicts that a $1 increase in the present value of future property taxes will lead to a $1 decline in house value (i.e. $\beta' = 1$), but it does not say that current tax differences will be fully capitalized (i.e. $\beta = 1$) *if they are not expected to persist*.
- Virtually all the literature estimates the capitalization of *current* property tax differences.

  - o Under the assumption that current tax differences will persist indefinitely, the assumption that $\beta = 1$ makes sense.
  - o In fact, however, current differences may not be expected to persist. In this case, we can use the result derived earlier, namely,

$$\beta = \beta'[1 - (1 + r)^{-N}]$$

  where N is the length of time current tax differences are expected to persist. The theory indicates that $\beta' = 1$, but the estimated β clearly need not equal to one, and indeed need not equal the same value under all circumstances.

- Research Issue 3 Examples

  - o If current property tax differences across (or within) communities are expected to disappear in 10 years and $r = 0.03$, then this equation implies that the estimated β will be only 26% even if $\beta' = 1$.

○ If revaluation is scheduled every 6 years, say, then the estimated β should decline as one moves closer to the year of revaluation.

1.3.6.4. Research Issue 4

- *Fourth*, because $t = T/V$, one must treat t as endogenous.

    ○ This endogeneity is both definitional (t is a function of the dependent variable) and behavioral (factors unobserved by the researcher but observed by the assessor may influence both T and V).

- PTHV uses a model of assessor behavior to identify some instruments and then uses either NL2SLS or 2SLS.

1.3.6.5. Research Issue 5

- *Fifth*, one must be careful about omitted variable bias.

    ○ Good data on housing traits are needed.
    ○ This is not quite such a big problem with double-sales data, which difference out time-invariant traits.
    ○ Even with double-sales data, it helps to control for renovations.
    ○ Deflating V eliminates the possibility that the estimated impact of a change in t is biased by the omission of other changes at the jurisdiction level.

1.3.6.6. Research Issue 6

- *Sixth*, one must consider itemization.
- If a taxpayer itemizes on her federal income taxes, then she gets to deduct property taxes. So a $1 increase in the present value of property taxes does not really cost this taxpayer $1. Estimated capitalization may reflect this effect.

    ○ However, mortgage interest payments are also deductible, so an income tax correction applies to both the numerator and denominator of the estimated coefficient, β/r. If s is the marginal income tax rate, this ratio with full deductibility of interest cam be written as $[\beta(1-s)]/[r(1-s)] = \beta/r$.

- One might also argue that the denominator is not the mortgage interest rate, but is instead the opportunity cost of investing in housing, which is the return on other low-risk, long-term investments and is unaffected by deductibility.

1.3.6.7. Evidence on Property Tax Capitalization

- Every reasonable study of property tax capitalization finds a statistically significant negative impact of property taxes on house values.

  ○ *Estimates of β vary from* 15 *to* 100%.
  ○ The main reason for this variation appears to involve *expectations*.

1.3.6.8. The Role of Expectations

- So far, current tax differences across houses are implicitly assumed to persist indefinitely.

  ○ But *if tax differences are not expected to persist, the capitalization of* current *differences, β, declines.*

    ■ A difference observed today that will disappear upon sale has no impact on V.
    ■ A difference observed today that is expected to last one year will have only a tiny impact on sales price.

1.3.6.9. The Case of Massachusetts

- In *Massachusetts*, revaluations were required by the state supreme court, but enforcement was weak.

  ○ Communities knew they could avoid revaluation for many years.
  ○ Existing tax differences were *expected to persist*, but not forever.

- PTHV finds that *current tax differences were capitalized at a rate of* 32%.

  ○ This is consistent with the expectation that current tax differences would disappear in 13 years.

Corrected Estimates of Capitalization in Waltham for *Property Taxes and House Values.*

	Nonlinear Version (Equation (8))	Linear Version (Equation (9))
Estimate of b	7.4233	7.0433
Value of	0.0420	0.0420
Value of $1 - b$	0.6882	0.7042
Original β	0.2227	0.2113
Corrected β	0.3236	0.3000
Understatement (%)	31.2	29.6
Implied N(years)	13.2	12.1

1.3.6.10. The Case of Syracuse

- In **Syracuse** in the early 1990s, revaluation had not occurred for decades and did not appear likely to happen any time soon.
- But the city council *unexpectedly* decided to revalue.
  - ○ A study of capitalization in Syracuse by a PA Ph.D. student (Eisenberg) found *capitalization rates near 100%* — exactly what the theory predicts when tax differences are expected to persist.
  - ○ This result applies when people are borrowing to the limit and not itemizing.

1.3.6.11. Stay or Go?

- If property taxes are fully capitalized, then any tax changes show up in house values immediately and *there is no way to escape* them.
  - ○ An owner with a *tax increase* must either stay and pay the higher tax or leave and suffer a *capital loss.*
  - ○ An owner with a *tax cut* gets a *capital gain.*
- Moreover, the loss is the *full present value* of the future increases in taxes.

1.4. *Property Tax Capitalization and Public Policy*

- Because of these gains and losses, tax capitalization has bizarre implications for *public policy*.
- Consider *revaluation*, which is a systematic revision of all assessed values.
- Revaluation leads to *capital gains* for homeowners who were over-assessed and to *capital losses* for homeowners who were under-assessed.

1.4.1. *Capitalization and policy*

- For *long-term residents*, these changes are fair.
  - A resident who has been under-assessed for a long time has been given, in effect, a loan from the city and *revaluation just claims back this "loan."*
- But for *new residents*, these changes are not fair.
  - If someone bought an under-assessed house one day and the change is announced the next, *this person has a capital loss even though she did not benefit* from the poor assessment system.
- Two ways to *minimize this fairness problem*:
  - First, introduce a *long lag* between announcement and implementation. This lag allows owners at the time of announcement to escape some of the burden of the tax changes.
  - Second, make sure houses are *revalued upon re-sale*, which they were not in Massachusetts or Syracuse.
- A revaluation imposes some unfair gains and losses but restores fairness in the near term and boosts faith in local government.
  - *This trade only makes sense if assessments are updated regularly.*
  - Otherwise, gains and losses are handed out each year as assessment errors mount.
- Poor assessments also lead to court cases, which the city usually loses.
  - People who buy over-assessed property pay low prices — and then can sue the city for a rebate because of unfairly high taxes.

○ This happened in Boston, to the tune of tens of millions of dollars.

○ The only way to avoid this crazy situation is to *keep assessments up to date!*

- *Proposition* 13 in California represents another unusual case.
- The proposition fixes assessment growth at 2%, so the assessment/sales ratio, and hence t, declines over time for long-term owners.
- *This cannot be turned into a capital gain* because houses are revalued upon sale.
- *But it represents a gift to long-term owners* and *it discourages mobility.*

  ○ The U.S. Supreme Court said this was legal. Voters in California and a few other states like this reward to long-term residents; I don't.

Lecture 11

Hedonics

1. Hedonic Regressions

- A regression of house value or rent on housing and neighborhood traits is called a *hedonic regression.*
- Hedonic regressions appear in markets for other products with multiple attributes, such as automobiles or computers.

  ○ But this class focuses on the application of hedonic analysis to *housing* markets.

- Many of the outcomes of interest in public finance, such as public services (e.g. education) or neighborhood amenities (e.g. air quality) are not traded in private markets.

  ○ As a result, we cannot directly observe demand for these outcomes or determine the value households place on changes in these outcomes (as in benefit–cost analysis, for example).

  ■ However, households have to compete for access to locations with desirable attributes, and their bids reveal something about the "missing" demand.

- o Thus, *hedonic regressions provide a key way for scholars to study household demand for public services and neighborhood amenities.*
- Hedonic regressions have been used, for example, to study household demand for:
  - o School quality;
  - o Clean air;
  - o Protection from crime;
  - o Neighborhood ethnicity;
  - o Distance from toxic waste sites;
  - o Distance from public housing.
- As we know from the theory of local public finance, different household types also compete against each other for entry into the most desirable neighborhoods.
- This competition takes place through bids on housing.
  - o So hedonic regressions also can, in principle, tell us something about the way different household types sort across locations — and therefore can give us insight into the nature of our highly decentralized federal system.

2. The Rosen Framework

- A famous paper by Sherwin Rosen (*JPE*, 1974) gives a framework everyone uses based on *bid-functions* and their mathematical *envelope*.
  - o A bid-function is the amount a household type would pay for housing at different levels of an amenity, holding their utility constant.
  - o The hedonic envelope is the set of winning bids; each point on the envelope is tangent to one of the underlying bid-functions.

2.1. *Rosen's Predecessors*

- Rosen did not, by the way, invent bidding and sorting.
  - o That honor goes to Johann Heinrich von Thünen in his 1826 book, *The Isolated State.* Modern treatment began with Alonso's 1964 book, *Location and Land Use.*

- Rosen cites Alonso and Tiebout, whose 1956 paper in the *JPE* raised the issue of community choice (with a simple model), along with early hedonic studies.

  o But Rosen's paper is justly famous because it provides a very general model.

2.2. The Rosen Picture

- Here is the Rosen picture, where z_1 is a product attribute, θ indicates a bid-function, and p is the *hedonic price function*, i.e. the envelope:

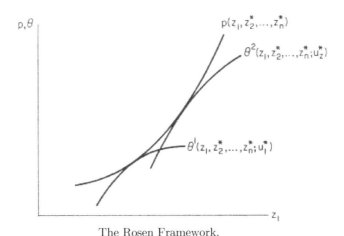

The Rosen Framework.

2.3. Household Heterogeneity

- Note that Rosen's framework is designed to consider *heterogeneous* households — i.e. households with different demands for the amenity as indicated by utility, u^*, in the bids.

  o If all households are alike, the hedonic price function is the same as the bid-function.

- But with heterogeneous households, we only observe one point — the tangency point — on each household type's bid-function.

- The tangency between the bid-functions and the hedonic price function is key.
- The slope of the hedonic price function is called the *implicit price* of the attribute on the X axis, Z_1.
- Maximizing households set the marginal benefit from Z_1 equal to their marginal cost which is equal to the implicit price.
- Households with different demand traits will have tangency points at different places on the hedonic price function.
- Note also, that in this set up, the hedonic price function is the mathematical envelope of the bid-functions. More on this later.

2.4. *Rosen and Housing*

- Rosen's paper is about hedonics in general, not just about housing.

  - But it is consistent with the bidding and sorting framework developed at about the same time in local public finance (as Rosen mentions).
  - However, many housing applications make two changes in the Rosen framework:
    - They ignore the supply side.
    - They look at bids *per unit of housing services*.

2.5. *Rosen's Supply Side*

- In Rosen's framework, each firm has an offer function, which is the amount it would pay to supply a given level of an attribute, holding profits constant.

  - With heterogeneous firms and households, the hedonic price function is the *joint envelope* of firm offer and household bid-functions.
  - Because amenities are not supplied by firms (and because most house sales are of existing housing), the supply side is not central in most housing applications and is simply ignored.

    - That is, the distribution of amenities is taken as given.

2.6. *Housing Services*

- Rosen treats all attributes the same way.
- But many housing scholars distinguish between *housing services*, H, which are a function of structural housing traits, X, and the *price per unit of housing services*, P, which is a function of public services and neighborhood amenities, S.
  - The value of a house is $V = P\{S\}H\{X\}/r$.
  - For a given set of $X's$, the index of housing services, $H\{X\}$, may be assumed not to vary across households.
- You need to look for this distinction when reading the literature.

2.7. *The Rosen Challenge*

- The Rosen framework is valuable because it brings together bidding and sorting.
- Just as in the local public finance literature, households with steeper bid-functions end up at places with higher amenities.
- But this framework also reveals an enormously difficult challenge:
  - The relationship we can observe — the hedonic price function — reflects both (a) the underlying bid-functions and (b) the factors that determine sorting across household types.
  - Because we only observe one point on each bid-function, there is no simple way to separate these two phenomena, i.e. to study either the determinants of household demand for amenities (bidding) or the determinants of household sorting across locations.

2.8. *Interpreting the Envelope*

- Many studies simply estimate the hedonic, i.e. the bid-function envelope.
  - For example, there is a large literature on school quality "capitalization" in which most studies simply regress house values on a measure of school quality (and controls).
  - We will review this literature in the next class.
- Two types of information can be gained from these studies.

- First, a positive, significant coefficient for an amenity indicates that people value that amenity.
  - If people do not care about an amenity, their bid-functions will be flat — and so will the envelope, regardless of sorting.
- Results must be interpreted with care.
  - One can say that a one unit increase in school quality leads to an x% increase in house values, all else equal.
  - One cannot say that people are willing to pay x% more for housing when school quality increases one unit, because the result does not refer to any particular household type and it mixes bidding and sorting.
- Second, as noted earlier, Rosen shows that a utility-maximizing household sets its marginal willingness to pay (MWTP) for an attribute equal to the slope of the hedonic price function.
  - This slope is called the implicit price of the attribute.
  - In our terms, it is $(\partial V/\partial S) = (\partial P^E/\partial S)H/r$.
- Hence, we can observe every household's MWTP at the level of the attribute they consume — and we can calculate the average MWTP.
  - But this average MWTP has a limited interpretation.
    - It indicates only what people would pay on average for a small, equal increase in the amenity at all locations, *starting from the current equilibrium.*
    - *This average cannot be compared across places or across time* because the equilibrium is not the same.

3. Separating Bidding and Sorting

- To go beyond this limited information from the hedonic itself, scholars must separate bidding and sorting.
- As just noted, this is inherently a very difficult issue because we only observe one point on each bid-function.
- Thus, there is no general solution to this problem.
  - *It is impossible to separate bidding and sorting without making some strong assumptions!*

- Scholars have come up with five different approaches to separating bidding and sorting, based on different assumptions with different strengths and weaknesses.

  ○ The Rosen two-step method.
  ○ The Epple *et al.* general equilibrium method.
  ○ Fancy econometric methods (often linked to Heckman and co-authors).
  ○ Discrete-choice methods.
  ○ The Yinger "derive the envelope" method.

3.1. *Method 1: The Rosen Two-step*

- Rosen proposes a two-step approach to estimating hedonic models.

  ○ Step 1: Estimate a hedonic regression using a general functional form (the envelope) and differentiate the results to find the implicit or hedonic price, V_S, for each amenity, S.
  ○ Step 2: Estimate the demand for amenity S as a function of V_S (and of income and other things).

3.1.1. *Rosen's step 1*

- The idea of the first step is to use as general an estimating method as possible to approximate the hedonic envelope.

  ○ Early studies used a Box–Cox form, which has linear, double-log, and semi-log forms as special cases. (We will return to this form later.)
  ○ Some more recent studies use a nonparametric technique, such as "local linear regression."
  ○ Some studies still just use linear, log, or semi-log, which are undoubtedly not nonlinear enough.

3.1.2. *Endogeneity in the Rosen step 2*

- As later scholars pointed out, the main problem facing the step 2 regression in the Rosen framework is that the implicit price is endogenous.

○ The hedonic function is almost certainly nonlinear, so households "select" an implicit price when they select a level of S.

○ Households have different preferences, so the level of S, and hence of V_S, they select depends on their observed and unobserved traits.

3.1.3. *Addressing endogeneity*

- Scholars have identified two ways to deal with this endogeneity in the step 2 of the Rosen procedure.
- The first is to find an instrument, which is, of course, easier said than done.

  ○ Some early studies pooled data for metropolitan areas and used construction cost as an instrument; however, hedonics operate at the level of a metropolitan area and this pooling is not appropriate.

  ○ Other studies (see the review by Sheppard in the *Handbook of Urban and Regional Economics*, Vol. 3) use nearby prices as an instrument; however, nearby prices may, because of sorting, reflect the same unobservables that cause the problem in the first place.

  ○ No general solution through instruments has been identified.

- The other approach is to assume that the price elasticity of demand for the amenity equal -1.0. See, e.g. Bajari and Kahn (*J. Bus. and Econ. Stat.*, 2004).
- In this case the demand for S can be written as follows:

$$S = KY^\theta (V_S)^{-1} \text{ or } S(V_S) = KY^\theta$$

where Y is income and K is other demand factors.

- Because the implicit price now appears on the left-side, nothing endogenous remains on the right side and endogeneity bias disappears.
- The problem with this approach, of course is that the price elasticity is the main thing we are trying to estimate!

3.1.3.1. Endogeneity in step 1?

- Some people argue that there is intrinsic endogeneity in the Rosen's first step, where people also seem to be picking a price-quantity combination.

  - This argument is based on a misunderstanding.

    - The hedonic envelope removes individual traits.
    - It depends on the distribution of those traits, but one observation (one house sale or rent) is a market outcome with bidding and sorting, not a selection by an individual.

  - This type of endogeneity does arise in two cases, however:

    - Some studies use community level data. Community-level amenities (e.g. school quality) may be determined by the demands of people in the community — and their unobserved traits. An insightful treatment of this case: Epple, Romer, and Sieg (*Econometrica*, 2001).
    - If determinants of the demand for S are included as controls, the apparent first step becomes a second step — and these determinants are endogenous.

3.2. *Method 2: General Equilibrium*

- Epple, Peress, and Sieg (*AEJ: Micro*, 2010)

  - These scholars derive a general equilibrium model of bidding and sorting with a specific functional form for the utility function; their model also includes an income distribution and a taste parameter with an assumed distribution.
  - They estimate this model using complex semi-parametric methods applied to housing sales data from Pittsburgh.
  - This technically sophisticated approach imposes a specific form on household heterogeneity (with parameters to be estimated); this form makes it possible to handle household heterogeneity within a jurisdiction.

- This approach obviously requires considerable technical skill in modeling and econometrics.

- It also makes some strong assumptions.

  ○ For our purposes, the most important weakness is that the model contains a single, linear index of public services and amenities.
  ○ Their index includes school quality, the crime rate, and distance to the city center, with estimated weights — an approach that violates standard utility postulates.

3.3. *Method 3: Fancy Econometrics*

- Another approach is to use non-parametric techniques that recognize the difference in curvature between bid-functions and their envelope.

  ○ Heckman, Matzkin, and Nesheim (*Econometrica* 2010).
  ○ This approach has not yet been applied to housing, so far as I know, and is, like the Epple *et al.* approach, limited to a single amenity index and technically complex.

3.4. *Method 4: Discrete Choice*

- Several scholars have pointed out that a hedonic price function can be estimated with a discrete-choice model of the allocation of household types to housing types as a function of housing traits.
- A well known article by Bayer, Ferreira, and McMillan (*JPE*, 2007) takes this logic a step farther.

  ○ They estimate a multinomial logit model of the allocation of heterogeneous households to individual houses.
  ○ This model directly addresses sorting — and makes it possible to simulate new sorting equilibria with other assumptions, such as equal income distributions for black and white households.

- This method is clever, but requires strong assumptions.

  ○ They assume that utility functions are linear!
  ○ They assume that housing prices 3 miles away are a good instrument for actual housing prices.
  ○ They assume that the hedonic price function is linear (which contradicts the first assumption).

3.5. *Method 5: Derive the Envelope*

- My paper (*JUE*, 2015) derives a new form for the hedonic equation using the standard bidding model with **constant-elasticity demand functions** for the amenity and housing.
- Then I draw on the standard theory of sorting to derive a **bid-function envelope** across households with different preferences.
- This approach can be generalized to any number of amenities and can be applied to the housing-commuting trade-off in a standard urban model.

  o My approach estimates the price elasticity of demand for S, μ, in the hedonic equation itself.

    ▪ Thus the main parameter of interest, μ, can be estimated without encountering the standard endogeneity problem.

- My approach allows for a general treatment of household heterogeneity, but then integrates out the determinants of this heterogeneity in deriving the bid-function envelope.

  o So this approach accounts for household heterogeneity without requiring data on household characteristics to estimate μ.

- I first assume that households have constant- elasticity demand functions for the amenity and housing:

$$S = K_S N^\delta Y^\theta W^\mu$$

$$H = K_H M^\rho Y^\gamma \left(P \left(1 + \frac{\tau}{r} \right) \right)^\nu$$

$$= K_H M^\rho Y^\gamma \hat{P}^\nu$$

where the "$\wedge$" indicates a before tax housing price.

- The bid-functions that result take a Box–Cox form.
- The Box–Cox form is

$$X^{(\lambda)} = \frac{(X^\lambda - 1)}{\lambda} \text{ if } \lambda \neq 0$$

and

$$X^{(\lambda)} = \ln\{X\} \text{ if } \lambda = 0$$

- To be more specific, the bid-functions are:

$$(\hat{P}\{S\})^{(1+\nu)} = C + \psi S^{((+\mu)/\mu)}$$

where C is a constant of integration and

$$\psi = ((K_S N^\tau)^{1/\mu} K_H M^\rho Y^{(\theta/\mu)+\gamma})^{-1}$$

- The next step is to bring in sorting.

  - A fundamental theorem is that **sorting depends on the slope of the bid-function**: a household class with a steeper slope sorts into a jurisdiction with a higher value of S.
  - The slope is $\hat{P}_S$; ψ contains all non-shared terms in $\hat{P}_S$ and is thus an index of this slope.
  - So a steeper slope (= higher ψ) is associated with a higher S as illustrated in the following graph.

- In this figure, the first panel illustrates bid-functions and their envelope.
- The second panel illustrates the associated slopes, i.e. the slope of the bid-functions and of the envelope.

  - The slope of the envelope is $\hat{P}_S$.

    - It depends on the level of S (i.e. movement down the demand = bid curve).
    - And on the value of ψ for the household type that wins the competition at each level of S.
    - The indicated upward shifts in the slope of the envelope indicate increases in ψ.

  - My approach is to assume that the equilibrium relationship between ψ and S can be approximated with the following equation:

$$S = (\sigma_1 + \sigma_2 \psi)^{\sigma_3}$$

  - Note that the σ_s are parameters to be estimated.

    - The sorting theorem predicts that $\sigma_2 > 0$, which can be tested.

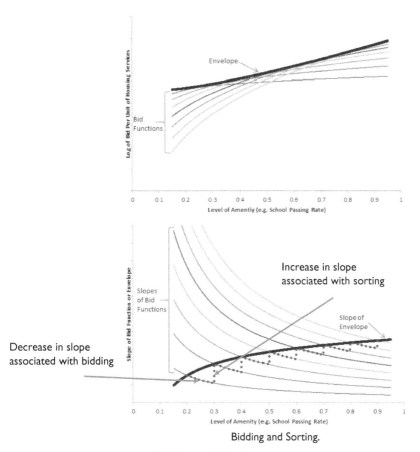

Bidding and Sorting.

- My paper and a companion paper (*JHE*, 2015) look into the types of assumptions that might lead to an equilibrium that takes this form.

  - I show that many assumptions about the distributions of ψ and S can lead to this form, especially (but not only) in the case of one-to-one matching, which is defined as a separate value of S for each value of ψ.

- Even if this form does not exactly describe the equilibrium, however, it is a polynomial form so that, with its estimated parameters, it can approximate the equilibrium.

- This assumption leads to the following form for the pre-tax hedonic envelope:

$$(\hat{P}E)(\lambda_1) = C_0 - \frac{\sigma_1}{\sigma_2}S^{(\lambda_2)} + \frac{1}{\sigma_2}S^{(\lambda_3)}$$

where

$$\lambda_1 = 1 + \nu; \quad \lambda_2 = \frac{(1+\mu)}{\mu}; \quad \lambda_3 = \lambda_2 + \frac{1}{\sigma^3}$$

Note: Left side is $\ln\{\hat{P}_S\}$ when $\nu = -1$.

3.5.1. *Extension to multiple amenities*

- So long as S_i is not directly a function of S_j, this approach can be extended to multiple amenities, with two terms in the bid-function for each amenity.
- This approach assumes that amenity space is dense enough so that we can pick up bidding for S_i holding other amenities constant.
- Similar, highly correlated amenities (e.g. two test scores) may need to be combined into an index.

3.5.2. *The final hedonic equation*

- The final estimating equation is

$$V - \frac{P^E\{S,t\}H\{X\}}{r} - \frac{\hat{P}^E\{S\}H\{X\}}{r + \beta\tau}$$

- To estimate this (nonlinear!) equation:
  - Use the form just derived for $\hat{P}^E$.
  - Assume a multiplicative form for $H\{X\}$.
  - Introduce the degree of property tax capitalization.

3.5.3. *Special cases*

- This general Box–Cox specification includes most of the parametric estimating equations in the literature as special cases.

Special Cases of Yinger Envelope.

Value of μ	Value of σ_3	Formula
$= -0.5$	$= \infty$	$\left(\frac{\sigma_1-1}{\sigma_2}\right)\left(\frac{1}{S}\right) =$ inverse
$= -1$	$= \infty$	$\left(\frac{1-\sigma_1}{\sigma_2}\right)\ln\{S\} =$ log
$= -\infty$	$= 1$	$-\frac{\sigma_1}{\sigma_2}S + \frac{1}{2\sigma_2}S^2 =$ quadratic
$= -\infty$	$= \infty$	$\left(\frac{1-\sigma_1}{\sigma_2}\right)S =$ linear
$< 0; \neq -1$	$= \infty$	$\left(\frac{1-\sigma_1}{\sigma_2}\right)\left(\frac{S^{(1+\mu)/\mu}-1}{(1+\mu)/\mu}\right) =$ Box–Cox

Note: $\mu = -\infty$ implies a horizontal demand curve; $\sigma_3 = \infty$ implies no sorting.

- ○ On the left side, the assumption that the price elasticity of demand for housing, ν, equals -1 leads to a log form, which is used by most studies.
  - ■ Studies that use this form do not recognize that they are making this assumption about ν.
  - ■ My *JUE* article cannot reject the assumption that ν equals -1.
- ○ On the right side, a wide range of functional forms are possible depending on the values of μ and σ_3.

4. Hedonic Vices

- Despite the fame of the Rosen article, many scholars have forgotten some of its key messages.
  - ○ What follows is my guide to "hedonic vices," i.e. to approaches that are not consistent with the Rosen framework and related literature.
- See Yinger/Nguyen-Hoang (*JBCA*, 2016).

4.1. *Functional Form Vices*

- The use of a linear (or semi-log or log-linear) form for the hedonic equation.

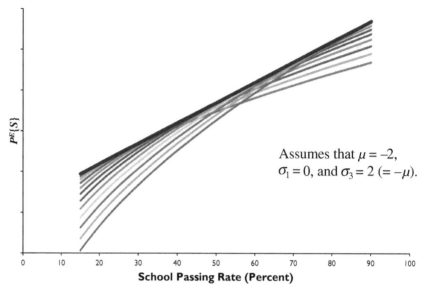

Example of a Linear Hedonic Envelope.

- ○ Unrelated parameters must somehow be equal to yield these forms.
- ○ With constant-elasticity demands, a linear form arises, e.g. in the bizarre case that $\sigma_1 = 0$ and $\sigma_3 = -\mu$; see figure "Example of a Linear Hedonic Envelope".
- ○ Contradictions between Rosen's step 2.
- • The envelope is mathematically connected to the bid-functions.
  - ○ It makes no sense to estimate a hedonic based on one assumption about the price elasticity and then to estimate the price elasticity in the next step.
  - ○ For example, a quadratic form assumes that $\mu = -\infty$, so it makes no sense to get implicit prices from this form and then to estimate μ.

4.2. *Control Variable Vices*

- • Using demand variables as controls.
  - ○ The Rosen framework implies that bid-functions depend on demand traits, such as income, but the hedonic envelope does not.

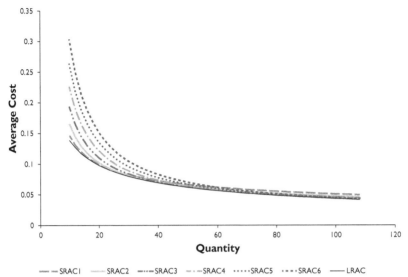

Short- and Long-Run Average Cost Curves, CES Production Function with Increasing Returns.

- o Adding demand variables therefore changes the estimation into a bid-function estimation, not an envelope estimation.
- • There is an exact analogy here to cost functions, as pictured above.
  - o The family of short-run average cost functions has plant size as a variable.
  - o The long-run average cost function, which is the envelope of the short-run functions, does not have plant size as an argument.
  - o Short-run average cost functions are analogous to bid-functions; plant size is analogous to demand factors; and long-run average cost functions are analogous to the hedonic envelope.
- • The addition of demand variables has two critical implications.
  - o First, the demand variables are endogenous; they bring the stage 2 endogeneity into the stage 1.
  - o Second, the demand variables must be interacted with the amenity variables; otherwise the coefficients of the amenities do not vary with demand traits (i.e. all bid-functions have the same slope) and there can be no sorting!

- One cannot avoid this problem by using small- neighborhood-level demand traits instead of household-level demand traits.

  ○ These two types of variables are highly correlated.
  ○ Traits of small neighborhoods remove the transitory component in household income and may thus be a better approximation to household permanent income than actual household income is.
  ○ But many studies still do this!

- One cannot avoid this problem by arguing that neighborhood-level demand traits, such as income, are neighborhood amenities and therefore need to be included.

  ○ Neighborhood income, education, and other demand traits might, indeed, be viewed as amenities by house buyers (although these traits cannot be observed directly).
  ○ But this possibility does not alter the fact that including them changes the meaning of the regression.

- This leaves researchers with two choices:

  ○ Leave out these traits and estimate a (possibly biased) hedonic regression.
  ○ Include these traits, treat them as endogenous, interact them with amenities, and interpret the regression as a bid-function regression.

- It is important to point out that this problem decreases as the size of the neighborhood unit increases.

  ○ The correlation between census block group traits and household traits is very high, so block group demand traits should never be included in a hedonic regression.
  ○ The correlation is much lower for census tracts, so researchers must use their judgment about the inclusion of census tract information.
  ○ The correlation is very small for zip codes or counties or other large-scale "neighborhood" units, so variables at this scale should not cause this problem.

- Neighborhood-level fixed effects with cross-section data.

○ One strategy for addressing omitted variable bias in Rosen's first step is to include geographic fixed effects, such as census block group fixed effects.

  ▪ The problem is that these fixed effects pick up the impact of demand factors, at least to some degree, especially if the geographic units are small, such as block groups.
  ▪ As a result, the use of small-area fixed effects runs into the same problem as the use of neighborhood-level demand variables.

• Neighborhood (or even house) fixed effects are fine with a panel; all coefficients are identified using amenity variation over time.

4.3. *Interpretation Vices*: *MWTP*

• Misinterpretation involving the mean MWTP.
• Many people interpret the coefficient of a linear hedonic as the mean MWTP.
• Even under this interpretation this concept indicates how much people would be willing to pay, on average, if they all received the same marginal increment in the amenity.
• This does not correspond to any reasonable policy situation.
• Moreover, this interpretation is usually based on misspecification of the regression.
• Many studies estimate a linear regression and assume that the coefficient is the mean MWTP.
• But a misspecified regression does not yield a unbiased estimate of this mean.
• *Example*: With the following nonlinear relationship, a linear specification understates true mean MWTP by 46%.
• Other studies compare the mean MWTP from a study in one location (or at one time) with the mean MWTP in another location (or at another time).
• These comparisons are not warranted, because one cannot assume that the underlying equilibria are the same at the two locations (or at the two times).
• The hedonic mean MWTP is a very limited concept!

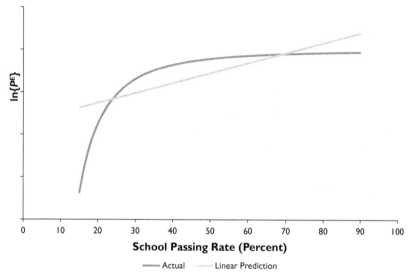

Error Using Linear Prediction for Mean MWTP.

4.4. *Interpretation Vices: Differences*

- Misinterpreting Difference Regressions

  ○ One common strategy for estimating the impact of an amenity
    that changes is to obtain panel data, identify double sale data,
    and then look at the change in house value, ΔV, as a function
    of the change in the amenity, ΔS.

  ○ This strategy is equivalent to the use of a fixed effect for each
    house, and therefore eliminates bias in the coefficient of ΔS from
    all time-invariant house and neighborhood traits.

  ○ The problem is that the coefficient of the ΔS variable could
    reflect any of three things:

    ■ The willingness to pay of existing residents for the change in
      S (which is what most people assume).

    ■ The willingness to pay of new residents (due to re-sorting) for
      the new S minus the WTP of previous residents for the old
      S, which is neither group's WTP.

    ■ Shifts in the distribution of households that have nothing to
      do with the change in S, such as those due to immigration.

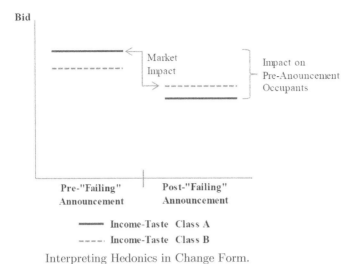

Interpreting Hedonics in Change Form.

- No method now available makes it possible to separate these possibilities.
- Example from Bogin (Maxwell Ph.D. Dissertation, 2012). The logic, but not figure, is in the revised version: Bogin/Nguyen-Hoang, *JRS*, 2014).
- One way to summarize this issue is to remember that the estimated coefficients in a hedonic regression reflect the current equilibrium in the area.
  - The coefficient of a change in an amenity variable reflects the changes in the equilibrium — not just changes in that variable.
- The change in the equilibrium cannot be accounted for simply by including control variables.

School Quality Capitalization

- **Class Outline**
  1. **Methodological Challenges**
  2. **Selected Recent Publications**
  3. **Procedures with a Derived Envelope**
  4. **Key Results with a Derived Envelope**
  5. **Conclusions About Estimates with a Derived Envelope**

1. Methodological Challenges

- Functional form
- Defining school quality (S)
- Controlling for neighborhood traits
- Controlling for housing characteristics

1.1. *Functional Form*

- As discussed in previous classes, simply regressing V on S (with or without logs) is not satisfactory.
  - Regressing $\ln\{V\}$ on S and S^2 is pretty reasonable — but cannot yield structural coefficients.
- To obtain structural coefficients, one must use either nonlinear regression or the Rosen 2-step method (with a general form for the envelope and a good instrument for the step 2).
- Both approaches are difficult!

1.2. *Defining School Quality*

- Most studies use a test score measure.
- A few use a *value-added* test score.
- A few use a graduation rate.
- Some use inputs (spending or student/teacher ratio).
  - The use of multiple output measures is rare — but sensible!
- We still do not know much about house buyer perceptions.

1.3. *Neighborhood Controls*

- Data quality varies widely; some studies have many neighborhood controls.
- Many fixed-effects approaches are possible to account for unobservables, e.g.:
  - Border fixed effects (BFE) (cross-section).
  - Neighborhood fixed effects (panel).
  - House-level fixed effects (panel with double sales).
- Another approach is to use an instrumental variable to account for unobservables, but one is needed for every amenity!

1.3.1. *Border fixed effects (BFE)*

- BFE were popularized by Black (1999); they appear in at least 16 subsequent studies.
- First, define elementary school attendance zone boundary segments.
- Second, define a BFE for each segment, equal to one for housing within a selected distance from the boundary.
- Third, drop all observations farther from boundary.
- The idea is that the border areas are like neighborhoods, so the BFEs pick up unobservables shared by houses on each side of the border.
- But bias comes from unobservables that are *correlated* with S; by design, BFEs are weakly correlated (i.e. take on the same value for different values of S).

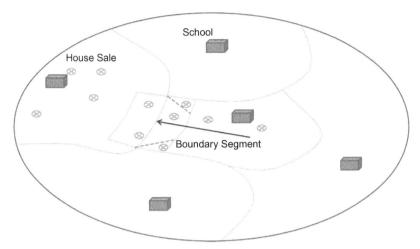

Border Fixed Effects.

- BFEs have three other weaknesses:

  - They shift the focus from *across-district* differences in S to *within-district* differences in S for elementary schools, which are less general because many elementary schools feed the same high school. This shift is not recognized in most studies.
  - They require the removal of a large share of the observations (and could introduce selection bias if demand for S is different for people who select border neighborhoods).
  - They do not account for *sorting*; i.e. they assume that neighborhood traits are not affected by the fact that sorting leads to people with different preferences on either side of the border.

1.3.2. *BFE and sorting*

- Two articles (Kane *et al.*, *ALER* 2006; Bayer *et al.*, *JPE*, 2007) find significant differences in demographics across attendance-zone boundaries.
- Bayer *et al.* then argue that these demographic differences become neighborhood traits, and they include them as controls.

- o I argue that these differences might be neighborhood traits, but are also measures of demand — which do not belong in an hedonic.

- As Rosen argued long ago (and as discussed in the last class), the envelope is not a function of demand variables.
- Including demand variables re-introduces the endogeneity problem and changes the meaning of the results.
- As discussed in a previous class, this is a tricky issue.
- Generally, we want to include controls that might measure (or be proxies for) amenities that people care about.

- o This argues for including neighborhood income.

- But we also want to exclude variables that change the meaning of the regression, in this case from a hedonic to bid functions.

- o This argues for excluding neighborhood income, at least when "neighborhood" is a small geographic area so that the average income is a good measure of household permanent income.

- One cannot solve a bias problem by changing the meaning of the regression.
- One cannot estimate a bid-function regression without interacting amenities with demand traits (to allow the slope to vary across households) and without treating amenities as endogenous.

1.3.3. *Other fixed effects*

- Other types of fixed effects are possible, e.g.,
  - o Tract fixed effects (with a large sample or a panel).
  - o School district fixed effects (with a panel).
  - o House fixed effects (with a panel).

- These approaches account for some unobservable factors, but may also introduce problems.

1.3.4. *Problems with fixed effects*

- They limit the variation in the data for estimating capitalization.

- ○ School district fixed effects, for example, imply that the coefficient of S must be estimated based only on *changes* in S.

- In a cross-section (not a panel) they may account for demand factors, such as income, that should not be included in a hedonic.

  - ○ Because household and block-group income are highly correlated, including BG dummies partially controls for household income.

- My interpretation is not popular.

  - ○ Many scholars seem to prefer fixed effects over other controls even if the fixed effects do not make theoretical sense.

1.3.5. *The IV approach*

- With omitted variables, the included explanatory variables are likely to be correlated with the error term.

  - ○ A natural correction is to use an instrumental variable — and 2SLS.

- However, credible IVs are difficult to find.

  - ○ The 2005 Chay/Greenstone article in the *JPE* estimates a hedonic for clean air using a policy *announcement* as an instrument.
  - ○ But many studies (some mentioned below) show that announcements affect house values so the C/G instrument fails the exogeneity test.

- Moreover, identification requires an instrument for every amenity — not just one.

1.3.6. *Two types of endogeneity*

- Note that this type of endogeneity comes from omitted variables.

  - ○ It is not the same as the inherent endogeneity problem that arises in the step 2 of Rosen's method.
  - ○ The endogeneity we are talking about here arises in Rosen's step 1.

- In principle, this type of endogeneity can be minimized with extensive controls for the structural characteristics of housing and neighborhood amenities.

1.4. *Controlling for Housing Traits*

- A housing hedonic requires control variables for the structural characteristics of housing.
- Because housing, neighborhood, and school traits are correlated, good controls for housing traits are important (but surprisingly limited in many studies).
- The B/F/M article in the *JPE* (2007) has only three housing traits: number of rooms, year built, and whether owner-occupied.
- If good data on housing traits are available, one strategy for a cross-section is to estimate the hedonic in two stages.
  - Stage 1: Define fixed effects for the smallest observable neighborhood type (e.g. block group or tract); regress V on housing traits and these FE's — with no neighborhood traits.
  - Stage 2: Use the coefficients of the FE's as the dependent variable in a second stage with neighborhood traits on the right side; the number of observations equals the number of neighborhoods.
- This approach has two advantages:
  - The coefficients of the housing traits cannot be biased due to missing neighborhood variables.
  - The stage 1 need not follow the same form as the first, so this approach adds functional-form flexibility.
- Note that the standard errors in the second stage must be corrected for heteroskedasticity.
  - The coefficient of each FE is based on a different number of observations and hence has a different standard error.

2. Selected Recent Publications

- Epple, Peress, and Sieg (*AEJ: Microeconomics*, 2010).
- Bayer, Ferreira, and MacMillan (*JPE*, 2007).

B/F/M Hedonic.

Key Coefficients from Baseline Hedonic Price Regressions				
	Sample			
	Within 0.20 Mile of Boundary ($N = 27{,}548$)		Within 0.10 Mile of Boundary ($N = 15{,}122$)	
Boundary fixed effects included	No	Yes	No	Yes
A. Excluding Neighborhood Sociodemographic Characteristics				
	(1)	(2)	(5)	(6)
Average test score (in standard deviations)	123.7 (13.2)	33.1 (7.6)	126.5 (12.4)	26.1 (6.6)
R^2	.54	.62	.54	.62
B. Including Neighborhood Sociodemographic Characteristics				
	(3)	(4)	(7)	(8)
Average test score (in standard deviations)	34.8 (8.1)	17.3 (5.9)	44.1 (8.5)	14.6 (6.3)
% census block group black	−99.8 (33.4)	1.5 (38.9)	−123.1 (32.5)	4.3 (39.1)
% block group with college degree or more	220.1 (39.9)	89.9 (32.3)	204.4 (40.8)	80.8 (39.7)
Average block group income (/10,000)	60.0 (4.0)	45.0 (4.6)	55.6 (4.3)	42.9 (6.1)
R^2	.59	.64	.59	.63

Note: All regression shown in the table also include controls for whether the house is owner-occupied, the number of rooms, year built (1980s, 1960–79, pre-1960), elevation, population density, crime, and land use (% industrial, % residential, % commercial, % open space, % other) in 1-, 2-, and 3-mile rings around cache location. The dependent variable is the monthly user cost of housing, which equals monthly rent for renter-occupied units and a monthly user cost owner-occupied housing, calculated as described in the text. Standard errors corrected for clustering at the school level are reported in parentheses.

- Clapp, Nanda, and Ross (*JUE*, 2008).
- Bogin (Syracuse Dissertation, 2011), building on Figlio and Lucas (*AER*, 2004), published as Bogin, Nguyen-Hoang (*JRS*, 2014).
- Yinger (*JUE*, 2015).

2.1. *B/F/M*

- B/F/M have census data from the San Francisco area.

- They estimate a *linear hedonic with BFE's*, pooling sales and rental data.
- They find that adding the BFE's cuts the impact of school quality on housing prices.

- They find that adding neighborhood income cuts the impact of school quality even more.

2.1.1. *B/F/M problems*

- They estimate a *linear* hedonic, which rules out sorting (in an article about sorting!) and is inconsistent with their own bid functions.
- They control for neighborhood (block group) income, which is not consistent with the Rosen framework.

  - They have only three housing traits and four other location controls (+BFE's).

2.2. *C/N/R*

- They use a panel of housing transactions in Connecticut between 1994 and 2004.
- They use *neighborhood demographics or tract fixed effects* to control for neighborhood quality.
- They look at math scores and cost factors (e.g. student poverty).
- They find that a model with tract fixed effects is almost identical to a model with town fixed effects plus income and other demographics.

2.2.1. *C/N/R problems*

- They use a semi-log form with only one term for S, which rules out sorting.
- They control for neighborhood (=tract) demographics or tract FEs.

  - This controls for time-invariant tract level traits.
  - But might introduce some demand variation.
  - Nobody has yet sorted this out.

C/N/R Hedonic.

Housing Price OLS and Fixed Effects Models

Controls	OLS	Town FE	Census Tract FE
Number of Rooms	0.024	0.023	0.023
	(10.07)	(9.97)	(10.79)
Number of Bedrooms	0.015	0.014	0.013
	(4.75)	(4.66)	(4.56)
Age in 100s	−0.817	−0.874	−0.883
	(−20.69)	(−23.52)	(−25.56)
(Age in 100s)^2	0.411	0.429	0.433
	(10.49)	(11.54)	(12.74)
Log (square footage < 2500 sq.ft.)	0.480	0.490	0.476
	(32.97)	(34.85)	(36.01)
Log (square footage ≥ 2500 sq.ft.)	0.076	0.057	0.070
	(2.40)	(1.87)	(2.25)
Math Test Score	0.074	0.014	0.013
	(8.99)	(2.53)	(2.45)
Fraction Student enrolled in Free	−0.363	0.049	0.019
Lunch program	(−6.19)	(0.75)	(0.31)
Fraction Student Non-English	0.419	0.165	0.085
Speakers	(4.93)	(1.24)	(0.79)
Fraction Student African-American	0.279	−0.152	−0.364
	(6.64)	(−0.77)	(−3.81)
Fraction Student Hispanics	0.128	−0.136	−0.308
	(1.22)	(−0.66)	(−1.90)
Effective Property Tax Rate	−0.531	−0.305	−0.299
	(−11.49)	(−8.30)	(−8.69)
Median Family Income	0.086	0.063	
in Tract	(24.56)	(20.43)	
Fraction African-American Persons	−0.265	−0.391	
in Tract	(−8.89)	(−14.61)	
Fraction Hispanic Persons in Tract	−0.295	−0.464	
	(−3.91)	(−6.53)	
Fraction Owner-occupied units	−0.011	0.030	
in Tract	(−0.50)	(1.61)	
Fraction Married Couple with	−0.866	−0.503	
Children in Tract	(−13.08)	(−8.79)	

- They have only four housing traits and two non-demand neighborhood traits.

2.3. *Bogin/Nguyen-Hoang*

- The Florida school accountability program hands out "failing" grades to some schools. The Figlio/Lucas paper (*AER*, 2004) looks at the impact of this designation on property values.
- The federal No Child Left Behind Act also hands out "failing" grades. The 2011 Bogin thesis and the 2014 Bogin/Nguyen-Hoang article (*JRS*, 2014) look at the impact of this designation on property values around Charlotte, North Carolina.

  ○ In both cases, the failing grades are essentially uncorrelated with other measures of school quality.
  ○ B/N-H find that a failing designation lowers property values by about 6%.

    ▪ This effect peaks about seven months after the announcement and fades out after one year.

- They also provide a clear interpretation of results with this "change" set-up.

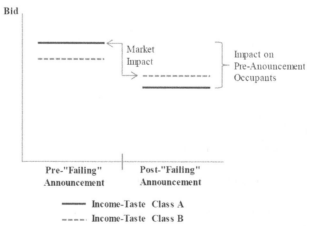

Pre and Post-"Failing" Announcement Bids: Re-Sorting.

Source: Bogin (2011).

○ Because of possible re-sorting, the change in house values cannot be interpreted as a willingness to pay.
○ A failing designation might change the type of people who move into a neighborhood.

3. Procedures with a Derived Envelope

- The study by Yinger (*JUE*, 2015) applies the "derive the envelope" method to data on house sales in the Cleveland area in 2000.

  ○ This method has several advantages:

    ▪ It avoids the endogeneity problem in the Rosen step 2 approach.
    ▪ It avoids inconsistency between the bid functions and their envelope (the hedonic equation).
    ▪ It includes most parametric forms for a hedonic as special cases.
    ▪ It allows for household heterogeneity.
    ▪ It leads to tests of key sorting theorems.

3.1. *My Envelope*

- The form derived in an earlier class:

$$(\hat{P}^E)^{(\lambda_1)} = C_0' - \frac{\sigma_1}{\sigma} S^{(\lambda_2)} + \frac{1}{\sigma} S^{(\lambda_3)}$$

where

$$\lambda_1 = 1 + \nu; \quad \lambda_2 = (1 + \mu)/\mu; \quad \lambda_3 = \lambda_2 + 1/\sigma_3;$$

and $X^{(\lambda)}$ is the Box–Cox form.
- A starting point is a quadratic form, which corresponds to

$$\mu = -\infty \text{ and } \sigma_3 = 1$$

3.2. *The Brasington Data*

- The data set contains all home sales in Ohio in 2000, with detailed housing characteristics and house location; compiled by Prof. David Brasington.

- Matched to:
  - School district and characteristics
  - Census block group and characteristics
  - Police district and characteristics
  - Air and water pollution data
- Yinger focuses on the five-county Cleveland area and adds many neighborhood traits.

3.3. *Yinger's Two-Step Approach*

- Step 1: Estimate the envelope using the above functional form to identify the price elasticity of demand, μ.
  - Step 1A: Estimate hedonic with neighborhood fixed effects using the *sample of house sales.*
  - Step 1B: Estimate $P^E\{S,t\}$ for *the sample of neighborhoods* with their coefficients from Step 1A as the dependent variable.
- Step 2: Estimate the impact of income and other factors (except price) on demand.

3.4. *Neighborhood Fixed Effects*

- Start with Census block groups containing more than one observation.
- Split block-groups in more than one school district.
- Total number of "neighborhoods" in Cleveland area sub-sample: 1,665.

3.5. *Step 1A: Run Hedonic Regression with Neighborhood Fixed Effects*

- Dependent variable: Log of sales price in 2000.
- Explanatory variables:
  - Structural housing characteristics.
  - Corrections for within-neighborhood variation in seven locational traits.
  - *Neighborhood fixed effects.*
- 22,880 observations in Cleveland subsample.
- $R^2 = 0.7893$.

Variable Definitions and Results for Basic Hedonic with Neighborhood Fixed Effects.

Variable	Definition	Coefficient	Std. Error
One Story	House has one story	−0.0072	0.0050
Brick	House is made of bricks	0.0153***	0.0052
Basement	House has a finished basement	0.0308***	0.0050
Garage	House has a garage	0.1414***	0.0067
Air Cond.	House has central air conditioning	0.0254***	0.0055
Fireplaces	Number of fireplaces	0.0316***	0.0038
Bedrooms	Number of bedrooms	−0.0082***	0.0028
Full Baths	Number of full bathrooms	0.0601***	0.0042
Part Baths	Number of partial bathrooms	0.0412***	0.0041
Age of House	Log of the age of the house	−0.0839***	0.0032
House Area	Log of square feet of living area	0.4237***	0.0086
Lot Area	Log of lot size	0.0844***	0.0037
Outbuildings	Number of outbuildings	0.1320***	0.0396
Porch	House has a porch	0.0327***	0.0073
Deck	House has a deck	0.0545***	0.0053
Pool	House has a pool	0.0910***	0.0180
Date of Sale	Date of house sale (January 1 = 1, December 31 = 365)	0.0002***	0.0000
Commute 1	Employment wtd. commuting dist. (house-CBG), worksite 1	−0.0952***	0.0272
Commute 2	Employment wtd. commuting dist. (house-CBG), worksite 2	−0.0991***	0.0321
Commute 3	Employment wtd. commuting dist. (house-CBG), worksite 3	−0.1239***	0.0302
Commute 4	Employment wtd. commuting dist. (house-CBG), worksite 4	−0.1012***	0.0295

(*Continued*)

(*Continued*)

Variable	Definition	Coefficient	Std. Error
Commute 5	Employment wtd. commuting dist. (house-CBG), worksite 5	−0.0942***	0.0344
Dist. to Pub. School	Dist. to nearest pub. elementary school in district (house-CBG)	−0.0032	0.0061
Elem. School Score	Average math and English test scores of nearest pub. elementary school relative to district (house-CBG)	0.0170	0.0197
Dist. to Private School	Distance to nearest private school (house-CBG)	−0.0168***	0.0057
Distance to Hazard	Dist. to nearest environmental hazard (house-CBG)	0.0332***	0.0082
Distance to Erie	Dist. to Lake Erie (if <2; house-CBG)	−0.0021**	0.0010
Distance to Ghetto	Dist. to black ghetto (if <5; house-CBG)	−0.1020***	0.0331
Distance to Airport	Dist. to Cleveland airport (if <10; house-CBG)	0.0259**	0.0122
Dist. to CBG Center	Distance from house to center of CBG	−0.0239***	0.0074
Historic District	In historic district on national register (house-CBG)	0.0120	0.0178
Elderly Housing	Within 1/2 mile of elderly housing project (house-CBG)	−0.0327*	0.0194
Family Housing	Within 1/2 mile of small family housing project (house-CBG)	0.0836**	0.0403
Large Hsg Project	Within 1/2 mile of large family housing project (>200 units; house-CBG)	−0.0568**	0.0257
High Crime	Distance to nearest high-crime location (house-CBG)	0.0701***	0.0246

Dependent variable = log of transaction amount; 22,880 observations; R^2 = 0.7893; *(**) [***] = significant at 10 (5) [1] percent level.
Source: Yinger (2015).

School Variables in Yinger.

Variables	Definition
Elementary	Average percent passing in 4th grade in nearest elementary school on five state tests (math, reading, writing, science, and citizenship) minus the district average (for 1998–1999 and 1999–2000).
High School	The share of students entering the 12th grade who pass all five tests (= the passing rate on the tests, which reflects students who do not drop out, multiplied by the graduation rate, which indicates the share of students who stay in school) averaged over 1998–1999 and 1999–2000.
Value Added	A school district's 6th grade passing rate (on the five tests) in 2000–2001 minus its 4th grade passing rate in 1998–1999.
Minority Teachers	The share of a district's teachers who belong to a minority group.

3.6. *Step 1B: Run Envelope Regression*

• Dependent variable: coefficient of neighborhood fixed effect.
• Explanatory variables:
  ○ Public services and neighborhood amenities
  ○ Commuting variables
  ○ Income and property tax variables
  ○ Neighborhood control variables
• Sample size: 1,665.
• $R^2 = 0.7169$.

3.7. *Cleveland and East Cleveland*

• The Cleveland School District is unique in 2000 because:
  ○ It was the only district to have private school *vouchers*.
  ○ It was the only district to have *charter schools* (except for one in Parma).
  ○ The private and charter schools tend to be located near low-performing public schools.

Descriptive Statistics for Key Variables in Yinger.

	Mean	Std. Dev.	Min.	Max.
CBG Price per unit of Housing	84835.6	23331.25	32215.8	345162.5
Relative Elementary Score	0.3148	0.0894	0.0010	0.6465
High School Passing Rate	0.3197	0.2040	0.0491	0.7675
Elementary Value Added	24.0021	9.4164	1.0000	49.6000
Share Minority Teachers	0.1329	0.1548	0.0010	0.6146
Share Non-Black in CBG	0.8022	0.3226	0.0010	1.0000
Share Non-Hispanic in CBG	0.9623	0.0810	0.3673	1.0000
Weighted Commuting Distance	13.2046	7.4567	7.2660	39.5236
Income Tax Rate	0.0091	0.0012	0.0075	0.0100
School Tax Rate	0.0309	0.0083	0.0172	0.0643
City Tax Rate[d]	0.0578	0.0140	0.0227	0.1033
Tax Break Rate[d]	0.0330	0.0121	0.0047	0.0791
No A-to-S	0.1339	0.3407	0.0000	1.0000
Not a City	0.1393	0.3464	0.0000	1.0000
Crime Low–high	0.0252	0.1569	0.0000	1.0000
Crime High–low	0.1291	0.3354	0.0000	1.0000
Crime High–high	0.1934	0.3951	0.0000	1.0000
Crime Hotspot1	0.0126	0.1116	0.0000	1.0000
Crime Hotspot2	0.0354	0.1849	0.0000	1.0000
Crime Hotspot3	0.0847	0.2785	0.0000	1.0000
Crime Hotspot4	0.2667	0.4423	0.0000	1.0000

- The East Cleveland School District is unique in 2000 because
  - It received a state grant for *school construction* in 1998–2000 that was triple the size of its operating budget.
  - No other district in the region received such a grant.

4. Key Results with a Derived Envelope

4.1. *Basic Results*

- In the case of the High School variable, housing prices are about 30% higher in a district with the highest value (77% passing) compared to a district with a 20% passing rate.

Definitions for Tax, Commuting, Crime, Pollution, and Ancillary School Variables in Yinger.

Variable	Definition
Income Tax Rate	School district income tax rate
School Tax Rate***	School district effective property tax rate
City Tax Rate	Effective city property tax rate beyond school tax
Tax Break Rate*	Exemption rate for city property tax
No A-to-S	Dummy: No A/V data
Not a City	CBG not in a city
Commute 1***	Job-weighted distance to worksites
Commute 2**	(Commute 1) squared
Crime Low–high***	Low property, high violent crime
Crime High–low**	High property, low violent crime
Crime High–high***	High property and violent crime
Crime Hotspot1***	CBG within $1/2$ mile of crime hot spot
Crime Hotspot2*	CBG $1/2$ to 1 mile from crime hot spot
Crime Hotspot3***	CBG 1 to 2 miles from crime hot spot
Crime Hotspot4***	CBG 2 to 5 miles from crime hot spot
Village**	CBG receives police from a village
Township***	CBG receives police from a township
County Police***	CBG receives police from a county
City Population***	Population of city (if CBG in a city)
City Pop. Squared***	City population squared/10000
City Pop. Cubed***	City population cubed/10000^2
City Pop. to 4th***	City pop. to the fourth power/10000^3
Smog***	CBG within 20 miles of air pollution cluster
Smog Distance**	(Smog) $\times$ Distance to cluster (not to the NW)
Near Hazard***	CBG is within 1 mile of a hazardous waste site
Distance to Hazard***	Distance to nearest hazardous waste site (if <1)
Value Added 1***	School district's 6th grade passing rate on five state tests in 2000–2001 less its 4th grade rate in 1998–1999
Value Added 2***	(Value Added 1) squared
Minority Teachers 1	Share of district's teachers from a minority group
Minority Teachers 2*	(Minority Teachers 1) squared
Rel. Elem. Cle. 1***	Average 4th grade passing rate on five state tests in nearest elem. school minus district average (1998–1999 and 1999–2000) for Cle. and E. Cle. only
Rel. Elem. Cle. 2***	(Rel. Elem. Cle. 1) squared
Cleveland SD	Dummy for Cleveland and E. Cleveland School Districts
Near Public	CBG is within 2 miles of public elem. school
Distance to Public*	(Near Public) $\times$ Distance to public school
Near Private	CBG is within 5 miles of a private school

- Prices are also about 3% higher at a 13% passing rate than at a 20% passing rate, but this result is not statistically significant (and involves only a few observations).

Definitions for Other Geographic Controls in Yinger.

Variable	Definition
Lakefront***	Within 2 miles of Lake Erie
Distance to Lake	(Lakefront) × (Distance to Lake Erie)
Snowbelt 1***	(East of Pepper Pike) × (Distance to Lake Erie)
Snowbelt 2***	(Snowbelt 1) squared
Ghetto	CBG in the black ghetto
Near Ghetto	CBG within 5 miles of ghetto center
Near Airport	CBG within 10 miles of Cleveland airport
Airport Distance	(Near Airport) × (Distance to airport)
Local Amenities***	No. of parks, golf courses, rivers, or lakes within 1/4 mile of CBG
Freeway	CBG within 1/4 mile of freeway
Railroad	CBG within 1/4 mile of railroad
Shopping	CBG within 1 mile of shopping center
Hospital	CBG within 1 mile of hospital
Small Airport	CBG within 1 mile of small airport
Big Park***	CBG within 1 mile of regional park
Historic District	CBG within an historic district
Near Elderly PH	CBG within 1/2 mile of elderly public housing
Near Small Fam. PH***	CBG within 1/2 mile of small family public housing
Near Big Fam. PH***	CBG within 1/2 mile of large family public housing (>200 units)
Worksite 2**	Fixed effect for worksite 2
Worksite 3***	Fixed effect for worksite 3
Worksite 4*	Fixed effect for worksite 4
Worksite 5	Fixed effect for worksite 5
Geauga County	Fixed effect for Geauga County
Lake County***	Fixed effect for Lake County
Lorain County***	Fixed effect for Lorain County

- The results for the Elementary variable in Cleveland are consistent with the view that parents care about elementary school quality, but also care about education opportunities, which are clustered in the neighborhoods with the worst regular public schools.

Specification Tests and Results for Key School Variables.

Variable	Linear	Quadratic	Nonlinear Estimation of μ's with $\sigma_3 = 1$
Relative Elementary Score Cle.			
First Term	-0606	-1.2976^{***}	0.3908^{***}
	(0.0722)	(0.3911)	(0.0229)
Second Term	—	1.6740^{***}	0.2979^{***}
		(0.4876)	(0.0875)
μ	$-\infty$	$-\infty$	$-\infty$
σ_3	∞	1	1
High School Passing Rate			
First Term	0.4826^{***}	-0.0862	0.2166^{***}
	(0.0600)	(0.2631)	(0.0342)
Second Term	—	0.6049^{**}	1.3255^{**}
		(0.2849)	(0.5366)
μ	$-\infty$	$-\infty$	-0.7511^{***}
			(0.2704)
σ_3	∞	1	1

Source: Yinger (2015).

4.2. *Graphical Results*

- These results are summarized in The Figures "Envelope for Relative Elementary Score" and "Envelope for High School Passing Rate."

4.3. *Tests for Normal Sorting*

- Once the envelope has been estimated, one can recover its slope with respect to S, which is a function of income and other demand variables (for S and H).
- The theory says that the income coefficient is

$$(-\theta/\mu - \gamma)$$

  - Normal sorting requires this coefficient to be positive.
  - Recall that the amenity price elasticity, μ, is negative.

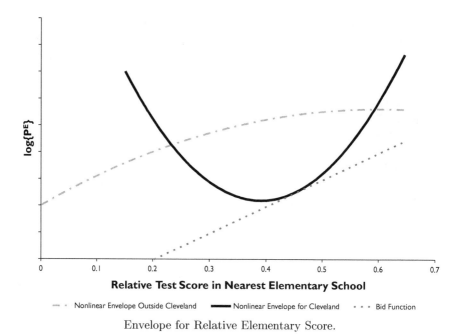

Envelope for Relative Elementary Score.

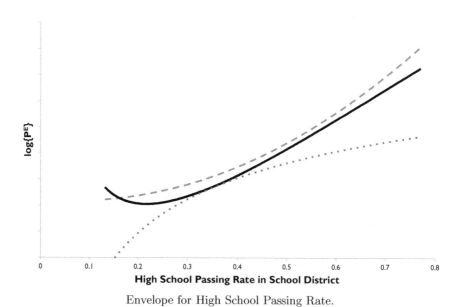

Envelope for High School Passing Rate.

Tests for Normal Sorting.

Type of Test	Relative Elementary Score in Cle.	High School Passing Rate
Indirect Test		
Income Coefficient	1.7699***	1.0189***
Standard Error	(0.5793)	(0.0564)
R^2	0.0849	0.2028
Observations	142	1113
Conclusion	Support	Support
Direct Test		
Income Coefficient	1.3540*	0.6426***
Standard Error	(0.8059)	(0.0906)
R^2	0.2236	0.2796
Observations	142	1113
Conclusion	Weak Support	Support

Source: Yinger (2015).

4.3.1. *Direct and indirect tests*

- Direct and indirect tests are possible.

  - A direct test looks at the income coefficient controlling for all other observable demand determinants.
  - An indirect test says that normal sorting for S may arise indirectly through the correlation between S and other amenities (and the impact of income on these other amenities).
  - Based on the omitted variable theorem, the indirect test comes from the sign of the income term in a regression *omitting all other demand variables*.

4.3.2. *Conclusions, normal sorting*

- Normal sorting is supported for relative elementary school when only positively sloped envelope segments in Cleveland are considered, although the support from the direct test is weak.
- Normal sorting is strongly supported for high school quality.

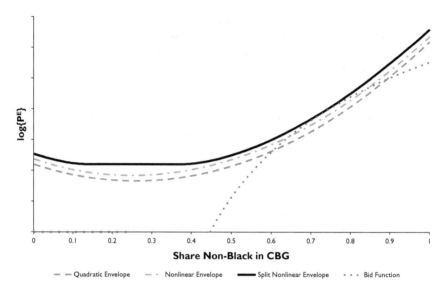

Envelope for Share Non-Black.
Source: Yinger (2015).

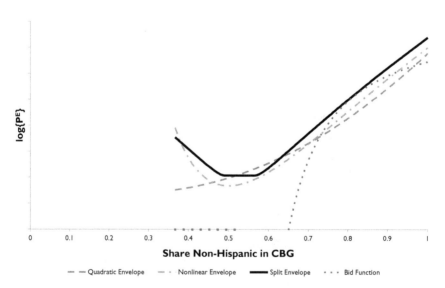

Envelope for Share Non-Hispanic.
Source: Yinger (2015).

The Impact of Amenities on Housing Prices.

| Amenity | Integrated Zone (%) | Change in Price of House Due to Raising the Amenity from: | |
		Minimum to Integrated Zone (%)	Integrated Zone to Maximum (%)
Share Non-Black	14.1–37.1	−1.7	24.6
Share Non-Hispanic	49.3–56.2	−17.6	30.4

Source: Yinger (2015).

4.4. *Neighborhood Ethnicity*

- The Figures "Envelope for Share Non-Black", "Envelope for Share Non-Hispanic" and Table "Tests for Normal Sorting" give the comparable results for neighborhood ethnicity variables.
- Preferences for neighborhood racial and ethnic composition are diverse.
  - Some households (the majority) prefer all-white neighborhoods.
  - But some prefer majority-black neighborhoods.
  - Results for Hispanic neighborhoods are similar but less precise.
  - I cannot link these results to the race/ethnicity of a household.

5. Conclusions About Estimates with a Derived Envelope

5.1. *Conclusions, Theory*

- The envelope derived in my paper:
  - Is based on a general characterization of household heterogeneity.
  - Makes it possible to estimate demand elasticities (and program benefits) from the first-step equation — avoiding endogeneity.
  - Ensures consistency between the envelope and the underlying bid functions.
  - Sheds light on sorting.

5.2. *Conclusions, Empirical Results*

- Willingness to pay for some aspects of school quality can be estimated with precision.

  ○ The price elasticity of demand for high school quality is about −0.75 and housing prices are up to 30% higher where high school passing rates are high than where they are low.

- The theory of sorting is strongly supported in some cases.

  ○ The σ_2 parameter is positive and significant for both the elementary and high school variables — as predicted with sorting based on bid-function slopes.

- Household seem to care about several dimensions of school quality, but precise demand parameters cannot be estimated in many cases.

  ○ The price elasticity and other parameters cannot be precisely estimated *for relative elementary scores.*

Lecture 13

Sales Taxes

- **Class Outline**
  1. **The Basics**
  2. **A New Era**
  3. **Tax Incidence**
  4. **Tax Distortion**
  5. **Recent Literature on Sales Tax Shifting**

1. The Basics

- The sales tax is really a *sales and use* tax.
  - States levy a tax on the purchase or use of a commodity or service within their boundaries.
  - States cannot levy a tax on the purchase or use of a commodity in another state. What counts is point of *delivery*. So wine shipped from one state to another is taxed where it is delivered.

2. A New Era

- Based on a 2018 U.S. Supreme Court decision, internet companies must collect the sales tax based on the delivery location.

- Before the 2018 Supreme Court decision, there was an effort to create standardized product definitions and even tax rates to minimize the burden on internet firms.
  - About 20 states have signed onto this Interstate Compact, and it was mentioned in the 2018 decision.

3. Tax Incidence

- Tax incidence has two meanings.
  - *Legal incidence* is about who has the legal obligation to pay a tax. With a sales tax, this is usually the seller. This is the meaning relevant for administration.
  - *Economic incidence* is about whose opportunities are constrained by a tax, that is, who bears the burden. This is the meaning relevant for evaluating the fairness of a tax.

3.1. *Analysis of Tax Incidence*

- An analysis of tax incidence has two steps.
  - Figure out which side of the market, demand or supply, bears the burden of the tax.
  - This is about tax shifting. Can the side on which the legal incidence falls shift it to the other side? If the legal incidence is on the seller, does P rise enough to compensate for the tax?
- Given the answer to step 1, figure out the distribution of the tax burden by income class.

3.1.1. *Market analysis*

- Standard incidence analysis begins by looking at the impact of a tax on the market for the taxed good or goods.
- This analysis does not apply to the market for one taxed good if other goods are being taxed, too.
  - This analysis is based on relative prices, which do not change for two goods that are both taxed.

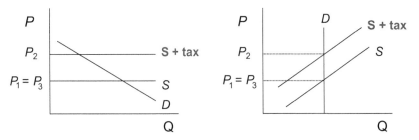

Possibility 1: Consumers Pay.

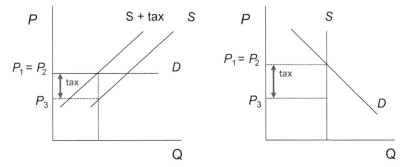

Possibility 2: Firms Pay.

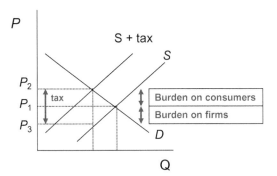

Possibility 3: The Burden is Shared.

3.1.2. *A simple model of incidence*

- Now consider the simplest possible supply and demand equations:

$$Q_S = a_s + b_S(P - T)$$

and

$$Q_D = a_D - b_D P$$

- Since Q_S must equal Q_D in equilibrium, we can equate the two right sides and solve for P:

$$P = \frac{a_D - a_S + b_S T}{b_S + b_D}$$

3.1.3. *Shifting*

- Now we can take the derivative of P with respect to T; i.e. we can ask how P changes as T changes.

$$\frac{dP}{dT} = \frac{b_S}{b_S + b_D} = \frac{1}{1 + \dfrac{b_D}{b_S}}$$

- From this it is clear that

$$\text{if} \quad b_D = b_S \quad \text{then} \quad \frac{dP}{dT} = \frac{1}{2} = \text{half shifted}$$

$$\text{if} \quad b_D = \infty \quad \text{then} \quad \frac{dP}{dT} = 0 = \text{not shifted at all}$$

$$\text{if} \quad b_S = \infty \quad \text{then} \quad \frac{dP}{dT} = 1 = \text{fully shifted}$$

  ○ This simple example refers to slopes. A more general version would refer to price elasticities. The degree of shifting depends on the relative price elasticities of demand and supply (in absolute value).
  ○ The intuition is about responsiveness. A more responsive curve, which suggests more alternatives, implies that a side of the market is better able to escape the tax.

3.2. Incidence, Step 2

- The second step is to translate to the distribution of income. This obviously depends on the incomes of suppliers vs. demanders. Either one could be higher.
- The result is usually summarized with a graph with T/Y on the vertical axis and Y on the horizontal axis. A flat curve indicates a *proportional* system; a rising curve indicates a *progressive* system, and a falling curve indicates a *regressive* system.

3.2.1. Incidence by income

- The concepts are given in the Figure "Alternative Tax Outcomes".

3.2.2. Equity principles

- In a policy setting, the positive analysis of tax incidence is combined with judgments about what is fair.
- The *ability to pay* principle says that people with a higher income should pay at least the same share of their income in taxes as people with a lower income.
  - People may disagree, of course, about how much progressivity is desirable.
  - Proportionality can be thought of as the lower bound on tax distributions consistent with this principle.
- The *benefit principle* says that people who benefit from the funded service should pay, but this does not rule out progressivity within this set of people.

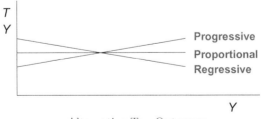

Alternative Tax Outcomes.

4. Tax Distortion

- Taxes affect behavior. This implies that taxes move outcomes away from the efficient level that is generated by a competitive private market (under some circumstances) — i.e. that taxes cause distortion.
- As before, the basic analysis applies to taxed markets relative to untaxed markets — not to one of many taxed markets.

4.1. *Excess Burden*

- Consider an elastic supply curve. The initial equilibrium is (P_1, Q_1). Because the tax is fully shifted, the new price, P_2, equals $P_1(1 + t)$, or $\Delta P = tP_1$.

    ○ Now if we draw the picture, we see that consumer surplus drops because of the tax revenue that is collected and because of a lost triangle = *excess burden.*

    ○ See the Figure "Market for Taxed Goods".

    ○ We do not consider the tax revenue as a loss of consumer surplus. Tax analysis usually compares the burden from alternative taxes, so this revenue will be lost no matter what we do.

    ■ Moreover, even if we were just evaluating a single possibility, the revenue collected presumably results in benefits in the form of public services.

- The triangle, called distortion or excess burden (EB), equals $(1/2)\Delta Q \Delta P = (1/2)\Delta Q(tP_1)$.

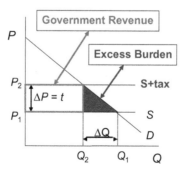

Market for Taxed Goods.

- Now the absolute value of the price elasticity of demand, say e, equals $(P_1 \Delta Q)/(Q_1 \Delta P)$. So

$$\Delta Q = (eQ_1)(\Delta P/P_1)$$
$$= (eQ_1)(tP_1)/P_1 = (eQ_1)t$$

and

$$EB = \tfrac{1}{2}(e)(t^2)(P_1 Q_1)$$

- This is a central result in tax analysis. Remember it!
- This result yields three important lessons in here:
  - EB increases with the size of the market being taxed (PQ).
  - EB increases with the price elasticity of demand. Lesson: tax products with a low price elasticity — that leads to minimal distortion (but may not lead to greatest fairness!).
  - EB increases with the square of the tax rate. The lesson: Have a diversified revenue system.
- Why the square of t? Doubling the tax rate more than doubles EB.

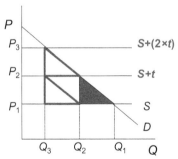

Tax Rate and Excess Burden.

- An additional important result arises in a market with an externality.
  - An example is the market for gasoline.
    - People buy gasoline in order to drive, and when they drive, they cause highway deterioration, pollution, and congestion.

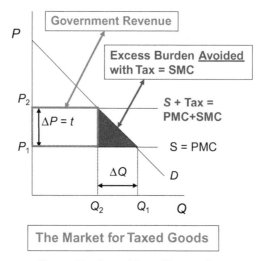

Excess Burden with an Externality.

■ Generally, gas taxes are set to cover maintenance only.
■ Raising the tax further would actually reduce distortion (i.e. lower excess burden).

5. Recent Literature on Sales Tax Shifting

- Several recent studies regress P on T in some form or another to see if P goes up dollar for dollar with T.
- Poterba (one of the stars of empirical public finance, an economist at MIT) does this for a few broad categories of goods in a few cities and finds approximately full forward shifting onto consumers.
- Besley and Rosen (two more stars; one a former editor of the *American Economic Review*, the other the author of a popular public finance textbook) conduct this analysis for many narrow categories of goods and find overshifting.

5.1. *Terminology*

- This research is a bit hard to get into because of terminology. Start with a tax rate of t.

   ○ The key is to distinguish between marginal cost (MC), the price "inclusive of tax" (Q), and the price "exclusive of tax" (P).

The *price inclusive of tax* is what one observes in a market once the tax is imposed. The *price exclusive of tax* is what the firm receives.

- So with no taxes and competitive markets, $P = Q = \text{MC}$. With taxes, competitive markets, and full shifting:

$$Q = P(1 + t) = \text{MC}(1 + t).$$

5.2. *Poterba (NTJ, 1996)*

The Poterba approach is to regress Q on national price changes and local taxes. In city i:

$$Q_i = Q_{US}(1 + t_i)$$

or

$$\ln(Q_i) = \alpha\ln(Q_{US}) + \beta\ln(1 + t) \approx \alpha\ln(\text{MC}) + \gamma t$$

- Poterba estimates this equation in change form.
  - He also uses "seemingly unrelated regression" technique to account for correlations across cities.
- With this specification, full shifting exists if the value of γ is 1.0. A value above 1.0 indicates over-shifting.
- How could there be over-shifting? The most plausible explanation is market power. With an elastic demand curve, a monopolist will raise the price by more than the tax.

5.2.1. *Poterba's results*

- Poterba uses data on categories of spending, namely, women's and girl's clothing, men's and boys' clothing, and personal care items. One data set is for 1947–1977, another is for 1925–1939.
  - He finds full shifting.
- Because the model is specified in difference form, the dependent variable is the percent change in the price for a spending category

in a city and the key explanatory variable is the change in the city's sales tax rate.

    o He has lagged values to pick up the phase-in of tax effects and finds small but significant lagged impacts. The total impacts imply full shifting.

5.3. *Besley/Rosen (NTJ, 1999)*

- The Besley/Rosen approach is to take market prices, Q, divide by $(1 + t)$ to get P, and regress P on t. With full shifting, the coefficient of t will be zero:

$$Q/(1 + t) = P = MC$$

or, in regression form,

$$P = MC + \beta t$$

- The predicted value of β is zero; a value above zero indicates overshifting onto consumers.

5.3.1. *Besley/Rosen results*

- They use data for the last 30 years for specific products (a Big Mac, a box of Kleenex, a Monopoly game, and a package of three boys cotton briefs). Their regressions include city and time effects and measures of real rental, wage, and energy costs — to capture MC.

    o The find full shifting for some (including Monopoly, Big Macs, and Kleenex) and over-shifting for others.

- They also do some dynamic analysis and find that the impact of taxes shows up very rapidly. They also reject Poterba's differencing approach.

5.4. *Young and Bielinska-Kwapisz*

- This paper is in the *NTJ* in 2002.
- They find over-shifting of excise taxes on beer and wine.
- So taxes are shifted and there is considerable evidence for market power!

5.5. *Hawkins*

- Finally, Hawkins, (*NTJ*, December 2002) provides some results on the distortion caused by various forms of the sales tax. See the Table "Hawkins Results".
- Hawkins estimates a demand system for all broad categories of consumption (nondurables, services, alcohol, gasoline, tobacco, home food, utilities, and autos and furnishings). This is done by assuming a pretty general functional form that yields structural parameters, that is, the parameters of the underlying utility functions — which makes it possible to calculate the EB from various forms of the sales tax.
- He looks at eight cases. The base case has no exemptions and no taxation of business inputs (which he calls pyramiding). The other cases add exemptions and/or taxation of (non-exempted) inputs: Here they are, with the excess burden that results (as a percent of revenue raised).

5.5.1. *Lessons from Hawkins*

- The exemptions do cause excess burden, as expected. Services and home food, which are usually exempted, have a significant excess burden. The equity gains must be worth it!

Hawkins Results.

Case	Excess Burden
1. Base	—
2. Services + Home food	23.3%
3. Case 2 + Utilities	30.6%
4. Case 3 + Gasoline	38.5%
5. Base + Pyramiding	0.4%
6. Case 2 + Pyramiding	17.9%
7. Case 3 + Pyramiding	22.1%
8. Case 4 + Pyramiding	26.7%

- Adding pyramiding actually lowers EB (except in case 5)! This is a surprise. But it happens because the taxed inputs produce goods that have inelastic demands and that tend to be exempt themselves. So ironically, pyramiding actually boosts efficiency by indirectly taxing exempt goods!

Property Tax Incidence

- **Class Outline**
  1. **Standard Incidence Analysis**
  2. **Alternative Approaches to Property Tax Incidence**
  3. **Property Tax Incidence and Public Policy**

1. Standard Incidence Analysis

1.1. *Question 1*

- The most basic question in property tax incidence is:
  - *Who bears the burden of a nationwide property tax (or, equivalently) of the average property tax rate?*

- Three answers have appeared:
  - *The Traditional View*
  - *The New View*
  - *The New New View*

1.1.1. *The traditional view*

- The traditional view is based on an analysis of the markets for individual types of property.

- It concludes that the property tax is *regressive*.

  o Business owners, who have many options, can escape the burden
    of the tax, and shift it onto consumers, workers, and renters.
  o Because business owners have relatively high incomes, this
    shifting makes the tax regressive.

- This view is focuses on the behavior of *responsive firms with
  property as an input*:

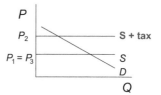

Product Markets (Commercial and Industrial Property is an Input) or Rental
Housing.

- Even in the Traditional View, *the property tax on land is progressive*:

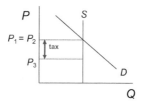

The Land Market.

1.1.2. *The new view*

- This view is based on a *general equilibrium* analysis of all markets.
- A property owner cannot escape a tax in one market if the *same
  tax is levied everywhere*.
- Since almost all property is taxed and the supply is fixed, *property
  owners cannot escape* the tax.

- Because property ownership (including commercial and industrial) increases with income, the *property tax is progressive.*
- Intuitively, the new view applies to the case when the supply of property in the nation is fixed:

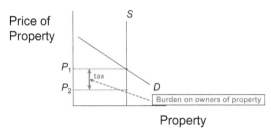

Tax on All Property.

- An alternative approach is to say that "property" is almost the same thing as "physical capital," K, so an equivalent graph is:

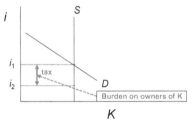

Tax on All Capital.

- The price in this case is the interest rate, i.

1.1.3. *The new new view*

- The "new new view" points out that the supply of property might respond to property taxes over time.

  o Decisions about how much property to build.
  o Decisions about demolition.

- This "correction" implies that the new view may be too extreme, but concludes that *most of the burden is still likely to fall on property owners.*
- This graph shows the New View (S-R) and the New New View (L-R)

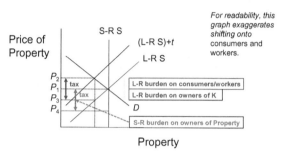

The New and New-New Views.

1.2. *Other Questions*

Some scholars say that the traditional view and the new view address different questions.

1.3. *The Traditional View*

- This view applies to the incidence of a property tax increase *in one place*, holding property taxes in other places constant.
- In this case, property owners can move from one place to another to escape the tax increase.
- Thus, the burden of a property tax increase in one place, such as a big city, may be *regressive.*

1.4. *The New View or the New New View*

- These views seems appropriate for the incidence of the property tax nationwide.
  - o Thus, most scholars agree that the property tax as a whole is *progressive.*
  - o This conclusion is relevant in deciding the extent to which a federal system should rely on local property taxes.

2. Alternative Approaches to Property Tax Incidence

2.1. *Approach 2: Focus on Owner-occupied Housing*

- Approach 2 is to focus on the property tax on owner-occupied housing.
- Because most owner-occupied housing sales involve existing housing, the two parties to the transaction are both households.

  o It follows that households bear the burden of the tax.
  o And the question is: How does the property tax burden change as household income changes?

2.1.1. *Approach 2: Property taxes and rents*

- For owner-occupied housing, property tax incidence depends on the income elasticity of demand for housing.

  o To see why, note that the property tax burden is:

$$\frac{T}{Y} = \frac{tV}{Y} = \frac{t\,(R/r)}{Y} = \left(\frac{t}{r}\right)\left(\frac{R}{Y}\right)$$

  where T is the property tax payment, t is the effective property tax rate, V is house value, R is the annual rental value of housing, r is a discount rate, and $V = R/r$.

2.1.2. *Approach 2: The Income elasticity of demand for housing*

- Holding t/r constant at the national average, this formula implies that the change in T/Y depends on the change in R/Y, which is measured by the income elasticity of demand for housing (θ):

$$\text{income elasticity} = \theta = \frac{\Delta(R)/R}{\Delta Y/Y}$$

- Differentiating T/Y with respect to Y and using this elasticity formula leads to:

$$\left(\frac{\Delta(T/Y)/(T/Y)}{\Delta Y/Y} \right) = \theta - 1$$

2.1.3. *Approach 2: Progressive or Regressive?*

- This result implies that

  o T/Y increases with income if $\theta > 1$;
  o T/Y is the same at all incomes if $\theta = 1$;
  o T/Y decreases with income if $\theta < 1$.

- There is a strong consensus that $\theta < 1$, so T/Y decreases with income and this portion of the tax is *regressive*.
- This analysis helps to explain why, as we will discuss later in the class, so many states have programs to lower property tax rates for lower-valued houses.
- Note that this approach is consistent with both the traditional and new views of the property tax.

2.1.4. *Approach 2: First conclusion*

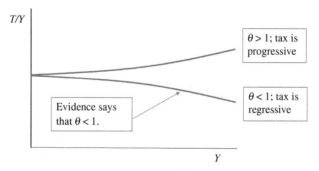

The Income Elasticity of Demand for Housing, θ, and the Progressively of the Property Tax on Owner-Occupied Housing.

2.1.5. *Approach 2: Variation in property taxes across jurisdictions*

- The property tax on owner-occupied housing is even more regressive when variation in tax bases across jurisdictions is considered.
- Some jurisdictions have high property values per household, while others do not.
  - Hence, some jurisdictions can obtain any given amount of revenue at a much smaller burden on their homeowners than can other jurisdictions.
  - These disparities are offset to some degree by state aid to local governments, which is considered in later classes.

2.1.6. *Approach 2: Second conclusion*

- Suppose school districts are expected to raise half of the state-wide average revenue for K-12 schools.
  - In New York State this amount is $9,443 per pupil (2014–2015 school year, without NYC). (*Source*: NY State Education Department).
- Property value pupil in New York State is $182,948 in the least wealthy decile of districts and $1,491,480 in the wealthiest.
  - As a result, the least wealthy districts would have to pay a property tax rate of 5.2% to reach this spending target, but the wealthiest districts would only need a rate of 0.6%.
  - This is obviously a very regressive outcome, but it is offset to significant degree by state aid, particularly if that aid uses a foundation formula, which was discussed in a previous class.

2.2. *Approach 3: Property Tax Incidence with Capitalization*

- A 3rd approach to property tax incidence is to consider the role of property tax capitalization.

- This capitalization shifts the focus to property owners at the time a tax increase (or decrease) is passed.

  ○ Owners at that time cannot escape the tax change.
  ○ If they stay in their house, they pay the tax change directly, and if they sell their house, they pay the tax change in the form of a capital gain or loss.
  ○ If they move, the people who buy their house do not bear any of the burden of the property tax increase because the tax change is offset by a change in sales price.

- According to this approach, therefore, the burden of any property tax change falls on the owners of property at the time of the change in the jurisdiction where the change took place.
- Capitalization arguments are often ignored.

  ○ The implications of this approach are quite counter-intuitive.
  ○ And the affected groups (e.g. homeowners at time t) may be quite similar to the unaffected groups (e.g. homeowners who buy a house after time t).
  ○ This distinction does not correspond to the categories in previous incidence analysis (such as owners, consumers, workers, and renters or rich and poor).

- Nevertheless the logic of this view and the evidence supporting it are quite strong.

  ○ Recall the strong evidence for property tax capitalization.

2.3. *Approach 4: The Property Tax as a Benefit Tax*

- A final approach to property tax incidence is the **Benefit View**.

  ○ According to this view, the property tax is simply the price a household pays to live in a community.
  ○ Households live where this price equals their benefits from the public services, so the property tax is fair according to the benefit principle.
  ○ In this context, the property tax is called a "benefit tax."

2.3.1. *Approach 4: Mixing positive and normative*

- This argument incorrectly mixes positive analysis (the property tax equals a household's benefits from the services it funds) with a normative principle (the benefit principle).
  - ○ A finding that the property tax is a benefit tax does not make the benefit principle any more or less compelling.
  - ○ One could agree that the property tax is a benefit tax and still reject the benefit principle as an appropriate fairness standard.
  - ○ One could conclude that the property tax is not a benefit tax, but still believe that the benefit principle is appropriate for judging the fairness of the tax.

2.3.2. *Approach 4: Evidence*

- The Benefit View implies that the value of public services will not be capitalized into the price of housing.
  - ○ Recall the analysis of the Hamilton model (a Tiebout model with housing and a property tax) in an earlier class.
  - ○ In his model, households all select their optimal community and the property tax is a benefit tax.
  - ○ Under these circumstances, households no reason to bid up the price of housing anywhere else.
- The extensive evidence of public service capitalization (discussed in an earlier class) therefore leads to a clear, unambiguous rejection of the Benefit View.

2.3.3. *Carroll/Yinger* (*NTJ, 1994*)

- In the case of rental housing, some evidence on these points is provided by C&Y.
- Tax shifting from landlords to tenants must take the form of higher rents.
- C&Y estimate the extent to which higher property taxes lead to higher rents in the Boston area, all else equal.

- Higher property taxes alone do not make an apartment more desirable to a tenant, so in the case of *mobile tenants*:

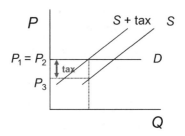

The Rental Housing Market (Within an Urban Area).

- However, even mobile tenants will pay higher rents *if they receive better public services.*

  o This effect will be larger where public service costs are lower.

- Thus, landlords can shift a property tax increase to tenants only to the extent that this increase leads to better public services.
- The question is: To what extent does this type of shifting occur?
- This is what happens when higher property taxes lead to better public services:

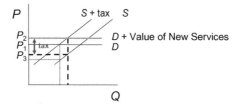

The Rental Housing Market (Within an Urban Area).

- C&Y estimate that a $1.00 increase in property taxes results in a rent increase of about $0.15, on average, which implies that landlords bear about 85% of the property tax burden.

- Thus, the conclusion from the Traditional View, namely, that tenants bear a large share of the burden of a property tax increase, is not correct, at least not in the Boston area.
- Neither is the benefit view: landlords pay a large share of the tax without receiving the benefits.

3. Property Tax Incidence and Public Policy

3.1. *Issue 1: When to Use Approach 3*

- The equity of tax provisions that have been in place a long time should be evaluated based on their progressivity or regressivity; gains and losses to property owners are not relevant.
- The equity of new tax provisions that are intended to be in place for a long time (e.g. a new property tax or income tax) should be evaluated primarily on the basis of their progressivity or regressivity, but gains or losses to specific groups are worth noting.
  - Gains to a politically connected group (e.g. homeowners on Long Island in the case of New York's STAR program) should be part of the discussion.
  - One way to minimize these gains and losses is to have a phase-in period.
- The equity of temporary tax policies should be framed primarily on the basis of the capitalization view.
  - The equity of a revaluation that is followed by a return to poor assessments should be evaluated on the basis of the (often unfair) gains and losses it generates.
  - The equity of a revaluation that is followed by the implementation of an accurate assessing system should be evaluated on the basis of the horizontal and vertical equity it generates.

3.2. *Property Tax Incidence and Public Policy: Application to Economic Development*

- One important application of capitalization is to economic development.

○ With full capitalization, lower property tax rates lead to higher property values and hence to no net advantage in attracting business for a low-tax jurisdiction.

- This argument helps to explain why scholars have not found consistent evidence to support the view that property tax rates affect economic development and why some careful studies do not find any such impact at all.

○ We will return to these issues in a later class.

3.3. Property Tax Incidence and Public Policy: Moderating Regressivity

- All views of property tax incidence say that taxes on homeowners are regressive.
- Voters want programs to cut this regressivity, which applies to the component of the property tax that is of greatest concern to voters.

○ Voters are particularly concerned about *elderly* homeowners and *veterans*.

3.4. Graduated Property Tax Rates

- Graduated property tax rates are possible (e.g. Minnesota) but do not make sense for nonresidential property.

○ The issue is regressivity across people, not across businesses.
○ A business with a small factory may be owned by a very rich person!

- So states turn to homestead exemptions and circuit breakers instead.

3.5. Homestead Exemptions

- **Design**
  ○ The formula:

$$T = t(V - X)$$

- o These exemptions may or may not lead to reimbursement by the state.
- o In New York's STAR program, X is higher in counties with expensive houses, which undermines both equity and efficiency, as it rewards (mostly wealthy) homeowners who move to high-cost locations.
- o The tax rate is zero below $V = X(\$52,500$ in the Figure "Property Tax Exemptions and Progressivity") and moves toward t^* (the legislated rate $= 2\%$) as V increases.
- An exemption also cuts regressivity when property taxes are compared to household income.

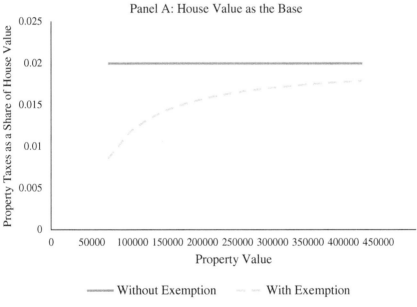

Property Tax Exemptions and Progressivity.

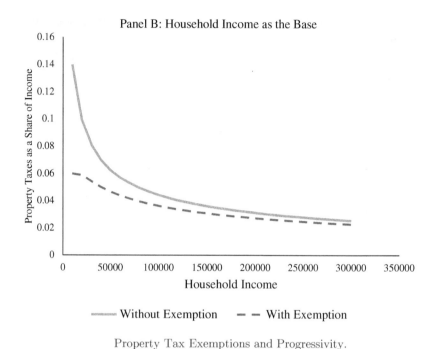

Property Tax Exemptions and Progressivity.

3.5.1. *Popularity of exemptions*

- Almost all states have some form of homestead exemption.
- Most states have *special exemptions*, usually for the elderly or veterans.
- Several states have *general exemptions*.
- A few states *reimburse local governments for the exemptions*.
- For details, go to http://www.lincolninst.edu.

3.5.2. *Strengths and weaknesses of exemptions*

- **Strengths**
  - Homestead exemptions cut the regressivity of the property tax on homeowners.

- **Weaknesses**
  - ○ Reimbursed homestead exemptions lower voters' tax prices and encourage property tax rate increases.
  - ○ Homestead exemptions cannot be given to renters without an assumption about the (unknown) extent to which landlords shift the property tax onto renters.

3.6. *Circuit Breakers*

- A **circuit breaker** provides a tax break (usually through an income tax rebate) if a person's property tax payment exceeds a given share of their income, Y.
Design:

$$CB = \alpha(tV - \beta Y) \quad \text{if } (tV - \beta Y) > 0$$
$$CB = 0 \quad \text{if } (tV - \beta Y) \le 0$$

with a typical $\alpha = 0.5$ and a typical $\beta = 0.035$.
- With an income elasticity of 0.5, the tax schedule with a circuit breaker is progressive up to the cut-off point.

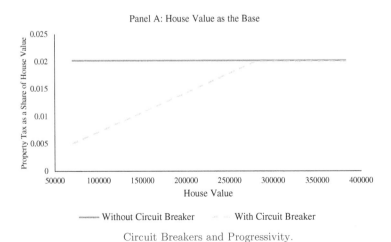

Circuit Breakers and Progressivity.

- This equation and figure describe a "single-threshold" circuit breaker.
- Some states use a "multiple-threshold" circuit breaker instead, which means that β is higher for lower-income households.
- Another design in some states is called a "sliding-scale" circuit breaker. It sets β equal to zero and sets higher values of α for lower-income households.
- A circuit breaker is also eliminates regressivity with respect to income — up to a point.

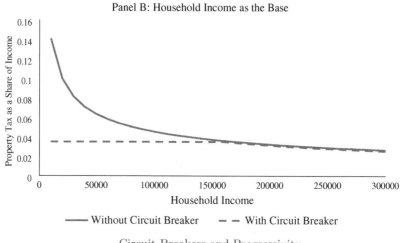

Circuit Breakers and Progressivity.

- But a circuit breaker also unfairly rewards people who buy an expensive house relative to their income (fixed at \$75,000 in this figure).

3.6.1. *Benefits of circuit breakers*

- **Popularity**
  - ○ About half of the states have circuit breakers for elderly homeowners or elderly renters.
  - ○ A few states have circuit breakers for all homeowners or all renters.
  - ○ For details, go to http://www.lincolninst.edu.

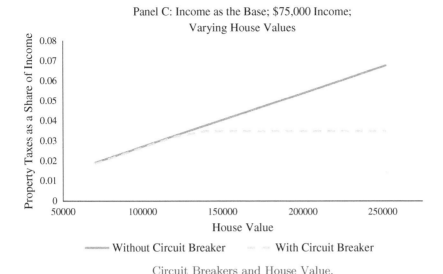

Circuit Breakers and House Value.

- **Strengths**
  - Circuit breakers provide tax relief for people who experience a negative income shock that makes it hard for them to pay property taxes out of their income.

3.6.2. *Problems with circuit breakers*

- **Weaknesses**
  - Circuit breakers help many home owners who do not need help.
    - Empty-nesters can borrow against their equity; the circuit breaker just subsidizes their children's inheritance.
    - Circuit breakers reward people who buy an expensive house.
  - Circuit breakers for all taxpayers lower tax prices for some voters and may have unintended consequences, such as higher spending.
  - Circuit breakers cannot be given to renters without an assumption about the (unknown) extent to which landlords shift the property tax onto renters.

3.6.3. *A better solution for regressivity*

- Many people like circuit breakers because they can add thresholds that make them very progressive with respect to income, not just with respect to property values.
- Exemptions could be made equally progressive with respect to income by setting a higher exemption amount for lower income households.
- This approach does not now exist, because one great advantage of exemptions is that they can be administered through property tax bills, whereas circuit breakers are administered through the income tax.
  - By switching the administration of exemptions to the income tax, the link between income and the size of the exemption would be easy to administer.
  - This design is like a sliding-scale circuit breaker except that the exemption gives the same tax break to all households in a given income bracket, whereas the sliding-scale circuit breaker gives a larger break to households who buy more expensive houses.

3.6.4. *A better solution for cash-flow problems*

- Many people like circuit breakers because they help empty nesters and people in vacation areas that experience rapid property-value growth.
  - In fact, however, these people have a valuable asset and do not need to be subsidized.
  - Instead, they need help with a cash-flow problem.
- A better solution for this cash-flow problem is a "tax deferral" program.
  - This type of program allows people in certain groups to postpone property tax increases until a house is sold or passed on to heirs; at that time all postponed payments are due, with interest.
  - About two dozen states currently have a limited program of this type, but eligibility is usually very limited, and this approach could be expanded.

Tax Competition

1. Introduction

- In a federal system like ours, the actions of one government are not independent of the actions of other governments.
  - This rule applies not only to the obvious case — intergovernmental aid — but also to decisions that do not involve any direct connection between governments.
- Governments' spending decisions are influenced by the spending decisions of their neighbors (or other jurisdictions with which they compare themselves).
  - This issue has already appeared as a guide to the choice of instruments for several studies, including Bill's and my work on school districts in New York.
- A government's taxing decisions may also be influenced by the extent to which its tax base is expected to flow into other jurisdictions.
- And perhaps by perceptions of what is acceptable based on what comparison jurisdictions do (= "yardstick" or "copy cat" competition).

- This is the topic for today.
- There is quite a large literature on this topic, both conceptual and empirical.
  - After a brief discussion of some technical issues, we are going to take a look at a couple recent empirical studies.

2. Conceptual Issues

- For an excellent review of the conceptual literature, see
  J. Wilson, "Theories of Tax Competition," *NTJ*, June 1999.
  - This is not a particularly technical article, but it is intellectually challenging. The issues are hard!
- The initial literature on this topic concluded that inter-jurisdiction competition was likely to lead to inefficiently **low** tax rates.
  - The basic intuition: The efficient level of taxation is one that provides public services at the level where marginal benefit equals marginal cost.
  - If tax decisions reflect an additional consideration — namely, the desire to attract business — then tax rates will be set below this optimal level.
- More recent work has identifies some circumstances under which tax competition might be useful.
  - In a "political economy" model, for example, in which public officials have their own agendas, tax competition might, in Wilson's words, "induce government officials to reduce waste in government."
- The impact of tax competition on important policy objectives, such as efficiency, is difficult to pin down.
  - Indeed, the set of issues raised by tax competition is amazingly complex.
  - At this point, there is no consensus as to whether tax competition has desirable outcomes or — if it does not — what to do about it.

2.1. *Rork (NTJ, 2003)*

Rork estimates a straightforward model:

$$T_{it} = X_{it}\beta + \theta\left(\sum_j w_{jt}T_{jt}\right) + \xi_i + \lambda_t + \mu_{it}$$

where T is a tax rate,
   i indicates a state (and j its neighbors),
   t stands for time,
   X is a vector of control variables,
   w is a set of weights (assumed, not estimated),
   β and θ are parameters to be estimated, and
   ξ, λ, and μ are error components for the state, the year, and random factors, respectively.

- This model can be estimated as a system of equations, since there is a T for each state.

  o So Rork stacks the equations, leaving a vector T on each side.

- He estimates this system with an IV procedure in which the weighted X's from other states, that is, the X's from other states multiplied by the appropriate w, are the instruments.

  o Rork does not provide tests for instrument validity.

2.1.1. *Rork's data*

- Rork obtains data from the Census (*State Government Finances*) and other sources for 1967 to 1996; the X variables include:

  o Fiscal stress (an exogenous measure?)
  o Per capita debt (a poor choice — endogenous!)
  o Per capita federal transfers
  o Political variables

    ■ Election year
    ■ Everyone (governor, both houses) Democrat
    ■ Everyone Republican

- State characteristics (affected by taxes?)
  - Unemployment rate
  - Per capita income
  - Percent elderly
- Fixed effects
  - State
  - Year
- The T variables are
  - Statutory rates.
    - For sales tax, gasoline, cigarettes taxes.
  - Average tax rates (revenue over base).
    - For income and corporate income taxes.

2.1.2. *Rork's result*

- The results are as follows, with everything statistically significant except the first result for income tax.

2.2. *Interpretation*

- A positive sign indicates that a higher tax in neighboring jurisdictions leads to a higher tax in state i.
- A negative sign means that a tax rate declines when neighbors' tax rates go up.
- Rork interprets these results, reasonably, as indications of the responsiveness of the tax base.

Impact of Neighbors' Tax Rates on Selected Tax Rates (Rork).

Tax	Equal Weights	Population-Based Weights
Cigarettes	0.636	0.416
Gasoline	0.600	0.463
Income	−0.048	−0.097
General Sales	−0.237	−0.164
Corporate Income	0.163	0.165

- o A positive sign, as in the case of cigarettes, gasoline, and corporate income, indicates that a state can only afford to have a high rate if its neighbors do, too.
- o If the tax base is not responsive (negative sign), as in the case of income and general sales taxes, a state can afford to behave differently than its neighbors.
- More on a negative sign:
  - o If a neighboring state lowers its tax, there will be some loss of revenue in a state, and the state will try to offset that loss by raising its own rate, knowing that the added loss in base will be minimal.
  - o If a neighboring state raises its tax, there will be some shift in base toward a state, and the state will maximize revenue by lowering its tax to make that shift as large as possible.
  - o This seems a bit odd. Perhaps he should have looked for asymmetric responses.
- Rork argues that states would do well to switch to unresponsive income and sales taxes and away from responsive excise and corporate taxes.
  - o But responsiveness is only one criterion!

2.3. *Tosun and Skidmore (NTJ, 2004)*

- This study looks at the impact of lottery competition on lottery revenue.
  - o The data are for West Virginia and the competition comes either from the introduction of lotteries in neighboring states or from the introduction of new lottery games in West Virginia.
- This study takes advantage of the fact that lotteries were introduced in Kentucky, Virginia, and Maryland after West Virginia already had a lottery.
- The basic equation is:

$$L_{it} = I_{it}\beta_1 + X_{it}\beta_2 + C_i + T_t + \varepsilon_{it}$$

where

- o L_{it} is the log of deflated per capita lottery sales in county i in year t;
- o I is the status of lottery games in neighboring states;
- o X is a set of control variables, including per capita income, unemployment, share of population over 65, proportion male, proportion non-white, and whether the county has *video lotteries*, which attract new customers from other states;
- o C is a county fixed effect, T is a time effect.

- Both the lottery in a neighboring *state and the video lottery variables are interacted with whether the county is on a state border.* Some regressions track these effects over time.
- The data are for all counties in West Virginia for 1987 to 2000 — 770 observations overall.
- They find that lottery revenue generally drops when lotteries are introduced in neighboring states.

  - o This is true for counties bordering on Kentucky, Virginia, and Maryland.
  - o But the results are not entirely clear: one of the results for Maryland is not significant; another result indicates that revenue in border counties increases in the years after introduction in Virginia.

- For some reason, the most obvious specification is not there: a shock in the first year followed by change in later years.

  - o They only estimate shocks or trends. THINK THROUGH YOUR SPECIFICATIONS! This one might have cleared everything up. I suspect the trend is important in Maryland, not the initial shock, and I suspect that there is an initial shock and then an offsetting trend in Virginia.

- They also find that the introduction of video lotteries increases revenue in border counties — i.e. steals revenue from neighboring states. (The same goes for casinos!)
- So there is intense competition for lottery revenues.

o This creates a *prisoner's dilemma.*

o If neighboring states all agreed to give up lotteries, they could move to more reasonable revenue sources.

o But so long as one keeps them, it is in the interest of others to keep them, too, because of their powerful ability to export taxes to nonresidents (or to prevent the importing of taxes from neighboring states).

3. Bonus Slides! State-Run Lotteries

- The first state lottery was in New Hampshire in 1964.
- Now every state except Hawaii and Utah have some form of legal gambling.
- Lotteries raise a small share of state revenue (1.1% of general revenue in 2011).
- Lotteries probably are a natural monopoly, as customers are attracted to very large prizes.

3.1. *Policy Issues Raised by Lotteries*

- *Legalization* (Should lottery gambling be allowed?).
- *Government Provision* (Should lotteries be a private or government monopoly?).
- *Rate of Taxation* (How much revenue should the state claim?).
- *Earmarking* (Should the revenue be earmarked for education?).
- *Promotion* (How should lotteries be designed and advertised?).

3.2. *Legalization*

- Lotteries generate *consumer surplus*, that is, many people pay for their entertainment value.
- Lotteries also generate *social costs*: gambling addiction for some people, increased crime, and, perhaps, undermining incentives to earn one's way.
- There is a consensus in this country that the benefits outweigh the costs (although the costs are high).

3.3. *Government Provision*

- Lotteries require large scale, so private lotteries would be huge companies that would be:
  - Difficult to regulate and tax (think of their political connections!).
  - Inviting to criminal elements.
- Thus, there is a broad consensus that legalized lotteries should be government monopolies.
- But a few states are now using private management or contemplating the sale of the lottery to a private company.

3.4. *Rate of Taxation*

- Lotteries provide a classic example of the trade-off between CS and revenue:
  - The analytical case for lotteries is based on the CS they generate, which is minimized by high implicit tax rates.
  - The political case for lotteries is based on the money they raise, which is maximized by high implicit tax rate.
- In this case (as in many others!) politics wins, that is, the implicit tax rates are very high.
- What is the implicit tax rate?
  - Answer: What the state keeps divided by the total costs of running the lottery.
  - Let t = implicit tax rate, R = state revenue, P = prizes awarded, C = administrative costs. Then

$$t = \frac{R}{P + C}$$

- The tax rate in the typical state is about 50%!
- In 2016 implicit lottery tax rates range from 16% (Idaho) to 288% (South Dakota) and are all far higher than the rates for any other type of tax.
- These high rates of tax cause enormous distortion between lotteries and other types of commodities.

- But they also cut back on the social costs (externalities) of lotteries and export taxes to nonresidents.
- Moreover, lottery taxes are very *regressive* — far more regressive than any other revenue source.
- One study: Low-income individuals earn 11% of total income but provide 25% of lottery revenue.
- Some games, such as instant games and lotto, are particularly regressive.
- Within income classes, the burden of lotteries is concentrated on a relatively small share of individuals.

Implicit Lottery Tax Rates, 2016.

Arizona	26.8%	Nebraska	35.1%
Arkansas	25.6%	New Hampshire	37.6%
California	46.1%	New Jersey	47.1%
Colorado	34.6%	New Mexico	45.1%
Connecticut	44.4%	New York	66.2%
Delaware	150.6%	North Carolina	39.8%
Florida	42.0%	North Dakota	40.0%
Georgia	37.5%	Ohio	42.6%
Idaho	16.0%	Oklahoma	57.6%
Illinois	33.6%	Oregon	192.3%
Indiana	33.1%	Pennsylvania	42.2%
Iowa	31.8%	Rhode Island	213.8%
Kansas	40.1%	South Carolina	36.9%
Kentucky	38.2%	South Dakota	288.1%
Louisiana	59.2%	Tennessee	66.8%
Maine	49.3%	Texas	41.3%
Maryland	43.9%	Vermont	29.5%
Massachusetts	32.7%	Virginia	45.3%
Michigan	42.6%	Washington	37.8%
Minnesota	36.5%	West Virginia	85.7%
Missouri	37.1%	Wisconsin	49.3%
Montana	47.9%	Wyoming	23.9%

Source: U.S. Census.

3.5. *Earmarking*

- Almost half of lottery states *earmark* the funds for education.
- This link is part of their political appeal: "Whatever their bad features, at least lotteries help fund out education system!"
- It is not clear, however, that lotteries increase net funds for education:
  - They facilitate cuts in state education aid.
  - They lower sales tax revenue.
- Even counting benefits from education, lotteries are still regressive.
- The people who run lotteries are paid to raise as much money as possible.
- Hence they resort to aggressive advertising: "All you need is a dollar and a dream."
- *Some of this advertising is misleading at best,* with no recognition of the low odds of winning.
- Moreover, *this advertising puts government in the position of undermining the work ethic.*
- The people who run lotteries sometimes resort to promoting games that are directed toward low-income communities.
  - These games maximize revenue because these people are more vulnerable to the misleading appeal of instant wealth.
  - But they also maximize both the regressivity of the lottery "tax" and the social costs of lottery addiction.
- Promotions of this type are, in my view, simply unethical.
- Illinois, Indiana, and New Jersey employ private companies to manage their lotteries; other states are considering this step.
- Private management is seen as a way to raise revenue.
- The easiest way to raise revenue is to exploit vulnerable populations.
- I look forward to studies of private management to see if this happens.

3.6. Conclusions About Lotteries

- Lotteries are here to stay.
- States cannot get rid of them without losing revenue to their neighbors.
- High implicit taxes discourage participation and cut direct CS but also cut the social costs.
- *So keep lotteries with high rates but use honest advertising and do not target vulnerable groups.*

Lecture 16

Tax Rates and Economic Development

- **Class Outline**
  1. **Introduction**
  2. **Conceptual Frames**
  3. **Recent Research**

1. Introduction

- Most state and local politicians run on the platform of "jobs, jobs, jobs," and it is important to try to figure out what policies actually affect the number of jobs (and the incomes they generate) in a given jurisdiction.
- Today we are going to focus on the most basic question: Can a jurisdiction promote economic development by lowering its tax rates?
  - We are going to look at one study (Bania and Stone) that answers "maybe," another (Wong) that answers "no" and (if time) another (Haughwout *et al.*) that answers "yes."
- Next class will focus on tax breaks for specific firms.

243

2. Conceptual Frames

2.1. *Profit Maximization*

- Two key conceptual frameworks appear in this literature.
- The *first* is that higher taxes mean lower profits, so if one controls for other things, one should find that jurisdictions with lower taxes attract/retain more firms and have more jobs and higher incomes.
- Of course firms also care about many other things, such as access to customers, access to the right kind of workers, access to energy or other inputs, access to transportation, and perhaps idiosyncratic factors.
- So this is ultimately an empirical question:
  - *How important are taxes in influencing firms' decisions and, ultimately, state and local economic development?*

2.2. *Capitalization*

- The *second* framework is that tax differences across locations are capitalized into land values.
  - As a result, firms moving into a location should not care about tax rates (or relevant service levels).
- When tax rates or relevant service levels are changed, they have an impact on current owners, but not on future owners.
  - Moreover, current owners cannot escape changes, so their behavior is not affected by them.
- Of course, capitalization may not be complete. So this is ultimately an empirical question:
  - *How important are taxes in influencing firms' decisions and, ultimately, state and local economic development?*

3. Recent Research

3.1. *Bania and Stone (JPAM, 2008)*

- Based on state panel for 1962–2002 (data every 5 years).

- They look at the growth rate in income (log change in real personal income per capita) as a function of taxes and spending.
- Because of the state budget constraint, they must leave one thing out.

  o They leave out "productive" spending, defined as spending on infrastructure, education, safety, and some other things.

Estimated Fiscal Effects on Economic Growth.

Variable	Linear Model (*OLS-FE*)	Nonlinear Model (*OLS-FE*)	Nonlinear Model (*GMM-FE*)
Constant	14.232**	−13.414	—
	(6.242)	(11.037)	
Taxes(−1)	0.175	5.102**	6.008**
	(0.427)	(1.557)	(1.081)
Taxes2(−1)		−0.216**	−0.257**
		(0.065)	(0.045)
Fees(−1)	0.180	0.368	0.012
	(0.696)	(0.662)	(0.290)
Other(−1)	2.561**	2.380**	1.889**
	(0.651)	(0.605)	(0.342)
H&W(−1)	−1.184	−1.216*	−0.844**
	(0.665)	(0.632)	(0.345)
Growth(−1)			−0.158**
			(0.042)
State fixed effects	yes	yes	yes
Period fixed effects	yes	yes	yes
R^2	0.649	0.663	0.658
J-statistic			25.547
Number of observations	392	392	343

Notes: Dependent variable is log change in personal income per capita Data are for 49 of the 50 states in the U.S. (Alaska is excluded) from 1962 to 1977 in five-year intervals. See text for sources and further details. Robust(panel-corrected, cross-section SUR) standard errors are in parentheses. The J-statistic is a test of the validity of the over-identifying restrictions in the GMM instrumental variables estimates in column (3).

**Significant at the 5 percent level; *at 10 percent level.

Source: Bania and Stone.

- ○ So they regress growth on tax rates and "unproductive" spending.
- ○ The coefficient of taxes indicates the impact on income of an increase in taxes *that goes into productive spending*.
- • "Unproductive" spending consists of health and welfare.
  - ○ In some regressions health is also treated as productive with little impact on the results.
- • There could be a serious endogeneity problem, so they:
  - ○ Lag the right-side variables 5 years.
  - ○ Add state fixed effects.
  - ○ Add period fixed effects.
  - ○ One version adds state trends.

State Revenue Hill (Bania and Stone)

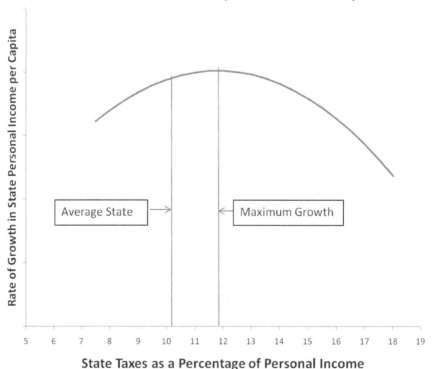

- Interpretation:

  - The right mix of productive spending and taxes raises the 5 year growth rate 2.3 percentage points above the median;
  - The wrong mix lowers this growth rate up to 4 points below the median.
  - The average state spends too little!

- B&S also do a policy experiment in which they raise taxes as a percentage of personal income by 1 percentage point in every state and assume the money goes to productive spending.
- This a not a very compelling experiment because it involves a much larger tax increase in NY and other high-income states than in low-income states.
- Why not have the same tax increase per capita?

3.2. *Srithongrung and Kriz* (*JPAM, 2014*)

- A more recent article in *JPAM* estimates a dynamic model of economic development that builds on the insights in Bania and Stone.
- "[T]axes have a slight negative effect on economic growth. In addition to current year effect, this tax effect is only a year lagged and is transient, rather than persistent."
- "Operational spending has a positive effect on growth approximately at about a one-to-one ratio. The positive effect of operational spending persists through the six-year estimation period."
- Public capital spending demonstrates a positive effect on economic growth for two years after the investment occurs. The effect is more than a one-to-one ratio and lasts for three years including the current year."
- "[T]he wisdom of cutting taxes as a way to boost a state economy must be seriously reexamined. While cutting taxes may produce a short-term boost in the economy, if those cuts are accompanied by cuts in spending (especially operational spending), the short-run gains are going to be offset and perhaps even exceeded by the drag on growth created by lower spending."

- "[T]he assertions that spending reduces growth ... must also be reexamined. Our results strongly support a view that spending on local public goods is complementary with private economic activity ... and provides strong multiplier effects."

3.3. *Wong*

- Wilson Wong's dissertation (Maxwell, 1998) looks at the impact of local property tax rates and public service quality on economic development in New York.
- This dissertation takes advantage of the variation in local tax rates generated by the Homestead Option.

  - This option gives cities the right to use a classified property tax, with a higher rate on business than on residential property, when they complete a revaluation.
  - In cities that adopt this option, therefore, there is a change in property tax rates that does not come from the usual budget processes.
  - This extra variation is like a natural experiment that gives the researcher some leverage to study the impact of property taxes on economic development.

- Wong estimates the following equation:

$$Y_{iy} = \beta_0 + \beta_t t_{iy} + \beta_s s_{iy} + \sum_k \beta_G^k G_{iy}^k + \mu_i + \lambda_y + \delta_i y + \varepsilon_{iy}$$

where

Y = a measure of economic development, such as jobs or payroll (in city i and time y)

t = effective property tax rate on commercial and industrial property

s = sales tax rate

G = a measure of performance (for government service k)

$\mu, \gamma, \delta, \varepsilon$ = error components for city, time, city time trend, and random stuff, respectively.

- He faces two challenging issues.

- The *first* is that effective tax rate may be endogenous, so he uses 2SLS.
- His instruments are of three types:
  - Deviations in the endogenous variable (from a city's own average).
  - Variable identifying above-median values (grouping method).
  - Variables that come from the Homestead Option (reassessment dummy, Homestead Option dummy, years since Homestead Option).
- He did not use all the fancy IV tests, which were not yet available.
- The *second* challenge is that government performance is hard to measure.
- He did an amazing job finding variables to measure government performance, including:
  - The crime rate.
  - Property loss from fire.
  - School test scores (from grades 3 through 6).

3.3.1. *Findings*

- He looks at employment and payroll in the following categories: total, manufacturing, trade, transportation and utilities, finance plus insurance plus real estate, and service.
- In the IV estimations, the property tax rate is statistically significant with a negative sign in almost every regression for both employment and payroll.
- The employment results are stronger than the payroll results.
- *Property taxes matter.*

3.3.2. *More findings*

- The crime rate is significant with a negative sign for total, trade, FIRE, and service.
- The education scores are significant with a positive sign in all employment regressions and for FIRE and service payroll regressions.

- The fire loss variable is negative and significant in about half the cases (including total) but in different cases for employment and payroll.
- *Public services matter.*

Impact of Eliminating the Property Tax (Based on Wong, 1998).

	Employment (%)	Payroll (%)
Total	1.36	3.23
Manufacturing	1.71	12.00
Trade	0.43	1.40
Transportation/Utilities	1.63	10.89
Finance, insurance, and real estate	7.00	6.22
Service	5.13	4.94

- The impact of taxes is amazingly small.
- Wong estimated the impact of eliminating the property tax altogether and replacing it with some other source with no impact (such as state in above table).
- Finally, remember that services matter, too.
- Wong's results indicate that one cannot cut property taxes and services and expect a boost in economic development.

  ○ Wong did not do any cost calculations, but the significant role of services suggest that such a step might undermine economic development because firms do care about safety and education.

3.4. Haughwout, Inman, Craig, and Luce (Restat, 2004)

- HICL start with a straightforward model of tax bases per capita (B) for five different taxes:

  ○ Property, in-city sales, resident wages, commuter wages, and in-city business receipts.
  ○ Each tax base depends on the vector of tax rates and on government services.
  ○ Along with prices and the opportunities households and businesses have elsewhere — which I am leaving out.

- In symbols:

$$B_t = B_t(\tau, G)$$

where

$$\tau = (\tau_p, \tau_s, \tau_w, \tau_m, \tau_x)$$

- The city budget constraint:

$$G = \frac{\sum_t \tau_t B_t(\tau, G) + Z}{c}$$

where Z is intergovernmental aid (from state and federal governments) and c is the cost of public services.
- Substituting the second equation into the first, we get

$$B_t = b_t(\tau, Z, c)$$

- Now differentiate this with respect to τ_t (assuming only B_t is affected).

$$dB_t = \frac{\partial B_t}{\partial \tau_t} d\tau_t = \left(\varepsilon_{tt} \frac{B_t}{\tau_t} \right) d\tau_t$$

- This is their estimating equation.
- They also point out that

$$T_t = \tau_t B_t = \tau_t b_t(\tau, Z, c)$$

and

$$\text{REV} = \sum_t \tau_t b_t(\tau, Z, c) + Z$$

- Again assuming the cross-base elasticities equal zero, this leads to

$$\Delta \text{REV} = B_j(1 + \varepsilon_{jj}) \Delta \tau_j$$

which is their "revenue hill."

- As they put it:

  o When a tax base's own rate-to-base elasticity is $\varepsilon_{jj} > -1$ (e.g. -0.5), then tax revenues increase with small increases in a tax's own tax rate and the city will be on a rising portion of its revenue hill ($\Delta R/\Delta \tau_j > 0$). When $\varepsilon_{jj} = -1$, the city is at the top of its revenue hill ($\Delta R/\Delta \tau_j = 0$), and when $-1 > \varepsilon_{jj}$ (e.g. -1.5), the city is on the falling side of the revenue hill ($\Delta R/\Delta \tau_j < 0$).

- They estimate this with time series data from five cities: Minneapolis (property tax only), Houston (property and sales taxes), New York (property, sales, and resident income), Philadelphia (property, resident and nonresident wage, and business receipts).
- Control variables (in change form) include

  o Z (aid minus city welfare spending, on the grounds that it does not affect bids for property),
  o c (measured by producer prices and interest rates — but not by poverty!),
  o wages (measured by local private wages, national unemployment, and national crime rates).

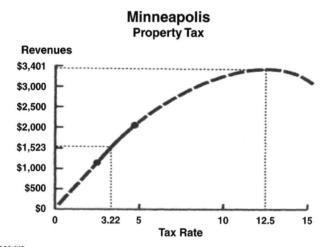

Source: HICL.

- They pay careful attention to time-series issues, which are important in a study like this, but, surprisingly, I could not find any information on the years covered by the study or even the number of observations.
- Results: They find very strong negative impacts of taxes on the base in most cases.
- One exception is Philly's wage tax, where the effects are not significant (so the "hill" never turns down).

  ○ They argue that this is because a higher tax drives out residents and therefore does not alter the tax base per capita.

- All cities except Minneapolis are near the top of their revenue hills.
- Here is a hill for New York City:

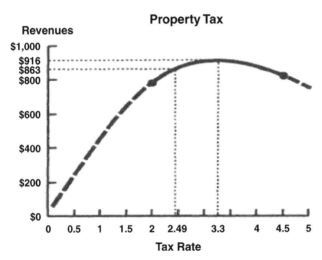

Source: HICL.

3.5. *Problem: Form*

- This approach is similar to the one used by Bania and Stone, except that it focuses specifically on tax bases instead of on an overall measure of economic wellbeing.
- I think this application is not nearly as compelling.

- Suppose one starts with the simplest possible base equation:

$$B_j = \alpha_{0j} + \alpha_{1j}\tau_j + \alpha_{2j}G + \alpha_{3j}Q$$

- Now take the steps outlined above to remove G with only one tax. The result:

$$B_j = \alpha_{0j} + \alpha_{1j}\tau_j + \alpha_{2j}\left(\frac{\tau_j(\alpha_{0j} + \alpha_{1j}\tau_j + \alpha_{3j}Q) + Z}{c - \alpha_{2j}\tau_j}\right) + \alpha_{3j}Q$$

- The estimating equation, which is the derivative of this equation with respect to τ_j, is not theirs!
  - It is not linear in τ_j.
  - It includes interaction between all the control variables and τ_j.
    - If there is more than one tax, it includes all the other tax bases, even with zero cross-base elasticities!
- In their estimating equation, the estimated coefficient (b) is

$$b_t = \left(\varepsilon_{tt}\frac{B_t}{\tau_t}\right)$$

- So this expression is assumed to be constant. They then derive the elasticity as:

$$\varepsilon_{tt} = b_t\left(\frac{\tau_t}{B_t}\right)$$

- This elasticity then goes into the "revenue hill" equation shown earlier.
- The problem is that this is rigged to generate a revenue hill.
  - The elasticity varies by definition — not due to an estimation of its variation (as in Bania and Stone).
  - Moreover, the elasticity must grow as the base shrinks!!
  - They never test this formulation!

3.6. *Problem: Endogeneity*

- HICL recognize that bases could affect rates. Their basic estimates use bases from the end of year and rates from the beginning. They also try lags and do IV.

- For instruments, they use "exogenous local political events thought to change the players or preferences setting local rates, as well as exogenous state and national-scale policies thought to change the overall attractiveness of local spending or the relative attractiveness of different local taxes."
- I don't find their analysis convincing for two reasons.
- First, their conceptual case for their instruments is not convincing. Political events can alter the base!
- Second, their instruments appear to be pretty weak (as they admit).

3.6.1. *Examples of instruments*

- The local election cycle.
- But aren't there give always, which might influence the base, at election time?
- Unexpected changes in state aid.
- Couldn't these be for subsidizing development?
- State-mandated changes in the relative assessments of residential and business property.
- Couldn't this affect the value of business property?

Tax Breaks and Economic Development

1. Basic Tools/Concepts

1.1. *Macroeconomic Models*

- This class focuses on microeconomics, i.e. on households and firms and single markets.
- But economic development involves macroeconomics, which is all markets put together.
- Today we will look at some highly simplified macroeconomic models: Keynesian, export-base, and input–output.

1.1.1. *A simple Keynesian model*

- A simple Keynesian model combines accounting identities and assumptions about behavior.
- The terms:
  Y = Income; E = Expenditures (= GNP);
  C = Consumption; I = Investment;
  S = Savings; X = Exports; M = Imports

- The identities:

$$E \equiv C + I + (X - M)$$
$$Y \equiv C + S$$
$$E \equiv Y$$

- The assumptions about behavior:

$$I = I_0; X = X_0$$
$$C = C_0 + cY; M = mY$$

- The equilibrium:

$$Y = \left(\frac{1}{1 - c + m} \right)(C_0 + I_0 + X_0)$$

- Interpretation:
  - Exports (and other exogenous factors) are multiplied into income.
  - These factors have a larger impact if the marginal propensity to consume (c) is larger.
  - These factors have a smaller impact if the marginal propensity to import (m = "leakage") is larger.

- Of course this model leaves out many things, such as:
  - Government
  - Prices and interest rates
  - Expectations

- But it introduces three key concepts:
  - Exports (= inflows)
  - Multipliers
  - Leakage

1.1.2. *Economic base models*

- *Economic base models* are the simplest possible macroeconomic models of a state or local economy.

- They are highly oversimplified and should be used with great care, but also provide some useful insights.

1.1.2.1. Export vs. Local Jobs

- The distinction between export and local jobs depends on the *context*.
- A famous restaurant or a retail store on a jurisdiction boundary may attract customers from other jurisdictions and therefore involve export jobs.

1.1.3. *An export base model*

- An export base model combines a *definition* and a simple *behavioral equation*.
- Let
T = Total jobs
L = Local jobs
E = Export jobs
- Then, the *definition* is:

$$T = L + E$$

- The *behavioral equation* is:

$$L = bE$$

- This equation indicates that *local jobs are created by resources flowing into an economy.*
- Putting these together, we have

$$T = bE + E = E(1 + b)$$

- In this equation, $(1 + b)$ is called the *"multiplier"*:
  - Export jobs are "multiplied up" into total jobs because they lead to income circulating around the local economy.

1.1.3.1. Alternative Export Base Model

- An alternative form of the behavioral equation is

$$L = (b^*)T$$

- In this case,

$$T = (b^*)T + E$$
$$T(1 - b^*) = E$$
$$T = E/(1 - b^*)$$

- Thus, $1/(1-b^*)$ is the multiplier.

1.1.3.2. Export Base Models, Lessons

- First, export jobs get "multiplied up" into total jobs.

  - If a government manages to attract another export job it adds more than one job to its economy.

- Second, "attracting" another local job (that is, giving it a subsidy) doesn't do anything except displace a local job on the other side of town.

  - Local jobs are determined by export jobs.

- *If you want to boost a local economy, attract export jobs!*

1.1.3.3. Export Base Models, Limits

- Export base models are highly simplified.
- For example, they ignore market failure. A state policy might be able to add local jobs by ending some form of market failure.
- But the *presumption* that economic development policy should focus on export jobs is a good place to start.

1.1.3.4. Input/Output Analysis

- Input/output analysis is a fancy export-base model.
- I/O analysis begins with $1 of *exogenous demand* for the products of industry A.
- Satisfying this demand requires contributions from all industries, say $.01 from A itself, $.05 from B, $.25 from C, and so on.
- Satisfying these demands requires additional contributions from each industry, etc.

- I/O analysis provides a formal way to summarize all these transactions.
- The more purchases are made locally, the higher the multiplier.
- Equivalently, the more purchases *leak* out to other jurisdictions, the lower the multiplier.

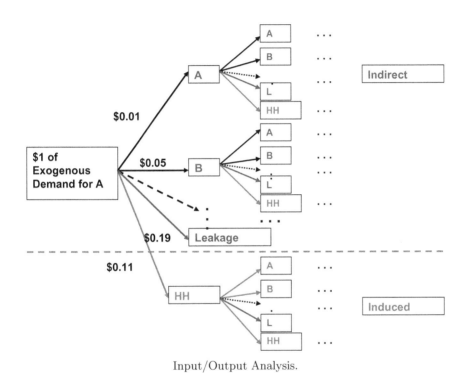

Input/Output Analysis.

1.1.4. *Input/Output models*

- In formal terms, an I/O model is a series of equations like:

$$Y_1 = a_{11}Y_1 + a_{12}Y_2 + \cdots + a_{1n}Y_n + X_1$$

where Y is output, X is exogenous demand, and a_{1j} is the amount of product 1 needed to produce the output for product j.

- Stacking these equations and using matrix notation:

$$Y = AY + X$$
$$(I - A)Y = X$$
$$Y = (I - A)^{-1}X$$

- Note that the $(I - A)^{-1}$ matrix is just the matrix-algebra version of the multiplier idea in the export-base model.

1.1.4.1. Types of I/O Models

- There are two types of I/O Model.
- The first treats the household sector as part of exogenous demand, X.

  ○ This is called an *open* model.

- With this model, the A matrix is just about purchases of non-labor inputs, and the multipliers reflect the *direct and indirect* requirements from each industry to meet exogenous demand.
- The second type treats households as an industry.

  ○ This is called a *closed* model.

- Households provide labor and make purchases from other industries.
- The household impact on multipliers is called an *induced* effect.

1.1.4.2. Contributions of I/O

- I/O adds two things to the debate:
- *First,* I/O provides a way to bring data to bear on the issue of multipliers.

  ○ The trouble is that the necessary data are not available at the local level, or even at the state level.
  ○ But regional I/O multipliers are available. See: http://www.be a.gov/regional/rims/index.cfm.
  ○ These multipliers are "based on 2007 national benchmark input/output data and 2015 regional data."

- *Second*, I/O introduces a distinction between *indirect* multipliers (based on purchases of inputs), and *induced* multipliers (based on purchases by households).
- The notion of indirect multipliers is critical: *The more inputs are produced locally, the less the leakage and the higher the multiplier.*

1.1.4.3. Estimating Multipliers

- Moretti (*AER*, 2010) points out that standard multipliers miss two key possibilities:
  - Increases in wages may lessen the impacts of exogenous demand.
  - Agglomeration economies may magnify the impacts of exogenous demand.
- Moretti also estimates city-level multipliers.

Local Multipliers for Tradables and Nontradables.

	Elasticity OLS	Elasticity IV	Additional Jobs for Each New Job
Model 1			
Effect of tradable on nontradable	0.554 (0.036)	0.335 (0.055) [8.2]	1.59 (0.26)
Model 2			
Effect of tradable durable on nontradable	0.283 (0.039)	0.006 (0.138) [3.21, 5.52]	0.73 (1.73)
Effect of tradable nondurable on nontradable	0.290 (0.024)	0.250 (0.072) [8.53 2.57]	1.89 (0.54)
Model 3			
Effect of tradable on other tradable	0.546 (0.069)	0.176 (0.156) [9.1]	0.26 (0.23)

Notes: Standard errors clustered by city in parentheses. First-stage *p*-values in brackets.
Data from this table reveals that 1 new "tradable" job leads to 1.59 "nontradable" jobs and (because of agglomeration economies?) 0.26 new tradable jobs.
Source: Moretti (*AER*, 2010).

Local Multipliers, by Skill Level.

	All Nontradable			Nontradable–skilled			Nontradable–unskilled		
	Dependent Variable								
Independent Variable	Elast. OLS (1)	Elast. IV (2)	Addit. Jobs (3)	Elast. OLS (4)	Elast. IV (5)	Addit. Jobs (6)	Elast. OLS (7)	Elast. IV (8)	Addit. Jobs (9)
Tradable	0.287	0.257	2.52	0.420	0.208	2.03	0.109	0.030	0.296
skilled	(0.037)	(0.157)	(1.54)	(0.044)	(0.176)	(1.72)	(0.039)	(0.172)	(1.68)
Tradable	0.292	0.115	1.04	0.125	−0.010	−0.09	0.510	0.367	3.34
unskilled	(0.033)	(0.109)	(0.99)	(0.042)	(0.133)	(1.21)	(0.037)	(0.117)	(1.06)

Notes: Data from this table reveals that 1 new tradable skilled job leads to 2.52 non-tradable jobs but 1 new tradable non-skilled job lead to only 1.04 new non-tradable jobs. Non-tradable jobs in construction, wholesale trade and personal services are most affected.
Source: Moretti (*AER*, 2010).

1.1.4.4. Moretti on Policy

- In addition, Moretti discusses the use of multipliers in policy.
  - He points out that new jobs may not be held by current residents.
  - But he misses another important issue, namely the misuse of multipliers.

1.1.4.5. Misuse of Multipliers

- A high multiplier for a particular industry says that attracting an export job in that industry will have a large positive impact on the economy.
- But multipliers can easily be misused because it is difficult to figure out what the world would be like *without* a program.
- An I/O analysis was used in a debate about subsidizing a Mazda plant in Michigan.
- The multipliers were high — 12! — because so many auto inputs are made in Michigan.
- The people who conducted the I/O analysis said almost any subsidy was worth it.

- But the sales from the plant exaggerate the change in exogenous demand.
- If the plant were not in Michigan, it would be in Indiana or Ohio and would still purchase many inputs from Michigan.
- *So one must compare income with the plant to income with these input purchases.*

2. Agglomeration Economies

- Another key concept for economic development is *agglomeration economies*, which come in two types:
  - ○ Localization economies = benefits from clustering within a given industry.
  - ○ Urbanization economies = savings that arise when the production costs of an individual firm decrease as the total output in its urban area increases.

2.1. *Examples of Localization Economies*

- From a report prepared for the 1900 U.S. Census:

  "Measured by the value of products, more than 85 per cent of the collar and cuff manufacture is carried on in Troy, N.Y.; more than 64 per cent of the oyster-canning industry in Baltimore, Md.; more than 54 per cent of the manufacture of gloves in the adjoining cities of Gloversville and Johnstown, N.Y.; more than 48 per cent of the coke manufacture in the Connellsville district, Pennsylvania; more than 47 per cent of the manufacture of brassware in Waterbury, Conn.; more than 45 per cent of the manufacture of carpets in Philadelphia, Pa.; more than 45 per cent of the manufacture of jewelry in Providence, R.I., and the adjoining towns of Attleboro and North Attleboro, Mass.; more than 36 per cent of the silverware manufacture in Providence, R.I.; more than 35 per cent of the slaughtering and meat packing industry in Chicago, Ill.; more than 32 per cent of the manufacture of plated and britannica ware in Meriden, Conn.; ....." Cited in a blog post by Paul Krugman on *The New York Times* website, August 9. 2015.

From (*The Guardian*, 2005): http://www.theguardian.com/busi ness/2005/may/25/china.g2.

- ○ "Qiaotou [in western China] has transformed itself from a farming village into a manufacturing powerhouse. . .
- ○ The first small workshop was established in 1980 by three brothers who picked up their first buttons off the street. Now the town's 700 family-run factories churn out 15 billion buttons and 200 million meters of zips a year. . . .
- ○ The local chamber of commerce estimates that three out of every five buttons in the world are made in the town. It ships more than two million zips a day, making it the biggest winner of China's 80% share of the international zip market."
- ○ Other Chinese cities specialize in toothbrushes or socks.

2.2. *Sources of Localization Economies*

- • Localization economies could arise from three sources:
  - ○ Sharing input suppliers.
  - ○ Economies of scale may arise when many firms are demanding the same inputs.
  - ○ Transportation costs may drop as more input firms locate nearby.

  Examples:

  - ○ High fashion firms cluster around specialized button and fabric producers.
  - ○ Corporate headquarters cluster around marketing firms.

- • Sharing a labor pool:

  - ○ A firm can make better matches if the labor pool is larger — and can make matches with lower transportation costs.

- • Sharing information (= knowledge spillovers):

  - ○ E.g., more innovative industries (as measured by patents per dollar of sales) are more likely to cluster.

2.3. *Evidence on Localization Economies*

- Rosenthal and Strange (*JUE*, 2001) find that firm births and new-firm employment in a zip code increase with nearby employment in the same industry.
- This effect declines with distance, but firms 15 miles away still have an effect in some industries.
- These authors also have a thorough literature review in Volume 4 of the (*Handbook of Regional and Urban Economics*, 2004).

2.4. *Urbanization Economies*

- Urbanization economies are agglomeration benefits that depend on the whole economy (not one industry) and fall upon the whole economy (not just one industry).
- Their sources are similar to those of localization economies.
- Intermediate Inputs:
  - There may be economies of scale in the banking, business services, insurance, and perhaps public services.
- Labor pooling:
  - As before, there could be better matches and lower search, moving, and transportation costs.
- Sharing information:
  - Some types of knowledge might spill over from one industry to others.

2.4.1. *Evidence on urbanization economies*

- Some studies find that labor productivity is linked to city size (see the survey article by Rosenthal and Strange).
- But, urbanization economies do not appear to arise for many industries, and, in general, do not appear to be as large as localization economies.
- However, cities would not exist without them — that is, without some reason to pay higher wages to offset higher housing costs.

2.5. *Agglomeration and Policy*

- Agglomeration economies imply that firm location decisions may involve an *externality*:
  - ○ The arrival of a firm may raise the productivity of other firms (in the same industry or the same region).
  - ○ Thus, government actions to encourage firms to locate where they cause agglomeration economies may enhance public welfare — at least in that location!
- The problem is that we do not yet know enough about agglomeration economies to accurately identify cases in which these externalities exist.
- And, as we will see next, we also do not know very much about how to attract firms.
- An interesting pair of columns by Rubin in the *Washington Post* looks at agglomeration economies and other aspects of cities, citing Glaeser, among others.
  - ○ https://www.washingtonpost.com/blogs/right-turn/wp/2017/03/08/trump-attacks-cities-but-theyre-the-lifeblood-of-our-country-part-1/?utm_term=.268d14ef8633.
  - ○ https://www.washingtonpost.com/blogs/right-turn/wp/2017/03/08/trump-attacks-cities-but-they-are-the-lifeblood-of-the-country-part-2/?utm_term=.6012e76609a1.

3. Research on Tax Breaks

- Research on tax breaks is limited by their heterogeneous nature. Many are negotiated on a case-by-case basis. They do not appear in any standardized data sets.
- The following slides review a few studies that make progress on studying tax breaks despite these challenges.

3.1. *NY Data*

- A recent report by the NYS Comptroller:

- o New York's Industrial Development Agencies (IDAs) provided $695 million in net tax exemptions in 2015, an increase of 10 percent from the prior year, according to a report issued today by New York State Comptroller Thomas P. DiNapoli.
- o http://www.osc.state.ny.us/press/releases/mar17/032717a.htm ?utm_source=weekly+news&utm_medium=email&utm_term= ida&utm_content=20170402&utm_campaign=fiscal+oversight.

3.2. *Wassmer/Anderson* (*Journal of Economic Development, Environment and People, 2001*)

- One hundred and twelve Cities in Detroit metropolitan areas; 4 years (1977, 1982, 1987, 1992).
- Outcomes: Employment rate, poverty rate, manufacturing property value, commercial property value.
- Key policy variables: Property tax abatements, IDBs, TIFA, DDA, municipal expenditures per capita, property tax rate.
  - o *Amazing data!*
- Abatements = cumulative real value of abatements for manufacturing or commercial developments.
- IDB = cumulative value of industrial development bonds.
- TIFA = tax increment financing authority exists.
- DDA = downtown development authority exists.
- Estimated simultaneously with assumed exclusion restrictions; second two dependent variables are in first two regressions; first two dependent variables are in second two regressions.
- Estimated with year and city fixed effects.
- Controls include socio-economic characteristics, percentage of property in various categories, and property composition of surrounding areas.
- Spending and property tax rate are treated as exogenous.
- Manufacturing abatements boost manufacturing property values — in the first year only.
  - o They guess that, since this is right after the program started, it is before other jurisdictions jumped in. (Capitalization or

development?) Commercial abatements actually lower commercial property value in 1992.

- TIFAs, DDAs, and municipal spending boost commercial property values.
  - TIFAs and DDAs may only makes sense when commercial property values are growing.
- Higher tax rate leads to higher commercial property values!
  - This could be a tax-price effect. High commercial property leads to low tax price and hence to a higher local property tax rate. Another reason to treat property taxes as endogenous!
- Higher residential employment rate leads to lower commercial property values. (Bizarre!)
  - This finding is discouraging; higher property values without employment is not the idea!
- They also find weak evidence that higher business property values lead to lower employment and lower poverty.
  - This could be displacement (as firm expansion drives out poor households).

3.3. *Kang, Reese, and Skidmore (JPAM, 2016)*

- A recent study of property tax abatements for new or improved industrial property in Southeast Michigan finds that the abatements increase industrial property values (= capitalization!) but also have small spillovers onto commercial and residential property values.
- However, this study also finds that the benefits from these abatements are very small relative to the foregone revenue. Under the most favorable scenario in this study, $1.00 of lost revenue brings in $0.03 in benefits.

3.4. *Nguyen-Hoang*

- "Tax Increment Financing and Education Expenditures: The Case of Iowa," *Education Finance and Policy*, Fall 2014.

- "This is the first study to directly examine the relationship between tax increment financing (TIF) and education expenditures, using the state of Iowa as a case study. I find that greater use of TIF is associated with reduced education expenditures. I also find little evidence to support the commonly held proposition that school spending increases when TIF districts expire. Finally, the negative price effect of TIF on education spending is increasingly larger for school districts in lower wealth or income groups compared with their counterparts in higher wealth or income groups. The negative, though small, effect of TIF on education spending, coupled with no gain from the often-claimed long-run benefits of TIF, justifies policy measures to protect school districts from TIF."

3.5. *Hanson (RSUE, 2009)*

- Andrew Hanson (2008 economics Ph.D. from Syracuse; *RSUE* 2009) studies the federal empowerment zone program (EZ). This program gave various tax breaks to firms locating in specified areas in Atlanta, Baltimore, Chicago, Detroit, Philadelphia/Camden, and New York.
- Table "Benefits on designation" lists the benefits of zone designation.
- Note that in to be "Enterprise Communities" (EC).
- They received a smaller set of benefits — and are the control group.
- He uses a triple-difference strategy.
- His method has two equations

$$Y_i = (Y_{\text{tract2000}} - Y_{\text{city2000}}) - (Y_{\text{tract1990}} - Y_{\text{city1990}}) \quad (17.1)$$

The estimating equation used to determine the effect of the EZ program on the percentage of residents employed and the percentage of residents with income below the national poverty level is:

$$Y_i = \alpha + \beta \text{EZ}_i + X_i'\delta + u \quad (17.2)$$

Where i indexes the census tracts, X is a vector of control variables, and EZ is a dummy variable for availability of the EZ wage tax

Benefits on Designation.

	Wage Credit	SS Block Grants	Cap Gains Exclusion	Stock Sale Exclusion	Facility Bonds	179 Expensing
Round I EZ	Yes	$100 million	Yes	Yes	Yes	Yes
Round I EC and EEC[a]	No	$3 million	No	No	Yes	No
Round I SEZ	No[b]	$450 million for LA, $177 million for CLE	Yes	Yes	Yes	Yes
Round II EZ	Yes[c]	None	Yes	Yes	Yes	Yes
Round III EZ	Yes[c]	None	Yes	Yes	Yes	Yes

Source: Tax Incentive Guide for Business (HUD, 2001).
[a] Enhanced EC differ from EC because they received some HUD grants and loan guarantees.
[b] Available starting in 2000.
[c] Available since 2002.

New York City EZ   Los Angeles EC

I compare the difference between the New York EZ and New York City before and after zone designation with the difference between the Los Angeles EC and Los Angeles before and after designation.

Location of EZs (Hanson).

credit. All variables are differenced as shown in Eq. (17.1). The unit of observation is the census tract, and I use data from the 1990 and 2000 censuses to estimate Eq. (17.2).

- He then points out that the EZ cities are not randomly selected and that the selection process in Congress could reflect anticipated economic health or growth.
- So he uses an IV approach. His instruments for the EZ variable are whether the city has a member of Congress on the Ways and

Effect of Empowerment Zone Tax Incentive on Zone Resident Employment (Standard Errors Clustered at the City Level are Shown in Parenthesis).

| | OLS | | IV | | |
| | (1) | (2) | (3) | (4) | (5) |
			Terms	Membership	Both
EZ	0.02**(0.01)	0.02**(0.01)	−0.03(0.07)	−0.09(0.25)	0.00(0.02)
% College educated		0.28***(0.06)	0.28***(0.06)	0.28***(0.06)	0.28***(0.06)
% Working age		0.02***(0.01)	0.03***(0.01)	0.02***(0.01)	0.02***(0.01)
% Non-White		−0.13***(0.04)	−0.14***(0.04)	−0.14***(0.04)	−0.14***(0.04)
N	1262	1262	1262	1262	1262
R^2	0.02	0.21			

Notes: ***Indicates significant at 1% level, **at 5% level.
Data are from the 1990 and 2000 Censuses Unit of observation is the census tract.
Source: Hanson.

Effect of Empowerment Zone Tax Incentives on Zone Resident Poverty (Standard Errors Clustered at the City Level are Shown in Parenthesis).

| | OLS | | IV | | |
| | (1) | (2) | (3) | (4) | (5) |
			Terms	Membership	Both
EZ	-0.02^{**}(0.01)	-0.02^{*} (0.01)	0.04 (0.07)	0.07 (0.20)	0.02 (0.03)
% College educated		-0.22^{**}(0.10)	-0.22^{**}(0.10)	-0.23^{**}(0.09)	-0.22^{**}(0.01)
% Working age		-0.02 (0.01)	-0.02 (0.02)	-0.02 (0.02)	-0.02 (0.01)
% Non-White		0.06 (0.09)	-0.06 (0.08)	0.06 (0.08)	0.06 (0.08)
N	1258	1258	1258	1258	1258
R^2	0	0.04			

Notes: ***Indicates significant at 5% level, *at 10% level.
Data are from the 1990 and 2000 Censuses.
Unit of observation is the census tract.
Source: Hanson.

Effect of Empowerment Zone Tax Incentives on Median Property Value (Standard Errors Clustered at the City Level are Shown in the Parenthesis).

| | OLS | | IV | | |
	(6)	(7)	(8) Terms	(9) Membership	(10) Both
EZ	4885 (8788)	6632 (9477)	116,681 (83,719)	140,094 (226,011)	105,305** (44,928)
% College educated		206,392*** (57,366)	200,946*** (75,155)	199,787** (78,520)	201,509*** (73,533)
% Working age		-243 (3274)	-1554 (5460)	-1833 (6613)	-1418 (5100)
% Non-White		-7969 (19,132)	-5417 (33,080)	-4874 (37,493)	-5681 (31,072)
N	1262	1262	1262	1262	1262
R^2	0.00	0.05			

Notes: ***Indicates significant at 1% level, ** at 5% level.
Data are from the 1990 and 2000 Censuses, property values are expressed in nominal changes, per capita income is expressed in 1999 dollars.
Unit of observation is the census tract.
Source: Hanson.

Means Committee (which selected the cities) and the tenure of that person on the committee.

- With OLS, the impacts on income and growth look positive; with IV these impacts go away.
- Note the positive impact on property values in the IV regressions.
- This result supports the notion that EZs provide a gift to property owners in the designated zone, because firms are willing to pay more for property to gain access to the EZ benefits.
- He detects no other impacts. Capitalization at work!
- Another study of EZ's appeared in 2013 (Busso, Gregory, and Kline, *AER*). It is neither cited Hanson nor used an IV. Here is the abstract:
- This paper empirically assesses the incidence and efficiency of Round I of the federal urban Empowerment Zone (EZ) program using confidential microdata from the Decennial Census and the Longitudinal Business Database. Using rejected and future applicants to the EZ program as controls, we find that EZ designation substantially increased employment in zone neighborhoods and generated wage increases for local workers without corresponding increases in population or the local cost of living. The results suggest the efficiency costs of first Round EZs were relatively modest.

3.6. *Bartik*

- Bartik has assembled an amazing data set of local economic development incentives.
- His preliminary analysis of these data finds no statistically significant impacts of these incentives on measures of economic well being.
- See: http://research.upjohn.org/reports/225/.

Lecture 18

Infrastructure

- **Class Outline**
  1. **What is Infrastructure?**
  2. **Capital Spending**
  3. **Paying for Infrastructure**
  4. **Benefit–Cost Analysis**

1. What is Infrastructure?

- Infrastructure is long-lived public investment:
  - Roads, bridges, transit
  - Dams, drinking water systems
  - Wastewater systems
  - Hazardous waste disposal sites
  - Navigable waterways, railroads
  - Energy production systems
  - Parks and recreation
- ASCE (civil engineers) gives lousy grades to American infrastructure (D+!).
- See: www.infrastructurereportcard.org.

2. Capital Spending

- Capital spending is difficult to study, largely because it varies greatly from one year to the next.

ASCE Grades, 2017.

Water and Environment

Dams	D
Drinking Water	D
Hazardous Waste	D$^+$
Levees	D
Solid Waste	C$^+$
Wastewater	D$^+$

Transportation

Aviation	D
Bridges	C$^+$
Inland Waterways	D
Ports	C$^+$
Rail	B
Roads	D
Transit	D$^-$

Public Facilities

Public Parks and Recreation	D$^+$
Schools	D$^+$

Energy

Energy	D$^+$

- Wang/Duncombe/Yinger (*NTJ*, 2011) find that school capital spending in New York has many of the same determinants as school operating spending:
  - Tax price (elasticity = −0.17);
  - Income (elasticity = 0.16).
- In New York, school building aid is provided through a matching grant, and most districts are quite responsive to the matching rate.
  - The estimated elasticity is −0.426.
- However, this response is about zero (elasticity = −0.023) for high-need districts.
  - Even strong price incentives cannot boost school capital spending in New York's neediest districts.

W/D/Y Regression Results for Capital Investment Models (New York School Districts).

Explanatory variables	Models		
	1	2	3
Cost variables			
Local capital share (all districts)	−0.394***	−0.426***	−0.426***
	(−11.94)	(−12.35)	(−12.34)
Local capital share (high-need urban/		0.403***	0.408***
suburban districts)		(6.43)	(6.20)
Local capital share (four large			0.371**
central cities)			(2.28)
Annual construction wages	0.120	0.068	0.068
	(0.87)	(0.55)	(0.55)
Teacher salary	1.798	2.394*	2.397*
	(1.32)	(1.73)	(1.73)
Enrollment	0.892*	0.824**	0.829*
	(1.91)	(1.74)	(1.74)
Enrollment squared	−0.075**	−0.076*	−0.077**
	(−2.36)	(−2.35)	(−2.36)
Share of students receiving	−0.001	0.000	0.000
subsidized lunch (%)	(−0.60)	(−0.51)	(−0.50)
Demand variables			
Local tax share	−0.186***	−0.171***	−0.171***
	(−3.64)	(−3.27)	(−3.27)
Income per pupil	0.216***	0.155**	0.155**
	(3.47)	(2.39)	(2.39)
Operating aid ratio	0.193	0.301	0.298
	(1.03)	(1.56)	(1.54)
Share of African American	−0.010***	−0.007**	−0.007**
students (%)	(−3.50)	(−2.39)	(−2.40)
Share of all African American	0.006**	0.004*	0.004*
students who live in a majority	(2.49)	(1.80)	(1.80)
African American district (%)			
Adjustment variables	−0.110**	−0.087	−0.086
Debt limit variable	(−1.97)	(−1.53)	(−1.52)
Enrollment change (last five year)	0.270***	0.259**	0.260**
	(2.67)	(2.50)	(2.50)
Change of superintendent (= 1 if	−0.025*	−0.028**	−0.028**
in last three years)	(−1.95)	(−2.16)	(−2.16)

(Continued)

(Continued)

Explanatory variable	Models		
	1	2	3
Consolidated school district	0.279***	0.227**	0.227**
(= 1 if year after consolidation)	(3.11)	(2.43)	(2.43)
Prob > F	0.00	0.01	0.00
RSME	0.44	0.44	0.44

Notes: Sample size is 12,042 (634 districts). The sample does not include New York City, districts with fewer than eight teachers, and districts serving special needs populations. The dependent variable is the estimated value of the capital stock from 1990–2008. The independent variables are lagged three years (1987–2005). All financial variables are inflation-adjusted and expressed in 2000$ using the consumer price index for urban consumers (CPI-U). All variables except for the operating and ratio, enrollment change, subsidized lunch, share of African American students, and dichotomous variables are expressed in natural logs. The model is estimated with linear 2SLS (with teacher salaries treated as an endogenous variable) with district and year fixed effects. z-statistics (in parentheses) are based on robust HAC standard errors. Asterisks denote statistical significance at the 1%(***), 5%(**), and 10%(*) levels.

- W/D/Y results from a model of the determinants of a school district's capital stock; e.g. demand variables affect desired capital stock — but must work through the production function.
- Capital stock is the dependent variable; the data cover 1990–2008; district fixed effects are included.

3. Paying for Infrastructure

- Many people think a government can pay for infrastructure through borrowing.
- This is not true.
- *Borrowing simply spreads the financing burden over time.*
- Taxes or fees are needed to pay for the infrastructure, with or without borrowing.
- The Trump Administration appears to think that you can pay for a lot of infrastructure with a relatively small federal budget ($200 billion).

- The idea is to give state and local governments and private companies an incentive to undertake projects.
- But:
  - State and local governments will focus on projects of local, not national importance.
  - Private companies will only take on profitable projects, which leaves out many projects with positive net benefits.
  - Turning to private companies leads to difficult contracting problems.
- See: https://www.nytimes.com/2018/02/12/business/trump-infra structure-proposal.html.
- Consider the (relatively simple!) case of residential infrastructure (streets, lights, sidewalks, water and sewer).
- Alternative sources of revenue are:
  - Property taxes.
  - Special assessments on homeowners.
  - User fees.
  - One-time fees charged to home buyers.
  - One-time fees charged to builder.
  - Requirement placed on builder.

3.1. *Incidence of Development Fees*

- Fees charged to home buyers and fees charged to builders sound quite different, but are, in fact equivalent.
  - Remember the theorem: Economic incidence does not depend on legal incidence.
- Because builders and home buyers are both mobile, they both must be compensated for fees paid.
  - Builders are compensated by a higher price (if they pay the fee).
  - Homeowners are compensated by receiving the benefits from the fees — i.e. **homeowners bear the burden of the fee** and receive the benefits from the infrastructure.
  - I will return to the case where the benefits and costs are not equal.
- Fees charged to builders and requiring builders to provide infrastructure sound the same, but may be quite different.

- Existing residents would like builders or new residents to pay not only for their infrastructure, but also for unrelated infrastructure, such as a marina.
- Courts require a **nexus** between fees and new infrastructure costs.
  - Local governments have negotiating room through their control of **zoning** and may "convince" builders to build other things.
- A recent U.S. Supreme Court decision appears to have changed the possibilities.
- A Florida water management district was denied a permit for a shopping center because the developer would not spend money on wetlands-restoration projects.
- The Supreme Court said a "rough proportionality" between the project and the requirements was needed.
- So fees and building requirements now look similar — and a key economic development tool may have been lost.
- If costs imposed on builders exceed benefits from the infrastructure, the price of undeveloped land will fall.
  - Builders will not build unless they make normal profits.
  - Homeowners will not pay more than the value of the infrastructure.
  - Landowners therefore cannot sell their land unless the price compensates builders.
- Thus, it is the owners of undeveloped land, not builders or new residents, who pay for unrelated infrastructure that is "financed" by new development.
- Finally, there is a subtle difference between fee imposed on developers and special assessments.
  - They appear to be the same, but aren't quite.
- A development fee is recouped through higher house values (which buyers pay because they get the services).
  - But because this house value increase is taxed by regular property taxes, it does not equal the full value of the fee.
- A special assessment has benefits = costs and hence no impact on house values.

- For more on this theory, see:
  - John Yinger, 1998. "The Incidence of Development Fees and Special Assessments." *National Tax Journal* 51(1): 23–42.
- For empirical tests (which support Yinger's theory!), see:
  - Keith R. Ihlanfeldt and Timothy M. Shaughnessy. 2004. "An Empirical Investigation of the Effects of Impact Fees on Housing and Land Markets." *Regional Science and Urban Economics* 34(6) (November): 639–661.

3.2. *Fees vs. Property Taxes, Normative Analysis*

- Development fees equal to costs place the burden on new residents.
  - This satisfies the benefit principle.
- Development fees above cost place an unfair burden on landowners.
- Property taxes spread the burden widely.
  - This is appropriate when a community is first being developed.
  - But violates the benefit principle (and gives a bonus to landowners) for fringe development.
- Development fees and property taxes for community-wide infrastructure are fair across generations.
- In either case, homeowners bear the burden through higher prices for the stream of benefits from infrastructure.
  - If a homeowner leaves the community, the household that purchases her house must pay for the remaining stream of benefits in the form of a higher house price.
  - Thus the person who actually receives the infrastructure benefits pays for them.
- Impacts on landowners, if any, are obviously not fair across generations.

3.3. *Infrastructure Decisions*

- When should a particular infrastructure project be built?
- Benefit–cost analysis is well suited to answering this question.
- Benefit–cost analysis is a set of tools that help to reduce a decision about a complex program to a manageable level.

4. Benefit–Cost Analysis

- Any government project has complex effects across (1) markets, (2) time and (3) groups.
- Benefit–cost analysis helps to simplify the analysis of each of these dimensions.
- Benefit-cost is very helpful, but it is not value free!

4.1. *Simplify across Markets*

- Benefit–cost analysis expresses everything in terms of willingness to pay, often measured with consumer surplus or cost savings.
  - The value of commuting time saved due to a new highway.
  - The consumer surplus from the new recreation opportunities created by a dam.
- In many cases, estimating benefits requires a demand curve.
- CS is the area under a demand curve.
  - The value of a new product is the area under the demand curve up to the quantity provided.
  - The CS from an increase in the provision of product is the area under the demand curve from the old quantity to the new quantity.
  - The CS from a decrease in the price of a product is the horizontal strip under the demand curve between the old and new price.
- Cost savings are also WTP measures.
- This B-C approach is based on the value judgment that it is appropriate to measure the impact of a program by the WTP of the people affected.
- This is a widely accepted approach, although it does raise equity questions, to which I will return.

4.2. *Simplify across Time*

- Benefit–cost analysis expresses everything in terms of present value; that is, it uses discounting.
  - The best discount rate is a long-term, low-risk rate, such as the rate for long term government bonds.

- The discount rate (the denominator) and the benefits and costs (the numerator) should both be either in real or in nominal terms. (More on this below).

- In B-C, a program is worth doing (ignoring equity) if the PV of net benefits is positive.
- If there is a budget constraint, the right criterion is to select the set of affordable programs that yield the highest present value of net benefits.
- A key issue: either real/real or nominal/nominal calculations require an estimate of inflation, which makes analysts uncomfortable.
- Consider **real/real**.

  - The numerator is easy Benefits and costs in each year are entered in real terms with no inflation adjustment. So a $1,000 benefit today that is expected to continue just stays at $1,000.
  - The denominator is hard. Any observed interest rate is nominal because it recognizes that money will be paid back in the future in dollars that are not worth as much.
  - So to get a real rate, anticipated inflation (not directly observed!) must be subtracted from a market rate.

- Consider **nominal/nominal**.
- Now the numerator is hard.

  - The $1,000 in the first year must be inflated with an expected inflation rate.

- The denominator is easy because market rates are in nominal terms.
- Note that real/real and nominal/nominal are equivalent.

  - If the numerator is inflated at rate a percent per year and the project has a long life, then the present value expression collapses to one with real benefits in the numerator and r-a, the real interest rate, in the denominator.

- Official B/C analysis uses real/real.
- The Office of Management and Budget requires calculations with a 3% rate and with a 7% rate.

- A 7% rate is undoubtedly too high.
- The Council of Economic Advisers defines the real social discount rate as "the difference between the nominal annual yield on the 10-year note less the five-year unweighted moving average of current and past annual inflation." This rate is below 1%.
- See: https://www.whitehouse.gov/sites/default/files/page/files /201701_cea_discounting_issue_brief.pdf.

4.3. *Highlighting Impacts across Groups*

- Benefit–cost analysis can highlight impacts on different groups.
- But it cannot save a decision maker from placing weights on these impacts.
- Programs designed to help a particular group should give them net benefits.
- Ignoring inter-group impacts is an implicit value judgment.
- Many economists argue that benefit–cost analysis should ignore the distribution of impacts across groups.
  - Bringing in such equity concerns would not be objective, they say.
- Nonsense! Equity concerns are built into B-C whether they like it or not.
  - If a project has a positive impact on a rich group and a negative impact on a poor group, then simply adding up benefits across groups may yield B > C, but this is not a good guide to policy unless one assumes that the distributional impacts are not relevant.
- A more subtle argument that distributional issues do not belong in B-C because there are other policies that explicitly address distribution.
  - This is not correct either. A willingness-to-pay metric reflects the current distribution of income. A project that makes sense under one distribution might not make sense with another.
  - So WTP calculations and distribution cannot be separated. One cannot ignore equity in B-C without assuming that the

distribution of income — and it implications for WTP — is just
fine the way it is.

- My position is that equity must be included in B-C.
  - ○ The logic of B-C requires that the CS in all affected markets be considered.
  - ○ If people care about distribution, then the CS from changes in distribution must be included.
  - ○ This is key when a program is designed to help certain people!

4.4. *Transfers*

- In my experience, this is the trickiest issue in all of B/C analysis. Pay attention!
- A transfer arises when a program shifts benefits or costs from one group to another.
  - ○ *Transfers do not represent real resources gained or lost — just real resources transferred.*
  - ○ So traditional B-C says they should be ignored.
  - ○ But transfers often have important equity consequences, so they should not be ignored at all.

Example 1: Taxes (or any government revenue)

- Taxes are *never* real resources created or lost from the point of view of citizens.
  - ○ They are only resources from the point of view of governments. B/C does not take the point of view of a government — it takes the point of view of the people.
  - ○ New taxes may solve the problem of a budget officer, but they take real resources away from some taxpayers and redistribute them, through the public budget, to other taxpayers (who get services or lower taxes).
- This is "just a transfer."
  - ○ We may care about the distributional consequences.
  - ○ If we are trying to help a particular group and all of their benefits are taxed away, it is not a very good program, even if B > C.

Example 2: Property Values

- Many programs affect property values.

  - Property values reflect real resources created that become accessible to people who own nearby property.
  - A park creates real benefits (esthetic and recreational), which are are transferred to nearby property owners.

- It follows that:

  - *We can measure the benefits by looking at impacts on property values.*
  - *But we cannot include both property value impacts and the direct measures of underlying CS as benefits.*
  - With direct CS measures, property values only matter if they connect with an equity concern.
  - A park may not help renters, for example, because it leads to higher rents (and values) so the benefits are transferred to property owners.

Example 3: Effects in Related Markets

- Producing a new good or service often has an effect in a related market.

  - These effects do not involve the creation of new resources; instead they are just a re-shuffling of existing resources that arises because of opportunities created by the new good.

- Suppose a government builds a park.

  - Ice cream cone venders will come to the park and sell ice cream cones; movie theatre owners will lose business.
  - These effects do not involve resources gained or lost — just re-shuffling.

- This can be confusing, because it looks like there is an increase in consumer surplus when the ice-cream-cone demand curve shifts out.

  - But in fact, the possibilities for consuming ice cream cones and movies are already built into the demand curve for visits to a park, so they are already taken care of by the consumer surplus calculation for parks.

Example 4: Effects in Input Markets

- Effects in input market are also just re-shuffling.
  - An irrigation project might raise the price of tractors, but only because the irrigation project leads to changes in the purchasing decisions of businesses — the tractors are not new resources created by the project.

Example 5: Displacement

- In general, local projects cannot influence the overall level of employment.
  - *If they could, we wouldn't have any unemployment!*
- So one should be suspicious about claims for jobs benefits.
  - A program may, indeed, hire some people, but there is very likely to be an associated loss of jobs somewhere else in the economy. So jobs are just transferred from one person to another.
- It is possible that a project results in the hiring of people who would otherwise be unemployed with no displacement. Some analysts would say this applies to a program for the long-term unemployed.

Benefit-Cost Example.

Group	Costs	Benefits	Net Impact
Participants	Higher taxes (T) Lost leisure (L)	Wages (W)	$W - L - T$
Taxpayers	Program Costs (C)	Higher Taxes	$T - C$
Society		Products (G)	G
Participants' Neighbors		Lower Crime (X)	X
NET IMPACT (with no equity weights!)			$W + G + X - L - C$

  o But even here, one must be careful, because the benefits are not as great as one might think.

  o Everyone puts some value on his or her leisure time, so the net benefits from the job equal *wages minus lost leisure*.

4.5. *Benefit–Cost Decisions*

- Benefit–cost analysis should not be blamed for the complexity of infrastructure decisions.
- Benefit–cost analysis can simplify a decision, but it cannot make value judgments or eliminate uncertainty.
- Try to frame benefit–cost analysis to focus on the factors that require analytical or value judgments.

An Example

- Consider a program that hires long-term unemployed workers to produce products.

  o The cost of the program consists of the employees that train and manage the participants.

  o Benefits: Suppose it leads to lower crime in the neighborhoods where the participants live.

- Now suppose impacts on participants are given twice the weight as impacts on others, because it is, after all, a program to help them.

  o Then the net benefits are

$$2(W - L - T) + G + X + T - C$$

which might give a different answer!

Lecture 19

Bond Markets

- **Class Outline**
  1. **Municipal Bonds**
  2. **Basic Bond Characteristics**
  3. **Types of Bonds**
  4. **The Market for Tax-Exempt Loanable Funds**
  5. **Issuing Bonds**

1. Municipal Bonds

- Today's topic is state and local bonds, usually lumped together as *municipal bonds.*
- This is an important topic because financing capital projects without borrowing would cause huge short-run shocks to state and local tax rates.
- Borrowing allows a jurisdiction to spread the budgetary impact of large capital projects over time.

1.1. *Bonds and Taxes or Fees*

- Municipal bonds are not a financing tool, they are a burden-spreading tool.
- A government cannot finance capital spending with bonds; instead, it must finance this spending with taxes or fees and then *spread the impact out over time* with bonds.
- Decisions about bonds therefore are connected to decisions about the best way to finance a project, that is, about the most appropriate taxes and fees (based on equity and efficiency.).

1.2. The Real Impact of Bonds

- Saying that bonds are a burden-spreading tool does not imply that they have no real impacts.
- In fact, *there is a cost to spreading out the impact of a project over time*, namely, interest costs, broadly defined.
- *Poor bond-issuing policies can boost interest costs above the minimum required level.*

1.3. The Volume of Bonds

Volume of State and Local Government Debt Issuances, 1992–2015.
Source: The Bond Buyer, 2015 *in Statistics: Annual Review*, February 2016.

1.4. Overview of Bond Market

- "Tax-Exempt Bonds: A Description of State and Local Government Debt," Grant A. Driessen, Congressional Research Service, December 23, 2016. Source of previous figure and other figures in this chapter can be accessed from this link: https://fas.org/sgp/crs/misc/RL30638.pdf.

1.5. *What is a Municipal Bond?*

- A *bond* is a *certificate of indebtedness*.
- The *issuer* agrees to pay interest to the *purchaser* in return for the use of the purchaser's money over a given period of time.
- A bond contrasts with a stock, in which a firm exchanges part ownership in a company for the use of an investor's money. Stocks are not relevant for government.

2. Basic Bond Characteristics

Three key things are stamped on a bond:

- *Face Value* = F (= par value or redemption value or value at maturity).
- *Coupon Rate* = c, which indicates the interest to be paid as a percentage of F and which can be either fixed or floating (i.e. tied to some other rate).
- *Years to Maturity* = N, which is the number of years until the bond can be redeemed and is also the number of years during which the investor is entitled to collect interest.
- Bonds are usually issued in *serial* form, which means that some bonds have $N = 1$, some have $N = 2$, some have $N = 3$, all the way up to the highest selected maturity, N^*.

  o This approach helps spread out the cost because it implies that only $1/N^*$ of the bonds have to be paid back each year.

- Bonds are usually issued with face values of $5,000 or multiples of $5,000.

  o In the past, this meant that only large investors tended to buy them, but now anyone can invest any amount in bonds through a *bond fund*.

- Other things that might be on a bond:
- *Call Option*, which gives the issuer the right to recall the bond before its maturity date (increasing the risk placed on the investor).

- *Put Option*, which allows the investor to redeem the bond before its maturity date (increasing the risk placed on the issuer).
- *Insurance*, against the possibility that the issuer cannot make the specified payments on time (lowering the risk placed on the investor, but imposing a cost on the issuer).

2.1. *The Price of a Bond*

- The first key to understanding bond markets is to think about the *market price* of a bond.
- This price equals the amount an investor would pay to purchase a bond.
- This market **price is not the same thing as a bond's face value!!**
- Suppose an investor has an alternative, similar investment, perhaps a U.S. Treasury Bill, that offers an interest rate r.
- Then r is the opportunity cost of investing in bonds, and the investor's willingness to pay is the present value of the benefits from holding the bond or

$$P = \frac{cF}{(1+r)} + \frac{cF}{(1+r)^2} + \cdots + \frac{cF}{(1+r)^N} + \frac{F}{(1+r)^N}$$

- With the help of some algebra, this formula can be simplified to the following:

$$P = \left(\frac{1 - (1+r)^{-N}}{r} \right) cF + \frac{F}{(1+r)^N}$$

$$= F \left(c \left(\frac{1 - (1+r)^{-N}}{r} \right) + \left(\frac{1}{(1+r)^N} \right) \right)$$

- See Yinger (forthcoming, Appendix A) for the details.
- In this equation, all terms except the last are interest payments.
- The last term indicates the present value of the bond when it is redeemed.
- If $P > F$, the bond is said to sell at a *premium*.
- if $P < F$, the bond is said to sell at a *discount*.

2.2. A Bond's Rate of Return

- The second key to understanding bond markets is to think about the *rate of return* on a bond that sells at price P.
- This rate of return is the value of r at which the above equation is true, given P.
- This is a standard type of present-value calculation; it is often called finding the *internal rate of return*.
- In the case of bonds, it is called calculating a bond's *yield to maturity*.

2.3. Calculating Yield to Maturity

- Calculating the yield to maturity is difficult because the equation is nonlinear.
- But most spreadsheet programs are set up to do this type of calculation, that is, to find an internal rate of return (IRR).
- Moreover, there is a simple approximation that indicates the key intuition.

2.4. Approximating Yield to Maturity

- This approximation starts with the recognition that the return on a bond has two parts:
  - *Interest Return* $= \mathbf{cF}$.
  - *Capital Gain* $= (\mathbf{F} - \mathbf{P})/\mathbf{N}$ **per year**.
- Thus, the total return, expressed as a share of the "price," is:

$$ r = \frac{cF + \frac{F-P}{N}}{\frac{P+F}{2}} $$

2.5. Price and Rate of Return

- The difference between these two ways of looking at bonds corresponds to what is unknown.
- In the first case r is known, but P is not. We use the present-value equation to solve for P.

- In the second case, P is known, but r is not. We use the present-value equation to solve for r.

3. Types of Bonds

Bonds come in many different types, including the following:

- *Zero Coupon Bond* = a bond that pays no interest. This bond obviously must sell at a huge discount because all of its return comes in the form of a capital gain.
- *Compound Interest Bond* = *Capital Appreciation Bond* = a bond that puts interest payments in an "account" and lets them accumulate, but does not pay them out until the maturity date. This bond changes the time pattern of payments by saving all the interest until the end.
- The prices of these types of bonds can be obtained with some algebra:

$$\text{Zero-coupon bond: } P = \frac{F}{(1+r)^N}$$

$$\text{Capital Appreciation Bond: } P = \frac{F + F((1+c)^N - 1)}{(1+r)^N}$$

$$= F\left(\frac{(1+c)^N}{(1+r)^N}\right)$$

- Some budget officials like these two types of bonds because they push the re-payment streams into the future.
- These bonds do not save money, however, because they do not change the present value of the re-payment stream.
- The Table "Payments on Three Types of Municipal Bond" gives an example.
- Zero-coupon bonds are generally avoided near a borrowing limit because they have the highest face values.
- *Perpetuity* = a bond with $N = \infty$, so it just pays interest and never gets to the redemption date.
- Perpetuities aren't used often because they put a perpetual burden on government. But they are interesting to evaluate.

Payments on Three Types of Municipal Bond.

Year	Standard Actual	Standard Present Value	Zero-Coupon Actual	Zero-Coupon Present Value	Capital Appreciation Actual	Capital Appreciation Present Value
1	$7,500.00	$7,142.86	$6,475.23	$6,166.88	$5,250.00	$5,000.00
2	$7,250.00	$6,575.96	$6,475.23	$5,873.22	$5,512.50	$5,000.00
3	$7,000.00	$6,046.86	$6,475.23	$5,593.55	$5,788.13	$5,000.00
4	$6,750.00	$5,553.24	$6,475.23	$5,327.19	$6,077.53	$5,000.00
5	$6,500.00	$5,092.92	$6,475.23	$5,073.51	$6,381.41	$5,000.00
6	$6,250.00	$4,663.85	$6,475.23	$4,831.92	$6,700.48	$5,000.00
7	$6,000.00	$4,264.09	$6,475.23	$4,601.82	$7,035.50	$5,000.00
8	$5,750.00	$3,891.83	$6,475.23	$4,382.69	$7,387.28	$5,000.00
9	$5,500.00	$3,545.35	$6,475.23	$4,173.99	$7,756.64	$5,000.00
10	$5,250.00	$3,223.04	$6,475.23	$3,975.23	$8,144.47	$5,000.00
Total	$63,750.00	$50,000.00	$64,752.29	$50,000.00	$66,033.94	$50,000.00

Note: The coupon rate and opportunity cost are set at 5%. The table presents the total payments on bonds of all maturities in each year. The face values of the standard and capital appreciation bonds are $5,000; the face values of the zero-coupon bonds are $6,475.23. The standard and capital appreciation bonds sell for $5,000, whereas the zero-coupon bonds sell for amounts between $4,761.91 (1-year maturity) and $3,069.57 (10-year maturity).

- With an infinite N, the present-value formula simplifies to:

$$P = \frac{cF}{r}$$

- So if $c = r$, then $P = F$; if $c < r$, the bond sells at a discount $(P < F)$; and if $c > r$, the bond sells at a premium. Discounts and premiums can arise even if a bond never matures!

3.1. Categories of Municipal Bond

- Bonds backed by full taxing authority of issuing government:
  - General Obligation Bonds (GO);
  - Moral Obligation Bonds;
  - Double Barreled GO Bonds.
- Bonds backed by Specific Revenue Source:
  - Revenue Bond;
  - Agency Bond;
  - Tax Increment Bond.

3.2. Categories of Municipal Bond (Driessen)

- Bonds backed by private revenue source:

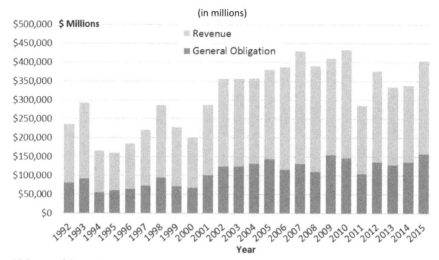

Volume of Long-Term Tax-Exempt Debt: General Obligation (GO) and Revenue Bonds, 1992–2015.

Source: The Bond Buyer (2015). *In Statistics: Annual Review*, February 2016.

- o Industrial Development Bonds;
- o Pollution Control Bonds;
- o Mortgage Revenue Bonds.

- Bonds to Smooth Timing Problems:

- o Tax Anticipation Notes (TANs);
- o Revenue Anticipation Notes (RANs);
- o Bond Anticipation Notes (BANs).

3.3. *Investments that Compete with Bonds*

- Governments must compete for investor's funds with many other types of investment, including:

- o Stocks;
- o Corporate Bonds;
- o Federal Bonds (savings bonds, treasury bonds, agency bonds);
- o Mortgages.

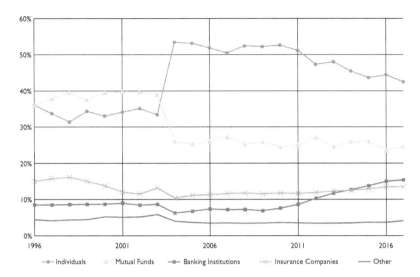

Holders of Municipal Debt, 1996–2017.

Source: Federal Reserve System (via www.sifma.org).

4. The Market for Tax-Exempt Loanable Funds

- **Demand**: State and local governments want loanable funds to smooth revenue flows.
- **Supply**: Investors with high marginal tax rates prefer tax-exempt investments, such as munis, for reasons explored later.

The Market for Municipal Bonds

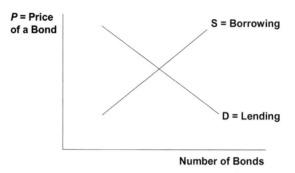

The Market for Municipal Bonds

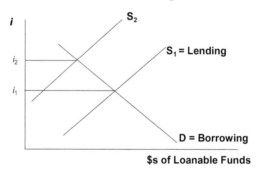

Impact of Tight Monetary Policy (or loss of confidence in munis or new tax-exempt savings options).

4.1. *Features of Municipal Bonds: Maturity*

- Because municipal bonds are serial issues, they have different maturities.
- In a market, *yields generally must rise with maturity*, because investors must be compensated for being locked in for a longer time.
- But,
  - *Call and put options* are equivalent to lowering maturity from the issuer or the investor's perspective, respectively.

The Market for Municipal Bonds

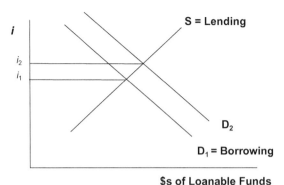

Initial Impact of Industrial Development Bonds. (or Mortgage Revenue Bonds).

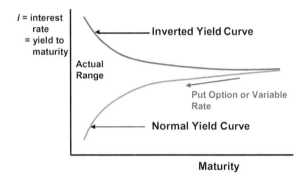

Yield Curves for Bonds.

o *Market conditions* are more volatile in the short-run than in the long-run, so an "inverted" yield curve (i.e. higher rates for shorter-term bonds) can arise under some circumstances.

4.2. *Features of Municipal Bonds: Tax Exemption*

- *Municipal bonds are free from federal tax* (and usually from state taxes if they are held by residents of the issuing state).
  - o The U.S. Supreme Court ruled that this is not a constitutional issue, but the federal government has kept this time-honored policy.

○ Some subsidies in the recent federal stimulus program were for taxable municipal bonds.
- This tax exemption implies that
  ○ Municipal bonds are particularly attractive to taxpayers with the highest federal marginal income tax rates.
  ○ The subsidy for municipal bonds is inefficient (but politically protected).

4.2.1. *Bonds and tax brackets*

- Suppose the taxable rate of return is 12% and the tax-free (i.e. municipal) rate is 9%.
- Then someone in the 25% income tax bracket is indifferent between taxable investments and munis:

$$12 \times (1 - 0.25) = 9$$

- Someone in the 35% tax bracket prefers munis:

$$12 \times (1 - 0.35) < 9$$

- Someone in the 15% tax bracket prefers a taxable investment:

$$12 \times (1 - 0.15) > 9$$

4.2.2. *The tax exemption is inefficient*

- Suppose a government issues $1 million in bonds and half are purchased by people in each of the top two brackets (25% and 50%).
- The savings to the issuing government is
  (.03)($1 million) = $30,000
- The cost to the federal government is
  ($500,000)(.12)(.5) = $30,000 (top bracket)
  + ($500,000)(.12)(.25) = $15,000 (middle br.)
  = $45,000 total
- This is **inefficient**, because the cost to the federal government exceeds the savings to the issuer.
- The federal subsidy for bonds is inefficient because anyone with a marginal tax rate above the "break-even rate" receives a benefit

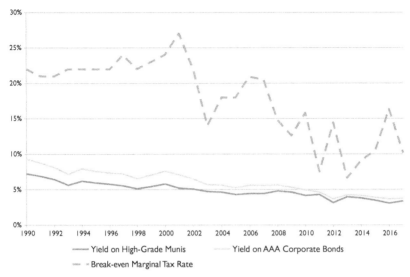

The Break-even Tax Rate, 1990–2017 (CEA).

greater than what is needed to induce them to buy a municipal bond.

- Direct subsidies would avoid this, but would have to go through the budget process, which is reviewed each year and is therefore less protected.

4.2.3. *Private purpose bonds*

- State and local governments have a strong incentive to use tax-exempt bonds for private purposes, such as economic development, education loans, and mortgages.
- This costs the federal government a lot of money and raises the price of bonds generally.
- So the use of tax-exempt bonds for private purposes is limited by the federal government.

4.3. *Features of Municipal Bonds: Ratings*

- Three companies, Moody's, Standard and Poor's, and Fitch provide 99% of muni ratings.

Percent of S&L Bonds for Private Activities, 2006.

Development	1.62%
Education	15.07%
Higher ed. student loans	9.76%
Other	5.32%
Electric power	4.27%
Healthcare	13.29%
Housing	10.12%
Public Facilities	2.81%
Convention centers	0.81%
Stadiums and arenas	1.32%
Theaters	0.10%
Parks, zoos, and beaches	0.27%
Other recreation	0.30%
Transportation	7.50%
Parking facilities	0.17%
Airports	2.73%
Mass transit	4.60%
Utilities	3.61%
Gas works	3.56%
Telephones	0.05%
Total Private	58.28%

Source: Gravelle and Gravelle, *NTJ*, September 2007.

- Several smaller firms, also designated "Nationally Recognized Statistical Ratings Organizations" by the SEC, rate a few specialized municipal bonds.
- Governments pay a fee to have their bonds rated because the ratings provide information to investors.
- Ratings are attached to bond issues, except in the case of GO bonds, where the issuing government has a rating.

4.3.1. *What do ratings measure?*

- The rating agencies say that *ratings measure default risk*, that is, the risk that the issuer will not make all the payments on time.

Investment Grade Ratings.

	Moody's	Standard and Poor's	Fitch
Best Quality	Aaa	AAA	AAA
High Quality	Aa1	AA$^+$	AA$^+$
	Aa2	AA	AA
	Aa3	AA$^-$	AA$^-$
Upper Medium Grade	A1	A$^+$	A$^+$
	A2	A	A
	A3	A$^-$	A$^-$
Medium Grade	Baa1	BBB$^+$	BBB$^+$
	Baa2	BBB	BBB
	Baa3	BBB$^-$	BBB$^-$

Growth in U.S. Municipal Ratings

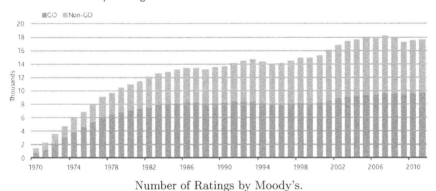

Number of Ratings by Moody's.

- Ratings are based on economic, financial, and political character-istics of the issuer, but the formulas are proprietary — and closely guarded.
- *Ratings may have a big impact on interest cost.* A highly rated bond might be able to pay one percentage point less in interest than a bond with a poor rating.
- Issuers do not have to buy a rating, but they usually do.

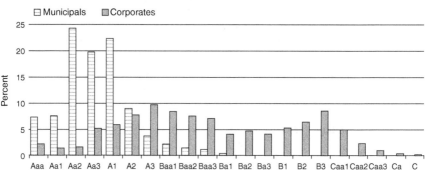

Distribution of Ratings by Moody's.

Revenue Bond Defaults, Standard and Poor's, 1990s.

Sector	# of Defaults	Defaulted Amount ($)	Avg. Time to Default	# Rated	# Non-Rated
Industrial Dev (IDBs)	288	2,839,915,892	88	33	255
Healthcare	239	1,994,158,951	58	24	215
Multifamily Housing	153	2,050,092,293	63	51	102
Land-Backed Debt	141	1,037,790,699	72	2	139
COPs/Lease Revs	30	146,505,781	57	2	28
Other Revenues	25	826,992,000	47	7	18
Single Family Housing	16	36,877,076	137	13	3
General Obligations	14	827,550,000	10	5	9
Utilities	8	39,450,000	70	0	8
Education	3	10,530,000	44	0	3
Totals	914	9,809,862,692	71	137	780

4.3.1.1. Default Risk

- Default risk is real, at least for revenue bonds.
- Consider the following tables from a Standard and Poor's document: "A Complete Look at Monetary Defaults During the 1990s."

  o http://www.kennyweb.com/kwnext/mip/paydefault.pdf.

GO Bond Defaults, Standard and Poor's, 1990s.

Year	# of Defaults	Defaulted Amount ($)	Avg. Time to Default	# Rated	# Non-Rated
1990	1	2,000,000	18	0	1
1995	3	800,000,000	12	3	0
1996	4	5,860,000	8	0	4
1997	1	2,800,000	11	0	1
1998	4	15,475,000	8	2	2
1999	1	1,415,000	9	0	1
Totals	14	827,550,000	10	5	9

Defaults in 1995 were tied to 3 short-term note deals issued by Orange County, California.

Seven out of the 14 monetary defaults were tied to late payments caused by administrative oversights and were not related to financial difficulties.

GO Default Settlements, Standard and Poor's, 1990s.

Settlement Type	# of Settlements	Avg. Time to Settlement	Avg. Recovery
Resumptions	7	1	N/A
Cash Distributions	3	11	100
Redemptions	2	4	100
Exchange	1	7	N/A
Totals	13	4	

Holders of the three Orange County, California note deals were made whole (recovered 100 cents on the dollar) through cash distributions when the County emerged from bankruptcy during June 1996.

- For perspective, outstanding muni debt in 2002 was about $1 trillion for revenue bonds and $600 million for GOs.

4.3.1.2. Impacts of Ratings

- Because high ratings lower interest costs, governments have in interest in obtaining a high rating.
- So many governments strive to meet the tax and management standards set by the rating agencies.

Moody's Defaults.

Default Counts by Sale Purpose, 1970–2011		
Purpose	Number of Defaults	Percentage (%)
Housing	29	40.8
Hospitals and Health Service Providers	22	31.0
Education	3	4.2
Infrastructure	4	5.6
Utilities	2	2.8
Cities	2	2.8
Counties	1	1.4
Special Districts	1	1.4
Water and Sewer	1	1.4
State Governments	1	1.4
Non General Obligation	66	93.0
General Obligation	5	7.0
Total	71	100

Source: Moody's.

- Many other governments buy *bond insurance*, which can raise ratings (and therefore save money).
- In some cases, states insure the bonds of their local governments.
- Some small governments form *bond pools* to broaden their resource base and lower the risk of default.
- Ratings also influence investor's response to events in the market place.
- When New York City defaulted in 1974, the premium paid for highly rated bonds went up noticeably.

  o When Cleveland defaulted in 1979, nobody noticed.
  o When Orange county defaulted in 1995, the impact was small and short-lived.

- From an investor's point of view, therefore, ratings also indicate *market risk*.

4.4. *Rating the Raters*

- The private rating agencies play an important public role — i.e. they influence the cost of infrastructure.
- Under these circumstances, one would think that they would be regulated, i.e. that some government agency would ask whether their actions are in the public interest.
- Regulation of ratings was prohibited by the Credit Rating Agency Reform Act of 2006.

  o The Dodd–Frank Act of 2010 gives the SEC some regulatory powers, but their impact is not yet clear.

- My 2010 article in the *American Law and Economics Review* suggests that some regulation may be needed.
- GO bonds essentially never default.
- As a result, no government characteristic has any value in predicting default.
- So any rating policy that puts cities with certain characteristics at a disadvantage cannot be justified by a connection to default risk.
- My work shows that all three ratings agencies hand out GO ratings that decline with the percentage of a city's population that is black.
- This is not fair, and a federal regulator should be looking into it.
- I have looked into the same issue with school bonds in California.
- Again I found this type of "redlining" also arises in this case.
- School districts with high black or Hispanic concentrations receive lower GO bond ratings than largely white districts — despite having the same probability of default.
- Lower ratings lead, of course, to higher interest costs for black and Hispanic than for white districts.
- http://cpr.maxwell.syr.edu/efap/about_efap/ie/June13.pdf.
- One might think that my focus on default risk is inappropriate because ratings also indicate market risk.
- But from society's point of view, this argument is circular — at least in the case of GO bonds.

- Ratings cannot predict default but they do predict market risk if investors believe they do. The link to market risk is therefore based on investor illusion.
- It makes no sense to justify unfair ratings for some cities because these ratings are successful in deluding investors!
- The point here is not that rating agencies are bad.
- In fact, they serve the public interest by encouraging governments to follow good practices.

  ○ Good practices lead to higher ratings and lower interest costs.
  ○ Or good practices lead to lower costs for bond insurance.

- Ratings provided by a higher level of government would undoubtedly not have as much credibility — or so much impact on government practices.
- But ratings agencies are out to make profits — not serve the public interest — and they should be regulated.

5. Issuing Bonds

- Many institutions are involved in issuing bonds.
- The issuing government hires an *adviser*:

  ○ An independent public finance advisor.
  ○ Or the underwriter (who must resign before buying the bonds).

- An *underwriter* buys the bonds from the issuing government.
- And then sells them to *investors*.

5.1. *Selecting a Bid*

- The issuing government must select a bid, which is a combination of prices, face values, and interest rates for a set of bonds.

  ○ Sometimes the bid is negotiated with a single underwriter.
  ○ Sometimes many underwriters bid and the issuing government decides which bid to accept.

- The amount raised by a bond is the price in the bid, not the face value.

- o But an issuing government typically includes a constraint requiring that the total amount of the bid (the sum of the prices) must be equal to (or nearly equal to) the amount that needs to be raised.
- The best bid is the one with the lowest true interest cost (TIC), which is the internal rate of return of the whole issue.
- This is found by solving the following equation for r:

$$\sum_{j=1}^{N} P_j = \sum_{j=1}^{N} \left(\sum_{t=1}^{M_j} \left(\frac{c_j F_j}{(1+r)^t} \right) + \frac{F_j}{(1+r)^{M_j}} \right)$$

- For a long time, local governments did not understand TIC and selected the bid with the lowest total interest payments.
- Underwriters did understand TIC and made bids with large interest payments up front where they had greater present value.
  - o This means higher interest rates on shorter maturities — the opposite of what one usually observes in a market.
- Restrictions, such as no interest rate inversion, can go a long way toward eliminating these problems, but TIC is better. Discounting matters!

5.2. *Competition vs. Negotiation*

- An issuing government must decide whether to use competitive bidding.
- If the bond issue is unusual and a certain underwriter has the needed expertise, negotiation makes sense.
- But competition, which is used for $3/4$ of bond issues, lowers costs.

5.3. *Robbins*

- In his PA dissertation from Maxwell (published in *PAR* 2001), Mark Robbins studies the impact of competitive bidding on interest costs.
- He also studies a twist in the middle of his sample period:
  - o A new regulation encouraged competitive bidding.

- o He asks whether this regulation lowered the benefit from competitive bidding by encouraging it when it was not appropriate.
- His dependent variable is "true interest cost" or TIC, which is the IRR of the serial issue.
- His key explanatory variables are whether the bond was issued with competitive bidding and this variable interacted with the time period with the new regulations.
- His control variables include:
  - o Market variables (average interest cost for two bond indexes).
  - o Issue variables (call provision, number of bids, amount, amount squared, maturity, whether refunding).
  - o Issuer variables (rating for issuer, whether insured — these are really issue characteristics!).
  - o And use of proceeds (dummies for type of project, such as health care facility).
- His equation is:

$$\text{TIC} = c + b_i\text{COMP} + b_i\text{COMPETITIVE} * \text{RESTRICTED}$$
$$+ b_i\text{MARKET} + b_i\text{ISSUE} + b_i\text{ISSUER} + b_i\text{USE} + e$$

- He does OLS with robust standard errors and GLS to account for clustering.
  - o The two approaches are similar and it is not clear which is preferable.
- Rating, maturity, and market conditions work as expected.
- Competition lowers costs 35 basis points $= 0.35$ percentage points.
- He also tries a model with number of bids.
  - o This model assumes that going from zero to 1 bid has the same impact as going from six to seven bids.
  - o He estimates that seven bids raises the savings to 46 basis points.
- The PV of the aggregate savings for the mean issue ($64.2 million over 23 years) is $1.4 million.
- The regulation had an insignificant impact.
- This approach treats the decision to go for competition as exogenous. Is this plausible?

Part II

STATE AND LOCAL PUBLIC FINANCE FOR MASTER'S DEGREE STUDENTS

Lecture 1

Introduction and Overview

1. The U.S. Federal System

- Broad Themes:
  - Legal framework defined by *constitutions*;
  - Details determined by politics.
- Units Defined by U.S. Constitutions:
  - The Federal Government;
  - State Governments.
- Units Defined by State Constitutions:
  - The State Government;
  - Counties and (usually) Townships;
  - Municipalities (Cities and Villages);
  - School Districts;
  - Special Districts.

1.1. *Variation at the Macro Level: States and Counties*

- We have gone, of course, from 13 to 50 states.
- State boundaries were often adjusted in the nation's early years.
- Counties were created — and revised.

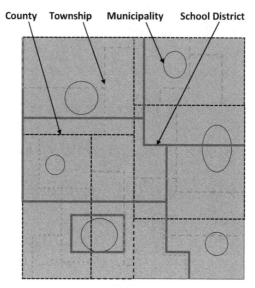

A Stylized Map of a State.

- Little change in state or county boundaries in recent years.
- https://www.youtube.com/watch?v=9UE9uu9fKSg.

1.2. *Variation in Local Governments across States (U.S. Census of Governments, 2012)*

- No townships in the South and West.
- No counties in Connecticut, Rhode Island, and the District of Columbia.
- DC, Maryland, North Carolina, Alaska, and Hawaii have no independent school districts. Hawaii has one state district.
- Sixteen states have dependent and independent school districts.
  - Virginia has one independent and 135 dependent school systems.
  - Louisiana has 69 independent school districts and one dependent school system.
  - New York has five dependent and almost 700 independent school districts.

1.2.1. *Special districts*

- The U.S. has 2012 independent special districts in 2012.

- Eleven states have over 1,000 special districts (California, Colorado, Illinois, Kansas, Missouri, Nebraska, New York, and Oregon, Pennsylvania, Texas, and Washington).
- Special districts vary greatly by state; the most common are:
  - Fire Protection Districts (5,865)
  - Water Supply Districts (3,522)
  - Housing and Community Development Districts (3,438)
  - Drainage and Flood Control Districts (3,248).

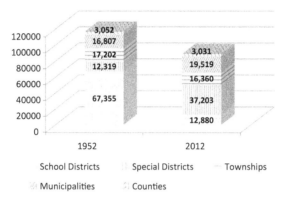

Number of Governments, by Type of Government, 1952 and 2012.

Source: U.S. Census of Governments.

State Examples, 2012.

State	Total	County	Town	Muni	School	Specl
Alaska	177	14	0	148	0*	15
California	4,425	57	0	482	1,025*	2,861
Hawaii	21	3	0	1	1(Dp)	17
Illinois	6,963	102	1,431	2,729	905	3,227
Mass.	857	5	298	53	84*	417
Nebraska	2,581	93	419	530	272	1,267
New York	3,453	57	929	617	679*	1,174
Penn.	4,897	66	1,546	1,015	514	1,756
Texas	5,147	254	0	1,214	1,079*	2,600
Virginia	518	95	0	229	1*	193

Note: *Includes some dependent districts; Muni = municipal; Specl = special district.

Source: U.S. Census of Governments.

1.3. *State and Local Revenue*

- States receive almost one-third of their revenue from the federal government, mainly for TANF and Medicaid.
- Local governments receive almost one-third of their revenue from their state, mainly for education; they also receive about 40% from fees and 40% from taxes.

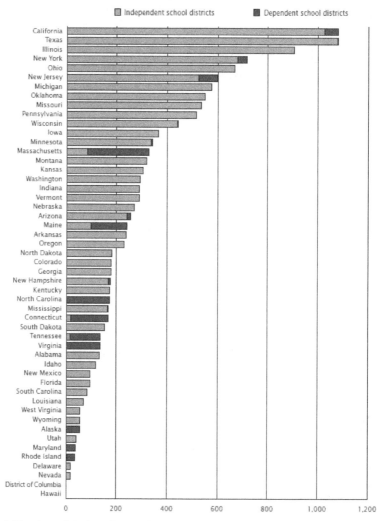

Total Number of Public School Systems by State.

Source: U.S. Census Bureau, 2012 Census of Governments.

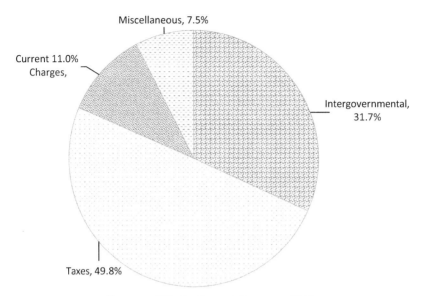

Sources of State General Revenue, 2015.

○ States cover about 47% of elementary and secondary education revenue; school districts cover about 45%, and the federal government covers about 8%.

• Local tax revenue comes mainly from the property tax.
• See: http://www.census.gov/govs/.

State Taxes, 2015.

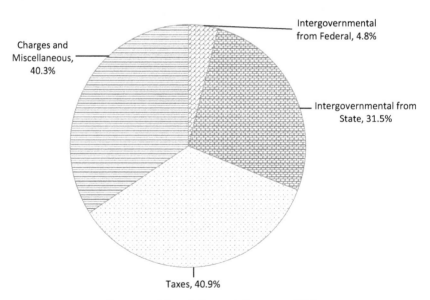

Sources of Local General Revenue, 2014.

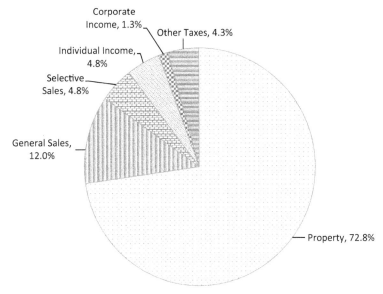

Local Taxes, 2014.

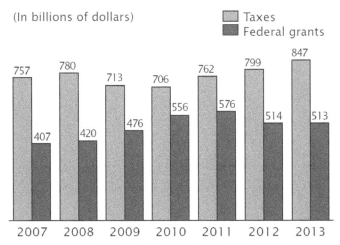

State Government Taxes Collected and Federal Grants Received: 2007–2013.
Source: U.S. Census Bureau, 2007–2013 Annual Survey of State Government Finances.

1.4. *State and Local Expenditure*

- State and local governments divide responsibility for education, highways, welfare.
- About one-third of state and local general spending is for education and about 20% is for elementary and secondary education.
- Highways are a surprisingly low 7% of state and local spending.

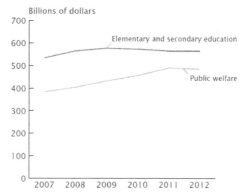

State and Local Government Select Expenditures: 2007–2012.

Source: U.S. Census Bureau, 2007 and 2012 Census of Governments: Finance — Surveys of State and Local Government Finances and intercensal estimates from the Annual Surveys of State and Local Government Finances.

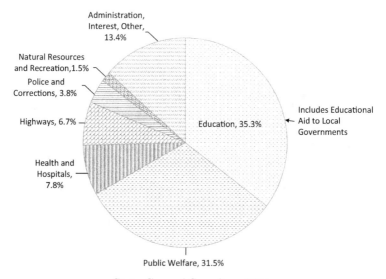

State General Spending, 2014.

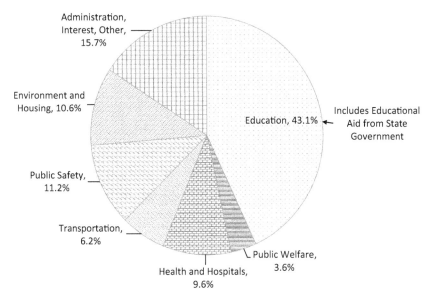

Local Direct General Expenditure, 2014.

2. Overview of Course Topics

- This course examines spending and taxation in the U.S. federal system.
  - Determinants of local spending;
  - Evaluating tax policies;
  - Fiscal aspects of economic development;
  - Intergovernmental fiscal relations.
- Many of the principles apply to the federal systems in other countries.

2.1. *Types of Analysis*

- The course covers both *positive* and *normative* analysis.
  - Positive analysis:
    - Examines the *behavior* of voters, businesses, and government officials.

- ■ In principle, positive statements can be *tested* against evidence.
  - ○ Normative analysis:
    - ■ Examines the *best choices* for public officials to make.
    - ■ Combines positive analysis with *values — yours!*

2.1.1. *Positive analysis, examples (which may or may not be true)*

- People with higher incomes vote for higher levels of local public services, all else equal.
- Communities with higher property tax rates have lower house values, all else equal.
- Lowering a city's property tax rate has little impact on its employment.
- School districts with more disadvantaged students have to spend more to achieve any given level of student performance.

2.1.2. *Normative analysis, examples (with which you may or may not agree)*

- Prison provision should be contracted out to private companies.
- A property tax is a better way to finance local public services than a local income tax.
- Cities should not use property tax exemptions to promote economic development.
- States should give more education aid to school districts with a high concentration of at-risk students.

2.2. *Intellectual Honesty*

- Separating positive and normative arguments may be the most difficult task in a public policy debate.
- Many people start with a favorite program and then cherry-pick the evidence that supports their position.
- This approach undermines their own objectives.

- *You should use the best available evidence to determine which programs best meet your objectives.*
- Thanks to the internet, you can find an amazing range of opinions about the effects of just about any public program.
- I urge you to make a habit of thinking about the credibility of every piece of evidence you receive.
  - The most credible evidence comes from a consensus among multiple peer-reviewed studies with strong methodologies.
  - But that type of evidence is very rare, so you have to think about the methods used by each study and the potential biases of study authors.
- Remember, the best way to meet you own objectives, whatever they are, is to base you policy choices on the best available evidence concerning each policy's impact.
- The need for good information (and the need to recognize fake news) are subjects of wide interest.
- Here are a couple websites I have come across that provide tips:
  - Stony Brook University Center for News Literacy: http://drc. centerfornewsliteracy.org/.
  - Stanford History Education Group: https://sheg.stanford.edu/.
- As the assistant director of the Center for News Literacy puts it: "One of the messages we've tried to stress more and more lately with the rise of fake news is this: Do you want to be fooled? Wouldn't you rather make up your own mind?"

2.3. *Intellectual Honesty vs. Politics*

- In our society, a person (or a person's party) has to be elected before they have a chance to implement any programs.
  - Sometimes the best choice may be to support a second-best policy (that is, one without the most desirable effects) in order to get something passed or in order to get elected.
- Nevertheless, compromising away from the first-best policy (that is, the one with the most desirable effects) should be a deliberate choice based on political calculations.

o One cannot make this choice without knowing the effects of the first- and second-best policies.

- This class is not about politics, which is beyond my expertise.

o Instead, it is about methods to identify the first- and second-best policies to achieve your objectives.

2.4. *Class Conference*

- At the end of this class, you will present your proposals for reform in state or local public finance; many of them will be more sensible than what is actually being discussed in state legislatures.
- After this class, some of you will be able to implement your proposals or develop other ones when your work in state and local governments.
- My hope is that your proposals will be at least a little better because you took this class!
- State and local governments face many challenges. You should have no trouble finding good topics. Recent examples:

o An Evaluation of Industrial Development Agencies.
o Private Prisons in New York.
o Chicago Parking Meter Privatization.
o Public School Facility Cost Relief.
o San Diego Chargers Stadium Proposal.
o The Costs and Benefits of Privatization of Wine and Spirits Sales in Pennsylvania.
o Privatization of New York City Subway Services.
o Financing California High-Speed Rail.
o Potential Atlanta Plastic Bag Tax.
o Proposal for D.C. Municipal Land Bank.

The Demand for Local Public Services

- **Class Outline**
  1. **The Determinants of Demand for Public Services**
  2. **Tax Price**
  3. **How is Demand Revealed?**

1. The Determinants of Demand for Public Services

- The demand for local public services (police, fire, education, and so on) is similar to the demand for a private good.
- Let S measure the quality of a local public service.
  - S is a function of *income, price*, the *prices of related goods*, and *preferences*.
  - The *demand curve for S* can be drawn as follows, where MB stands for marginal benefit.

1.1. The Demand Curve for Local Public Services

S = Local public service quality; D = Demand; MB = Marginal benefit from S

1.2. Features of Public Demand

- Three twists arise in studying the demand for local public services:
- First, the *output* must be defined.

  - Ultimately, we want to measure the quality of local public services.
  - For today, we will define output as spending per household.

- Second, the *price* must be defined.

  - Public services are not usually sold directly to individuals.
  - The price arises through the tax system.

- Third, the *salience* of the price must be determined.

  - People do not respond to price differences they cannot observe.

2. Tax Price

- Because it operates through the tax system, the price for a local public service is called a *tax price*.
- A tax price varies with the tax used; we examine a tax price with a *property tax*, which is the main local tax in the U.S.
- A tax price is defined as the amount a taxpayer would have to pay for another unit of services if the property tax rate were raised to pay for it.

2.1. Property Taxes

- A property tax *payment* equals a *tax rate* multiplied by a property's *assessed value*.

  - The tax rate is selected by elected officials.
  - The assessed value is determined by an assessor, who may be elected or appointed.

- In symbols, homeowner i's property tax payment (T_i) equals the property tax rate (t) multiplied by the assessed value of her house (V_i):

$$T_i = t V_i$$

2.2. The Community Budget Constraint

- The community must set spending = revenue.
- Define:
  - S = spending per household
  - N = number of households
  - $\bar{V}$ = average assessed value

$$(S)(N) = t\sum_i V_i \text{ or } S = \frac{t\sum_i V_i}{N} = t\bar{V}$$

$$\text{or } t = \frac{S}{\bar{V}}$$

2.3. Solving for Tax Price

- Put these two equations together:

$$T_i = tV_i = \left(\frac{S}{\bar{V}}\right) V_i = S\left(\frac{V_i}{\bar{V}}\right)$$

- Note that T_i/S equals taxes paid per unit of S — the "price" of S.

$$\text{"Price"} = \left(\frac{T_i}{S}\right) = \frac{V_i}{\bar{V}}$$

- So for every unit of S, homeowner i pays $(V_i/\bar{V})$; that is, $(V_i/\bar{V})$ is her tax price.

2.4. Examples of Tax Price (= $\bar{V}_i/V$)

- A house with the average V in its community has a tax price of 1.0.
- A house worth twice the average in its community has a tax price of 2.0.
- A house worth half the average in its community has a tax price of 0.5.

2.5. Tax Price and Demand

- Compare 2 owners of $100,000 houses, one in a city where $\bar{V}$ is $50,000 and the other in a city where $\bar{V}$ is $200,000.
  - The first owner has a tax price of 2.0; the second a tax price of 0.5.

○ All else equal, the second owner faces a lower tax price and demands more public services as a result!

2.6. *The Salience of Tax Price Differences*

• Homeowners are not trained in public finance, so how do they figure out about tax price?

 ○ They observe what happens to their property taxes when a large shopping center in their town goes out of business, lowering $\bar{V}$ and raising their tax price.

 ○ Owners of relatively small houses may recognize that any property tax increase will be largely born by people with much more expensive houses.

 ○ These and other sources of information are not exact, but as we will see they are sufficient to cause significant behavioral responses — but perhaps smaller responses than those to private market prices.

3. How is Demand Revealed?

• The demand for local public services is revealed in three ways:

 ○ Voting.
 ○ Choice of a community in which to live.
 ○ The purchase of related private goods (such as private schools or private security).

• The next class examines voting.

• This class ends with a brief analysis of community choice; for more see Yinger, *Housing and Commuting*, Chapter 13, "Bidding and Sorting" (World Scientific, 2018).

3.1. *The Tiebout Hypothesis*

• A famous 1956 article by an economist named *Tiebout* made two points:

 ○ People consider the public service-tax package when they decide where to live (a *positive* statement).

○ The choice of a community is like the choice of a private good, so this process allocates resources in an efficient manner (a *normative* statement).

3.2. Developments Since Tiebout

- The literature since Tiebout has identified two key implications of his positive analysis:
- First, better public services or lower property taxes lead to higher house values, all else equal.

  ○ This phenomenon is known as *capitalization.*
  ○ We study property tax capitalization in a later class.

3.2.1. *Public service capitalization*

- Dozens of studies establish that, all else equal, the price of housing is higher in a community with better schools or better police protection.
- A recent review finds, for example, that all 50 studies of school quality capitalization published since 1999 find evidence of capitalization (Nguyen-Hoang and Yinger, *Journal of Housing Economics* (2011)).
- Several studies also find that lower crime leads to significantly higher house values, controlling for other things.
- If a policy changes the distribution of local public services, it will alter house values and therefore affect current homeowners!

3.2.2. *Income sorting*

- Second, people compete for entry into communities with desirable service tax packages.

  ○ High-income people win this competition.
  ○ This leads to *sorting*: high- and low-income people tend to live in different places, with richer people in places with better public services and, often, lower property tax rates.

o Income sorting is a key feature of the U.S. federal system — and a key cause of continuing inequality. This inequality is passed from one generation to the next.

3.2.3. Sorting in Cleveland

- My recent research (*Journal of Urban Economics*, 2015), based on all house sales in the Cleveland area in 2000, focuses on these two points.
  - o I find that housing prices are up to 30% higher in school districts where more entering 12th graders pass state tests.
  - o I find (with a new method) that higher-income people do, indeed, sort into school districts with higher-quality schools — a key source of inequality.
  - o A one standard deviation increase in homeowner income leads, purely because of income sorting, to a 1.30 standard deviation increase in the rate at which entering 12th graders pass state tests.
- It is also possible to estimate the overall value in the housing market of a house's neighborhood traits, including school quality and safety and other traits that cannot be observed. This value can be called "neighborhood quality" or "neighborhood housing value."
- The following figure shows the relationship between neighborhood quality and income in the Cleveland area.
- The horizontal axis is the median income of a homeowner in a neighborhood (in log form); the vertical axis is neighborhood quality (also in log form); on average, a one percent increase in homeowner income leads to a 0.524% increase in neighborhood quality.
- This income sorting is a central cause of inequality in local public service outcomes.

3.3. Housing Conversion and Zoning

- Two further points about sorting are helpful for understanding community change:

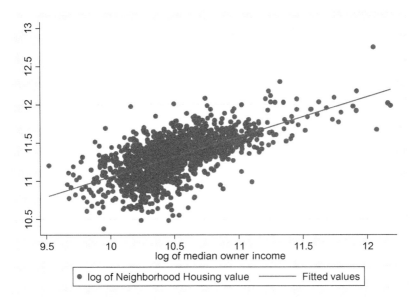

Income Sorting in the Cleveland Area, 2000.

○ Some communities experience housing conversion (houses split into apartment or small apartments combined into large condos) when the type of household moving into a community changes.

○ Some communities use large-lot zoning or some other restriction to prevent lower-income household from moving in, but sorting happens even without zoning.

3.4. *Sorting and Allocative Efficiency*

• On Tiebout's normative point, most scholars believe that having many local governments is more efficient than having just one.

• But, they disagree about:

○ Whether the current federal system could be made more efficient.

○ Whether the efficiency advantages of choice outweigh the equity costs of sorting.

• *These are key issues in the design of any federal system.*

Local Voting

- **Class Outline**
  1. **Voting and Demand**
  2. **Tax Limits**

1. Voting and Demand

- In most cases, citizens cannot directly express their demand for local public services.
- So they express their demand through their voting, either for public officials or on referenda.
- In this class, we explore how an understanding of demand helps us understand the choices local governments make.

1.1. *The Median Voter*

- The *median voter* always votes on the winning side.
  - Line voters up by the strength of their preference for public services.
  - Identify the voter in the middle — the median voter.
  - A majority vote must include the median voter.

```
-------------------------M-----------------------------
        weakest                    strongest
        preference                 preference
```

1.1.1. *Identifying the median voter*

- But voters do not line up, so the median voter is not identified!
- The *median voter model* shows how to identify the median voter assuming preferences are driven by demand factors.
  - The median voter has the median income and the median tax price.
  - This model places certain restrictions on *preferences*.
  - This model assumes political *institutions* are neutral.

1.1.2. *Using the median voter model*

- The median voter model is widely used because:
  - It explains community decisions based the demand function for a single voter — the median voter.
  - It makes use of widely available data at the community level: spending (or performance), median income, median tax price (median divided by mean house value).
  - *It works!*

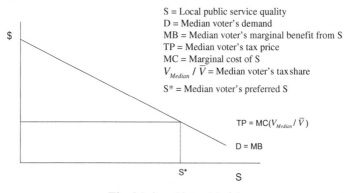

S = Local public service quality
D = Median voter's demand
MB = Median voter's marginal benefit from S
TP = Median voter's tax price
MC = Marginal cost of S
$V_{Median} / \bar{V}$ = Median voter's tax share

S* = Median voter's preferred S

$TP = MC(V_{Median}/\bar{V})$

D = MB

The Median Voter Model.

1.1.3. *Example: Eom, Nguyen-Hoang, Duncombe and Yinger, Education Finance and Policy, 2014*

- 1991–2011 data for over 600 school districts in New York State.
- Service quality measured by high school exams and drop-out rates.

- *Income elasticity = 0.17* (based on income per pupil).
- *Price elasticity = −0.22* (based on median tax price).
- Significant preference variables include share of housing that is owner-occupied and share of population age 65 or older.

1.1.4. *Other examples*

- The median voter model works well for local governments, particularly school districts.
- Recent applications include:
  - ○ Massachusetts (Nguyen-Hoang and Yinger, *Journal of Education Finance*, Spring 2014).
  - ○ California (Duncombe and Yinger, *International Tax and Public Finance*, June 2011).

1.1.5. *Preference assumptions*

- Median voter models need "single-peaked" preferences.
  - ○ Consider two communities with a high demand for education, one (City A) with a good private school and the other (City B) without.
  - ○ In City A, the high demand for education may not show up as a high demand for *public* education.
  - ○ In this case, which is extreme, the median voter model breaks down.

1.1.6. *The role of institutions*

- Scholars disagree about the importance of institutions.
  - ○ Some scholars believe institutions are fairly neutral in most cases, particularly outside large cities.
  - ○ Other scholars believe bureaucrats can have a large impact on spending and service quality — the *leviathan* view.
  - ○ In some cases, it is possible to control for institutions, such as whether a city as a mayor or a city manager.

2. Tax Limits

- Tax limits challenge the median voter model: Why do voters need to limit taxes if they control spending anyway?
- Some scholars believe that most tax limits make a political point with little impact on spending.
- Others believe that tax limits reveal voters' belief in leviathan — and their desire to reign in bureaucrats.

2.1. *Evidence about Tax Limits*

- The research on tax and expenditure limits (TELs) leads to five main conclusions.
- *First*, TELs come in many different forms.
  - Some limit property tax rates; some limit property tax levy increases; some limit expenditure increases.
  - Some include limits on assessment increases, which, over time, lower taxes for long-term residents. (More on this in a later class.)
  - For a thorough catalogue of the various types of limits, see Kioko, *Public Budgeting and Finance*, 2011.
- *Second*, TELS that focus on the property tax shift the tax burden away from property taxes to other revenue sources.
  - This shift was very large right after *Proposition 13* in CA and *Proposition 2¹/₂* in MA but has moderated since then.
  - Some of the new revenue sources, especially fees, are very regressive, but others, such as income taxes in a few cases, are not.
- *Third*, TELs have not stopped the growth in state and local government spending.
- According to the Urban Institute:
  - "Direct state and local spending on general government increased from approximately $1.1 billion in 1977 (in inflation-adjusted 2015 dollars) to $2.8 billion in 2015 — a 170% increase over 38 years. Similarly, per capita expenditures increased from about $4,900 a person to $8,800 a person, an increase of 82%."

- ○ https://www.urban.org/policy-centers/cross-center-initiatives/ state-local-finance-initiative/state-and-local-backgrounders.
- *Fourth*, there is no compelling evidence that TELs have boosted the efficiency of state and local governments.
  - ○ States with strong TELs have experienced a decline in the quality of public services.
  - ○ The performance by California's students on national tests has dropped significantly, for example, since Proposition 13.
  - ○ For a review of this literature, see Downes and Figlio (*Handbook on Education Finance and Policy*, 2nd Edition 2015).
- *Fifth*, voter demand factors still matter even with a strong TEL.
- California has severe limits, e.g.
  - ○ But Duncombe and Yinger (*ITPF*, 2011) find that voters with higher incomes or lower tax prices still pick higher school quality.
  - ○ Through active monitoring of school officials or the use of secondary revenue sources, such as parcel taxes or private foundations.
- *Sixth*, TELs push governments to use special districts, which are generally not included in tax caps.
- For evidence on this point, see the article by P. Zhang, *Economics of Governance*, 2018.
- This is an unintended consequence and its benefits and costs are not well understood.

2.2. *The New Tax Cap in NY*

- A couple years ago Governor Cuomo proposed and the legislature passed a cap on tax levy increases for all local governments.
- The cap is the lesser of 2% and inflation, with technical exceptions.
- The cap exempts new construction (to preserve incentives for development and growth).
- The legislation allows jurisdictions to override the cap with a 60% vote, but few districts try to override (and fewer succeed).
  - ○ In 2018, 662 districts proposed budgets within the cap and 98.6% passed.

- o Also 14 districts proposed budgets that needed an override and only 50% passed.
- o Nobody should expect this cap to make local governments more efficient.
- o Without more state aid (unlikely) or many overrides (also not likely) this cap will cut local services.
- o Source of data: http://www.nyssba.org/.

- This cap is likely to increase disparities across jurisdictions in education and other public services.
- Richer school districts are more likely to override the cap.
- Because poorer school districts receive more state aid, they have lower property tax levies.

  - o This fact implies that poorer districts need larger percentage increases in revenue just to keep up with richer districts.

- Some wealthy school districts raise about \$30,000 in property taxes per pupil; Buffalo, Rochester, and Syracuse (the Upstate Big 3) raise about \$3,700.
- In 20 years, the allowable annual revenue will go up by \$30,000 $\times$ $[(1.02)^{20} - 1] = \mathbf{\$14{,}578}$ in these rich districts.
- But by only \$3,700 $\times$ $[(1.02)^{20} - 1] = \mathbf{\$1{,}798}$ in the Upstate Big 3.

Public Sector Costs Concepts

1. Key Concepts

- *Production functions* translate inputs into outputs.
- *Cost functions* indicate the spending required to reach a given level of output.
- Understanding public production and cost functions is critical to understanding public spending and performance.

2. Public Production and Cost Functions

- Private Production Function:

$$Q = q\{\text{Inputs}\}$$

- Private Cost Function:

$$C = c\{Q, \text{ Input Prices}\}$$

2.1. *Government Production Function (Bradford/Malt/Oates, National Tax Journal, 1969)*

- Intermediate Output (G depends on inputs)

$$G = g\{\text{Inputs}\}$$

- Final Output (S depends on G and the Environment, N)

$$S = s\{G, \text{Environment}\}$$
$$= s\{G, N\}$$

- Inverted Final Output (required G depends on N and on desired S)

$$G = s^{-1}\{S, N\}$$

2.2. *Government Cost Functions (B/M/O, NTJ, 1969)*

- Cost of Intermediate Output (depends on G and input prices, W)

$$C_G = c_G\{G, W\}$$

- Cost of Final Output (depends on S, N, and W)

$$C = c\{G \text{ needed for } S, W\}$$
$$= c\{s^{-1}\{S, N\}, W\}$$
$$= c'\{S, N, W\}$$

2.3. *Public Outputs*

- Public cost functions focus on the cost of government *performance.*
  - Police: Crime rate.
  - Fire: Probability of loss from fire.
  - Education: Test scores, graduation rates.
- Public cost functions are influenced by the *environment* in which the services are delivered.

3. Examples of "Environment"

- *Police*: Poor people are more likely to be victims of crime and to be desperate enough to turn to crime.
- *Fire*: Old houses catch fire more often and burn faster; fire spreads faster when housing is closely packed.
- *Education*: Children from poor families are more likely to bring health or behavioral problems to school, and less likely to have lessons reinforced at home.

3.1. *Estimates of "Environment"*

- Ladd and Yinger (*America's Ailing Cities*, 1991) find that police costs increase with *poverty and city population*.
- Duncombe and Yinger (*Journal of Public Economics*, 1993) find that fire costs increase with *industrial and utility property and tall buildings*.
- Many scholars find that education costs increase with the *share of students from poor families or with limited English proficiency*. (See, for example, the following table from Duncombe and Yinger, *Economics of Education Review*, 2005.)

Estimated Pupil Weights (= extra costs for at-risk pupils).

	Simple Average	Pupil-Weighted Average	Directly Estimated
Without Special Education			
Child Poverty	1.415	1.491	1.667
LEP	1.007	1.030	1.308
With Special Education			
Child Poverty	1.224	1.281	1.592
LEP	1.009	1.033	1.424
Special Education	2.049	2.081	2.644

Source: Duncombe/Yinger (*EER*, 2005).

3.2. Duncombe/Yinger Study of California (International Tax and Public Finance, 2011)

- Cost factors in education:
  - Share of student from poor families.
  - Share of students with limited English proficiency.
  - Share of students with a severe disability.
  - Required wage to attract teachers.
  - Enrollment (economies of scale).
  - Enrollment change.
  - Grade level (higher costs for high school).

4. Cost vs. Spending

- A cost function describes technology, and implicitly is based on *best practices*.
- In fact, however, we cannot observe *costs*, we can only observe *spending*.
- The final step in the logic is to link costs and spending.

4.1. Government Expenditure Function

- To link cost (C) and spending (E), we can write:

$$E = C/e = c\{S, N, W\}/e$$

4.1.1. Definition of efficiency (e)

- An efficient government $(e = 1)$ uses *best practices* to spend as little as possible in delivering S.
- Spending more than this minimum $(e < 1)$ is inefficient.
- Alternative measures of S yield alternative definitions of e.

4.1.2. Examples of efficiency

- Suppose we define S as *student performance* on basic math and reading tests.

- *Many rich, suburban schools will be inefficient* despite their high scores because they spend a lot on art, music, science, and social studies.
- *Some poor, urban schools will be efficient* despite their low scores because they focus most of their spending on the basics.
- Some schools also may be inefficient because they are *wasteful* — a type of inefficiency that cannot be separated from the above.

4.1.3. *Measuring efficiency*

- Efficiency cannot be measured directly.
- Scholars disagree on the best way to account for efficiency in estimating an expenditure function.
- One method (D/Y):
  - The *efficiency-related behavior* of voters (monitoring, demand for public services not in S) and public officials (waste) responds to *incentives*.
  - Control for variables that describe these incentives.

4.2. *Examples of Incentives That May Influence Efficiency*

- **Tax Price:** Voters monitor public officials more carefully when paying a higher share of tax revenue.
- **State Aid:** State aid shifts the financing burden away from voters and weakens their incentive to monitor public officials.
- **Competition:** Public officials may be more efficient when they face competition.

4.3. *Duncombe/Yinger Study of California*

- Efficiency factors in education (with state's test score index as the measure of performance)
  - Median income.
  - Tax price (based on parcel tax).
  - State aid for education.
  - Federal aid for education.

- ○ Migration into district.
- ○ Categorical aid as a share of total aid.

4.4. *Other Recent Cost Studies*

- **New York**: Eom, Duncombe, Nguyen-Hoang, and Yinger, *Education Finance and Policy*, Fall 2014.
- **Massachusetts**: Nguyen-Hoang and Yinger. *Journal of Education Finance*, Spring 2014.
- **Missouri**: Duncombe and Yinger, *Peabody Journal of Education*, 2011.
- **California, Kansas, Missouri, and New York**: Lukemeyer, Duncombe, and Yinger. In *Improving on No Child Left Behind*, R. D. Kahlenberg (ed.), The Century Foundation, 2008.

4.5. *Allocative vs. Productive Efficiency*

- Note that we have defined two different efficiency concepts:
  - ○ **Allocative efficiency** = whether goods and services are allocated to the people who value them most.
  - ○ **Productive efficiency** = whether goods and services are produced using best practices.
- *You can improve public welfare by boosting either type of efficiency!*

Public Sector Costs: Policy

- **Class Outline**
  1. **Baumol's Disease**
  2. **Boosting Productive Efficiency**
  3. **Competition and Costs**

1. Baumol's Disease

- Today we will discuss ways to promote productive efficiency in the public sector.
- Before turning to this topic, however, we will gain some perspective on it by discussing something called *"Baumol's Disease."*
  - This is a misnomer — it's not really such a bad thing!

1.1. *Baumol's Assumptions*

- In 1967, an economist named Baumol (my micro professor) analyzed a two-sector economy.
- His model has **four** key assumptions:
  - One sector has productivity gains, the other does not.
  - The labor market is competitive, so the wage in each sector must equal MRP (also called VMP).
  - Labor is mobile between sectors.
  - The demand for goods in the unproductive sector is inelastic (as estimated for local governments!).

1.2. *Baumol's Conclusions*

- Wages rise with labor productivity in the productive sector.
- But also must rise in the unproductive sector because of labor mobility.
- This leads to some startling conclusions:
  - The relative cost of goods in the unproductive sector steadily rises.
  - Employment steadily shifts into the unproductive sector.

1.3. *Mobility between Sectors*

- First, what happens in the labor market when productivity rises [MRP = $(P_Q)(MP_L)$]:

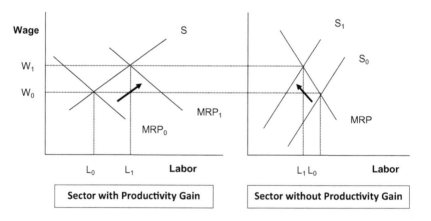

1.4. *Responses to Price Increases*

- Second, consider what happens in **product markets** when labor costs rise:

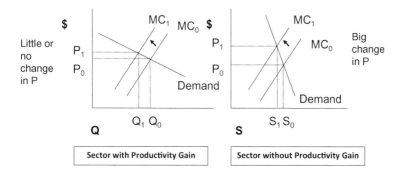

Sector with Productivity Gain   Sector without Productivity Gain

1.5. *Net Impacts in Labor Markets*

- Third, go back to **labor markets** to consider price increases
  $[\mathrm{MRP} = (\mathrm{P_Q})(\mathrm{MP_L})]$:

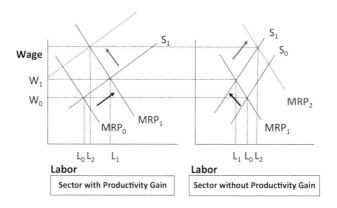

Sector with Productivity Gain   Sector without Productivity Gain

1.6. *Leviathan or Baumol's Disease?*

- Spending and employment in state and local government have been steadily rising for decades.
- Some commentators say this is evidence of **leviathan** — of increasing inefficiency by bureaucrats.
- Their policy prescription is to boost accountability programs and privatization.
- But a more likely explanation is that these trends reflect "Baumol's Disease",
  - Which is nothing more than an inter-sector shift as productivity gains make a society richer.
- In this view, the cost of the public sector does increase over time, but this trend just preserves levels of local public services — and we can afford it!

1.7. *Other Examples of Baumol's Disease*

- Baumol's disease does not apply only to public services.
- Several scholars have applied it to the arts:
  - Technology cannot replace the actors in one of Shakespeare's plays.
- A column in the *New York Times* applies it to higher education:
  - Mankiw, "Three Reasons for those Hefty College Bills" http://www.nytimes.com/2015/12/20/upshot/three-reasons-for-tho se-hefty-college-tuition-bills.html?hpw&rref=upshot&action=c lick&pgtype=Homepage&module=well-region&region=bottom -well&WT.nav=bottom-well&_r=0.

2. Boosting Productive Efficiency

- Regardless of the role played by "Baumol's Disease," productive efficiency is a good thing.
- So how can public officials lower costs and hence cut taxes (or raise service quality without raising costs)?

- The answer:
  - Observe
  - Experiment
  - Evaluate!

2.1. *Step 1: Use Your Judgment*

- Formal evaluation of programs or management reforms are usually not available.
- Thus, it is appropriate for you (when you become public officials!) to **use your own judgment:**
  - to select programs and reforms that appear to have worked in other places;
  - to design new programs and reforms.

2.2. *Step 2: Use Evaluation Studies and Principles*

- But evaluation should always be in the back of your mind.
  - Search for evaluations of the programs or reforms you are interested in.
  - Make an honest judgment about the quality of existing evaluations.
  - Informally apply basic evaluation principles to programs and reforms you are considering.
  - Implement formal evaluations whenever possible!

2.3. *Further Reading*

- For more on evidence-based policy making, see:
  - Commission on Evidence-Based Policy Making, "The Promise of Evidence-based Policy Making." https://www.cep.gov/conte nt/dam/cep/report/cep-final-report.pdf.
  - Sara Dube and Darcy White, "Key Findings from 50-State Assessment of Evidence-Based Policy Making." http://www. routefifty.com/2017/01/key-findings-50-state-assessment-evid ence-based-policymaking/135042/?oref=rf-home-latest-top.

o Gordon Berlin, "Comments to the Commission on Evidence-Based Policymaking." https://www.mdrc.org/sites/default/file s/CEP_comments_MDRC_111416.pdf.

2.4. The With–Without Principle

- What is the basic problem facing someone wanting to evaluate any public program?
  - o What you want is to know how one place differs with and without the program.
  - o What you observe is either (a) what the world is like after and before the program or (b) what one place is like with the program and another is without it.
  - o Thus, you cannot be sure that the effects you observe are not due to non-program differences over time or across places.

2.5. Approaches to Program Evaluation

- The two ways to solve this problem are:
  - o Random assignment;
  - o Statistical control.
- Random assignment insures that differences across time and place are not correlated with participation in the program.
- Statistical controls can account for observable (and some unobservable!) differences across place or time.

2.5.1. Random assignment

- Random assignment is the preferred method in most cases.
  - o It provides results that are intuitively compelling and scientifically sound.
  - o If you believe in cutting costs, become an advocate for evaluation using random assignment!
  - o However, results from a random assignment study may not apply to different circumstances.
    - o A random-assignment finding that lower class size boosts student performance (holding teacher quality constant) does

not imply that student performance will improve if low-quality teachers are hired to bring class sizes down.

2.5.1.1. Random Assignment Examples

- Random assignment has been used to study (among other things):
  - Welfare-to-work programs;
  - Unemployment insurance;
  - Job training;
  - Income maintenance;
  - Housing assistance;
  - Electricity pricing;
  - Education (e.g. Charter Schools);
  - Early childhood development;
  - Criminal justice policy;
  - Child health and nutrition.

2.5.2. *Statistical control*

- Random assignment is not always feasible.
- The best statistical studies:
  - Must have extensive data to ensure that differences aren't due to unobservable factors.
  - Must have comparable treatment and control groups based on observable factors, which often requires new "matching" methods.
  - May have multiple observations over time so they can "difference out" unobservable factors.
- High quality research designs include:
  - **Difference in differences**: Is the change over time in a key outcome greater in the treated location than in a comparable location where the program was not implemented.
  - **Regression discontinuity**: Were outcomes significantly different for people who were just above an eligibility cut-off (and hence participated in the program) than for those who were just below the cut-off (and hence did not get in).

3. Competition and Costs

- You all learned in micro-economics how private prices are driven down by competition.
- With some important qualifications, the same lesson applies in the public sector.
- Three issues are particularly important.

3.1. *Provision vs. Production*

Issue 1: The distinction between provision and production

- Each unit of government is legally obligated to provide certain services, i.e. to ensure that these services are available.
- In many cases, however, the unit of government responsible for provision does not actually have to produce the service itself.

3.1.1. *Production examples*

- Production Arrangements Include:
  - Contracting out to a private firm.
  - Contracting out to another government agency.
  - Outsourcing, i.e. purchasing from a private company.
  - Use of vouchers to finance private production.
  - Intergovernmental cooperation (to gain economies of scale).

3.2. *Competition vs. Privatization*

Issue 2: The distinction between competition and privatization

- Competition generates incentives to cut costs so as to maintain business, funding, or reputation.
- Privatization substitutes private incentives (profit) for public incentives (public service).
- They do not necessarily go together.

3.2.1. *Alternatives to public delivery by one agency*

- Consider the following ways to move away from delivery by a single public agency:

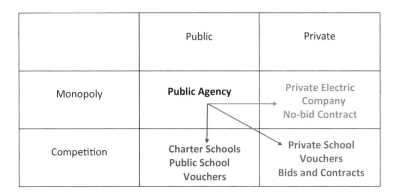

3.2.2. *The benefits and costs of privatization*

- Although competition is likely to cut costs, the impact of privatization on costs is not so clear:
  - Private firms are probably more likely to innovate because it boosts their profits.
  - But private firms are also more likely to cut corners or to neglect social concerns — if their contract allows — in order to boost profits.

3.3. *Defining Performance*

Issue 3: The Need for a Clear Definition of Performance

- The key to harnessing competition and private firms' desire for profits is to write a contract that:
  - Specifies performance standards.
  - Provides clear incentives to meet those standards.

3.3.1. *The requirements for successful privatization*

- Contracting out to private firms can work well if:
  - The relevant market is competitive and bidding is possible.
  - The performance objectives can be clearly specified in the contract.
  - A firm's performance can be monitored.
  - Financial rewards and/or penalties can be written into the contract, too.

3.3.2. *Incomplete contracts*

- The 2016 Nobel prize in economics was awarded to Oliver Hart (my graduate school classmate!) for his work on contracts.
- A key concept in his work is the notion of incomplete contracts.

  - If the contract cannot be fully specified, particularly with respect to the quality of service, then it matters who controls decisions that impact production costs.
  - If the government is the provider contracting with a private producer, then the government can approve or deny a money-saving policy, based on its impact on service quality.
  - With privatization, the firm has the control rights and can implement money-saving policies even if they damage service quality (at least service quality that is not completely specified in the contract).
  - Hart and his co-authors argue, for example, that privatization is not a good idea for prisons because contracts are inevitably incomplete.

3.4. *Additional Problems*

3.4.1. *Big problem number 1: Documenting cost savings*

- Cost savings are almost impossible to document.
- Cost savings only exist when full costs are lower, **holding performance constant**.
  - But many costs are hidden.

o And performance usually cannot be measured.

- *Beware of cost-savings claims!*

3.4.2. *Big problem number 2: The role of politics*

- Contracting to private firms often yields political benefits (i.e., campaign contributions from the firms in the industry) even when it does not boost efficiency.
- In the case of services with well-funded lobbying activities and/or voiceless beneficiaries, contracting is likely to go too far.
- *Be careful with this tool!*

3.4.3. *Big problem number 3: Loss of sovereignty*

- Politicians desperate for short-term savings may go too far.
  o "First, 'compensation event' clauses require the government to pay the contractor when certain triggering events occur, such as an emergency road closure.
  o Second, non-compete clauses prevent the government from building or repairing competing infrastructure.
  o Third, adverse action clauses allow the contractor to retain the right to object to government decisions that affect the profitability of the contract."
  o *Source*: Matthew Titolo, "Leasing Sovereignty: On State Infrastructure Contracts," *University of Richmond Law Review*, 2013, pp. 631–693. http://lawreview.richmond.edu/wp/wp-content/uploads/2013/01/Titolo-472.pdf.

3.5. *Further Reading*

- A Nice Overview:
  o http://www.nytimes.com/2013/01/16/business/when-privatization-works-and-why-it-doesnt-always.html?_r=0.
- Examples of Privatization that Went Wrong.

- Private Prisons: https://www.nytimes.com/2018/04/10/us/private-prisons-escapes-riots.html?hp&action=click&pgtype=Homepage&clickSource=story-heading&module=first-column-region&region=top-news&WT.nav=top-news http://www.thenation.com/article/end-abuse-in-our-privatized-immigrant-only-prisons/.
- Private Highway: http://www.washingtonpost.com/local/trafficandcommuting/how-virginia-paid-more-than-250-million-for-a-road-that-never-got-built/2015/05/30/39a1a222-062d-11e5-a428-c984eb077d4e_story.html?tid=hpModule_13097a0c-868e-11e2-9d71-f0feafdd1394&hpid=z12.

Lecture 6

Local Public Revenue

- **Class Outline**
  1. **Tax Policy Principles**
  2. **Tax Equity**
  3. **Allocative Efficiency**
  4. **Introduction to the Property Tax**

1. Tax Policy Principles

- When deciding on the best taxes to use, you should think about which tax (or set of taxes) is:
  - Fairest;
  - Least distortionary;
  - Able to raise sufficient revenue;
  - Least costly to administer;
  - Most transparent.

- Here we focus on the first two principles.

2. Tax Equity

- Any analysis of tax equity must address two questions, one positive and one normative.

- The positive question: Who pays the tax?
- The normative question: Is the distribution of the tax burden fair?

2.1. *Tax Incidence*

- The **positive** analysis of tax equity must begin with a distinction between legal and economic incidence:

  o **Legal incidence**: Who is responsible for writing the tax checks to the government?
  o **Economic incidence**: Whose real income is diminished because of the tax?

- *Legal and economic incidence need not be the same!*

2.2. *Measuring Economic Incidence*

- A tax alters real incomes by changing market prices — and hence consumers' opportunities.
- The following figures examine tax incidence with a variety of assumptions about the shapes of supply and demand curves.
- These figures examine a tax in a single market with the legal incidence on suppliers. Other cases are considered below.

2.2.1. *Taxed vs. untaxed goods*

Important Note:

- The following pictures show the market for taxed goods.
- In the background, there is a market for untaxed goods.
- If all markets were taxed, the agents bearing the legal incidence could not shift the tax to anyone else.

2.2.2. *Case 1: Shifting to consumers*

- In some cases, the tax burden falls entirely on **consumers**, who pay the tax in the form of a higher price:

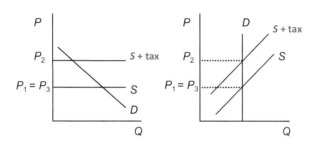

2.2.3. *Case 2: No shifting to consumers*

- In some cases, the tax burden falls entirely on **firms**, because the price does not change:

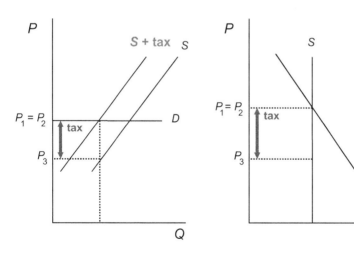

2.2.4. *Case 3: Shared incidence*

- In other cases, the burden is **shared**:

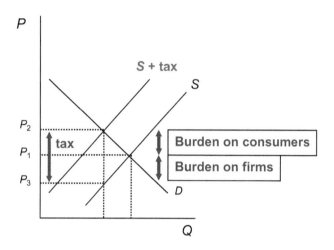

2.2.5. *What determines incidence?*

- Incidence is determined by **responsiveness** (= price elasticity).
- Economic actors are responsive to price if they have good alternatives.
- The side of the market with better alternatives escapes more of the tax.
- If one side of the market has poor alternatives, it cannot escape the tax.

2.2.6. *The irrelevance of legal incidence*

- Two further points about incidence.
- *First*: Legal incidence does not affect economic incidence.
  - ○ Economic incidence is determined by supply and demand curves, not by institutions.
  - ○ Legal incidence should be selected on administrative grounds (not based on misperceptions about economic incidence!).

- This result can be seen by comparing both forms of legal incidence:

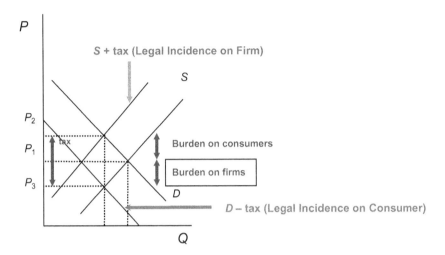

- Second, be careful: these figures only compare **taxed** and **untaxed** **markets.**

  o They show the incidence of a tax on Beer A if other brands of beer are not taxed.
  o They show the incidence of a tax on beer of other forms of alcohol are not taxed.
  o They show the incidence of a tax on alcohol if non-alcoholic beverages are not taxed.

2.3. *Distributional Impact*

- The final step in positive analysis of tax equity is to translate the above incidence analysis into a **distributional impact**.

  o The supply side may represent rich (corporations) or poor (low-wage craftspeople).
  o The demand side may represent poor (buyers of necessities) or rich (buyers of fine crafts).

2.3.1. *Progressive vs. regressive taxes*

- The end result is a distribution of tax burden by income.
- As shown in the figure, this distribution can be proportional, progressive, or regressive.

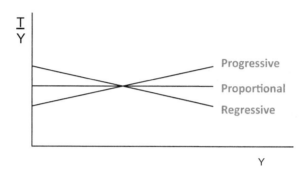

2.4. *Principles of Tax Fairness*

- To compare the fairness of different taxes, incidence analysis must be combined with a value judgment.
- Most people rely on one or both of two well-known principles:
  - **The Ability to Pay Principle**: People with higher incomes should pay a larger share of their income in taxes.
  - **The Benefit Principle**: People who receive more benefits from the public services funded by a tax should pay more in taxes.

2.4.1. *The ability to pay principle*

- The ability to pay principle is linked to the notions of progressivity and regressivity.
- A strong version of this principle calls for a highly progressive tax.
- A regressive tax is not consistent with this principle.
  - If your believe in this principle, therefore, you should not pick such a tax unless it has advantages over progressive alternatives.
- This principle is not incompatible with the benefit principle.

2.4.2. *The benefit principle*

- The benefit principle leads to the taxation of a group of beneficiaries.
  - ○ Some people want to go farther and make tax payments proportional to benefits.
  - ○ But this is impossible because an individual's benefit from a public service cannot be measured.
- The benefit principle is often used as a justification for **earmarking**, such as the use of the gasoline tax for road maintenance and repair.
- The benefit principle provides an argument for taxing suburban commuters, who benefit from city services but do not pay city income or property taxes.

3. Allocative Efficiency

- Taxes **distort** economic decisions because they lead people to make choices based on taxes instead of just on real resource costs.
- All else equal, the best tax is more neutral, i.e. less distortionary.
- Scholars measure tax distortions with a concept called **excess burden**, which is lost consumer surplus.

3.1. *Excess Burden*

Figure "The Excess Burden from a Tax" shows the excess burden from a tax.

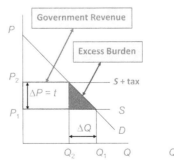

The Excess Burden from a Tax.

3.2. Tax Revenue and Efficiency

- **Tax revenue** $(= tQ_2)$ represents the choice to provide something through the public sector, not a distortion of private choices by a particular tax.
- In this context, we need to raise the same revenue regardless of which tax we select, so we want the tax with the lowest excess burden, all else equal.
- Selecting the right level of public services is a separate issue, not considered here.

3.3. Determinants of Excess Burden

- **Excess burden (EB)** is the shaded triangle.
  - The formula for a triangle yields following formula for EB, where t is the tax rate and e is the price elasticity of demand for Q.

$$\text{EB} = \left(\frac{1}{2}\right) \Delta P \Delta Q$$

$$= \left(\frac{1}{2}\right) (t^2) \, |e| \, (P_1 Q_1)$$

3.3.1. Excess burden and the tax rate

- Doubling the tax rate quadruples the number of EB triangles

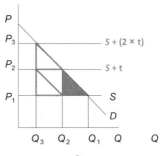

Why Does t^2 Matter?

3.3.2. *Excess burden and the price elasticity of demand*

- Why excess burden increases with the absolute value of the demand elasticity.

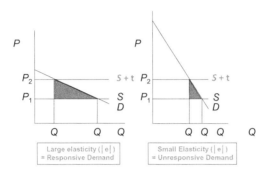

3.4. *Policy Implications*

- Because excess burden increases with the square of the tax rate, a balanced tax system is less distortionary than one relying on a single tax.
- All else equal, taxes on unresponsive tax bases are less distortionary (but not necessarily more fair!) than taxes on responsive tax bases.

  ○ For example, consider a tax on medicine.

4. Introduction to the Property Tax

- The property tax is a tax on the **market value** of property.

  ○ It applies to real estate, unless owned by a non-profit.
  ○ It sometimes applies to business equipment.
  ○ It occasionally applies to personal property.
- Market value is widely accepted as an objective, fair tax base.

4.1. *Implementation of the Property Tax*

- Two institutions are involved in implementing the property tax:
  - An assessor determines the **assessed value** of each property (A), i.e. the value for tax purposes.
  - Elected officials select the **nominal tax rate or "mill rate"** (m) to be applied to assessed value.
- The **tax payment** (T) is:

$$T_i = m\, A_i$$

4.2. *Assessment Methods*

- Depending on the available data, assessors use one of three methods to assess property, that is, to estimate a property's market value:
  - The market value method, which uses information on the sales price of properties that sell to estimate the value of properties that did not sell — an application of regression analysis!
  - The cost method, which estimates market value based on the cost of reproducing a building, minus depreciation.
  - The income method, which estimates value based on the present value of the flow of net income from a property.
- See: https://www.tax.ny.gov/research/property/reports/cod/2013mvs/index.htm.

4.2.1. *Accounting for assessment practices*

- Assessing practices and assessing accuracy vary across jurisdictions and even across property within a jurisdiction.
- Because market value is the intended tax base, a comparison of tax rates across houses must be based on an **effective tax rate** (t), not the nominal rate (m):

$$t_i \equiv \frac{T_i}{V_i} = \frac{m\, A_i}{V_i} = m\left(\frac{A_i}{V_i}\right)$$

4.2.2. *Measuring assessment quality*

- Assessment quality is measured by variation in the assessment-sales ratio, A/V, within a jurisdiction.
- Assessing has become more professional (and more data driven) over time, and the quality if assessments has gradually improved.
- The following chart shows improvement in NY State, where assessments are not very regulated.

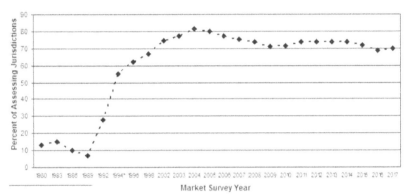

* In measuring assessment equity for 1994 and subsequent survey years, acceptable levels of the coefficient of dispersion (COD) statistic were increased for the more rural assessing units. Recent reassessment programs that were reviewed and verified for the 1996 and subsequent surveys were deemed uniform.

Assessment Quality in New York State.
Source: NY State Dept. of Taxation and Finance, *Assessment Equity in New York: Results from the 2017 Market Value Survey*. https://www.tax.ny.gov/research/property/reports/cod/2017mvs/index.htm.

4.3. *Comparing Property Tax Rates across Jurisdictions*

- Suppose the **nominal tax rates** are the same in two communities, but the **assessment/sales ratio** equals 0.5 on one community and 1.0 in the other.
- Then the **effective tax rate** is only half as large in the first community (since it effectively applies to only half of property value).

4.4. *Comparing Property Tax Rates Within a Jurisdiction*

- Suppose two houses have the same market value but one is assessed at twice the value of the other.
- Then the first house has an effective tax rate that is twice as high.
- *Poor assessments lead to unfair variation in effective taxes within the same jurisdiction!*

4.5. *Classification*

- Some local governments are given the authority to charge different nominal (and hence different effective) tax rates for different types of property.
- Typically, this "classification" option leads to a higher rate for commercial and industrial property than for residential property.
- This type of classification works against standard economic-development arguments, which call for lower taxes on business. We will return to this topic in a later class.

Lecture 7

Property Tax Capitalization

- **Class Outline**
  1. **Tiebout and Oates**
  2. **What is Property Tax Capitalization?**
  3. **How Does Tax Capitalization Arise?**
  4. **Property Tax Capitalization and Public Policy**

1. Tiebout and Oates

- In 1969, an economist named Oates (my public finance professor) tested Tiebout's positive hypothesis that people care about services in their community (*JPE*, 1969).
- Tiebout's hypothesis implies, said Oates, that better public services and lower property taxes will lead to higher property values.
- This phenomenon is known as *capitalization*.
- Using data for suburbs in New Jersey, Oates found evidence of capitalization — and inspired a huge literature.

2. What is Property Tax Capitalization?

- This class explains property tax capitalization and discusses its policy implications.

- A more detailed discussion of property tax capitalization is available in

  o Yinger, J. "Property Tax Capitalization," Chapter 14 in *Housing and Commuting: The Theory of Urban Residential Structure* (World Scientific, 2018).

2.1. *Asset Pricing*

- The value of an asset equals the present value of the expected net benefits from owning it.
- Without property taxes, the amount someone is willing to pay for a house is the expected present value of the rental benefits, or

$$V = \sum_{y=1}^{L} \frac{PH}{(1+r)^y} = \frac{PH}{(1+r)} + \frac{PH}{(1+r)^2} + \cdots + \frac{PH}{(1+r)^L}$$

where P is the pre-tax price of housing services, H is housing services, r is the real discount rate, and L is the expected lifetime of a house.

2.1.1. *The pricing of a long-lived asset*

- If the expected real value of rental services is constant over time and L is large, this equation reduces to:

$$V = \frac{PH}{r}$$

- The value of a house equals its expected annual rental value divided by a discount rate.
- Because housing lasts a long time, this is a reasonable — and obviously helpful — simplification.

2.2. *Property Taxes*

- A property tax payment, T, is the product of a nominal tax rate, m, and an assessed value, A.
- It is also the product of an effective tax rate, t, and a market value, V.

- In symbols

$$T = mA = tV$$

- Property taxes represent an annual expense for a homeowner.

2.2.1. *House values with property taxes*

- Adding property taxes as an expense, the house value equation becomes:

$$V = \sum_{y=1}^{L} \frac{PH}{(1+r)^y} - \sum_{y=1}^{L} \frac{tV}{(1+r)^y}$$
$$= \frac{PH}{r} - \frac{tV}{r}$$

- Note that property taxes are added as a *flow* because they must be paid every year.

2.3. *What is Capitalization?*

- Now you can see the source of the term *"capitalization."*
- The annual *flow* of property tax payments shows up in a *"capital"* or *asset value*, namely V, using the logic of discounting.
- The denominator in an asset pricing expression, r here, is often called the *capitalization rate*.

2.4. *The Degree of Property Tax Capitalization*

- This equation assumes that property taxes are fully capitalized.
  - As we will see, this might not be the case, so a more general form is:

$$V = \sum_{y=1}^{L} \frac{PH}{(1+r)^y} - \sum_{y=1}^{L} \frac{\beta tV}{(1+r)^y}$$
$$= \frac{PH}{r} - \frac{\beta tV}{r}$$

where β is the "degree of property tax capitalization;" i.e., the impact of a \$1 increase in the present value of property taxes on the value of a house.

2.4.1. *Interpreting β*

- A value of β equal to 1.0 corresponds to *full capitalization.*
- A value of β equal to 0.0 corresponds to *no capitalization.*
- If β equals 0.5 a \$1 increase in the present value of property taxes leads to a \$0.50 decrease in the value of a house.
- The value of β need not be the same under all circumstances.

2.5. *The Capitalization Equation*

- Solving the above for V yields the final capitalization equation:

$$V = \frac{PH}{r + \beta t}$$

- Thus, houses with higher effective property tax rates (t) will have lower values (V).
- The strength of this relationship depends on β.

2.5.1. *A change form for the capitalization equation*

- One can also derive a change form of the capitalization equation:

$$\frac{\Delta V}{V_1} = \frac{-\beta \Delta t}{r + \beta t_2}$$

where Δ stands for change and 1 and 2 indicate time periods.
- Thus, an increase in $\boldsymbol{t}$ (relative to other houses) will result in a decrease in $\boldsymbol{V}$.

2.5.2. *Sources of variation in $\boldsymbol{t}$*

- These equations apply *within* a community.
  - *Poor assessments* result in higher assessment-sales ratios, and hence higher effective tax rates, for some houses than for others.

- These equations also apply *across* communities, which may have very different effective tax rates due, for example, to differences in commercial and industrial property.

3. How Does Tax Capitalization Arise?

- Real estate brokers indicate anticipated property tax payments so buyers can make comparisons across houses.
- Lenders require mortgage plus tax payments to equal a fixed percentage of an applicant's income.
  - An increase in T must be offset by a drop in the mortgage, and hence a drop in how much the applicant can pay for the house, V.

3.1. Evidence on Property Tax Capitalization

- Every reasonable study of property tax capitalization finds a statistically significant negative impact of property taxes on house values.
- Estimates of β vary from 15 to 100%.
- The main reason for this variation appears to involve *expectations*.

3.1.1. The role of expectations

- So far, current tax differences across houses are implicitly assumed to persist indefinitely.
- But if tax differences are not expected to persist, the capitalization of *current* differences, β, declines.
  - A difference observed today that will disappear upon sale has no impact on V.
  - A difference observed today that is expected to last one year will have only a small impact on sales price.

3.2. The Case of Massachusetts

- In Massachusetts, revaluations were required by the state supreme court, but enforcement was weak.

○ Communities knew they could avoid revaluation for many years.

○ Existing tax differences were expected to persist, but not forever.

- A study of capitalization in Massachusetts (by myself and three other scholars) found that current tax differences were capitalized at a rate of 32% (Yinger *et al.*, *Prop. Taxes and House Values*, 1988).

- This is consistent with the expectation that current tax differences would disappear in 13 years.

3.3. *The Case of Syracuse*

- In Syracuse in the early 1990s, revaluation had not occurred for decades and did not appear likely to happen any time soon.
- But the city council unexpectedly decided to revalue.
- A study of capitalization in Syracuse by Eisenberg (in his PA Ph.D. dissertation) found capitalization rates near 100% — exactly what the theory predicts when tax differences are expected to persist.

3.4. *The Capitalization Trap*

- If property taxes are fully capitalized, then any tax changes show up in house values immediately and there is no way to escape them.

○ An owner with a tax increase must either stay and pay the higher tax or leave and suffer a capital loss.

○ An owner with a tax cut gets a capital gain.

- Moreover, the loss is the full present value of the future increases in taxes.

4. Property Tax Capitalization and Public Policy

- Because of these gains and losses, tax capitalization has bizarre implications for public policy.
- Consider revaluation, which is a systematic revision of all assessed values.

- Revaluation leads to capital gains for homeowners who were over-assessed and to capital losses for homeowners who were under-assessed.

4.1. *Capitalization and Fairness*

- For long-term residents, these changes are fair.
  - A resident who has been under-assessed for a long time has been given, in effect, a loan from the city and revaluation just claims back this "loan."
- But for new residents, these changes are not fair.
  - If someone bought an under-assessed house one day and the change is announced the next, this person has a capital loss even though she did not benefit from the poor assessment system.

4.2. *Minimizing the Impact of Capitalization*

- Two ways to minimize this fairness problem:
  - First, introduce a long *lag* between announcement and implementation. This lag allows owners at the time of announcement to escape some of the burden of the tax changes.
  - Second, make sure houses are *revalued upon re-sale*, which they were not in Massachusetts or Syracuse.

4.3. *The Case for Regular Assessments*

- So a revaluation imposes some unfair gains and losses but restores fairness in the near term and boosts faith in local government.
  - This trade only makes sense if assessments are updated regularly.
  - Otherwise, gains and losses are handed out each year as assessment errors mount.
- Poor assessments also lead to court cases, which the city usually loses.
  - People who buy over-assessed property pay low prices — and then can sue the city for a rebate because of unfairly high taxes.

- o This happened in Boston, to the tune of tens of millions of dollars.
- o The only way to avoid this crazy situation is to keep assessments up to date!

4.4. *Proposition 13*

- *Proposition 13* in California represents another unusual case.
  - o The proposition fixes assessment growth at 2%, so the assessment/sales ratio, and hence t, declines over time for long-term owners.
  - o This cannot be turned into a capital gain because houses are revalued upon sale.
  - o But it represents a gift to long-term owners and it discourages mobility.
  - o The U.S. Supreme Court said this was legal. Voters in California and a few other states like this reward to long-term residents; I don't.

4.5. *Looking Ahead*

- Property tax capitalization is a critical issue in economic development policy.
- If property tax breaks are capitalized into the price of business property, then owners of this property at the time a tax break is announced may receive all the benefits even if they do not change their behavior,
- And future owners (exactly the people the policy is intended to attract) may receive no benefits at all.

Lecture 8

Property Tax Incidence

- **Class Outline**
  1. **Four Approaches to Property Tax Incidence**
  2. **Property Tax Incidence and Public Policy**

1. Four Approaches to Property Tax Incidence

1.1. *Property Tax Incidence: Approach 1*

- The first approach to property tax incidence is to ask:
  - Who bears the burden of a nationwide property tax (or, equivalently) of the average property tax rate?
- The standard answer to this question, often called the "New View," is that the property tax falls on the owners of real estate, including residential, commercial, and industrial property.
  - Because property ownership is concentrated among high income households, this answer implies that the property tax is **progressive**.

1.1.1. *Approach 1: The new view*

- In contrast to traditional analysis, the **New View** is based on a general equilibrium analysis of all markets.

- A property owner cannot escape a tax in one market if the same tax is levied everywhere.
- Since almost all property is taxed, property owners cannot escape the tax by turning to another type of property.
- The inability of property owners to shift the tax combined with the concentration of property ownership at high incomes leads to the conclusion that the property tax is progressive.

1.1.1.1. Approach 1: The National Market for Property

- Although it is often expressed in a mathematical model, the intuition of the **New View** is simply that the supply of property in the nation is fixed and taxes on property therefore cannot be shifted:

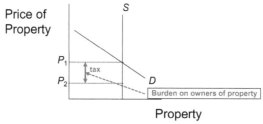

National Market for Property.

1.1.2. *Approach 1: The new new view*

- An amended new view (the **New New View**?) points out that the amount of property can change slowly over time due to construction, remodeling, and demolition.

  ○ Alternatively, some scholars argue that the property tax is roughly a tax on physical capital and the supply of physical capital can vary in the long run based on investment responses to the rate of return.

- This amendment implies that the New View may be too extreme but that most of the burden is still likely to fall on property owners.

○ Because changes in the amount of property are small relative to the stock of property, only a small share of the burden can be shifted to renters, consumers, and workers.

1.1.2.1. Approach 1: The Long-Run and the Short-Run

- The **New View** (S-R) and the **New New View** (L-R)

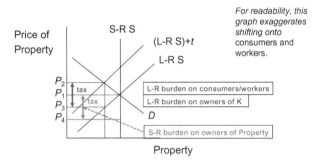

The New View in the Long Run.

1.2. *Approach 2: Focus on Owner-Occupied Housing*

- A second approach is to focus on the property tax on owner-occupied housing.
- Because most owner-occupied housing sales involve existing housing, the two parties to the transaction are both households.
  ○ It follows that households bear the burden of the tax.
  ○ And the question is: How does the property tax burden change as household income changes?

1.2.1. *Approach 2: Property taxes and rents*

- For owner-occupied housing, property tax incidence depends on the income elasticity of demand for housing.
  ○ To see why, note that the property tax burden is:

$$\frac{T}{Y} = \frac{tV}{Y} = \frac{t(R/r)}{Y} = \left(\frac{t}{r}\right)\left(\frac{R}{Y}\right)$$

where T is the property tax payment, t is the effective property tax rate, V is house value, R is the annual rental value of housing, r is a discount rate, and $V = R/r$.

1.2.2. *Approach 2: The income elasticity of demand for housing*

- Holding t/r constant at the national average, this formula implies that the change in T/Y depends on the change in R/Y, which is measured by the income elasticity of demand for housing (θ):

$$\text{income elasticity} = \theta = \frac{\Delta(R)/R}{\Delta Y/Y}$$

- These formulas imply that the change the average tax rate, T/Y, in percentage terms is

$$\left(\frac{\Delta(T/Y)/(T/Y)}{\Delta Y/Y} \right) = \theta - 1$$

1.2.3. *Approach 2: Progressive or regressive?*

- This result implies that

  ○ T/Y increases with income if $\theta > 1$;
  ○ T/Y is the same at all incomes if $\theta = 1$;
  ○ T/Y decreases with income if $\theta < 1$.

- There is a strong consensus that $\theta < 1$, so T/Y decreases with income and this portion of the tax is *regressive.*
- This analysis helps to explain why, as we will discuss later in the class, so many states have programs to lower property tax rates for lower-valued houses.

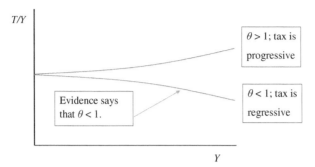

The Income Elasticity of Demand for Housing, θ, and the Progressivity of the Property Tax on Owner-occupied Housing.

1.2.4. *Approach 2: Variation in property taxes across jurisdictions*

- The property tax on owner-occupied housing is even more regressive when variation in tax bases across jurisdictions is considered.
- Some jurisdictions have high property values per household, while others do not.

  - Hence, some jurisdictions can obtain any given amount of revenue at a much smaller burden on their homeowners than can other jurisdictions.
  - These disparities are offset to some degree by state aid to local governments, which is considered in later classes.

- Suppose school districts are expected to raise half of the state-wide average revenue for K-12 schools.

  - In New York State this amount is $9,443 per pupil (2014–2015 school year, without NYC). (Source: NY State Education Department.)

- Property value pupil in New York State is $182,948 in the least wealthy decile of districts and $1,491,480 in the wealthiest.

    ◦ As a result, the least wealthy districts would have to pay a property tax rate of 5.2% to reach this spending target, but the wealthiest districts would only need a rate of 0.6%.

    ◦ This is obviously a very regressive outcome, but it may be offset to some degree by state aid formulas that give more aid to lower-wealth districts.

1.3. *Approach 3: Property Tax Incidence with Capitalization*

- A third approach to property tax incidence is to consider the role of property tax capitalization.
- This capitalization shifts the focus to property owners at the time a tax increase (or decrease) is passed.

    ◦ Owners at that time cannot escape the tax change.

    ◦ If they stay in their house, they pay the tax change directly, and if they sell their house, they pay the tax change in the form of a capital gain or loss.

    ◦ If they move, the people who buy their house do not bear any of the burden of the property tax increase because the tax change is offset by a change in sales price.

- According to this approach, therefore, the burden of any property tax change falls on the owners of property at the time of the change in the jurisdiction where the change took place.
- Capitalization arguments are often ignored.

    ◦ The implications of this approach are quite counter-intuitive.

    ◦ And the affected groups (e.g. homeowners at time t) may be quite similar to the unaffected groups (e.g. homeowners who buy a house after time t).

- Nevertheless the logic of this view and the evidence supporting it are quite strong.

    ◦ Recall the strong evidence for property tax capitalization.

1.4. *Approach 4: The Property Tax as a Benefit Tax*

- A final approach to property tax incidence is the *Benefit View.*
  - According to this view, the property tax is simply the price a household pays to live in a community.
  - Households live where this price equals their benefits from the public services, so the property tax is fair according to the benefit principle.
  - In this context, the property tax is called a "benefit tax."

1.4.1. *Approach 4: Mixing positive and normative*

- This argument incorrectly mixes positive analysis (the property tax equals a household's benefits from the services it funds) with a normative principle (the benefit principle).
  - A finding that the property tax is a benefit tax does not make the benefit principle any more or less compelling.
  - One could agree that the property tax is a benefit tax and still reject the benefit principle as an appropriate fairness standard.
  - One could conclude that the property tax is not a benefit tax, but still believe that the benefit principle is appropriate for judging the fairness of the tax.

1.4.2. *Approach 4: Evidence*

- The Benefit View implies that the value of public services will not be capitalized into the price of housing.
  - If households all select their optimal community, they have no reason to bid up the price of housing anywhere else.
- The extensive evidence of public service capitalization (discussed in an earlier class) therefore leads to a clear, unambiguous rejection of the Benefit View.

2. Property Tax Incidence and Public Policy

2.1. *Issue 1: When to Consider Capitalization*

- The equity of tax provisions that have been in place a long time should be evaluated based on their progressivity or regressivity; gains and losses to property owners are not relevant.
- The equity of new tax provisions that are intended to be in place for a long time (e.g. a new property tax or income tax) should be evaluated primarily on the basis of their progressivity or regressivity, but gains or losses to specific groups are worth noting.
- The equity of short-term tax provisions (e.g. revaluation followed by fixed assessments) should be evaluated on the basis of gains and losses to current property owners.

2.2. *Issue 2: Application to Economic Development*

- One important application of capitalization is to economic development.
  - ○ With full capitalization, lower property tax rates lead to higher property values and hence to no net advantage in attracting business for a low-tax jurisdiction.
- This argument helps to explain why scholars have not found consistent evidence to support the view that property tax rates affect economic development and why some careful studies do not find any such impact at all.
  - ○ We will return to these issues in a later class.

2.3. *Issue 3: Moderating Regressivity*

- All views of property tax incidence say that taxes on homeowners are regressive.
- Voters want programs to cut this regressivity, which applies to the component of the property tax that is of greatest concern to voters.

○ Voters are particularly concerned about *elderly* homeowners and *veterans*.

2.4. Graduated Property Tax Rates

• Graduated property tax rates are possible (e.g. Minnesota) but do not make sense for nonresidential property.

  ○ The issue is regressivity across people, not across businesses.
  ○ A business with a small factory may be owned by a very rich person!

• So states turn to homestead exemptions and circuit breakers instead.

2.4.1. *Homestead exemptions*

• **Design**
  ○ The formula, where X is the exemption, is:

$$T = t(V - X)$$

  ○ These exemptions may or may not lead to reimbursement by the state.
  ○ In New York's STAR program, X is higher in counties with expensive houses, which undermines both equity and efficiency, as it rewards (mostly wealthy) homeowners who move to high-cost locations.

• The tax rate is zero below $V = X(\$40,000)$ and moves toward t^* (the legislated rate = 2%) as V increases.

• An exemption also cuts regressivity of the property tax relative to income.

2.4.1.1. Popularity of Exemptions

• Almost all states have some form of homestead exemption.
• Most states have *special exemptions*, usually for the elderly or veterans.
• Several states have *general exemptions*.
• A few states *reimburse* local governments for the exemptions.
• For details, go to http://www.lincolninst.edu.

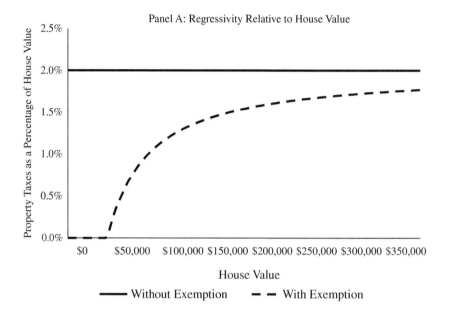

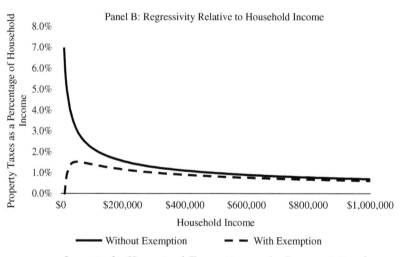

Impact of a Homestead Exemption on the Progressivity of
the Property Tax.

2.4.1.2. Strengths and Weaknesses of Exemptions

- **Strengths**
  - o Homestead exemptions cut the regressivity of the property tax on homeowners.
- **Weaknesses**
  - o Reimbursed homestead exemptions lower tax prices and encourage property tax rate increases.
  - o Homestead exemptions cannot be given to renters without an assumption about the (unknown) extent to which landlords shift the property tax onto renters.

2.4.2. *Circuit breakers*

- A *circuit breaker* provides a tax break (usually through an income tax rebate) if a person's property tax payment exceeds a given share of their income, Y.
- Design:

$$\text{CB} = \alpha(tV - \beta Y) \quad \text{if } (tV - \beta Y) > 0$$
$$\text{CB} = 0 \qquad\qquad\quad\; \text{if } (tV - \beta Y) \leq 0$$

  with a typical $\alpha = 0.5$ and a typical $\beta = 0.035$.
- This equation (and the following figures) describe a "single-threshold" circuit breaker.
- Some states use a "multiple-threshold" circuit breaker instead, which means that β is higher for lower-income households.
- Another design in some states is called a "sliding-scale" circuit breaker. It sets β equal to zero and sets higher values of α for lower-income households.
- A CB has a progressive element (rebates start at lower house values for lower-income households) and a regressive element (at any given income level, relief increases with house value).
- A circuit breaker also eliminates regressivity with respect to income — up to a point.
- But a circuit breaker also unfairly rewards people who buy an expensive house relative to their income (fixed at \$75,000 in the

Figure "Impact of a Circuit Breaker on the Progressivity of the Property Tax").

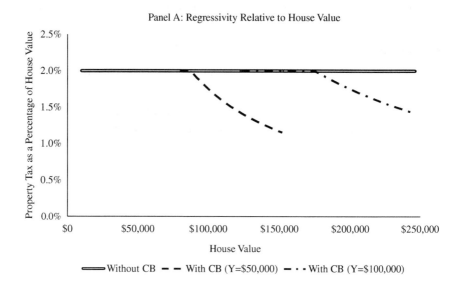

Impact of a Circuit Breaker on the Progressivity of the Property Tax.

2.4.3. *Benefits of circuit breakers*

- **Popularity**
  - About half of the states have circuit breakers for elderly homeowners or elderly renters.
  - A few states have circuit breakers for all homeowners or all renters.
  - For details, go to http://www.lincolninst.edu.
- **Strengths**
  - Circuit breakers provide tax relief for people who experience a negative income shock that makes it hard for them to pay property taxes out of their income.

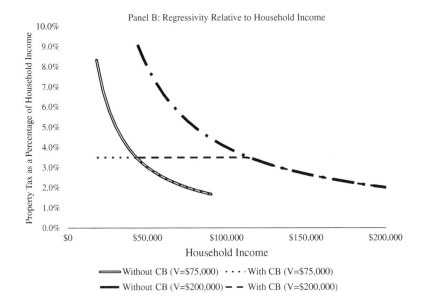

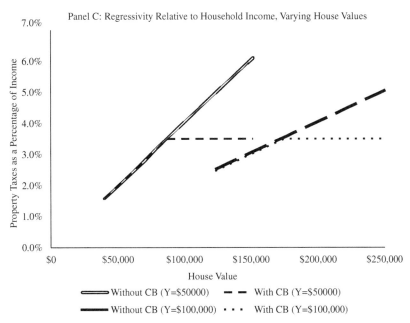

Impact of a Circuit Breaker on the Progressivity of the Property Tax.

2.4.4. *Problems with circuit breakers*

- **Weaknesses**

  - Circuit breakers help many home owners who do not need help.

    - Empty-nesters can borrow against their equity; the circuit breaker just subsidizes their children's inheritance.
    - Circuit breakers reward people who buy an expensive house.

  - Circuit breakers for all taxpayers lower tax prices for some voters and may have unintended consequences, such as higher spending.
  - Circuit breakers cannot be given to renters without an assumption about the (unknown) extent to which landlords shift the property tax onto renters.

2.4.5. *A better solution for income inequity*

- Many people like circuit breakers because they can be progressive with respect to income, not just with respect to property values.
- Exemptions could be made progressive with respect to income by setting a higher exemption amount for lower income households.
- This approach does not now exist, because one great advantage of exemptions is that they can be administered through property tax bills, whereas circuit breakers are administered through the income tax.

  - By switching the administration of exemptions to the income tax, the link between income and the size of the exemption would be easy to administer.
  - This design is like a sliding-scale circuit breaker except that the exemption gives the same tax break to all households in a given income bracket, whereas the sliding-scale circuit breaker gives a larger break to households who buy more expensive houses.

2.4.6. *A better solution for cash-flow problems*

- Many people like circuit breakers because they help empty nesters and people in vacation areas that experience rapid property-value growth.
  - ○ In fact, however, these people have a valuable asset and do not need to be subsidized.
  - ○ Instead, they need help with a cash-flow problem.
- A better solution for this cash-flow problem is a "tax deferral" program.
  - ○ This type of program allows people in certain groups to postpone property tax increases until a house is sold or passed on to heirs; at that time all postponed payments are due, with interest.
  - ○ About two dozen states currently have a limited program of this type, but this approach should be expanded.

Lecture 9

Income and Sales Taxes

- **Class Outline**
  1. **Sales Taxes**
  2. **The Federal Income Tax**
  3. **Links between Federal and State Income Taxes**

1. Sales Taxes

1.1. *Sales Tax Distortion*

- All taxes cause distortion (i.e. inefficiency), measured by *excess burden.*
- The sales tax is no exception.
- A sales tax distorts choices between taxed and untaxed items.
- All else equal, the best tax has the lowest excess burden.

1.1.1. *Excess burden and policy*

- Distortions are smallest for taxed goods with inelastic demand, such as medicine or cigarettes (but equity effects differ!).
- Distortions arise when goods are taxed and services are not.
- Distortions may arise when intermediate goods or services (i.e. inputs) are taxed.
- Taxes can reduce distortions when there are externalities.

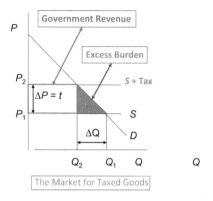

Excess Burden from Taxation.

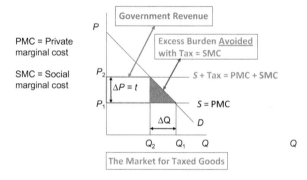

Excess Burden Saved in a Market with Externalities.

- Driving (= gasoline use) causes air pollution and emits greenhouse gases; a gas tax therefore promotes efficiency by discouraging driving!
- The federal gas tax has declined 40% in real terms since 1993.
- One study finds that new fuel-efficiency standards for new cars will cost the U.S. six times as much for the same reduction in gas use as setting the gas tax at $0.45 per gallon. See Karplus, *New York Times*, February 2013. https://www.nytimes.com/2013/02/22/opinion/the-case-for-a-higher-gasoline-tax.html.

1.2. Sales Tax Incidence

- Some sales taxes are specific, such as so-called "sin" taxes, and may not distort due to externalities.
- General sales taxes sometimes exempt certain things, such as many services, and therefore cause distortion between taxed and untaxed items.
- Sales taxes can be seen as a tax on consumption, and therefore distort the choice between work and leisure.

  ○ The labor supply elasticity is small, so little shifting into leisure occurs, and the tax falls mainly on consumers.

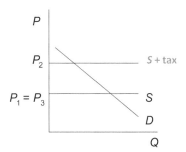

Incidence of a Sales Tax.

- Many goods have elastic supply curves, so most of the burden of sales tax differences falls on consumers.
- The ratio of consumption to income declines as income rises.
- In other words, rich people save a larger share of their income.
- So a sales tax is regressive overall.

  ○ Some components of a sales tax (e.g. a sales tax on luxury goods or services) might be progressive.

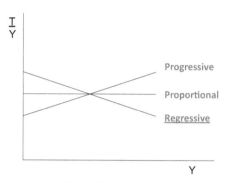

A Sales Tax is Regressive.

1.3. A Key Administrative Issue in the Design of a Sales Tax

- According to a famous U.S. Supreme Court decision, sales taxes on mail order or internet sales could only be collected if the seller has a business "nexus" in a state.
  - This decision was based on the inter-state commerce clause of the U.S. Constitution, which prohibits one state from placing an undue burden on businesses in other states.
  - It cost the states billions of dollars and was a major source of distortion.
- This decision was overturned in June 2018.
  - Internet companies can now be required to collect sales tax for every state, regardless of their presence in the state.
- The sales tax is actually a sales and use tax.
  - A resident of State X owes the sales tax to State X even if he or she buys something subject to the sales tax in State Y and then brings it home.
  - The new Supreme Court decision helps with internet sales, but does not eliminate all administrative problems.
- The use tax is still hard to administer in some cases:
  - Massachusetts police parked at New Hampshire liquor stores.

○ Interstate agreements to share credit card information for large purchases in one state delivered to another without collection of sales taxes (unless the new Supreme Court decision is applied to these sales).

• States were working on common definitions of goods and services and common rates to try to get around the burden argument at the heart of the old Supreme Court decision.

○ This effort was called the Streamlined Sales Tax Project and 22 states had joined.

• The question now is whether these burden-minimizing efforts will continue now that internet firms can be required to collect sales taxes even if the current burdens remain.

2. The Federal Income Tax

• We start with the federal income tax because most state taxes are linked to it.
• We will discuss the broad issues in the design of the federal income tax.
• Then we will turn to state and local income taxes.

2.1. *Federal Income Tax Design*

• **Comprehensive Income**
  ○ Exclusions
• **Adjusted Gross Income**
  ○ Exemptions
  ○ Deductions (Itemized or Standard)
• **Taxable Income**
  ○ Tax Table
    ■ **Gross Tax**
  ○ Tax Credits
    ■ **Net Tax**

2.1.1. *Exclusions and Exemptions*

Exclusions

- Interest income on municipal bonds.
- Implicit rent on owner-occupied housing.

Exemptions (Eliminated by the 2017 Tax Cuts and Jobs Act, TCJA)

- Personal exemptions **($4,050 in 2016)**.
- Exemptions for dependents.
- Exemptions for age and some categories of disability.

2.1.2. *Deductions*

- **Itemized Deductions**
  - Mortgage interest on primary residence (and some secondary).
  - Property taxes on primary residence (and some secondary).
  - State income taxes (or state sales taxes — but not both!).
  - State and local tax deductions *are limited to $10,000 by TCJA*.
  - Charitable contributions.
  - Excess medical expenses.
- **Standard Deduction**
  - Fixed amount (used by most taxpayers).
  - $12,700 for joint return in 2016 (*increased to $24,000 by TCJA*).

2.1.3. *Tax calculations*

- **Tax Tables**

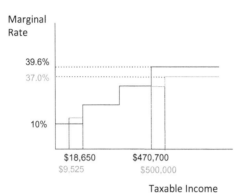

Tax Table, Joint Returns, 2017 (2018).

- ○ Separate tables for married and single.
  - ■ A marriage penalty for equal-earning couples due to standard deduction.
  - ■ A marriage bonus for one-earner couples due to broader brackets.
- ○ The alternative minimum tax (AMT) tries to ensure that exemptions and deductions do not push the average tax rate too low.
  - ■ The AMT affects fewer taxpayers with the TCJA.
  - ■ But still serves to reclaim some revenue lost to other provisions.

- **Tax Credits**

  ○ Earned income tax credit.

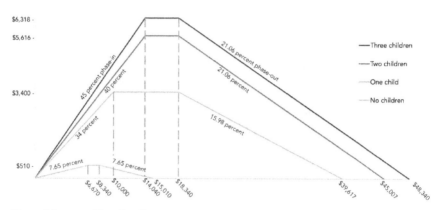

Earned Income Tax Credit.

Note: Assumes all income comes from earnings. Amounts are or taxpayers filing a single of head-of-household tax return. For married couples filing a joint tax return, the credit begins to phase out at income $5,590 higher than shown.

Source: Tax Policy Center, IRS Rev. Proc. 2016–55.

2.1.4. *Marginal to average rates*

- The translation from marginal to average rates is complicated.

  ○ Marginal rate tables are misleading due to the *EITC*.
  ○ All the other features of the tax code affect *average rates*.
  ○ *Deductions* are particularly powerful at the highest income levels.

- State income taxes are less progressive than the federal income tax.

  ○ States worry about scaring away high-income residents, although I have not seen any evidence that this is a large effect.

- State top rates go as high as 13.3% (California), and eight states have a flat rate.

3. Links between Federal and State Income Taxes

3.1. *State Income Taxes*

- Seven states do not have an income tax, and two states only tax investment income.
- For more, see: http://www.taxpolicycenter.org/statistics/state-in dividual-income-tax-rates-2000-2018.

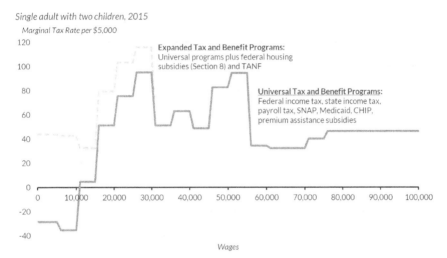

Single adult with two children, 2015

Effective Marginal Tax Rates.

Note: Average effective marginal tax rates facing a single parent with two children living in Colorado. The effective marginal rate is the marginal tax rate is calculated using changes in net income after taxes and transfers given changes in total compensation, which includes employee wages and the employer share of payroll taxes. The tax rate is then smoothed in $5,000 increments.

Source: C. Eugene Steuerle and Caleb Quakenbush. Urban Institute. 2015.

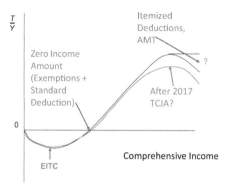

Possible Average Rates.

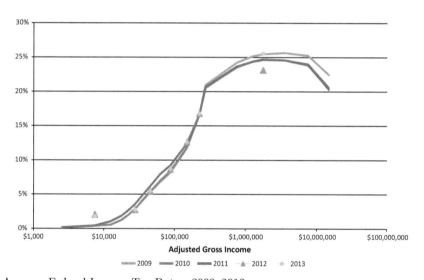

Average Federal Income Tax Rates, 2009–2013.
Source: IRS. Note that negative rates form the EITC cannot be identified in the IRS data.

3.2. Tax Reform Act of 1986 (TRA)

- Remarkable bi-partisan reform that closed loopholes (favored by liberals) and lowered marginal rates (favored by conservatives).
- These two are linked — broadening the base makes lower rates possible.

- Since then loopholes have been added at a furious pace.
- This reform also shifted the burden from individuals to corporations.

3.2.1. *Link to state income taxes*

- Most state income taxes either
  - use federal taxable income and their own tax tables, or
  - set their tax as a percentage of federal tax.
- The "A" states gained from base broadening in the 1986 TRA.
- The "B" states lost from the shift away from individual income taxes in the 1986 TRA.

3.3. **The Tax Cuts and Jobs Act of 2017 (TCJA)**

- The same issues arise with TCJA. Possible revenue raisers for states:

  "Personal Exemption Elimination

  The federal tax bill will repeal personal exemptions. Ten states currently couple their state personal exemption with the federal personal exemption. Given that the federal personal exemption was eliminated, these states could see a revenue gain, absent a change in state law.

  Alternative Inflation Measure

  The legislation eliminates the use of the traditional CPI-U (consumer price index for all urban consumers) measure for inflationary adjustments to the tax system. Instead, the bill imposes the slower growing, chained CPU measure. This will affect tax brackets, the standard deduction, the Earned Income Tax Credit (EITC) phasein/phaseout thresholds.

  Modifications to Other Deductions

  Modifications to the deduction for home mortgage interest, non-disaster casualty losses, and moving expenses have been

estimated to increase federal revenues. This would also increase revenues in the states that incorporate these changes."
See: http://www.ncsl.org/research/fiscal-policy/federal-tax-ref orm-and-the-states.aspx.

- Possible revenue losers for states:

"Standard Deduction

Twelve states conform to the federal standard deduction [and will lose revenue from its increase]. For states that use federal taxable income as their starting points, the increase in the standard deduction will decrease revenues unless actions are taken to decouple.

Pass-Through Deduction

The new law will allow a new deduction of 20% of qualified business income from certain pass-through entities [with income limits]. The deduction is only allowed in computing and reducing taxable income, not federal AGI, so only the few states that conform to FTI would be affected by this change, which would reduce revenues unless they decouple from this provision or switch to federal AGI as a starting point.

[This provision may encourage some business entities to switch from the corporate to the individual income tax.] State corporate income tax is already declining rapidly as a revenue source for states, so this could potentially add to that trend with more businesses moving to the individual tax code. Some tax experts *have speculated* that states may consider eliminating the corporate income tax entirely and look at broader taxes imposed on all forms of business entities, such as Ohio's commercial activity tax or Texas' margin tax." See: http://www.ncsl.org/ research/fiscal-policy/federal-tax-reform-and-the-states.aspx.

3.4. State Responses

- Some states have responded to TCJA by changing their tax code.
- To offset the loss of itemized deductions for state taxes, New York passed an optional employer-base payroll tax as an alternative to the state income tax.
  - With this approach, state income taxes are paid by the employer but the incidence probably falls on the worker.
  - As a result, the worker's income is equivalent to income after state taxes and hence to income with a deduction for state taxes.
- However, some experts caution against major changes in state taxes.
  - See: Burman and Sammartino, http://www.taxpolicycenter.org taxvox/state-responses-tcjas-salt-deduction-limit-may-be-costl y-and-favor-high-income-residents and Leachman and Mazerov https://www.cbpp.org/research/state-budget-and-tax/how-sho uld-states-respond-to-recent-federal-tax-changes.

3.5. Local Income Taxes

- A few cities (e.g. Baltimore, Detroit, New York) have income taxes of their own, usually linked to their state tax.
- Most local income taxes are limited to wages and salaries and take the form of either
  - an earnings tax (with the legal incidence on the worker);
  - a payroll tax (with the legal incidence on the firm).
- Ohio allows school districts to levy an income tax (at a specified rate).

3.5.1. Commuter taxes

- A few cities (e.g. Newark, San Francisco, Cleveland, Philadelphia) collect taxes on the wages and salaries earned by non-residents within the city.
  - Payroll taxes do this automatically.

- Commuter taxes only work if cities have access to them but suburbs do not.
- The first claim on taxable resources goes to the jurisdiction of residence. So if a city passes an income tax, the suburbs can pass one and claim all the taxes paid by their commuting residents — with no increase in the tax on those residents!
- This happened in Pittsburgh.
- Commuter taxes have the advantage that they can help satisfy the benefit principle — people who benefit from the services in the city where they work help pay for these services.
- Commuter taxes have the disadvantage that they may encourage firms (not households) to leave a city (so they can pay lower wages), although the evidence on this effect is mixed.

Revenue from Government Monopoly

- **Class Outline**
  1. **Why have Government Monopolies?**
  2. **State-run Liquor Stores**
  3. **State-sponsored Gambling**
  4. **Legal Narcotics Stores?**

1. Why have Government Monopolies?

1.1. *Reason 1: Natural Monopoly*

- A declining long-run AC curve gives large firms a competitive advantage — and leads to monopoly.
- Unregulated private monopolies select inefficient levels of output.
- So governments either:
  ○ regulate private monopoly or
  ○ set up a government monopoly.

1.1.1. *Monopoly pricing*

- If the government monopoly uses the private monopoly price it:
  ○ Maximizes its revenue.
  ○ Causes the same distortion as the private monopoly!
  ○ Transforms monopoly profits into government revenue.

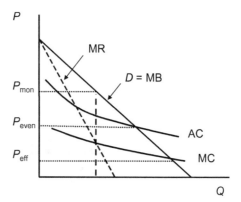

Pricing with Government Monopoly.

- *Note*: Government monopoly can raise revenue by setting price anywhere between the break-even price (P_{even}) and the private monopoly price (P_{mon}). It loses money at the efficient price (P_{eff}).
- Even at the monopoly price, consumer surplus (CS) is generated, but there is a clear *trade-off* between CS and government revenue.
- If the government sets the efficient price, it

  ○ Maximizes consumer surplus in this market.
  ○ But it loses money.
  ○ And must raise revenue elsewhere, undoubtedly causing distortion (i.e. lost consumer surplus) in other markets.

- We will pursue these issues in the next class.

1.2. *Reason 2: Regulation*

- Governments sometimes decide to monopolize a good or service on policy grounds.
- Hence they prohibit private production and provide the product themselves.
- This case involves the same trade-off between CS and government revenue.
- *Note*: Government monopoly can raise revenue by setting price anywhere between the break-even price (P_{even}), which is the efficient price (P_{eff}), and the private monopoly price (P_{mon}).

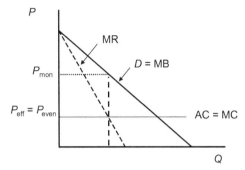

Pricing with Government Monopoly and Fixed MC.

2. State-run Liquor Stores

- According to the Census, 16 states have a state-run liquor monopoly, sometimes at the wholesale level, sometimes for both wholesale and retail.
- This reflects the prohibition tradition in some states — not a natural monopoly.
- It gives the state control over advertising and sales.
- It boosts exporting because a state can charge a high price to non-residents even if it cannot tax them.

3. State-sponsored Gambling

- States now sponsor many kinds of gambling, including casinos and lotteries.
- Now every state except Hawaii and Utah has some form of legal gambling.
- Gambling now provides roughly 5% of state general revenue.

3.1. State-Run Lotteries

- The first state lottery was in New Hampshire in 1964.
- Now 43 states have a lottery.

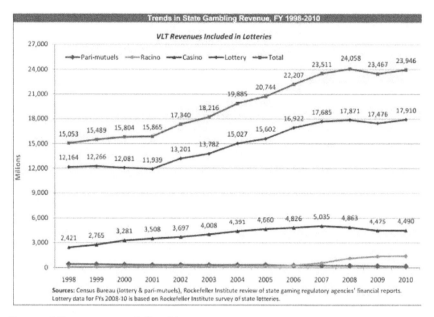

Types of State-sponsored Gambling.

Sources: Census Bureau (lottery and pari-mutuels), Rockefeller Institute review of state gaming regulatory agencies' financial reports. Lottery data for FYs 2008–10 is based on Rockefeller Institute survey of state lotteries.

- Lotteries raise 2 to $2^{1}/_{2}\%$ of general revenue in a typical lottery state, and somewhat more in a few states.
- Lotteries probably are a natural monopoly, as customers are attracted to very large prizes.
- For more on lotteries, see: http://rockinst.org/wp-content/uploa ds/2017/11/2016-04-12-Blinken_Report_Three-min.pdf.

3.2. *Policy Issues Raised by Lotteries*

- Legalization (Should lottery gambling be allowed?)
- Government Provision (Should lotteries be a private or government monopoly?)
- Rate of Taxation (How much revenue should the state claim?)
- Earmarking (Should the revenue be earmarked for education?)
- Promotion (How should lotteries be designed and advertised?)

3.2.1. *Legalization*

- Lotteries generate *consumer surplus*, that is, many people pay for their entertainment value.
- Lotteries also generate *social costs:* gambling addiction for some people, increased crime, and, perhaps, undermining incentives to earn one's way.
- There is a consensus in this country that the benefits outweigh the costs (although the costs are high).

3.2.2. *Government provision*

- Lotteries require large scale, so private lotteries would be huge companies that would be:
  - Difficult to regulate and tax (think of their political connections!).
  - Inviting to criminal elements.
- Thus, there is a broad consensus that legalized lotteries should be government monopolies.
- But many states are debating private management or even the sale of the lottery to a private company.
- In January 2011, Illinois turned the management of its lottery over to a private firm. Indiana and New Jersey have also gone this route.
- In Illinois, the firm agreed to large payments to the state if it does not increase lottery revenue, which it apparently has not.
- Without comprehensive contracts, this approach is a recipe for exploitation (discussed below).
- A former governor of Massachusetts says:
  - Illinois ... appears to be ending its experiment nearly half a billion dollars behind the revenue projections promised by the winning bidder and with no truly game-changing innovations in the way the lottery performs. New Jersey ... missed on already-lowered revenue projections last year, and is running further behind this year. Indiana was viewed as a relative success ...,

but the private operator missed its targets last year, too and the Hoosier Lottery is now on track to miss its 2015 targets by $50 million.

- See: http://www.forbes.com/sites/realspin/2015/02/24/where-lo ttery-privatization-went-wrong/#466a94214f18.

3.2.3. *Rate of taxation*

- Lotteries provide a classic example of the trade-off between CS and revenue:
  - The analytical case for lotteries is based on the CS they generate, which is minimized by *low* implicit tax rates.
  - The political case for lotteries is based on the money they raise, which is maximized by *high* implicit tax rate.
- Tax rates are very high.
- What is the implicit tax rate?
  - Answer: What the state keeps divided by the total costs of running the lottery.
  - Let t = implicit tax rate, R = state revenue, P = prizes awarded, C = administrative costs.

Then

$$t = \frac{R}{P + C}$$

- According to the Census, the values of these variables for the U.S. as a whole in 2016 (per $1.00 of sales) are:
  - $R = \$0.315$;
  - $P = \$0.640$;
  - $C = \$0.045$.
- Thus the average implicit tax rate in the U.S. in 2003 was:

$$t = \frac{0.315}{0.640 + 0.045} = 0.461 = 46.1\%$$

- This is analogous to a sales tax rate.

- This is not a typo: The tax rate in the typical state was 46.1%!
- In 2016, implicit lottery tax rates range from 16% (Idaho) to 288% (South Dakota) and are all far higher than the rates for any other type of sales tax.
- These high rates of tax cause enormous distortion between lotteries and other types of commodities.
- But they also cut back on the social costs (externalities) of lotteries and export taxes to nonresidents.
- Moreover, lottery taxes are very *regressive* — far more regressive than any other revenue source.
- One study: Low-income individuals earn 11% of total income but provide 25% of lottery revenue.

Implicit Lottery Tax Rates, 2016.

Arizona	26.8%	Nebraska	35.1%
Arkansas	25.6%	New Hampshire	37.6%
California	46.1%	New Jersey	47.1%
Colorado	34.6%	New Mexico	45.1%
Connecticut	44.4%	New York	66.2%
Delaware	150.6%	North Carolina	39.8%
Florida	42.0%	North Dakota	40.0%
Georgia	37.5%	Ohio	42.6%
Idaho	16.0%	Oklahoma	57.6%
Illinois	33.6%	Oregon	192.3%
Indiana	33.1%	Pennsylvania	42.2%
Iowa	31.8%	Rhode Island	213.8%
Kansas	40.1%	South Carolina	36.9%
Kentucky	38.2%	South Dakota	288.1%
Louisiana	59.2%	Tennessee	66.8%
Maine	49.3%	Texas	41.3%
Maryland	43.9%	Vermont	29.5%
Massachusetts	32.7%	Virginia	45.3%
Michigan	42.6%	Washington	37.8%
Minnesota	36.5%	West Virginia	85.7%
Missouri	37.1%	Wisconsin	49.3%
Montana	47.9%	Wyoming	23.9%

Source: U.S. Census.

- Some games, such as instant games and lotto, are particularly regressive.
- Within income classes, the burden of lotteries is concentrated on a relatively small share of individuals.

3.2.4. *Earmarking*

- Almost half of lottery states *earmark* the funds for education.
- This link is part of their political appeal: "Whatever their bad features, at least lotteries help fund our education system!"
- It is not clear, however, that lotteries increase net funds for education:
  - They facilitate cuts in state education aid.
  - They lower sales tax revenue.
  - See: https://www.brookings.edu/blog/brown-center-chalkboar d/2018/05/09/who-wins-and-who-loses-when-states-earmark-l ottery-revenue-for-higher-education/.
- Even counting benefits from education, lotteries are still regressive.

3.2.5. *Promotion*

- The people who run lotteries are paid to raise as much money as possible.
- Hence they resort to aggressive advertising: "All you need is a dollar and a dream."
- Some of this advertising is misleading at best, with no recognition of the low odds of winning.
- Moreover, this advertising puts government in the position of undermining the work ethic.
- The people who run lotteries sometimes resort to promoting games that are directed toward low-income communities.
  - These games maximize revenue because these people are more vulnerable to the misleading appeal of instant wealth.
  - But they also maximize both the regressivity of the lottery "tax" and the social costs of lottery addiction.
- Promotions of this type are, in my view, simply unethical.

- Quick Draw is a game played in bars and some stores in NY.
- Governor Cuomo has proposed expanding the set of places to play and lowering age limits.
- "The restrictions have proved cumbersome and unnecessary, and have substantially reduced the amount of earnings that would otherwise be generated by the game."
- So let's get more kids hooked on video gambling to raise a few $s?
- Illinois, Indiana, and New Jersey employ private companies to manage their lotteries; other states are considering this step.
- Private management is seen as a way to raise revenue.
- The easiest way to raise revenue is to exploit vulnerable populations.
- I look forward to studies of private management to see if this happens.

3.3. Conclusions About Lotteries

- Lotteries are here to stay.
- States cannot get rid of them without losing revenue to their neighbors.
- High implicit taxes discourage participation and cut direct CS but also cut the social costs.
- So keep lotteries with high rates but use honest advertising and do not target vulnerable groups.

3.4. The Latest from New York

- NY has lotteries and "racinos" and Native-American casinos.
- In November 2014, voters passed a constitutional amendment to permit a limited number of private (but taxed) casinos; projects have been selected, and some built.
- Casinos ($\approx$ addictive slot machines) are a growth industry; they exist in 39 states.
- Casinos will compete with other forms of gambling and other entertainment spending — with an unclear net impact on state revenue.

- Casino taxes and fees are a particularly regressive source of state revenue.
- Unlike lotteries, casinos would give the gambling industry a new source of political power.
- My views in these casinos appear in an op-ed posted on my website.

4. Legal Narcotics Stores?

- The question of legalizing narcotics is conceptually similar to that of legalizing gambling.
- Several states have taken a step in this direction by legalizing recreational marijuana; Colorado and Washington were the first states; Alaska, California, Maine, Massachusetts, and Nevada have now joined them.
- This may all be moot if the Trump Administration decides to enforce federal law, which still prohibits recreational use of marijuana.
- The impact of legal recreational marijuana is not yet known.
- Colorado and Washington have collected more revenue than expected, but no one has calculated net revenue after lost sales taxes from purchases of other items that would be made without legal marijuana.
- Although the legalization of marijuana is a significant change, it is a difficult change to evaluate.

  ○ Some studies count the number of traffic accidents in which a driver tested positive for marijuana, but these studies cannot determine whether marijuana was the cause of an accident.
  ○ Changes in behavior due to marijuana are difficult to determine.

- At this point, legalization of marijuana is popular in several states, but we still do not know the costs and benefits.
- See: http://taxfoundation.org/article/marijuana-legalization-and -taxes-federal-revenue-impact.
- What about "harder" drugs, such as cocaine?
- In this case the *social costs* may be much higher.

  ○ More people may become addicted.

- ○ The consequences of addiction for an individual are more severe.
- ○ The consequences of addiction for society are more severe.
- In addition, *economies of scale* may not be large, so it may be difficult to keep out private firms.
- This may lead to a Hobson's choice for governments after legalization:
  - ○ If government (or legal private) stores set high prices to discourage narcotics use and minimize social costs, unregulated private firms could offer narcotics at lower prices.
  - ○ If government stores set low prices to drive out private competition, violence would drop, but addiction might become a major social problem.
- With these behavioral responses, the social costs of narcotics might go up either way.
- A contrary view is that the main social cost issue is the violence associated with the drug trade.
- If private firms who enforce contracts through violence are driven out of business by low-cost narcotics in government (or government regulated) stores, the savings to society might be huge.
- Those believe the benefits from lower violence exceed the costs from higher addiction support legalizing narcotics.
- Problems of poisoning also might be eased.

Lecture 11

User Fees

1. Why Use Public Pricing?

- Public pricing, i.e. the use of user fees, is an alternative to taxation.
- It has three key justifications:
  - Some public monopolies are used as revenue sources (the subject of the last class).
  - The benefit principle justifies linking payments to the people who use a service.
  - Fees are needed to ensure efficient usage of a public service.

1.1. *Equity and Efficiency*

- Today we focus on setting efficient public prices, i.e. prices to support an efficient allocation of resources.
- Public pricing often raises equity issues, as well.
- In some cases, high prices may discourage the use of a public facility, such as a zoo, by low-income groups.
- In other cases, high public prices may hit vulnerable groups hard. An example is the impact of a subway fare hike on "captive riders," namely, low-income workers who cannot afford a car.

2. Basic Rule for Public Prices

- To promote efficiency, a public price (P) should be set equal to marginal cost (MC).
- If $P = $ MC, then consumers base their usage decisions on the true resource cost.
- As in a private market, decisions based on true resource costs lead to efficient outcomes.

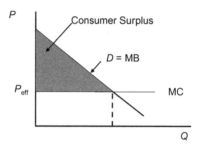

Efficient Pricing with Known MC.

Note: The basic rule for public pricing is that the efficient price is one that maximizes consumer surplus, namely, a price equal to marginal cost (MC).

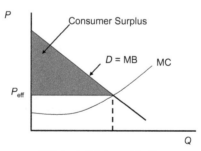

Efficient Pricing with Known
MC Schedule and Demand Curve.

Note: The basic rule may be difficult to apply; if MC is not constant, the rule cannot be applied without knowing the shapes of the demand and MC curves.

2.1. *What is the Margin?*

- In some cases, the margin is not well defined and some judgment is required.
- Consider the case of public transit.

  o One could say that the *last rider* is the margin, in which case MC is essentially equal to zero.
  o One could say (more reasonably) that the *last bus route* is the margin, because that is what the provider controls, in which case MC could be set to the cost of the route divided by the average number of passengers.

2.2. *Special Cases*

- Pricing rules need to be adjusted in the presence of:

  o Externalities (which, as discussed in an earlier class, also affect taxing rules).
  o Variation in usage over time, which is usually called a "peak load" problem.

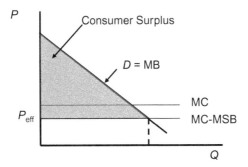

Public Pricing with Externalities.

Note: When a public service generates positive externalities (such as lower pollution and congestion on roads due to public transit), the efficient price equals MC minus marginal social benefits (MSB).

3. Peak-load Pricing

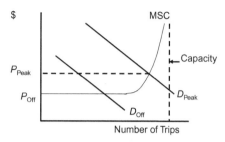

Peak-load Pricing.

Note: When congestion drives up the marginal social cost (MSC) or travel during peak times, the efficient price for the peak period (P_{Peak}) exceeds the efficient price for the off-peak period (P_{OFF}).

3.1. *Peak-load Pricing and Capacity*

- This figures holds transit capacity constant, but this capacity (and hence this pricing scheme) might not be optimal in the long run.
- The optimal capacity is the one at which the marginal benefits equal the marginal costs. This is an example for the next class!
- A pricing scheme consistent with this capacity decision is given in the Figure "Long Run Peak-Load Pricing".

3.1.1. *Long-run peak-load pricing*

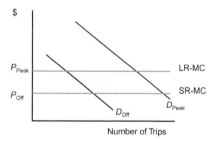

Long Run Peak-load Pricing.

Note: When extra capacity must be added to accommodate peak travel, a pricing rule that recognizes the capacity decision is to set the peak price at the long-run MC, which equals the short-run MC plus the marginal cost of added capacity.

3.1.2. *Optimal departures from MC pricing*

- Covering a deficit for a *natural monopoly*.
- Responding to *distorted prices* in related markets.

3.1.3. *Pricing for a natural monopoly*

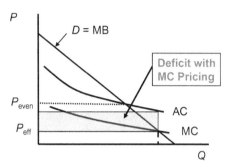

Deficit with Peak-Load Pricing.

Note: When the government service is a natural monopoly, setting $P = MC$ results in a deficit, which must be closed with tax revenue or by raising the price! The trick is to find the least distortionary financing.

3.2. **Ways to Cover a Deficit**

- Use the break-even price (Average cost (AC) pricing).
- Use non-distortionary taxes.
- Use distortionary taxes.
- Set different prices for different services.
- Use a two-part tariff.
- Use some combination of the above.

3.2.1. *Average-cost pricing*

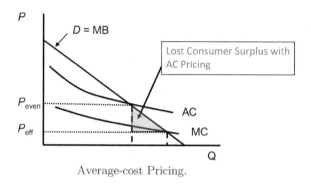

Average-cost Pricing.

Note: Using the break-even price instead of the efficient price covers the deficit, but results in a loss of consumer surplus.

3.2.2. *Covering a deficit with taxes*

- Non-distortionary taxes would be optimal, but they do not exist. Even a local head-tax distorts the decision about where to live.
- A distortionary tax is a good option if the excess burden from the tax is less than the lost consumer surplus from AC pricing.
- Taxes may violate the benefit principle because they are not limited to people who use the priced service.

3.2.3. *Pricing with multiple services*

- Recall that excess burden depends on the price elasticity of demand.

$$\text{EB} = \left(\frac{1}{2}\right)(t^2)\,|e|\,(P_1 Q_1)$$

- For any two services, i and j, prices should deviate from MC according to the following rule:

$$\left(\frac{P_i - \text{MC}_i}{P_i}\right)e_i = \left(\frac{P_j - \text{MC}_j}{P_j}\right)e_j$$

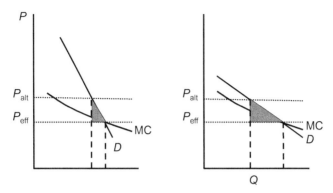

Deviations from MC pricing with two services.

Note: If a government provides two services, it can cover its deficit with less distortion if it sets a higher gap between P and MC for services with less elastic demand (unlike this picture!).

3.2.4. *Two-part tariff*

- Some services involve stages, such as buying a phone and then using the phone. (This used to be a public sector business!)
- These two stages may involve different elasticities.

  - For example, almost everyone used to buy a phone, but the number of calls clearly depends on the price.
  - So using the logic for multiple services, set a higher deviation from MC pricing for the less elastic stage (buying a phone).

3.3. *Distorted Private Prices*

- Efficiency requires consumers' MRS to equal firms' MRT for any two goods (where MRS = marginal rate of substitution is the ratio of the marginal utilities for the two goods and MRT = marginal rate of transformation is the ratio of their marginal costs).
- Competitive markets achieve efficiency because consumers set their MRS and firms set their MRT equal to the same market price ratio for the two goods.
- The P = MC rule simplifies this by looking at only one good, implicitly assuming that all other goods are priced properly.

- But if other goods are not priced properly, this simplification is not correct.
- We will examine *two* cases with distorted private prices:
  - An externality in a private market that is related to the government good being priced.
  - A private monopoly (or, indeed, any kind of market power) in a market that is related to the government good being priced.

3.3.1. *Case 1: Externalities*

- With a negative externality from the private good, the private price falls short of marginal social cost (MSC).
- Thus, if the government sets $P = $ MC, the ratio of the government to private price is above the ratio of the government to private MC.
- Because households respond to prices,

$$MRS = \frac{P_G}{P_P} > MRT$$

- Because the price ratio is "too high," consumers under-consume the public good relative to the private good.
- This could be fixed by pricing the externality in the private market — as in the gas tax case discussed in an earlier class.
- Or by setting a price for the public good that is below its marginal cost.

3.3.1.1. Externalities Example

- Automobiles cause pollution and congestion, which are not priced.
- Drivers pay the gas tax, but (as discussed in an earlier class) this just covers road maintenance.
- Thus the price of driving is below the marginal social cost.
- One way to fix this is to lower the price of public transit below MC.

3.3.2. *Case 2: Private monopoly*

- A private monopoly sets the price of its product above MC.
- Thus, if the government sets $P = $ MC, the ratio of the government to private price is below the ratio of the government to private MC.

- Because households respond to prices,

$$MRS = \frac{P_G}{P_P} < MRT$$

- Because the price ratio is "too low," consumers over-consume the public good relative to the private good.
- This could be fixed by regulating the monopoly's price.
- Or by setting a price for the public good that is above its marginal cost.

4. When Pricing Principles Conflict

- Pricing decisions can get very complicated.
- Consider transit fares:
  - Raise fares to eliminate a deficit.
  - Lower fares to protect captive riders.
  - Raise fares at rush-hour to account for congestion on public transit.
  - Lower fares at rush-hour to account for the positive externalities of transit (lower pollution and congestion on highways) and the unpriced externalities (pollution and congestion) from driving.
- The key lesson: One cannot achieve many objectives with one pricing tool!
- In general, a policy maker needs as many policy tools as objectives:
  - Raise fares to lower a deficit (and/or raise taxes to pay for transit since the entire area benefits from the transit system).
  - Provide discount cards for low-income people to protect captive riders.
  - Use peak-load pricing to account for congestion on public transit.
  - Raise parking fees or raise gas taxes or charge tolls or implement a rush-hour pricing scheme in some zones (as in London or Singapore) to address pollution and congestion.

4.1. *Income-based Discounts*

The New York Times, February 2015.

Seattle:

- "ORCA Lift" gives discounts on public transportation to people whose household income is no more than 200% of the federal poverty level.
- Subsidy is over 50% of peak fares.

San Francisco:

- Muni Lifeline has fewer than 20,000 card holders in a system that serves about 350,000 people a day.

Green County (near Dayton):

- Social service agencies buy travel vouchers and distribute them to their clients.

4.2. *Transit Fares in NYC — The Reduced Fare*

- Cost: The base subway or local bus fare is $2.75. Reduced fare is half the base fare, $1.35 or less with Reduced-Fare MetroCard discounts.
- Who's eligible: Customers who are 65 years of age or older or have a qualifying disability.
- Where and when you can ride:
  - MTA New York City Transit and MTA Bus: local buses anytime.
  - MTA New York City Transit and MTA Bus: express buses anytime except weekday rush hours: Monday through Friday, 6 a.m. to 10 a.m. and 3 p.m. to 7 p.m.

Transit Fares in NYC, 2017.

Unlimited Ride MetroCard	Pay-Per-Ride MetroCard
The more you ride, the less each ride costs.	5% bonus on purchase of $5 or more.
All free transfers included.	Free subway-to-bus, bus-to-subway, or bus-to-bus transfer within 2 hours of paying your fare (Some exceptions apply).
Refill as often as you like, until card expires.	Refill as often as you like, until card expires.
Can only be used by one person at a time.	Can be used to pay for up to four people at a time.
Cannot be used again at the same station or same bus route for 18 minutes.	

4.3. *Transit Fares in NYC — Analysis*

- Basic pricing similar to two-part tariff: High price for entry, but reductions for frequent travelers.
- Basic pricing also helps captive riders, who can lower their cost per ride.
- Reduced fares help seniors and people with disabilities — but are not fully available during rush hour to minimize impact on congestion.
- Fares are higher for express buses to account for higher MC associated with longer trip (and perhaps lower price elasticity).
- In 2016, fares cover only 40% of revenue, which accounts for externalities, but MC is unknown.

Best Values in NYC System.

How Often Do You Ride? Get the Best Value			
If you ride the sub-way or local bus	**Choose this option**	**Cost**	**Your cost per ride**
Fewer than 13 rides per week or 48 rides per month	Pay-Per-Ride	$5.50($6.11 value)	$2.48 (effective fare with 11% bonus)
13 rides per week	7-Day Unlimited	$31.00	$2.38
15 rides per week			$2.07
20 rides per week			$1.55
48 rides per month	30-Day Unlimited	$116.50	$2.43
60 rides per month			$1.94
75 rides per month			$1.55
If you ride the express bus Fewer than 10 rides per week	Pay-Per-Ride	$6.50 ($7.22 value)	$5.86 (effective fare with 11% bonus)
10 rides per week	Express Bus 7-Day	$57.25	$5.73

- Tolls on MTA's 7 within-city bridges encourage transit use — and shift 12% of costs to drivers (who benefit from transit).
- Dedicated taxes (36%) and governmental subsidies (8%) shift revenue to state taxpayers and to city taxpayers, which accounts for the benefits non-riders receive.
- See: http://web.mta.info/mta/news/books/docs/MTA_2016_Adopted_Budget_February_Financial_Plan_2016_2019.pdf.

Lecture 12

Infrastructure

- **Class Outline**
  1. **What is Infrastructure?**
  2. **Capital Spending**
  3. **Infrastructure Decisions**
  4. **Paying for Infrastructure**

1. What is Infrastructure?

- Infrastructure is long-lived public investment:
  - Roads, bridges, transit;
  - Dams, drinking water systems;
  - Wastewater systems;
  - Hazardous waste disposal sites;
  - Navigable waterways, railroads;
  - Energy production systems;
  - Parks and recreation.
- ASCE (civil engineers) estimates that the U.S. needs $3.6 trillion investment in infrastructure over the next 5 years.
- It is a great time to invest in infrastructure:
  - Infrastructure needs are great;
  - Borrowing costs are very low.

ASCE Infrastructure Grades, 2017.

Water and Environment	
Dams	D
Drinking Water	D
Hazardous Waste	D$^+$
Levees	D
Solid Waste	C$^+$
Wastewater	D$^+$
Transportation	
Aviation	D
Bridges	C$^+$
Inland Waterways	D
Ports	C$^+$
Rail	B
Roads	D
Transit	D$^-$
Public Facilities	
Public Parks and Recreation	D$^+$
Schools	D$^+$
Energy	
Energy	D$^+$

Source: www.infrastructurereportcard.org.

1.1. *Infrastructure Needs*

- Recent years have seen numerous examples of danger from deteriorating bridges, poorly maintained rail lines, and outdated water systems.
- These issues led to the formation of the Building America's Future Education Fund (BAFuture) to try to boost awareness of infrastructure needs.
- See: http://bafuture.org/.
- One of the co-chairs of BAFuture, Ray LaHood, who was Secretary of Transportation, clearly made the main points in a 2016 op-ed in *Time Magazine*.

○ "The irony of letting our infrastructure slide into a state of disrepair for financial reasons, besides the fact that it is terribly unsafe, is that it is also fiscally unsound. Routine maintenance is much less expensive than enormous repairs or building a new bridge. When a municipality lacks funding and has to defer routine maintenance year after year, they end up with an expensive crisis on their hands."

○ "Roads and highways aren't the only piece of infrastructure starved by underfunding. Our cities are built on water systems that are a century old. The aviation sector relies on World War II era radar technology. And funding for public transportation, like Amtrak, is routinely cut to the bone by a fickle Congress more interested in a press release announcing they saved a buck than in investing in our country's future."

- See: http://time.com/3860397/ray-lahood-amtrak-tragedy-infrastructure/.

2. Capital Spending

- Capital spending is difficult to study because of its variability from year to year.
- Wang/Duncombe/Yinger (*National Tax Journal*, 2011) find that school capital spending in New York has many of the same determinants as school operating spending:
  ○ Tax price (elasticity = -0.22);
  ○ Income (elasticity = 0.2).
- In New York, school building aid is provided through a matching grant, and most districts are quite responsive to the matching rate.
  ○ The estimated price elasticity is -0.42.
- However, this response is about zero (elasticity = -0.023) for high-need districts.
  ○ Even strong price incentives cannot boost school capital spending in New York's neediest districts.

3. Infrastructure Decisions

- When should a particular infrastructure project be built?
- *Benefit–cost analysis* is well suited to answering this question.
- Benefit–cost analysis is a set of tools that help to reduce a decision about a complex program to a manageable level.

3.1. *Benefit–cost Analysis*

- Any government project has complex effects across

  ○ markets,
  ○ time, and
  ○ groups.

- Benefit–cost analysis helps to simplify the analysis of each of these dimensions.

3.1.1. *Benefit–cost analysis — markets*

- To simplify across markets, benefit–cost analysis expresses everything in terms of *willingness to pay,* often measured with consumer surplus or cost savings.

  ○ The value of commuting time saved due to a new highway or subway stop.
  ○ The consumer surplus from the new recreation opportunities created by a dam.

3.1.2. *Benefit–cost analysis — time*

- To simplify across time, benefit–cost analysis expresses everything in terms of present value; that is, it uses discounting.

  ○ The best discount rate is a long-term, low-risk rate, such as the rate for long-term government bonds.

○ The discount rate (the denominator) and the benefits and costs (the numerator) should both be either in real or in nominal terms.

- Consider *real/real*.

  ○ The numerator is easy. Benefits and costs in each year are entered in real terms with no inflation adjustment. So a $1,000 benefit today that is expected to continue just stays at $1,000.
  ○ The denominator is hard. Any observed interest rate is nominal because it recognizes that money will be paid back in the future in dollars that are not worth as much.
  ○ So to get a real rate, anticipated inflation (not directly observed!) must be subtracted from a market rate.

- Consider *nominal/nominal*.

  ○ Now the numerator is hard. The $1,000 in the first year must be inflated with an expected inflation rate for later years.
  ○ The denominator is easy because market rates are in nominal terms.
  ○ Note that real/real and nominal/nominal are equivalent. If the numerator is inflated at rate a percent per year and the project has a long life, then the present value expression collapses to one with real benefits in the numerator and $r - a$, the real interest rate, in the denominator.

- Official B/C analysis uses real/real.
- The Office of Management and Budget requires calculations with a 3% rate and with a 7% rate.

  ○ A 7% rate is undoubtedly too high.
  ○ The Council of Economic Advisers defines the real social discount rate as "the difference between the nominal annual yield on the 10 year note less the 5 year unweighted moving average of current and past annual inflation." This rate is below 1%.
  ○ See: https://www.whitehouse.gov/sites/default/files/page/file s/201701_cea_discounting_issue_brief.pdf.

3.1.3. *Benefit–cost analysis — groups*

- Third, benefit–cost analysis can highlight impacts on different groups.
- But it cannot save a decision maker from placing weights on these impacts.
- Programs designed to help a particular group should not be implemented if they do not give this group net benefits.
- Ignoring inter-group impacts is an implicit value judgment.

3.1.4. *Benefit–cost analysis — transfers*

- A final key issue is: *transfers.*
  - ○ In my experience, this is the trickiest issue in all of B/C analysis: A transfer arises when a program shifts benefits or costs from one group to another.
  - ○ *Transfers do not represent real resources gained or lost — just real resources transferred.* Traditional B-C says they should be ignored, but transfers often have important *equity* consequences, which should be considered.

3.1.4.1. Transfer Example 1: Taxes (or **Any Government Revenue**)

- Taxes are *never* real resources created or lost from the point of view of citizens.
  - ○ They are only resources from the point of view of governments. B/C does not take the point of view of a government — it takes the point of view of the people.
  - ○ New taxes may solve the problem of a budget officer, but they take real resources away from the taxpayer and redistribute them, through the public budget, to other taxpayers.
  - ○ We may care about the distributional consequences; if we are trying to help a particular group and all of their benefits are taxed away, it is not a very good program, even if B > C.

3.1.4.2. Transfer Example 2: Property Values

- Many programs affect property values.

○ Property values reflect real resources created that become accessible to people who own nearby property.

○ A park creates real benefits (esthetic and recreational), which are transferred to nearby property owners.

○ We can measure the benefits by looking at impacts on property values, but we cannot include *both* property value impacts and the direct measures of underlying CS as benefits.

○ With direct CS measures, property values only matter if they connect with an equity concern; a park may not help renters, for example, because it leads to higher rents (and values) so the benefits are transferred to property owners.

3.1.4.3. Transfer Example 3: Effects in Related Markets

• Producing a new good or service often has an effect in a related market.

○ These effects do not involve the creation of new resources; instead they are just a re-shuffling of existing resources that arises because of opportunities created by the new good.

○ Suppose a government builds a park. Ice cream cone venders will come to the park and sell ice cream cones; movie theatre owners will lose business. These effects do not involve resources gained or lost — just re-shuffling.

○ It looks like there is an increase in consumer surplus when the ice-cream-cone demand curve shifts out. But in fact, the possibilities for consuming ice cream cones and movies are already built into the demand curve for visits to a park, so they are already taken care of by the consumer surplus calculation for parks.

3.1.4.4. Transfer Example 4: Displacement

• In general, local projects cannot influence the overall level of employment. *If they could, we wouldn't have any unemployment!*

○ A program may, indeed, hire some people, but there is very likely to be an associated loss of jobs somewhere else in the economy. So jobs are just transferred from one person to another.

    o It is possible that a project results in the hiring of people who would otherwise be unemployed with no displacement. Some analysts would say this applies to a program for the long-term unemployed.

    o But even here, one must be careful, because the benefits are not as great as one might think. Everyone puts some value on his or her leisure time, so the net benefits from the job equal *wages minus lost leisure*.

3.1.5. *Using benefit-cost*

- Benefit–cost analysis should not be blamed for the complexity of infrastructure decisions.
- Benefit–cost analysis can simplify a decision, but it cannot make value judgments or eliminate uncertainty.
- Try to frame benefit–cost analysis to focus on the factors that require analytical or value judgments.

4. Paying for Infrastructure

- Many people think a government can pay for infrastructure through borrowing.
- This is not true.
- Borrowing simply spreads the financing burden over time.
- Taxes or fees are needed to pay for the infrastructure, with or without borrowing.
- President Trump announced an infrastructure plan in early 2018.

    o His plan calls for $200 billion in federal funds to encourage infrastructure projects by state and local governments and private companies.

- Few scholars think this is a viable strategy.

    o The source of the federal money is not specified.

    o Because of across-state spillovers and economies of scale, national infrastructure projects should be funded at the federal level.

    o Private companies will select projects based on profitability, not on the net benefits to households, so key projects will not be funded.

- The plan runs into the "incomplete contracts" problem discussed earlier in the class.

- See: https://www.nytimes.com/2018/02/12/business/trump-infr astructure-proposal.html.
- Now consider the (simpler!) case of residential infrastructure (streets, lights, sidewalks, water and sewer).
- Alternative sources of revenue are:

  - Property taxes;
  - Special assessments on homeowners;
  - User fees;
  - One-time fees charged to home buyers;
  - One-time fees charged to builder;
  - Requirement placed on builder.

4.1. *Incidence of Development Fees*

- Fees charged to home buyers and fees charged to builders sound quite different, but are, in fact equivalent.

  - Remember the theorem: Economic incidence does not depend on legal incidence.

- Because builders and home buyers are both mobile, they both must be compensated for fees paid.

  - Builders are compensated by a higher price (if they pay the fee).
  - Homeowners are compensated by receiving the benefits from the fees — i.e. *homeowners bear the burden of the fee* and receive the benefits from the infrastructure.
  - I will return to the case where the benefits and costs are not equal.

- Fees charged to builders and requiring builders to provide infrastructure sound the same, but used to be quite different.

  - Existing residents would like builders or new residents to pay not only for their infrastructure, but also for unrelated infrastructure, such as a marina.

- Courts require a *nexus* between fees and new infrastructure costs:
  - But local governments have had negotiating room through their control of *zoning* and could "convince" builders to build other things.
- A recent U.S. Supreme Court decision appears to have changed the possibilities.
- A Florida water management district was denied a permit for a shopping center because the developer would not spend money on wetlands-restoration projects.
- The Supreme Court said a "rough proportionality" between the project and the requirements was needed.
- So fees and building requirements now look similar — and a key economic development tool may have been lost.
- If costs imposed on builders exceed benefits from the infrastructure, the price of undeveloped land will fall.
  - Builders will not build unless they make normal profits.
  - Homeowners will not pay more than the value of the infrastructure.
  - Landowners therefore cannot sell their land unless the price compensates builders.
- Thus, it is the owners of undeveloped land, not builders or new residents, who pay for unrelated infrastructure that is "financed" by new development.

4.2. *Fees vs. Property Taxes*

- Property taxes are sometimes used to pay for new infrastructure.
  - This approach places the burden on all residents, not just new residents.
- This approach also provides a bonus to the owners of undeveloped land.
  - The price of new housing goes up by more than the cost of infrastructure.
  - So landowners can sell the land to builders for a higher price.

4.2.1. *Fees vs. property taxes, normative analysis*

- Development fees equal to costs place the burden on new residents.
  - This satisfies the benefit principle.
- Development fees above cost place an unfair burden on landowners.
- Property taxes spread the burden widely.
  - This is appropriate when a community is first being developed.
  - But violates the benefit principle (and gives a bonus to landowners) for fringe development.
- Development fees and property taxes for community-wide infrastructure are fair across generations.
- In either case, homeowners bear the burden through higher prices for the stream of benefits from infrastructure.
  - If a homeowner leaves the community, the household that purchases her house must pay for the remaining stream of benefits in the form of a higher house price.
  - Thus the person who actually receives the infrastructure benefits pays for them.
- Impacts on landowners, if any, are clearly not fair across generations.

4.2.2. *Fees vs. Property taxes, positive analysis*

- The use of fees vs. property taxes is driven by the relative power of homeowners and landowners.
- Expect property tax financing where landowners are politically powerful.
- Expect the use of development fees or construction requirements (sometimes for unrelated projects) where homeowners are well organized (or taxes limited).

Lecture 13

Municipal Bonds Markets

1. Municipal Bonds

- Today's topic is state and local bonds, usually lumped together as municipal bonds or munis.
- This is an important topic because financing capital projects without borrowing would cause huge short-run shocks to state and local tax rates.
- Borrowing allows a jurisdiction to spread the impact of large capital projects over time.

1.1. *Bonds and Taxes or Fees*

- Municipal bonds are not a financing tool, they are a burden-spreading tool.
- A government cannot finance capital spending with bonds; instead, it must finance this spending with taxes or fees and then spread the impact out over time with bonds.

445

- Decisions about bonds therefore are connected to decisions about the best way to finance a project, that is, about the most appropriate taxes and fees (based on equity and efficiency).

1.2. *The Real Impact of Bonds*

- Saying that bonds are a burden-spreading tool does not imply that they have no real impacts.
- In fact, there is a cost to spreading out the impact of a project over time, namely, interest costs, broadly defined.
- Poor bond-issuing policies can boost interest costs above the minimum required level.

1.3. *Overview of the Muni Bond Market Update*

- In 2017, state and local governments issued $360.4 billion of tax-exempt municipal debt (and $34.2 billion of taxable debt).

  ○ We will cover the issue of "taxability" in the next class.

- This debt was used to spread out the burden of paying for, among other things, general purpose projects ($178.4 billion), K-12 schools ($126.2 billion), higher education ($70.4 billion), hospitals ($31.2 billion), mass transit ($20.3 billion), tunnels ($19.8 billion), housing($18.3 billion), and airports.
- For more information, see: https://www.sifma.org/wp-content/uploads/2018/02/US-Municipal-Report-2018-02-23-SIFMA.pdf.

1.4. *What is a Municipal Bond?*

- A bond is a certificate of indebtedness.
- The issuer agrees to pay interest to the purchaser in return for the use of the purchaser's money over a given period of time.
- A bond contrasts with a stock, in which a firm exchanges part ownership in a company for the use of an investor's money. Stocks are not relevant for government.

2. Basic Bond Characteristics

- Three things are always stamped on a bond:

  - *Face Value* $= F$ ($=$ par value or redemption value or value at maturity).
  - *Coupon Rate* $= c$, which indicates the interest to be paid as a percentage of F and which can be either fixed or floating (i.e. tied to some other rate).
  - *Years to Maturity* $= N$, which is the number of years until the bond can be redeemed and is also the number of years during which the investor is entitled to collect interest.

- Bonds are usually issued in serial form, which means that some bonds have $N = 1$, some have $N = 2$, some have $N = 3$, all the way up to the highest selected maturity, N^*.

  - This approach helps spread out the cost because it implies that only $1/N^*$ of the bonds have to be paid back each year.

- Bonds are usually issued with face values of $5,000 or multiples of $5,000.

  - In the past, this meant that only large investors bought them, but now anyone can invest any amount in bonds through a bond fund.

- Other things that might be on a bond:

  - *Call Option*, which gives the issuer the right to recall the bond before its maturity date (increasing the risk placed on the investor).
  - *Put Option*, which allows the investor to redeem the bond before its maturity date (increasing the risk placed on the issuer).
  - *Insurance* against the possibility that the issuer cannot make the specified payments on time (lowering the risk placed on the investor, but imposing a cost on the issuer).

2.1. *The Price of a Bond*

- The first key to understanding bond markets is to think about the market price of a bond.
- This price equals the amount an investor would pay to purchase a bond.
- This market price is not the same thing as a bond's face value!
- Suppose an investor has an alternative, similar investment, perhaps a U.S. Treasury Bill, that offers an interest rate r.
- Then r is the opportunity cost of investing in bonds, and the investor's willingness to pay is the present value of the benefits from holding the bond or

$$P = \frac{cF}{(1+r)} + \frac{cF}{(1+r)^2} + \cdots + \frac{cF}{(1+r)^N} + \frac{F}{(1+r)^N}$$

- With the help of a little algebra, this equation can be simplified to:

$$P = F\left(c\left(\frac{1-(1+r)^{-N}}{r}\right) + \left(\frac{1}{(1+r)^N}\right)\right)$$

- The first term is like a mortgage (where P is the mortgage amount and cF is the monthly payment), but a bond, unlike a mortgage, retains its principal until it is redeemed (the second term).
- Thus, regardless of the split between interest (the first term) and redemption value (the second term), P is proportional to F.

  ○ If $P > F$, the bond is said to sell at a *premium*.
  ○ If $P < F$, the bond is said to sell at a *discount*.

2.2. *A Bond's Rate of Return*

- The second key to understanding bond markets is to think about the rate of return on a bond that sells at price P.
- This rate of return is the value of r at which the above equation is true, given P.
- This is a standard type of present-value calculation; it is often called finding the internal rate of return.

- In the case of bonds, it is called calculating a bond's *yield to maturity.*

2.3. *Calculating Yield to Maturity*

- Calculating the yield to maturity is difficult because the equation is nonlinear.
- But most spreadsheet programs are set up to do this type of calculation, that is, to find an internal rate of return (IRR).
- Moreover, there is a simple approximation that indicates the key intuition.

2.4. *Approximating Yield to Maturity*

- This approximation starts with the recognition that the annual return on a bond has two parts:
  - Interest Return $= cF$.
  - Capital Gain $= (F - P)/N$ per year.
- Thus, the total return, expressed as a share of the "price," is:

$$r = \frac{cF + \frac{F-P}{N}}{\frac{P+F}{2}}$$

2.5. *Price and Rate of Return*

- The difference between these two ways of looking at bonds corresponds to what is unknown.
  - In the first case r is known, but P is not. We use the present-value equation to solve for P.
  - In the second case, P is known, but r is not. We use the present-value equation to solve for r.

3. Types of Bonds

- Bonds come in many different types, including the following:
- Zero Coupon Bond $=$ a bond that pays no interest. This bond obviously must sell at a huge discount $(P < F)$ because all of its return comes in the form of a capital gain.

o Its price:

$$\text{Zero-coupon bond: } P = \frac{F}{(1+r)^N}$$

- Compound Interest Bond or Capital Appreciation Bond = a bond that puts interest payments in an "account" and lets them accumulate, but does not pay them out until the maturity date. This bond changes the time pattern of payments by saving all the interest until the end.

  o Its price:

$$\text{CAB} : P = F\left(\frac{(1+c)^N}{(1+r)^N}\right)$$

  o If $c = r$, then $P = F$.

- Some budget officials like zero-coupon or capital appreciation bonds because they push the re-payment streams into the future — and hence make it easier to balance the budget today.
- These bonds do not save money, however, because they do not change the *present value* of the re-payment stream.
- Moreover, zero-coupon bonds are generally avoided near a borrowing limit because they have the highest face values.
- The following table shows the actual payments and the present value of payments for standard, zero-coupon, and capital-appreciation bond serial issues, each with a present value of $50,000.
- Actual payments are the budget amounts for interest and redemption.
- The present value columns account for the fact that payments made in the future have a lower true impact than payments made today.
- Bond decisions should be based on present values!

Note that CABs have illusory savings (= lower payments) in the first few years — but the same present value overall!

Payments on Three Types of Municipal Bond.

	Standard		Zero-Coupon		Capital Appreciation	
Year	Actual ($)	Present Value ($)	Actual ($)	Present Value ($)	Actual ($)	Present Value ($)
1	7,500.00	7,142.86	6,475.23	6,166.88	5,250.00	5,000.00
2	7,250.00	6,575.96	6,475.23	5,873.22	5,512.50	5,000.00
3	7,000.00	6,046.86	6,475.23	5,593.55	5,788.13	5,000.00
4	6,750.00	5,553.24	6,475.23	5,327.19	6,077.53	5,000.00
5	6,500.00	5,092.92	6,475.23	5,073.51	6,381.41	5,000.00
6	6,250.00	4,663.85	6,475.23	4,831.92	6,700.48	5,000.00
7	6,000.00	4,264.09	6,475.23	4,601.82	7,035.50	5,000.00
8	5,750.00	3,891.83	6,475.23	4,382.69	7,387.28	5,000.00
9	5,500.00	3,545.35	6,475.23	4,173.99	7,756.64	5,000.00
10	5,250.00	3,223.04	6,475.23	3,975.23	8,144.47	5,000.00
Total	63,750.00	50,000.00	64,752.29	50,000.00	66,033.94	50,000.00

Note: The coupon rate and opportunity cost are set at 5%. The table presents the total payments on bonds of all maturities in each year. The face values of the standard and capital appreciation bonds are $5,000; the face values of the zero-coupon bonds are $6,475.23. The standard and capital appreciation bonds sell for $5,000, whereas the zero-coupon bonds sell for amounts between $4,761.91 (1-year maturity) and $3,069.57 (10-year maturity).

- Perpetuity = a bond with $N = \infty$, so it just pays interest and never gets to the redemption date.
- Perpetuities aren't used often because they put a perpetual burden on government. But they are interesting to evaluate.

  o With an infinite N, the present-value formula simplifies to:

  $$P = \frac{cF}{r}$$

  o So if $c = r$, then $P = F$; if $c < r$, the bond sells at a discount $(P < F)$; and if $c > r$, the bond sells at a premium. Discounts and premiums can arise even if a bond never matures!

- Although perpetuities are rare, a case of bonds with very long maturities appeared in *The New York Times* a couple years ago.
- In 1868, Winston Churchill's grandfather, Leonard W. Jerome, came up with the idea of building a road to a new racetrack in what is now the Bronx.

- Two villages issued the bonds at a 7% interest rate and with maturities up to 279 years; the resulting street was initially called Central Avenue, but it is now called Jerome Avenue.
- When NYC annexed these villages, it inherited the bonds and will keep paying 7% interest to remaining bondholders until the last bond is redeemed in 2147!
- See: http://www.nytimes.com/2009/02/13/nyregion/13jerome. html.

3.1. *Categories of Municipal Bond*

- Bonds backed by full taxing authority of issuing government:
  - General Obligation Bonds (GO);
  - Moral Obligation Bonds;
  - Double Barreled GO Bonds.
- Bonds backed by Specific Revenue Source:
  - Revenue Bond;
  - Agency Bond;
  - Tax Increment Bond.
- Bonds backed by a private revenue source:
  - Industrial Development Bonds;
  - Pollution Control Bonds;
  - Mortgage Revenue Bonds.
- Bonds to Smooth Timing Problems:
  - Tax Anticipation Notes (TANs);
  - Revenue Anticipation Notes (RANs);
  - Bond Anticipation Notes (BANs).

3.2. *Investments that Compete with Bonds*

- Governments must compete for investor's funds with many other types of investment, including:
  - Stocks;
  - Corporate Bonds;
  - Federal Bonds (savings bonds, treasury bonds, agency bonds);
  - Mortgages.

3.3. The Market for Tax-exempt Loanable Funds

- *Demand*: State and local governments want loanable funds to smooth revenue flows.
- *Supply*: Investors with high marginal tax rates prefer tax-exempt investments, such as munis, for reasons explored next class.

3.4. Purchasers of Munis

- For reasons discussed in the next class, the purchasers of munis are mostly high-income individuals, mutual funds, banks, and insurance companies. According to www.sifma.org:
  - The share of munis owned by high-income individuals went from 11.8% in 1996 to 42.5% in 2017.
  - The shares for mutual funds are 11.8% in 1996 and 24.6% in 2017; the shares for commercial banks are 2.8% in 1996 and 15.4% in 2017; and the shares for insurance companies are 4.9% in 1996 and 13.4% in 2017.

3.5. Analyzing the Municipal Bond Market

The following figures provide a brief review on the analysis of the municipal bond market.

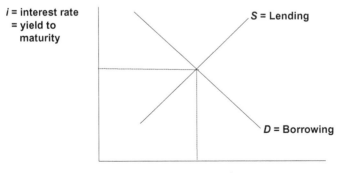

The Supply and Demand for Tax-Exempt Loanable Funds.

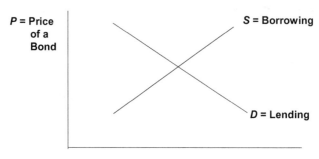

The Supply and Demand for Municipal Bonds.

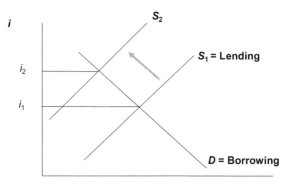

Impact of Tight Monetary Policy (or Loss of Confidence in Munis or New Tax-exempt Savings Options).

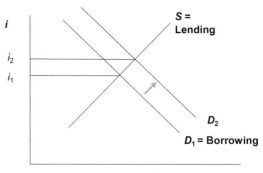

Initial Impact of Industrial Development Bonds (or Mortgage Revenue Bonds).

Lecture 14

Issuing Municipal Bonds

- **Class Outline**
  1. **Market Overview**
  2. **Features of Municipal Bonds**
  3. **Issuing Bonds**

1. Market Overview

- "Tax-Exempt Bonds: A Description of State and Local Government Debt," Grant A. Driessen, Congressional Research Service, February 15, 2018. https://fas.org/sgp/crs/misc/RL30638.pdf.

2. Features of Municipal Bonds

2.1. *Maturity*

- Because municipal bonds are serial issues, they have different maturities.
- In a market, yields generally must rise with maturity, because investors must be compensated for being locked in for a longer time. But:
  - Call and put options are equivalent to lowering maturity from the issuer or the investor's perspective, respectively.
  - Market conditions are more volatile in the short-run than in the long-run, so an "inverted" yield curve (i.e. higher rates for shorter-term bonds) can arise under some circumstances.

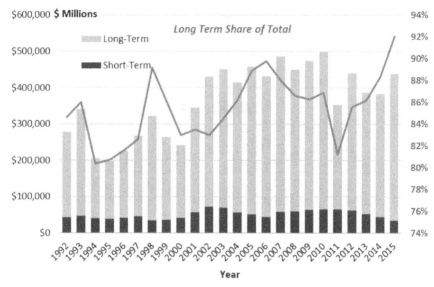

Volume of State and Local Government Debt Issuances, 1992–2015.

Source: The Bond Buyer, 2015 in Statistics: Annual Review, February 2016.

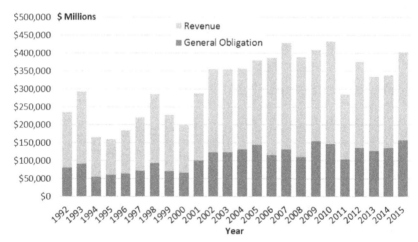

Volume of Long-Term Tax-Exempt Debt: General Obligation (GO) and Revenue Bonds, 1992–2015.

Source: The Bond Buyer, 2015 in Statistics: Annual Review, February 2016.

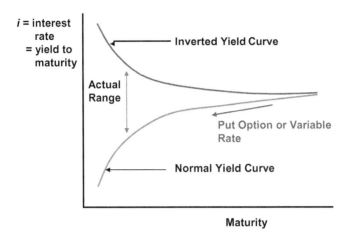

Yield Curves for Bonds.

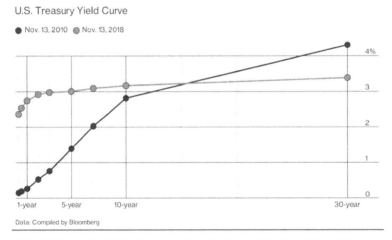

Yield Curves for U.S. Treasury Bonds (from *The New York Times*).

2.2. Tax Exemption

- Municipal bonds are free from federal tax (and usually from state taxes if they are held by residents of the issuing state).

○ The U.S. Supreme Court has ruled that this is not a constitutional issue, but the federal government has declined to alter this time-honored policy.

• This tax exemption implies that:

○ Municipal bonds are particularly attractive to taxpayers with the highest federal marginal income tax rates.

○ The subsidy for municipal bonds is inefficient (but politically protected).

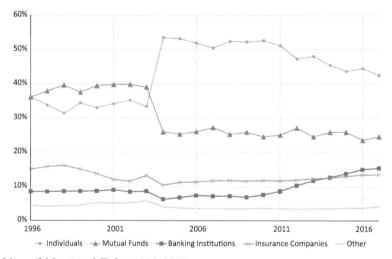

Holders of Municipal Debt, 1996–2017.

Source: Federal Reserve Board via www.sifma.org.

2.2.1. *Bonds and tax brackets*

• Suppose the taxable rate of return is 12% and the tax-free (i.e. municipal) rate is 9%.

○ Then someone in the 25% income tax bracket is indifferent between taxable investments and munis:

$$12 \times (1 - 0.25) = 9$$

○ Someone in the 35% tax bracket prefers munis:

$$12 \times (1 - 0.35) < 9$$

○ Someone in the 15% tax bracket prefers a taxable investment:

$$12 \times (1 - 0.15) > 9$$

- The actual break-even tax rate has varied a great deal over the last 30 years, with a high of 27% in 2001 and a low of 7% in 2013.
- The lower the break-even tax rate, the greater the share of taxpayers who will benefit from the tax exemption.
- A large drop in the break-even tax rate from 2002 to 2003, combined with new access to information about municipal bonds on the internet, led to the large increase in 2004 in the share of bond holders who are individuals.

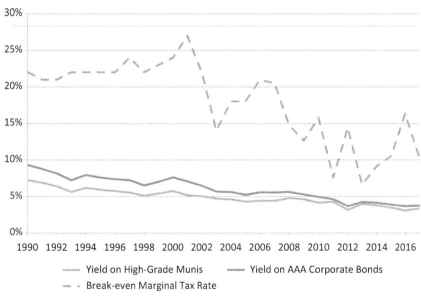

The Break-Even Tax Rate, 1990–2017 (CEA).

2.2.2. *The tax exemption is inefficient*

- Suppose a government issues $1 million in bonds and half are purchased by people in each of the top two brackets (25% and 50%).

    o The savings to the issuing government is

    $$(0.03)(\$1 \text{ million}) = \$30,000$$

    o The cost to the federal government is

    $$(\$500,000)(0.12)(.5) = \$30,000 \text{ (top bracket)}$$
    $$+ \qquad\qquad = \$15,000 \text{ (middle br.)}$$
    $$(\$500,000)(0.12)(.25) = \$45,000 \text{ total}$$

- This is inefficient, because the cost to the federal government exceeds the savings to the issuer.
- The federal subsidy for bonds is inefficient because anyone with a marginal tax rate above the "break-even rate" receives a benefit greater than what is needed to induce them to buy a municipal bond.
- Direct subsidies would avoid this, but would have to go through the budget process, which is reviewed each year and is therefore less protected.

2.2.3. *Removing the subsidy*

- Last year some Republicans in Congress proposed eliminating the interest rate subsidy.

    o See: http://www.routefifty.com/finance/2017/02/state-local-leaders-defend-tax-exempt-muni-bonds/135679/.

- This would save the U.S. Treasury about $617 over 10 years, but would obviously cost state and local governments the same amount.

- Moreover, this change would reverse a long-standing policy to subsidize state and local infrastructure because of its importance to the national economy.

2.2.4. *Private purpose bonds*

- State and local governments have a strong incentive to use tax-exempt bonds for private purposes, such as economic development, education loans, and mortgages.
- This costs the federal government a lot of money and raises the price of bonds generally.
- So the use of tax-exempt bonds for private purposes is limited by the federal government.

2.3. *Ratings*

- Three companies, Moody's, Standard and Poor's, and Fitch provide 99% of the ratings for municipal bonds.

Private-Activity Bond Volume by Type of Activity in 2014 and 2015 (Driessen).

	Allocation in Billions ($)		Percent of Capacity Available (%)	
Capacity Allocation	2014	2015	2014	2015
Total Volume Capacity Available	87,223.50	90,036.20	100.00	100.00
New Volume Capacity	32,748.30	34,878.90	37.55	38.74
Carry Forward from Previous Years	56,445.30	58,478.60	64.71	64.95
Total Carryforward to Next Year	60,220.00	54,584.90	69.04	60.63
Total PABs Issued	8,824.30	13,139.80	10.12	14.59
Mortgage Revenue	1,828.20	4,566.30	2.10	5.07
Multi-family Housing	4,722.30	6,605.80	5.41	7.34
Exempt Facilities	6,076.00	7,614.10	6.97	8.46
Other Activities	84.20	27.10	0.10	0.03
Student Loans	480.20	688.10	0.55	0.76
Industrial Development	355.80	244.30	0.41	0.27
Abandon Capacity	11,751.60	10,460.10	13.47	11.62

Source: "CDFA's 2015 Annual Volume Cap Report," July 2014; and "CDFA's 2015 Annual Volume Cap Data." August 2016. The data are available at http://www.cdfa.net/.

- o Several smaller agencies are also designated "Nationally Recognized Statistical Ratings Organizations" by the SEC and rate a few municipal bonds.
- o See: https://www.sec.gov/ocr/reportspubs/annual-reports/201 7-annual-report-on-nrsros.pdf.
- Governments pay a fee to have their bonds rated because the ratings provide information to investors.
- Ratings are attached to bond issues, except in the case of GO bonds, where the issuing government has a rating.

2.3.1. *What do ratings measure?*

- The rating agencies say that ratings measure default risk, i.e. the risk that the issuer will not make all the payments on time.
- Ratings are based on economic, financial, and political characteristics of the issuer, but the formulas are proprietary — and closely guarded.
- Ratings have a big impact on interest cost. A highly rated bond might be able to pay one percentage point less in interest than a bond with a poor rating.
- Issuers do not have to buy a rating, but they usually do.

2.3.2. *Default risk*

- Default risk is real, at least for revenue bonds.
- Consider the following tables from a Standard and Poor's document: "A Complete Look at Monetary Defaults During the 1990s." http://www.kennyweb.com/kwnext/mip/paydefault.pdf.
- For perspective, outstanding muni debt in 2002 was about $1 trillion for revenue bonds and $600 billion for GOs.

2.3.3. *Impacts of ratings*

- Because high ratings lower interest costs, governments have in interest in obtaining a high rating.
- So many governments strive to meet the tax and management standards set by the rating agencies.

Investment Grade Ratings.

	Moody's	Standard and Poor's	Fitch
Best Quality	Aaa	AAA	AAA
High Quality	Aa1	AA$^+$	AA$^+$
	Aa2	AA	AA
	Aa3	AA$^-$	AA$^-$
Upper Medium Grade	A1	A$^+$	A$^+$
	A2	A	A
	A3	A$^-$	A$^-$
Medium Grade	Baa1	BBB$^+$	BBB$^+$
	Baa2	BBB	BBB
	Baa3	BBB$^-$	BBB$^-$

Growth in U.S. Municipal Ratings

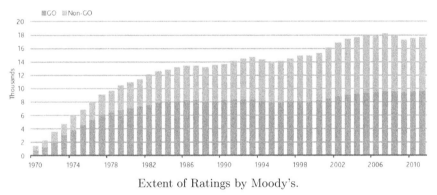

Extent of Ratings by Moody's.

- Many other governments buy bond insurance, which can raise ratings (and therefore save money).
- In some cases, states insure the bonds of their local governments.
- Some small governments form bond pools to broaden their resource base and lower the risk of default.
- Ratings also influence investor's response to events in the market place.

Ratings Distributions: Municipals vs. Corporates, Year End 2011

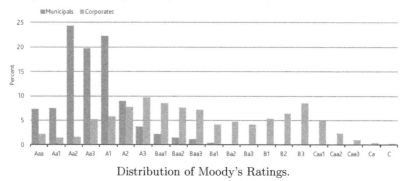

Distribution of Moody's Ratings.

Revenue Bond Defaults, 1990s.

Sector	# of Defaults	Defaulted Amount $	Avg. Time to Default	# Rated	# Non-Rated
Industrial Dev (IDBs)	288	2,839,915,892	88	33	255
Healthcare	239	1,994,158,951	58	24	215
Multifamily Housing	153	2,050,092,293	63	51	102
Land-Backed Debt	141	1,037,790,699	72	2	139
COPs/Lease Revs	30	146,505,781	57	2	28
Other Revenues	25	826,992,000	47	7	18
Single Family Housing	16	36,877,076	137	13	3
General Obligations	14	827,550,000	10	5	9
Utilities	8	39,450,000	70	0	8
Education	3	10,530,000	44	0	3
Totals	914	9,809,862,692	71	137	780

- When New York City defaulted in 1974, the premium paid for highly rated bonds went up noticeably.

  ○ When Cleveland defaulted in 1979, nobody noticed.
  ○ When Orange County in California defaulted in 1995, the impact was small and short-lived.

Go Bond Defaults, 1990s.

Year	# of Defaults	Defaulted Amount ($)	Avg. Time to Default	# Rated	# Non-Rated
1990	1	2,000,000	18	0	1
1995	3	800,000,000	12	3	0
1996	4	5,860,000	8	0	4
1997	1	2,800,000	11	0	1
1998	4	15,475,000	8	2	2
1999	1	1,415,000	9	0	1
Totals	14	827,550,000	10	5	9

Defaults in 1995 were tied to 3 short-term note deals issued by Orange County, California.

Seven out of the 14 monetary defaults were tied to late payments caused by administrative oversights and were not related to financial difficulties.

Go Default Settlements, 1990s.

Settlement Type	# of Settlements	Avg. Time to Settlement	Avg. Recovery
Resumptions	7	1	N/A
Cash Distributions	3	11	100
Redemptions	2	4	100
Exchange	1	7	N/A
Totals	13	4	

Holders of the three Orange County, California note deals were made whole (recovered 100 cents on the dollar) through cash distributions when the County emerged from bankruptcy during June of 1996.

- From an investor's point of view, therefore, ratings also indicate *market risk*.

2.3.4. *Rating the raters*

- The private rating agencies play an important public role — i.e. they influence the cost of infrastructure.

Moody's Default.

Default Counts by Sale Purpose, 1970–2011

Purpose	Number of Defaults	Percentage (%)
Housing	29	40.8
Hospitals and Health Service Providers	22	31.0
Education	3	4.2
Infrastructure	4	5.6
Utilities	2	2.8
Cities	2	2.8
Counties	1	1.4
Special Districts	1	1.4
Water and sewer	1	1.4
State Governments	1	1.4
Non General Obligation	66	93.0
General Obligation	5	7.0
Total	71	100

- Under these circumstances, one would think that they would be regulated, i.e. that some government agency would ask whether their actions are in the public interest.
- Regulation of ratings was prohibited by the Credit Rating Agency Reform Act of 2006.
  - The Dodd–Frank Act of 2010 gives the SEC some regulatory powers, but their impact is not yet clear.
- My 2010 article in the *American Law and Economics Review* suggests that some regulation may be needed.
- GO bonds essentially never default.
- As a result, no government characteristic has any value in predicting default.
- So any rating policy that puts cities with certain characteristics at a disadvantage cannot be justified by a connection to default risk.
- My work shows that all three large ratings agencies hand out GO ratings that decline with the percentage of a city's population that is black.

- This is not fair, and a federal regulator should be looking into it.
- I have looked into the same issue with school bonds in California.
- Again I found this type of "redlining" also arises in this case.
- School districts with high black or Hispanic concentrations receive lower GO bond ratings than largely white districts — despite having the same probability of default.
- Lower ratings lead, of course, to higher interest costs for black and Hispanic than for white districts.
- http://cpr.maxwell.syr.edu/efap/about_efap/ie/June13.pdf.
- One might think that my focus on default risk is inappropriate because ratings also indicate market risk.
- But from society's point of view, this argument is circular — at least in the case of GO bonds.
- Ratings cannot predict default but they do predict market risk if investors believe they do. The link to market risk is therefore based on investor illusion.
- It makes no sense to justify unfair ratings for some cities because these ratings are successful in deluding investors!
- The point here is not that rating agencies are bad.
- In fact, they serve the public interest by encouraging governments to follow good practices.

  ○ Good practices lead to higher ratings and lower interest costs.
  ○ Or good practices lead to lower costs for bond insurance.

- Ratings provided by a higher level of government would undoubtedly not have as much credibility — or so much impact on government practices.
- But ratings agencies are out to make profits — not serve the public interest — and they should be regulated.

3. Issuing Bonds

- Many institutions are involved in issuing bonds.
- The issuing government is required by the Consumer Finance Protection Bureau to hire an independent public finance advisor to help figure out the characteristics of the bond issue.

- An underwriter buys the bonds from the issuing government, and then sells them to investors.
- In rare cases, the issuing government uses a broker to sell directly to investors.

3.1. *Selecting a Bid*

- The issuing government must select a bid, which is a combination of prices, face values, and interest rates for a set of bonds.

  ○ Sometimes the bid is negotiated with a single underwriter.
  ○ Sometimes many underwriters bid and the issuing government decides which bid to accept.

- The amount raised by a bond is the price in the bid, not the face value.

  ○ But an issuing government typically includes a constraint requiring that the total amount of the bid (the sum of the prices) must be equal to (or nearly equal to) the amount that needs to be raised.

- The best bid is the one with the lowest true interest cost (TIC), which is the internal rate of return of the whole issue.
- This is found by solving the following equation for r:

$$\sum_{j=1}^{N} P_j = \sum_{j=1}^{N} \left(\sum_{t=1}^{M_j} \left(\frac{c_j F_j}{(1+r)^t} \right) + \frac{F_j}{(1+r)^{M_j}} \right)$$

- For a long time, local governments did not understand TIC and selected the bid with the lowest total interest payments.
- Underwriters did understand TIC and made bids with large interest payments up front where they had greater present value.

  ○ This means higher interest rates on shorter maturities — the opposite of what one usually observes in a market.

- Restrictions, such as no interest rate inversion, can go a long way toward eliminating these problems, but TIC is better. Discounting matters!

3.2. Competition vs. Negotiation

- An issuing government must decide whether to use competitive bidding.
- If the bond issue is unusual and a certain underwriter has the needed expertise, negotiation makes sense.
- But competition, which is used for $3/4$ of bond issues, lowers costs.
- In his PA dissertation from Maxwell and later work, Mark Robbins (now at University of Connecticut) found that competition lowers TIC by about 35 basis points (= 0.35 percentage points).

Economic Development: Concepts

- **Class Outline**
  1. **Introduction**
  2. **Macroeconomic Models**
  3. **Input/Output Analysis**
  4. **Agglomeration Economies**

1. Introduction

- Economic development is an important topic in state and local public finance.
- After all, most state and local politicians run on the platform of "jobs, jobs, jobs".
- The question is: What policies actually affect the number of jobs (and the incomes they generate) in a given jurisdiction.
- This class examines some basic concepts in state and local economic development.
- The next class looks at the impact of fiscal policies, including taxes and public spending, on local economic development.
- This topic is complex and frustrating: Although there is a great deal of research, there is no consensus about the best policies to follow.

2. Macroeconomic Models

- This class has focused on microeconomics, that is, on the analysis of households and firms and single markets.

- But economic development involves macroeconomics, which is all markets put together.
- Today we will look at some highly simplified macroeconomic models: Keynesian, export-base, and input–output.

2.1. *A Simple Keynesian Model*

- A simple Keynesian model combines accounting identities and assumptions about behavior.
- The terms:

  $Y =$ Income;
  $E =$ Expenditures (=GNP);
  $C =$ Consumption;
  $I =$ Investment;
  $S =$ Savings;
  $X =$ Exports;
  $M =$ Imports.

- The identities:

$$E \equiv C + I + (X - M)$$

$$Y \equiv C + S$$

$$E \equiv Y$$

- The assumptions about behavior:

$$I = I_0; \quad X = X_0$$

$$C = C_0 + cY; \quad M = mY$$

- The equilibrium:

$$Y = \left(\frac{1}{1 - c + m} \right) (C_0 + I_0 + X_0)$$

- Interpretation:

  ○ Exports (and other exogenous factors) are multiplied into income.

- These factors have a larger impact if the marginal propensity to consume (c) is larger.
- These factors have a smaller impact if the marginal propensity to import (m = "leakage") is larger.

- Of course this model leaves out many things, such as:
  - Government
  - Prices and interest rates
  - Expectations
- But it introduces three key concepts:
  - Exports (=inflows)
  - Multipliers
  - Leakage

2.2. *Economic Base Models*

- Economic base models are the simplest possible macroeconomic models of a state or local economy.
- They are highly oversimplified and should be used with great care, but also provide some useful insights.

2.3. *Export vs. Local Jobs*

- Export base models start with a distinction between "export jobs" and "local jobs."
- *Export jobs* are associated with goods or services sold on a national market.
  - Manufacturing jobs are a key example.
- *Local jobs* are jobs associated with goods or services that compete only in local markets.
  - Jobs in grocery stores, fast food restaurants, or dry cleaners are examples.
- The distinction between export and local jobs depends on the context.
- A famous restaurant or a retail store on a jurisdiction boundary may attract customers from other jurisdictions and therefore involve export jobs.

2.3.1. *An export base model*

- An export base model combines a definition and a simple behavioral equation.
- Let:

  T = Total jobs;
  L = Local jobs;
  E = Export jobs.

- Then, the definition is:

$$T = L + E$$

- The behavioral equation is:

$$L = bE$$

- This equation indicates that local jobs are created by resources flowing into an economy.
- Putting these together, we have

$$T = bE + E = E(1 + b)$$

- In this equation, $(1 + b)$ is called the *"multiplier"*:

  ○ Export jobs are "multiplied up" into total jobs because they lead to income circulating around the local economy.

2.3.1.1. Alternative Export Base Model

- An alternative form of the behavioral equation is

$$L = (b^*)T$$

- In this case,

$$T = (b^*)T + E$$
$$T(1 - b^*) = E$$
$$T = E/(1 - b^*)$$

- Thus, $1/(1 - b^*)$ is the multiplier.

2.3.1.2. Export Base Models, Lessons

- First, export jobs get "multiplied up" into total jobs.

  ○ If a government manages to attract another export job it adds more than one job to its economy.

- Second, "attracting" another local job (that is, giving it a subsidy) doesn't do anything except displace a local job on the other side of town.

  ○ Local jobs are determined by export jobs.

- If you want to boost a local economy, attract export jobs!

2.3.1.3. Export Base Models, Limits

- Export base models are highly simplified.
- For example, they ignore market failure. A state policy might be able to add local jobs by ending some form of market failure.
- But the presumption that economic development policy should focus on export jobs is a good place to start.

3. Input/Output Analysis

- Input/output (I/O) analysis is a fancy export-base model.
- I/O analysis begins with $1 of exogenous demand for the products of industry A.
- Satisfying this demand requires contributions from all industries, say $.01 from A itself, $.05 from B, $.25 from C, and so on.
- Satisfying these demands requires additional contributions from each industry, etc.
- I/O analysis provides a formal way to summarize all these transactions.
- The more purchases are made locally, the higher the multiplier.
- Equivalently, the more purchases leak out to other jurisdictions, the lower the multiplier.

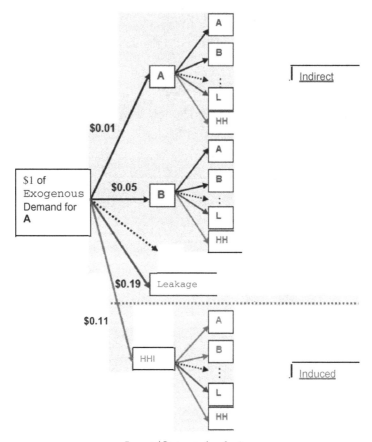

Input/Output Analysis.

3.1.1. *Input/output model*

- In formal terms, an I/O model is a series of equations like:

$$Y_1 = a_{11}Y_1 + a_{12}Y_2 + \cdots + a_{1n}Y_n + X_1$$

where Y is output, X is exogenous demand, and a_{1j} is the amount of product 1 needed to produce the output for product j.

- Stacking these equations and using matrix notation:

$$Y = AY + X$$

$$(I - A)Y = X$$

$$Y = (I - A)^{-1}X$$

- Note that the $(I - A)^{-1}$ matrix is just the matrix-algebra version of the multiplier idea in the export-base model.

3.1.2. *Types of I/O models*

- There are two types of I/O Model.
- The first treats the household sector as part of exogenous demand, X.

  o This is called an *open* model.
  o With this model, the A matrix is just about purchases of non-labor inputs, and the multipliers reflect the *direct and indirect* requirements from each industry to meet exogenous demand.

- The second type treats households as an industry.

  o This is called a *closed* model.
  o Households provide labor and make purchases from other industries.
  o The household impact on multipliers is called an *induced* effect.

3.1.3. *Contributions of I/O*

- I/O adds two things to the debate:
- *First*, I/O provides a way to bring data to bear on the issue of multipliers.

  o The trouble is that the necessary data are not available at the local level, or even at the state level.
  o But regional I/O multipliers are available, See: http://www.be a.gov/regional/rims/index.cfm.

- These multipliers are "based on 2007 national benchmark input–output data and 2015 regional data."

- *Second,* I/O introduces a distinction between *indirect* multipliers (based on purchases of inputs), and *induced* multipliers (based on purchases by households).

  - The notion of indirect multipliers is critical: The more inputs are produced locally, the less the leakage and the higher the multiplier.
  - Even informal analysis of economic development programs should consider inter-connections in a local economy.

3.1.4. *Misuse of multipliers*

- A high multiplier for a particular industry says that attracting an export job in that industry will have a large positive impact on the economy.
- But multipliers can easily be misused because it is difficult to figure out what the world would be like without a program.

  - Remember: The correct question for program evaluation is how the world differs *with and without* the program.

- An I/O analysis was used in a debate about subsidizing a Mazda plant in Michigan.
- The multipliers were high — 12! — because so many auto inputs are made in Michigan.
- The people who conducted the I/O analysis said almost any subsidy was worth it.
- But the sales from the plant exaggerate the change in exogenous demand.
- If the plant were not in Michigan, it would be in Indiana or Ohio and would still purchase many inputs from Michigan.
- So one must compare income with the plant to income with these input purchases.

- You should always think about the appropriate counter-factual situation!
- A more complicated problem is that I/O multipliers are static, but the world is dynamic.
- When an Mercedes-Benz plant was built in Alabama (thanks to huge subsidies from the state government subsidies), no automobile inputs were produced in Alabama.
- Once the plant was built, however, many auto input firms moved to Alabama.
- Because Alabama had no auto firms to begin with, a large share of the people hired by M-B and by the auto input firms came from out of state.
- So predict input-firm responses, but think about whether current taxpayers should subsidize people from other states.

4. Agglomeration Economies

- Another key concept for economic development is agglomeration economies, which come in two types:

  ○ Localization economies = benefits from clustering within a given industry.
  ○ Urbanization economies = savings that arise when the production costs of an individual firm decrease as the total output in its urban area increases.

- These economies can be striking, but need not be permanent.

4.1. *Localization Economies*

4.1.1. *Examples of localization economies*

- From a report prepared for the 1900 U.S. Census:

"Measured by the value of products, more than 85 per cent of the collar and cuff manufacture is carried on in Troy, N.Y.; more than 64 per cent of the oyster-canning industry in Baltimore, Md.; more than 54 per cent of the manufacture of gloves in the adjoining cities of Gloversville and Johnstown, N.Y.; more than 48 per cent of the coke manufacture in the Connellsville district, Pennsylvania; more than 47 per cent of the manufacture of brassware in Waterbury, Conn.; more than 45 per cent of the manufacture of carpets in Philadelphia, Pa.; more than 45 percent of the manufacture of jewelry in Providence, R.I., and the adjoining towns of Attleboro and North Attleboro, Mass.; more than 36 per cent of the silverware manufacture in Providence, R.I.; more than 35 per cent of the slaughtering and meat packing industry in Chicago, Ill.; more than 32 per cent of the manufacture of plated and britannica ware in Meriden, Conn.; . . . ." Cited in a blog post by Paul Krugman on *The New York Times* website, August 9. 2015.

- From *The Guardian,* 2005: http://www.theguardian.com/busines s/2005/may/25/china.g2.

  ○ "Qiaotou [in western China] has transformed itself from a farming village into a manufacturing powerhouse.
  ○ The first small workshop was established in 1980 by three brothers who picked up their first buttons off the street. Now the town's 700 family-run factories churn out 15 billion buttons and 200 million meters of zips a year.
  ○ The local chamber of commerce estimates that three out of every five buttons in the world are made in the town. It ships more than two million zips a day, making it the biggest winner of China's 80% share of the international zip market."
  ○ Other Chinese cities specialize in toothbrushes or socks.

- Localization economies could arise from three sources:

  ○ Sharing input suppliers

    ■ Economies of scale may arise when many firms are demanding the same inputs.
    ■ Transportation costs may drop as more input firms locate nearby.

- Examples
  - Auto firms cluster to be near steel, plastic, fabric and other input firms (as in Detroit, at least until recently).
  - Corporate headquarters cluster around marketing firms.
  - Sharing a labor pool
    - A firm can make better matches if the labor pool is larger — and can make matches with lower transportation costs.
  - Sharing information (= knowledge spillovers)
    - For example, more innovative industries (as measured by patents per dollar of sales) are more likely to cluster.

4.2. *Evidence on Localization Economies*

- Rosenthal and Strange (*Review of Economics and Statistics*, 2003) find that firm births and new-firm employment in a zip code increase with nearby employment in the same industry.
- This effect declines with distance, but firms 15 miles away still have an effect in some industries.

4.3. *Urbanization Economies*

- Urbanization economies are agglomeration benefits that depend on the whole economy (not one industry) and fall upon the whole economy (not just one industry).
- The help to explain why wages are higher in larger cities (as agglomeration economies boost worker productivity).
- Their sources are similar to those of localization economies.
  - Intermediate Inputs
    - There may be economies of scale in the banking, business services, insurance, and perhaps public services.
  - Labor pooling
    - As before, there could be better matches and lower search, moving, and transportation costs.

- Sharing information
  - Some types of knowledge might spill over from one industry to others.

4.3.1. *Evidence on urbanization economies*

- Some studies find that labor productivity is, as expected, linked to city size.
- But, urbanization economies do not appear to arise for many industries, and, in general, do not appear to be as large as localization economies.

4.4. *Agglomeration and Policy*

- Agglomeration economies imply that firm location decisions may involve an *externality*:
  - The arrival of a firm may raise the productivity of other firms (in the same industry or the same region).
  - Thus, government actions to encourage firms to locate where they cause agglomeration economies may enhance public welfare — at least in that location!
- The problem is that we do not yet know enough about agglomeration economies to accurately identify cases in which these externalities exist.
- And, as we will see next class, we also don't know very much about how to attract firms.
- The examples given earlier are mainly driven by random events — not government policy — but sometimes a government gets lucky.

4.5. *Moretti on Multipliers*

- A recent study by Moretti (*American Economic Review*, 2010) points out that standard multipliers miss two key possibilities:
  - Increases in wages or housing prices may lessen the impacts of exogenous demand.
  - Agglomeration economies may magnify the impacts of exogenous demand.
- Moretti also estimates city-level multipliers.

Local Multipliers for Tradables and Nontradables.

	Elasticity OLS	Elasticity IV	Additional Jobs for Each New Job
Model 1			
Effect of tradable on nontradable	0.554 (0.036)	0.335 (0.055) [8.2]	1.59 (0.26)
Model 2			
Effect of tradable durable on nontradable	0.283 (0.039)	0.006 (0.138) [3.21, 5.52]	0.73 (1.73)
Effect of tradable nondurable on nontradable	0.290 (0.024)	0.250 (0.072) [8.53, 2.57]	1.89 (0.54)
Model 3			
Effect of tradable on other tradable	0.546 (0.069)	0.176 (0.156) [9.1]	0.26 (0.23)

Notes: Standard errors clustered by city in parentheses. First-stage p-values in brackets.

So 1 new "tradable" job leads to 1.59 "non-tradable" jobs and (because of agglomeration economies?) 0.26 new tradable jobs. Note: "tradable" = "manufacturing."

- Another table shows multipliers by skill level.
  So 1 new tradable skilled job leads to 2.52 non-tradable jobs but 1 new tradable non-skilled job lead to only 1.04 new nontradable jobs. Non-tradable jobs in construction, wholesale trade and personal services are most affected.

Local Multipliers, by Skill Level.

| | Dependent Variable | | | | | | | | |
| | All Nontradable | | | Nontradable–skilled | | | Nontradable–unskilled | | |
Independent Variable	Elast. OLS (1)	Elast. IV (2)	Addit. Jobs (3)	Elast. OLS (4)	Elast. IV (5)	Addit. Jobs (6)	Elast. OLS (7)	Elast. IV (8)	Addit. Jobs (9)
Tradable	0.287	0.257	⟨2.52⟩	0.420	0.208	2.03	0.109	0.030	0.296
skilled	(0.037)	(0.157)	(1.54)	(0.044)	(0.176)	(1.72)	(0.039)	(0.172)	(1.68)
Tradable	0.292	0.115	⟨1.04⟩	0.125	−0.010	−0.09	0.510	0.367	3.34
unskilled	(0.033)	(0.109)	(0.99)	(0.042)	(0.133)	(1.21)	(0.037)	(0.117)	(1.06)

- In addition, Moretti discusses the use of multipliers in policy.
  - He points out that new jobs may not be held by current residents.
  - But his estimates apply to manufacturing, not all tradables.
  - He cannot account for variation across cities.
  - He misses the importance of the counterfactual.

Lecture 16

Economic Development Policy

- **Class Outline**
  1. **Taxes and Economic Development**
  2. **Specific Tax Breaks**
  3. **Public Services and Economic Development**
  4. **The Art of Economic Development Policy**

1. Taxes and Economic Development

- *Two* conceptual frameworks are often used for thinking about the impact of taxes on economic development.
  - Taxes and firm profitability;
  - Capitalization.
- The trouble is that these two frameworks lead to virtually opposite policy conclusions!

1.1. *Taxes and Profitability*

- The *first* framework focuses on the idea that profit-making firms care about the level of taxation.
  - Higher taxes mean lower profits.
  - So, all else equal, jurisdictions with lower taxes should attract/ retain more firms and have more jobs and higher incomes.

- Firms also care about many other things, of course.
  - In surveys, firms mention access to customers, access to the right kind of workers, access to energy or other inputs, access to transportation, and other things before they mention taxes.
  - The owners of firms also may base their decisions on idiosyncratic factors, such as their own personal interest in a particular location.
- So ultimately the question is:
  - How important are taxes in influencing firms' decisions and, ultimately, state and local economic development?
- As we will see, this has proven to be a difficult question to answer.

1.2. *Capitalization*

- The *second* framework starts with the observation that tax differences across locations are likely to be capitalized into land values.
- As a result, firms moving into a location may not care about tax rates:
  - That is, firms are compensated for higher tax rates in the form of lower property values.
- Capitalization may also imply that firms do not care about relevant service levels.
- Capitalization also implies that when tax rates or relevant service levels are changed, they have an impact on current owners, but not on future owners.
- Moreover, current owners cannot escape changes, so their behavior is not affected by them.
- Of course, capitalization may not be complete, so this complete-capitalization story may not be quite right.
- Once again, we are back at the empirical question: To what extent do taxes (and services) matter for economic development?

1.2.1. *Studies of taxes and economic development*

- In the literature on taxes and economic development, there is a rough consensus that

○ Tax differences probably matter, particularly within an urban area, **but**

■ the impacts of taxes on economic development are not very large, and
■ service quality differences matter, too.

1.3. *Evidence*

1.3.1. *State-level evidence*

- Bania and Stone (*JPAM*, 2008) look at the determinants of growth in state personal income per capita.
- They find that raising taxes and using it for education, transportation, public safety, the environment, or housing raises growth at first, then lowers it.
- The impacts are more negative if the taxes are used for health or welfare.
- The right mix raises the 5 year growth rate 2.3 percentage points above the median; the wrong mix lowers it 4 points below the median.
- A more recent article Srithongrung and Kriz (*JPAM*, 2014) estimates a complex, dynamic model of economic development.
- This article finds that taxes have a slight, short-lived negative effect on economic growth, that operating and public-capital spending have long-lived, larger impacts on economic growth.
- The authors say it is appropriate to "reexamine" both the wisdom of cutting taxes to boost a state economy and the assertion that spending reduces growth.

1.3.2. *Local-level evidence*

- Wai-Ho Wilson Wong's dissertation (Maxwell, PA, 1998) looks at the impact of property tax rates and public services on economic development in New York.
- It takes advantage of variation in local tax rates due to the Homestead Option.

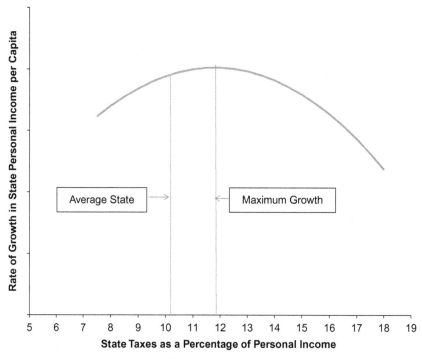

State Revenue Hill (Based on Bania and Stone).

- o Recall that this option gives cities the right to use a classified property tax, with a higher rate on business than on residential property, when they complete a revaluation.
- o This extra variation in tax rates is like a natural experiment for studying the impact of property taxes on economic development.

- Wong estimates the impact of property tax rates and public services on employment and payroll (overall and by sector) for cities in New York.
- The property tax rate has a significant negative impact in almost every regression for both employment and payroll. Property taxes matter!
- Student test scores usually have a significant positive impact, and fire loss has a significant negative impact in about half the cases. Public service levels matter, too!

- Although the impact of property taxes on economic development is negative, it turns out to be amazingly small.
- Wong calculated the impact of eliminating the property tax altogether and replacing it with some other source with no impact on economic development (such as state aid). Here is what he found:

The Impact of Eliminating Property Taxes.

	Employment Increase (%)	Payroll Increase (%)
Total	1.36	3.23
Manufacturing	1.71	12.00
Trade	0.43	1.40
Transportation/Utilities	1.63	10.89
Finance, insurance, and real estate	7.00	6.22
Service	5.13	4.94

Note: Based on Wong (1998).

1.3.3. *Tax cuts and economic development*

- Cutting property taxes usually requires cutting public services.
- Wong's study finds that service levels matter, too, and therefore does not support the view that cutting property taxes helps economic development.
- Indeed, raising taxes and improving schools might be (and probably is) a better economic development strategy!

2. Specific Tax Breaks

- Wong's study, and most of the literature, looks at the impact of tax rates and service levels.
- Most economic development programs give specific tax breaks or provide specific services.
- What do we know about the impact of specific tax breaks? Not much!

- Because every case is unique and because they are not included in any standard data set, specific tax breaks are difficult to study.
- Wassmer and Anderson's (*Economic Development Quarterly*, 2001) study of the Detroit area: property tax abatements raise manufacturing property value (MPV) in 1977 (but not in 1982, 1987, or 1992) and higher MPV leads to a lower employment rate and more poverty!
- A report by Bartik finds no significant link between economic development incentives and economic development outcomes (http://www.upjohn.org/models/bied/report.php).
- Another good study (Hanson, (*RSUE*, 2009)) finds no employment impact from the federal empowerment zone program, which gives specific tax breaks to firms locating in high-poverty zones.
- The main analytical problem that arises with specific tax breaks is that a government generally does not know which firms are "at the margin."

  ○ A firm "at the margin" is potentially influenced by the incentive provided by the specific tax break.
  ○ A firm that is not "at the margin" will locate in the jurisdiction even without the tax break.

- If a firm is not at the margin, then any tax break it receives is a waste of government funds because it has no impact on the firm's behavior.
- Unfortunately, a public official can claim credit for attracting any firm that receives a tax break, even if that firm was not "at the margin."
- The firm is located in the jurisdiction, the firm received the tax break, and there is no way to tell if the tax break made a difference.
- This feature of specific tax breaks implies that they are often misused.
- Public officials offer specific tax breaks to gain favor with the electorate and with the subsidized firm even when these tax breaks have no impact on economic development.
- Of course, if a firm is "at the margin," then a specific tax break might be a powerful economic development tool.

- Attracting an export firm with a tax break boosts the local economy, and the tax break does not represent lost revenue because the firm would not have been in the jurisdiction without the tax break.
- Moreover, specific tax breaks have a large advantage over general tax breaks, at least in principle.
  - General tax breaks are not cost-effective by definition because they automatically go to every firm, regardless of whether they are at the margin or not.
- But giving a large specific break to one firm that is not at the margin is not as cost effective as giving a small general tax break to all firms, a few of which are at the margin!
- Overall, the potential gain from specific tax breaks continues to make them popular.
- But politicians are insured against misuse of this tool because nobody can prove that a particular tax break did not matter.
- This insurance guarantees misuse, but does not help us identify the cases in which misuse occurs.
- A recent study (Kang, Reese, and Skidmore, *JPAM*, 2016) of property tax abatements for new or improved industrial property in southeast Michigan finds that the abatements increase industrial property values (= capitalization!) but also have small spillovers onto commercial and residential property values.
- However, this study also finds that the benefits from these abatements are very small relative to the foregone revenue. Under the most favorable scenario in this study, $1.00 of lost revenue brings in $0.03 in benefits.

2.1. *A Framework*

- We can make a little more progress on this topic by setting up a two-way table:
  - The rows are the two ways of looking at economic development: profits or capitalization.
  - The two columns indicate whether or not we have evidence that the firm is "at the margin."

A Framework for Thinking About Economic Development.

	Government knows if the firm is "at the margin"	Gov't has no insight into firm's decision
Profit view	Specific tax breaks can work	Breaks = gifts to firm (or lucky guesses)
Capitalization view	Breaks = gifts to landowners	Breaks = gifts to landowners

- The "gifts to landowners" entries require further comment.
  - ○ If the firm already owns the land and the tax break would not be offered to any other firm, then it only receives the break if it stays; in this case, the break affects firms at the margin.
  - ○ In the bottom left cell, breaks can work if the government owns the land and sells it below market price. A case for business parks or land banks!

3.   Public Services and Economic Development

- Good public services promote economic development.
- Firms care about good schools and good safety — on business grounds and to please their employees.
- Government services interact with business decisions in important ways.

3.1.   *Glaeser's View (Author of Triumph of the City)*

- "The best local economic development strategy is to work on attracting smart, entrepreneurial people and then … get out of their way."
- "*Be a Consumer City*: Cities thrive by attracting workers with quality of life and excitement. This leads to a focus both on bread-and-butter urban issues — like safe streets and short commutes — and on eliminating any barriers to innovation in the entertainment sector, like overregulation of restaurants, bars and my personal pet cause: the food truck."
- "*Make Entrepreneurship Easy*: I would urge every older city to set up a task force charged with making sure that their town is about the easiest place in the world to open a new start-up.

- *Get Physical*: Declining cities should make sure that private developers who want to remake urban spaces have a relatively easy time of it. They should also work to ensure that unoccupied structures are turned into more attractive and usable urban space.
- *Straighten Out Your Books*: Replace defined benefit retirement plans with defined contribution plans."
- "And finally, don't forget that better schools can reward a city more quickly than they can graduate students, by attracting skilled parents."
- Quotes from Leonhardt (2011).

4. The Art of Economic Development Policy

- Focus on the economic base.
  - The best way to boost a local economy is by increasing the flow of resource into it.
  - Subsidizing local jobs usually leads to displacement.
  - Don't go beyond economic base without good evidence.
- Don't expect tax cuts accompanied by service cuts to boost economic development.
  - The available research does not support this position. Remember Bania/Stone and Wang.
  - Of course, it is possible to spend too much, but the quality of services in big cities (and, indeed, in most states) falls below the optimal level.
  - Tax cuts are not a magic bullet!
- Strive for good management.
  - Good management keeps tax rates down without sacrificing services.
  - Good management can directly aid economic development by supporting business development and identifying unnecessary regulatory barriers.
  - This is consistent with Glaeser: Don't let bad management get in the way of business start-ups.
- Avoid specific tax breaks unless 3 conditions are met:
  - They are given to a firm "at the margin."

- o The firm adds to the economic base (or otherwise boosts the economy).
- o You are confident the benefits will not be capitalized away.
- o More extensive use is an invitation to "corruption."
- Use looser rules if you are trying to help a specific group.
  - o Adding local market jobs in certain neighborhoods might help certain groups, for example.
  - o But don't forget to think about the costs of likely displacement.
- Don't forget about the expenditure side.
- Many types of public spending have been shown to help economic development:
  - o Infrastructure;
  - o Education and training;
  - o Public safety;
  - o Technical assistance;
  - o Improving public spaces (as suggested by Glaeser).
- Be skeptical of financing programs.
  - o Private capital markets work reasonably well.
  - o Public financing programs usually have problems.
  - o They pick likely successes (who could get private financing), or
  - o They pick likely failures (and therefore have little impact).

4.1. *Economic Development Policy in New York State*

- The focus at the state level has been on subsidies and tax breaks for specific firms.
- Nanotechnology initiative.
- Start-up New York.
- Regional competitions.
- The focus on the local level has been on property tax breaks for specific firms, such as Destiny.
  - o The nanotechnology initiative.
  - o The good news is that state subsidies for university expertise in nanotechnology (manipulating matter at the atomic level, as

in semiconductors) appear to have helped to create a thriving and growing nanotechnology sector first in Albany and now throughout upstate. See: https://www.ncbi.nlm.nih.gov/books/NBK158826/.

○ The bad news is that the subsidies have been given to prominent supporters of the governor, and eight people (not including the governor) have been indicted for participating in this "pay to play" scheme. See: https://buffalonews.com/2016/11/22/eight-indictments-handed-statewide-pay-play-scheme/.

- Start-up New York:

○ This program provides tax breaks for firms and their workers if the forms move onto or near a university campus.

○ The first official report indicated that the program created 408 jobs, which is not a resounding success. See: https://cdn.esd.ny.gov/Reports/2015_ESD_Business_Incentives_Report.pdf.

○ Moreover, this jobs count does not net out jobs that would have been created anyway.

- Regional Competitions (which help a region if not the state)

○ Governor Cuomo has devoted billions of dollars to an Upstate Revitalization Initiative, which is a competition for state economic development funds.

○ Central New York won $500 million (over 5 years) in the first round of this competition in 2015. For details of the plan, see: https://www.ny.gov/sites/ny.gov/files/atoms/files/CNYREDC_URI_FinalPlan.pdf.

○ Projects in the plan include:

  ▪ A veteran's center at Syracuse University.
  ▪ A spa and conference center in Aurora.
  ▪ A silicone coating production line in Pulaski.

Lecture 17

Intergovernmental Fiscal Relations

1. U.S. Constitutional Structure

- The federal government and the states have equal standing as constitutional units, with separate rights and responsibilities.
- Counties, townships, cities, villages, school districts, and special districts are creatures of the states.

1.1. *Rough Distribution of Responsibilities*

- The federal government provides national defense, social insurance, and social welfare.
- The states provide higher education, social services, and highways.
- Local governments provide elementary and secondary education, police and fire protection.

1.2. *The Role of Intergovernmental Grants*

- Higher levels of government provide extensive financial assistance to lower levels of government in the form of intergovernmental aid.

497

- The federal government gives grants to states and to local governments.
- State governments give grants to local governments.

1.3. Federal Grants to State and Local Governments

- Federal grants peaked in 1978 at over one-fourth of state and local general revenue.
- Federal grants declined rapidly in the Reagan years, but have usually increased since, mainly due to Medicaid — to almost the 1978 level.
- According to the U.S. Census Bureau, federal grants now provide 22.5% of state and local general revenue (2015), 31.9% of state revenue (2015), and 8.1% of local school revenue (2016).
- See: http://www.census.gov/govs/.

1.4. State Grants to Local Governments

- States provide 31.8% of local general revenue (2015).
- This share rose slowly for a long time but is now falling.
- The state share is higher for elementary and secondary education (47.4% in 2016, down from 48.3% in 2008).
  - This share ranges from 30.2% in South Dakota to 90.2% in Vermont.
  - http://census.gov/content/dam/Census/library/publications/2016/econ/g14-aspef.pdf.

1.5. Mandates and Rules

- Higher levels of government also affect lower levels of government in other ways.
- The federal government can give financial incentives for state or local governments to do certain things (e.g. NCLB).
- The federal government cannot impose requirements on states, however.
- State governments can impose unfunded spending mandates on local governments.

- State governments can alter the assignment of spending responsibilities or taxing rules.
  - For example, some cities must provide ports, airports, hospitals, or higher education.
  - For example, some cities have access to a commuter tax.

2. Principles to Guide the Assignment of Responsibilities

- A famous framework developed by an economist named Richard Musgrave, divides the responsibilities of government into three "branches":
  - Stabilization;
  - Allocation;
  - Distribution.

2.1. *Stabilization*

- Everyone agrees that the main responsibility for stabilization policy (i.e. monetary and fiscal policy) should fall on the federal government.
- Nevertheless, states can alter the impact of economic fluctuations on their citizens through rainy day funds or similar policies.
  - If you want to know more about this, see Professor Yilin Hou's 2013 book: *State Government Budget Stabilization.* https://www.springer.com/us/book/9781461460602.

2.2. *Allocation*

- All levels of government address issues involving the allocation of resources.
- Allocation questions involve both of the types of efficiency discussed in this class:
  - Productive or technical efficiency.
  - Allocative efficiency.

2.2.1. *Productive efficiency, economies of population scale*

- The per-capita cost of a public service may depend on the number of people being served.
  - ○ Economies of population scale, also called publicness, arise when the per-capita cost declines with population.
  - ○ Diseconomies of population scale, also called congestion, arise when the per-capita cost increases with population.
- Defense is a pure public good; there are diseconomies of scale for police.
- Elementary and secondary education has U-shaped cost functions.
  - ○ The estimated minimum-cost size is 3,000 pupils in New York and 58,000 in California (based on my work with Bill Duncombe).
  - ○ This difference reflects different measures of school performance emphasized in each state and perhaps other factors.

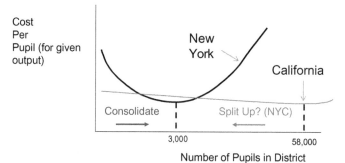

Economics of Pupil Scale in Education

2.2.1.1. Economies of Population Scale in Public Education

- All else equal, the responsibility for a public service should be assigned to the unit of government with the scale closest to the minimum-cost scale.
  - ○ Suburban school districts meet this test.
  - ○ Rural districts are too small, and, on cost grounds, at least, they should consolidate.

○ Urban districts may be too large and, on cost grounds, it may make sense to split them up.

- Different public services have different optimal scales — a reason for layers of government — but evidence is limited!
- Cost considerations may, of course, be offset by other concerns.

2.2.1.2. Economies of Population Scale and Consolidation

- The existence of returns to population scale contribute to a case for consolidation since the cost per person is lower with larger units.
- But be careful. To estimate returns to population scale, one must

  ○ Control for variation in service quality across jurisdictions.
  ○ Control for cost differences across jurisdictions.

- If larger jurisdictions spend less because they provide lower quality services, for example, one cannot conclude that there are economies of population scale.
- Outside of education, few studies have good information on service quality or costs.
- Bill Duncombe and I estimated economies of population scale for fire services in NY State (*Journal Public Economics*, 1993).

  ○ We measured fire services output by the dollar value of losses per fire and the number of fires per dollar of property value.
  ○ We identified several important cost factors, including

    ■ The share of houses built before 1940.
    ■ The poverty rate.
    ■ The share of property classified as commercial and industrial.
    ■ The percentage of apartment buildings more than 2 stories high.

  ○ We found no evidence of economies or diseconomies of population scale; the per capita cost of fire services does not change as population changes.

    ■ These results imply that there would not be any cost savings from the consolidation of fire districts in New York.

2.2.2. *Allocative efficiency*

- Recall the normative argument by Tiebout: A federal system is efficient if there are many local governments and people are able to choose their preferred service-tax package.
- This argument calls for assigning service responsibilities to small local governments, all else equal.

2.2.2.1. Allocative Efficiency — Spillovers

- Spillovers from public services are an *externality*.
  - ○ Example: Benefits from a state highway system to people in surrounding states.
- One way to address spillovers is to assign service responsibility to a level of government high enough to internalize the externality.
  - ○ Example: An air- or water-pollution district that encompasses an entire air- or water-shed.
- Another way to address spillovers is with *intergovernmental grants*.
  - ○ Examples: Federal matching grants for highways, state aid for education.

2.3. *Distribution*

- Most analysts call for the assignment of distribution to higher levels of government:
- Truly equal opportunity requires a higher level of government.
  - ○ E.g., national programs for social insurance or civil rights.
- Redistribution may involve spillovers:
  - ○ People in State A who believe in equality benefit from equality in State B.
- Redistribution at lower levels of government may be undermined by mobility:
  - ○ Wealthy individuals can escape progressive state and local taxes.
  - ○ Needy individuals may move to generous cities or states.
  - ○ Evidence says these effects are small.
- Consolidation also raises complex questions about distribution.

- Rich and poor jurisdictions generally do not consolidate with each other because this type of consolidation raises taxes on the rich partner and lowers taxes on the poor partner.
  - In other words, the rich district votes against consolidation.
- Consolidation also raises issues of political power and control over spending.
  - A poor city might not want to consolidate with rich suburbs despite the above tax changes, because city residents' influence on spending in the city will be diluted.

3. Behavioral Responses to Grants

- Intergovernmental grants are intended to influence the choices made by lower levels of government.
- The impacts of grants on the behavior of recipient governments has been widely studied.
- Policy makers who design grants should know about this research!

3.1. *Lump-Sum Grants as Income*

- In theory: In a median-voter model, $1 of grants is equivalent to an increase in voter income that equals $1 multiplied by median tax-price.

Fisher's Intergovernmental Grant Table.

Conditions on Use	Categorical Grants				General Grants	
Allocation Method	Formula		Project		Formula	
Matching?	Lump-Sum	Lump-Sum	Matching		Lump-Sum	Revenue Sharing (Matching)
Limits?			Closed-Ended	Open-Ended		
	1	2	3	4	5	6

Source: Fisher (2015).

- o $1 of aid only saves the voter its share of a $1 property tax cut, which is the same thing as the voter's tax price.
- o In a town with a shopping center that cuts the tax-share in half, e.g. $1 of aid is only worth $0.50 to voters.
- o This is often called the Bradford/Oates equivalence theorem after their article in the *American Economic Review* in 1971.

- In practice: Grants have consistently been found to have a larger-than-predicted impact on public spending.

  - o This is called *the flypaper effect.*

3.1.1. *The flypaper effect*

- After accounting for the Bradford/Oates theorem, my working paper with Phuong Nguyen-Hoang (another PAIA graduate) (2019a) finds that it would take $12 to $14 of household income to have the same impact on school spending as $1 of appropriately adjusted state aid.
- This result implies that, on average, $1 of state aid will lead to a $0.30 increase in spending on schools and a $0.70 tax cut.
- State officials should not expect $1 of aid to result in $1 more local spending.

  - o A "maintenance of effort" clause can do this for one year, but not after that because the base spending amount is not known.

- Hines and Thaler (*Journal of Economic Perspectives*, 1995) argue that the main cause of the flypaper effect is the behavioral economics concept of *framing,* which has to do with the way a policy is presented to households.

  - o Aid is framed as part of the school budget (where it "sticks").
  - o But income is framed as part of the overall household budget, which is not primarily devoted to school spending or property taxes.

- My working paper with Nguyen-Hoang finds support for this hypothesis.

  - o In New York, the Bradford/Oates correction must include both the standard tax share and the STAR tax share.

○ As discussed in an earlier class, the STAR exemptions in New York, which appear on tax bills, lower voters' tax shares, and must be included in the Bradford/Oates correction.

○ In 2007–2009 the exemptions were supplemented with STAR rebates, which had the same algebraic form, but arrived as a check in the mail.

● We show that because of the difference in the way they are framed, these two tax-price change have different impacts on the perceived value of aid to voters.

○ The STAR exemptions, which are framed as part of the school budget, alter the perceived value of aid to voters in the manner predicted by the Bradford/Oates theorem.

○ The STAR rebates, which are framed as unlabeled household income, have no impact at all on the perceived value of aid to voters.

○ In this case, framing matters.

3.2. *Impact of Grants on Efficiency*

● An issue at the frontier of knowledge is whether grants affect governmental efficiency.

● This issue has two parts:

○ A grant to promote service A (math and English scores) may also boost service B (music education).

○ A grant may lead to bureaucratic waste.

● In our analyses of education finance in several states, Bill Duncombe and I found indirect evidence of both effects.

● So *grants funds are transferred in a leaky bucket!*

3.3. *Categorical vs. General Grants*

● The decision as to which type of grant to use is analogous to that of cash versus food stamps.

● There is no evidence that the flypaper effect (or the efficiency impacts) are different for general and categorical grants, so the standard graph applies.

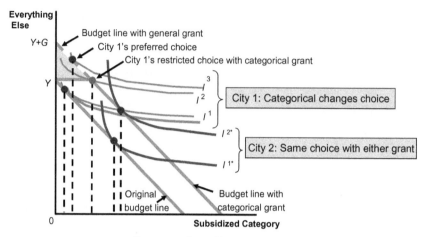

Categorical vs. General Grant.

- Making a grant "categorical" does not alter its impact, unless the size of the grant is large relative to what the recipient would otherwise have spent on the designated category.

3.4. *Matching vs. Lump-Sum Grants*

- In deciding which of these grants to use, the standard figure for income and price subsidies is often used.
- This figure implies that a matching grants has a larger impact on local performance than does a lump-sum grant with the same cost to the granting government.
- This effect reflects the fact that a matching grant, unlike a lump-sum grant, has both an *income effect* and a *price effect*.
- But this theorem ignores (a) the flypaper effect and (b) the impact of grants on efficiency.
- Because their price component lowers a voter's tax share, matching grants also lower voter's incentive to monitor public officials and might lower governmental efficiency.
- The implicit flypaper effect in matching grants and the impact of matching grants on efficiency are not well understood, but they may prove to be important because they lead to the possibility

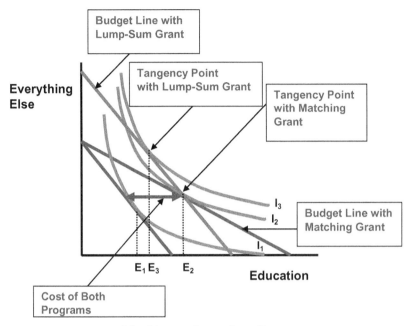

Matching vs. Lump-Sum Grant.

that lump-sum grants might be more stimulative than matching grants, at least under some circumstances.

4. Fiscal Health

- Fiscal health is the extent to which a jurisdiction's ability to provide reasonable services at a reasonable tax rate is constrained by factors outside its control (see Ladd and Yinger, 1991).
  - Fiscal health is relevant for policy.
  - It provides perspective on spending/performance differences.
- It helps in designing aid to local governments, particularly schools.
- The key philosophical issue here is whether a state should accept some responsibility for the fiscal disparities its actions help to create.
- Fiscal health equals the difference between a jurisdiction's expenditure need and its revenue-raising capacity, both based on factors outside the jurisdiction's control.

- A deficit is a poor measure of fiscal health because forecasting methods and assumptions are not outside a jurisdiction's control.
  - ○ A wealthy, low-cost district may still overestimate its revenue at budget time and run up a deficit during the year.
  - ○ A poor, high-cost district may still use very conservative revenue and expenditure projections and thereby have a balanced budget.

4.1. *Expenditure Need*

- Expenditure need depends on expected service quality (constant across jurisdictions), assigned responsibilities, and public service costs.
- In symbols:

$$\text{EN}_j = (\bar{E})(R_j)(C_j)$$

4.2. *Revenue-Raising Capacity*

- RRC = the ability of a jurisdiction to raise revenue based on factors outside its control.
- The Income-Plus-Exporting approach holds tax burden constant across jurisdictions.
  - ○ How much could a jurisdiction raise if it placed the same tax burden on its residents as the average jurisdiction?
- The Representative Tax System approach holds tax rates constant.
  - ○ How much could a jurisdiction raise if it levied the same tax rates as the average jurisdiction?

4.3. *Income-Plus-Exporting Approach*

- Define for jurisdiction j and tax i:
  - ○ b = tax burden
  - ○ Y = income per capita
  - ○ e = taxes raised from nonresidents for every dollar raised from residents = export ratio
  - ○ s = expected revenue share for given tax

- Then with an "overbar" to indicate an average across jurisdictions:

$$\mathrm{RRC}_j = \bar{b}Y_j \left(1 + \sum_i \bar{s}_i e_{ij} \right)$$

4.4. *Representative Tax System Approach*

- Define for jurisdiction j and tax i:
  - t = tax rate
  - B = tax base per capita
- Then

$$\mathrm{RRC}_j = \sum_i \bar{t}_i B_{ij}$$

- In short:
  - States influence fiscal health by setting service responsibilities, access to taxes, and tax rules.
  - Fiscal health is also influenced by a city's economy.
  - Fiscal health varies widely across large cities and across school districts.

$$\mathrm{FH}_j = \mathrm{RRC}_j - \mathrm{EN}_j$$

State Aid to Education

- **Class Outline**
  1. **Education Finance Reform and the Courts**
  2. **Key Questions in Education Finance Reform**
  3. **Types of State Aid Formula**

1. Education Finance Reform and the Courts

- State elected officials make the rules for elementary and secondary education.
- State elected officials also design the education finance system:
  - State aid (about 47% of total in average state in 2016).
  - Property taxes and perhaps other local taxes (about 44% of total).
  - Compensation for homestead exemptions.
- The federal government provides a little funding (about 8%), income tax breaks for property taxes, and some incentives (through NCLB).
- The broad rules are laid out in a state constitution, which has phrases such as "a system of free public schools" or "a sound, basic education."
- State elected officials design a system that meets their objectives, which usually (but not always!) do not involve extensive re-distribution.

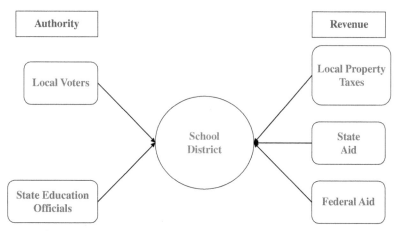

Education Finance in the U.S.

- People in low-performing districts bring suits into the state courts, and the state courts rule on the constitutionality of the system designed by elected officials.
- The voters added strong language to the Florida constitution in 2002.
- "The education of children is a fundamental value of the people of the State of Florida. It is, therefore, a paramount duty of the state to make adequate provision for the education of all children residing within its borders. Adequate provision shall be made by law for a uniform, efficient, safe, secure, and high quality system of free public schools that allows students to obtain a high quality education and for the establishment, maintenance, and operation of institutions of higher learning and other public education programs that the needs of the people may require." Fla. Const. art. IX, § 1(a).
- As a result of the 2002 amendments, Florida's constitution also requires the legislature to make adequate provision for reduced class sizes, and provides that every four-year-old child in the state have access to a "high quality pre-kindergarten learning opportunity." Fla. Const. art. IX, § 1(b).
- Prior to 1998, the constitution simply required the state to make "[a]dequate provision . . . for a uniform system of free public schools."

1.1. *The Role of the Courts*

- 1971: *Serrano* decision by California Supreme Court rejected California's education finance system based on U.S. and California Constitutions.

  ○ It is unfair, the court said, for a child's education to depend on the wealth of his/her school district.

- 1972: *Rodriquez* decision by the U.S. Supreme Court ruled out education claims based on the U.S. Constitution.

Since 1971

- At least 43 state courts have heard challenges to their state's education finance system.
- Twenty more education finance systems have been declared unconstitutional, at least in part, by a state supreme court.
- Court decisions have led to major education finance reforms in many states, including California, Kentucky, New Hampshire, New Jersey, Texas, Vermont.
- Several states have implemented major reforms without a court mandate, including Kansas, Maryland, and Michigan.

The latest decision

- In March 2017, the Kansas Supreme Court ruled that the state's education funding system is "not reasonably calculated to have all Kansas public education students meet or exceed the minimum constitutional standards of adequacy," and required the state to come up with a new funding system by June 30.
- If this deadline is met, the court said that "will mean that the state's education financing system is constitutionally invalid and therefore void" — and the schools will be shut down.
- http://schoolfunding.info/2017/03/kansas-supreme-court-rules-th hat-states-funding-system-does-not-meet-constitutional-adequacy -standards/.
- One careful accounting of all the court cases can be found in the following references:

-   S.P. Corcoran and W. N. Evans, "Equity, Adequacy, and the Evolving State Role in Education Finance," *Handbook of Research in Education Finance and Policy*, 2015.
-   For the latest developments, see: http://schoolfunding.info/.

1.2. *Educational Disparities*

- What the courts are responding to are enormous disparities in both resources and student performance across school districts within a state.
- This disparities arise because districts vary widely in both available resources and educational costs.
- Large cities, which often contain many poor families, have particularly low student performance.

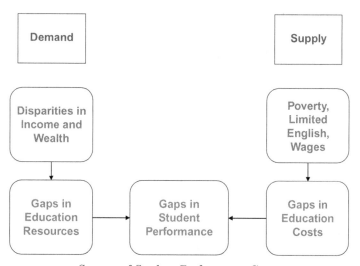

Sources of Student Performance Gaps.

1.3. *Educational Disparities, Example*

- The following 17 cities volunteered to participate in the National Educational Assessment Program (NAEP) tests in 2015.
- Many disadvantaged cities (e.g., Buffalo, Rochester, Syracuse, Milwaukee, Newark) are not included.

NAEP 4th Grade Math, 2015.

| City | Percent Proficient | | |
	City	State	City/State (%)
Albuquerque	28	27	103.7
Atlanta	26	35	74.3
Austin	47	44	106.8
Baltimore	12	40	30.0
Boston	33	54	61.1
Charlotte	51	44	115.9
Chicago	30	37	81.1
Cleveland	13	45	28.9
Dallas	34	44	77.3
Detroit	5	34	14.7
Fresno	14	29	48.3
Houston	36	44	81.8
Los Angeles	22	29	75.9
Miami	41	42	97.6
NYC	26	35	74.3
Philadelphia	15	45	33.3
San Diego	31	29	106.9

Source: www.nationsreportcard.gov.

- The state averages include the cities; if the city is a large share of state population, the score for "rest of state" could be very different from the score for the state as a whole.
  - In the case of NYC, e.g., which has 39.3% of New York State's students, the city proficiency rate is only 63.7% of the rate in the rest of the state.
- Similar disparities exist for 8th grade math and for 4th and 8th grade reading.
- The next two figures describe disparities in New York state.

2. Key Questions in Education Finance Reform

- What is the best way to measure the education provided by a school district?
  - What do we want schools to provide?

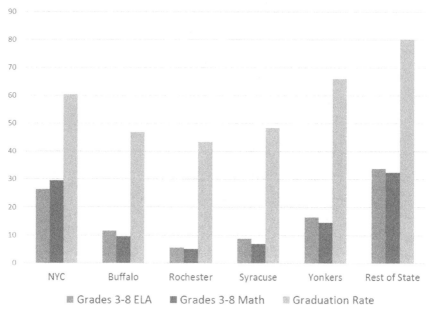

Passing and Graduation Rates in New York, 2013.
Source: New York State Education Department.

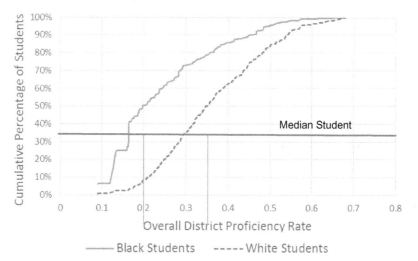

Distribution of Students by Overall District Proficiency Rate, New York State Excluding NYC, 2014.
Source: http://cpr.maxwell.syr.edu/efap/about_efap/ie/April_2015.pdf.

- What is the appropriate equity standard?

  ○ How would we recognize a fair outcome if we saw it?

2.1. *Measuring Education*

- Spending per pupil is a poor measure of education.

  ○ Easy to measure, but hard to interpret.
  ○ Rejected by most courts.
- Spending ignores variation in the cost of education due to:

  ○ Concentrated disadvantage among students.
  ○ The high cost of attracting teachers to some districts.
- Pupil performance, such as test scores and drop-out rates, provides a better measure of education.

  ○ It corresponds with what parents want.
  ○ It is consistent with the trend toward setting higher standards.
  ○ It is consistent with accountability programs (discussed next class).
- An education cost index provides a bridge between performance and spending.

  ○ An equivalent approach is using higher "weights" for disadvantaged students.

2.2. *Educational Adequacy*

- *Adequacy* is the equity standard emphasized in most recent court decisions and by most policy makers:

  ○ Every student should be in a school that delivers an adequate average student performance.
- An adequacy standard does not eliminate all disparities:

  ○ Districts are allowed to provide above-adequate educations if they can.
- Adequacy is achieved by a foundation aid program (discussed below).

2.3. *Other Equity Standards*

- Access Equality:
  - ○ The education provided by a district should depend only on its property tax rate.
  - ○ Refers to fairness for *taxpayers*, not students.
  - ○ Is achieved by power-equalizing aid (discussed below).
  - ○ Was the main issue in *Serrano*.
- Wealth Neutrality:
  - ○ Educational outcomes should not be correlated with school district wealth.
  - ○ Difficult to achieve.
- Equality:
  - ○ All school districts should provide the same level of education.
  - ○ Impossible to achieve, even with state provision, as in Hawaii.

3. Types of State Aid Formula

3.1. *The Foundation Aid Formula*

- Thirty six states use a foundation aid formula, designed to achieve educational adequacy (and several others have foundation-like components). See Verstegen and Knoeppel, *Journal of Education Finance*, Fall 2012.
- The foundation aid formula is:

$$A_j = E^* - t^* V_j$$

where

$A_j =$ aid per pupil to school district j;

$E^* =$ foundation spending per pupil (state-selected; the same in every district);

$t^* =$ minimum required property tax rate (state-selected; the same in every district);

$V_j =$ actual property tax base per pupil in district j.

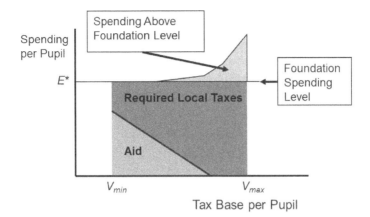

A Basic Foundation Aid Formula.

- A foundation aid formula can easily be adjusted for educational costs (that is, focused on performance):

$$A_j = S^* C_j - t^* V_j$$

where S^* = foundation spending level per pupil in a district with average costs; C_j = educational cost index for district j.
- Pupil weights can also be used; replace number of pupils with number of weighted pupils, with higher rates for pupils from poor families.
- This formula is equivalent to offsetting fiscal disparities across schools.
- A foundation formula must address four issues:
  ○ How much spending is "adequate"?
  ○ Should the foundation level be adjusted for variation in education costs across districts?
  ○ Should a minimum local property tax rate be required?
  ○ How should burden of funding an adequate education be distributed?

3.2. What Spending is Adequate?

3.2.1. Rose decision in Kentucky

- "sufficient oral and written communication skills to enable students to function in a complex and rapidly changing civilization"
- "sufficient understanding of governmental processes to enable the student to understand the issues that affect his or her community, state, and nation"
- "sufficient levels of academic or vocational skills to enable public school students to compete favorably with their counterparts in surrounding states, in academics or in the job market"

3.2.2. CFE decision in NY

- "meaningful high school education, one which prepares them to function productively as civic participants"

3.3. Adjust for Costs?

- Districts with higher costs must spend more to achieve any given performance level.
- So a cost adjustment is needed to combine a *performance* definition of education with an *adequacy* standard.
- According to Verstegen and Knoeppel (*JEF*, 2012), 36 states adjust aid for student poverty and 42 states adjust for English language learners.
  - But no state does a comprehensive, estimated cost adjustment.
  - Full cost adjustment leads to extensive re-distribution, which is politically difficult, and requires statistical procedures.

3.4. Require Minimum Tax Rate?

- To reach foundation spending, E^*, a district must levy at least the selected tax rate, t^*.
- But when a school district receives state aid, it only spends some of the money on education — the rest goes to relief from local taxes.

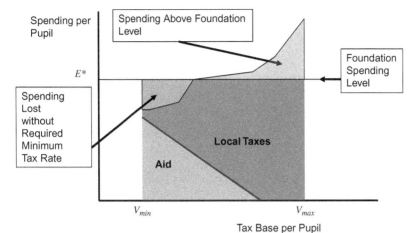

Foundation Aid Without Minimum Tax Rate Requirement.

- Thus, the foundation level of spending will not be achieved unless a minimum rate of t^* is required!
- *Behavioral responses to public policies matter!*
- Note that if the required minimum tax rate is set high enough, the property tax effectively becomes a state tax.
- If this minimum tax is accompanied by a spending limit, then rich districts may contribute more through the minimum tax rate applied to their high tax base than they receive back in the form of the maximum spending they are allowed to impose.
- This type of system was in place in Kansas before the state lost its collective mind over education (and other things).
- This is a kind of *recapture*, that is, a form of redistribution through the property tax system.

3.5. *Power-Equalizing Aid*

- Power-equalizing (or guaranteed tax base, GTB) aid, is the main program in three states and a supplementary program in 10 others.
- The idea behind GTB aid is that a district's spending should depend on tax effort, not tax base:

$$E_j = t_j V^*$$

- The associated aid formula is:

$$A_j = E_j \left(1 - \frac{V_j}{V^*} \right)$$

- GTB is matching aid; the state share of spending decreases with V_j.
- If $V^* <$ maximum V_j, then matching rates are negative in rich districts.

  o This is another form of *recapture*.
  o Vermont is an example.

- Raising V^* raises the cost of GTB aid.

  o To offset this effect, set matching rates at a fraction of the value in the above formula.
  o That is, flatten the line in the following picture.

- GTB aid can be adjusted for costs (but rarely is):

$$A_j = E_j \left(\frac{S^* C_j}{S^* \bar{C}} - \frac{V_j}{V^*} \right) = E_j \left(C_j - \frac{V_j}{V^*} \right)$$

- Using GTB as a supplement to foundation aid is misguided:

  o Foundation aid already requires poor districts to set tax rates above their desired level.
  o Adding GTB aid is unlikely to induce any further tax rate increases.

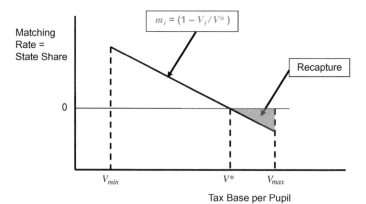

Power-Equalizing Aid.

3.5.1. *Comparing foundation and GTB aid*

- GTB aid is often thought to be more equalizing than foundation aid.
- In fact, however, price elasticities are small, so the response to GTB aid is small, even for poor districts.
- So:
  - Foundation aid is much more equalizing at the bottom of the property value distribution (and is the only way to ensure adequacy).
  - GTB aid is more equalizing at the top of the property value distribution — at least if it includes recapture.

3.5.2. *Options for spreading the burden*

- Local property taxes in districts that receive aid.
  - In a foundation formula, the higher the required t^*, the greater the local contribution.
  - Without a required t^*, many districts will use increase aid for tax relief.

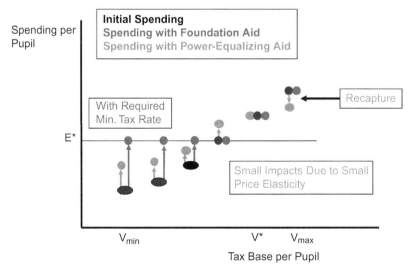

Comparing Foundation and GTB Aid.

- Broad-based state taxes, such as the income tax.
  - The higher E^* and the lower t^*, the greater the state contribution.
- Contributions by low-need school districts.
  - Financial burden: recapture.
  - Non-financial burden: prohibit or limit supplementation of foundation spending.

3.5.3. *The frontier*

- There is some evidence that state aid lowers school district efficiency.
  - Some aid goes to educational activities not valued by the state.
  - Aid leads to less monitoring by voters and hence more wasteful spending.
- Thus, to some degree, aid to school districts is transferred with a leaky bucket.
  - The frontier issue is how to minimize these leaks.

3.5.4. *The Latest from New York*

- After the CFE decision, which applied only to NYC, New York passed a major reform of education aid in 2007 to be phased in for the entire state.
  - The new foundation formula had major improvements to cost adjustments.
  - Which were offset to some degree by changes in the expected local contribution.
- When the recession hit, the phase-in stopped and "gap elimination adjustment" (= GEA = aid cuts) arrived.
  - GEA was finally eliminated in 2016, but aid remains below the 2007 target.
  - See my testimony to Governor Cuomo's New NY Education Reform Commission at: http://cpr.maxwell.syr.edu/efap/about_efap/ie/Nov13.pdf (December 2013 "It's Elementary"

column) or my 2016 testimony at: http://faculty.maxwell.syr.
edu/jyinger/Videos/index.html (October 2016 "It's Elementary
column).

- According to the New York State Association of School Business
  Officials, it will take $4.2 billion more state aid (on top of the
  2017–2018 budget) to reach the aid amounts promised in the fully
  phased in foundation aid formula of 2007. The 2018–2019 budget
  increases foundation aid by $618 million, leaving a gap of almost
  $3.6 billion.
- See: http://www.nysasbo.org and https://stateaid.nysed.gov/.
- New York is also slowly watering down its foundation aid program
  by transforming some of it into categorical grants, called set-asides,
  that must be spent to support "community schools." These set-
  asides now add up to about $200 million.

Education Accountability

- **Class Outline**
  1. **State Aid Reform and Accountability**
  2. **State Aid Reform and School Choice**
  3. **State Aid Reform and Capital Spending**

1. State Aid Reform and Accountability

- Policy makers must decide whether reforms in an education aid formula should be linked to an accountability program.
- All states already have some type of accountability program.

  o And a majority of states have a program that imposes some type of financial rewards and punishments.

1.1. *The Courts and Accountability*

- The courts did not link accountability to state aid reform until recently.
- In 1989, the Kentucky Supreme Court's Rose decision threw out the state's system of school governance and brought new visibility to accountability programs.
- Moreover, the recent state aid reforms in Kentucky, Michigan, and Texas have all been accompanied by accountability programs that include district-level rewards and sanctions.

1.2. *The Role of Accountability*

- State officials are reluctant to give more money to schools without assurances that the money will be well spent.
- Some scholars, including Bill Duncombe and me, have found that increases in state aid may lower school district efficiency.
- In this context, efficiency measures a school district's success in translating inputs into student performance (as specified in the accountability system), after accounting for factors outside the district's control, such as concentrated poverty among its students.

1.3. *Does Money Matter?*

- Some scholars, especially Eric Hanushek, have argued that aid increases are unlikely to boost student performance at all.
- Extensive evidence rejects this position:

  - Lafortune, Rothstein, and Schanzenbach (*NBER Working Paper*, 2016) find that "In the long run, over comparable time frames, states that send additional money to their lowest-income school districts see more academic improvement in those districts than states that don't."
  - Jackson, Johnson, and Persico (*Quarterly Journal of Economics*, 2016), found that "for poor children, a 10% increase in per-pupil spending each year of elementary and secondary school was associated with wages that were nearly 10% higher, a drop in the incidence of adult poverty and roughly six additional months of schooling."
  - Quotes from: http://www.nytimes.com/2016/12/12/nyregion/ it-turns-out-spending-more-probably-does-improve-education. html?_r=0.

- So the question is: How can a state maximize the impact of aid increases on student performance?

  - Give aid to the districts that really need it (based on high costs or low revenue-raising capacity).

○ Provide data, identify good programs, run experiments to help districts figure out best practices for their circumstances.
○ Hold districts accountable if they fail to improve despite adequate funding and good program information.

1.4. *Accountable for What?*

• An accountability program should hold schools responsible for things they control.
• Student performance depends not only on a district's efficiency but also on its wage environment and disadvantages of its students.
• It makes no sense to punish a district because it is located in a high-wage environment or has a high concentration of disadvantaged students.

○ But that is what is done by any program that bases rewards and sanctions on student performance alone.
○ Many state programs and the original federal No Child Left Behind Act (NCLB) fall into this category.

• Some states were trying to build accountability systems that focused on a district's role by comparing its performance to others with the same wealth and student poverty.

○ This experimentation was cut off by NCLB.

• The original NCLB let states set the standards but then imposed severe sanctions if they are not met.

○ This led many states to lower their standards.

• NCLB required all states to have 100% passing rates on state tests by 2014.

○ This totally unreasonable standard (and other aspects of NCLB) led many states to ask for waivers of NCLB requirements — and replacement with state-determined requirements.
○ By 2015, 42 states plus D.C. had been granted waivers.

• NCLB was replaced with the Every Student Succeeds Act (ESSA) at the end of 2015.

- o ESSA places the 100% passing rate in its title, but removes it from its requirements.
- o In effect, ESSA gives a waiver to every state to set up its own accountability system.

- Some people claim that using test score *gains* not levels solves these problems by adjusting for a district's starting point. This is not true.
- *First,* test score gains have a random element, reflecting differences in ability across cohorts.

  - o In small schools a few high (or low) ability students have a large impact on scores.
  - o Small schools dominate the good and bad categories in states that use test score gains.

- *Second,* school districts facing relatively high costs also must pay more to achieve any given test score gain.
- *Third,* using test score gains is unfair to districts that did a good job in the past.

1.5.   Hold Teachers Accountable?

- The latest effort is to *hold teachers accountable* using estimates of a teacher's average contribution to test-score gains of his/her students.

  - o Many scholars think this is a promising approach for identifying the worst teachers.

- However, test score gains for an individual teacher are difficult to estimate because one must control for student traits in his/her classroom, such as the share of students in poverty.
- The latest evidence indicates that basing teacher rewards on test-score gains will not boost student achievement: https://www.rand.org/pubs/research_reports/RR2242.html.
- NCLB required states to do this; ESSA removed this requirement.

1.6. *Hold Students Accountable?*

- Finally, some states hold students accountable by turning their tests into "high stakes" tests.

  - Some states will not let a student graduate unless he or she passes certain tests.
  - Other states give different diplomas to students who pass all the tests than to those who do not.

- The impacts of this approach on student achievement and graduation are also not known.
- And I find it ironic (and unfair!) that a state would punish a student because the state failed to help him or her pass state tests.

1.7. *Hold States Accountable?*

- An alternative approach is to shift the focus of accountability programs to states.
- If a school is not performing, the state should provide the needed resources and expertise.

  - The education finance system should be fair.
  - The state should have a research and analysis department to determine what programs work under various circumstances.

- If a school district has sufficient funding and does not implement the appropriate programs in a responsible way, then its teachers and administrators should be held accountable.

2. State Aid Reform and School Choice

- Expanded school choice is linked to education finance reform in some states, and is likely to become an emphasis of federal policy.
- School choice plans allow parents to send their children to public schools outside their attendance zone or even outside their district.
- Charter schools, public schools subject to fewer restrictions than existing public schools, now exist in most states.

- Vouchers are payments, usually to parents in low-performing schools, that can be used to send children to other public or even to private schools.
- These plans provide new choices for parents.
- In theory, this choice might lead to innovation and increased effort in the competition to attract students.
- New schools might come up with innovative methods that improve student performance and that regular public schools (or teacher unions) have been unwilling to try.
- Existing schools might improve their practices (or copy successful alternative schools) in order to retain their students.
- But enhanced choice does not guarantee improvements in school performance because school choice plans face several major limits:

  o They are subject to capacity restrictions — and all schools can give preference to students in their attendance zone.
  o Politics usually prevents them from working across district lines, except on a small scale.
  o Low-income families may not be able to afford the transportation costs to send their children to the best schools.
  o New choice schools may shut down, causing disruption in the education of the children who attend them.

2.1. *Charter Schools*

- Some school districts have dozens of charter schools, others have none.
- Some states allow out-of-district students to attend charter schools, which are concentrated in big cities.
- Charter schools are difficult to evaluate because they are so heterogeneous.

  o One can find examples of terrific charter schools and of terrible ones — and of ones that fail.

- A recent report found that 17% of charter schools boosted student test scores year after year (http://credo.stanford.edu/research-reports.html).

- Most charter schools lead to lower scores and do not improve over time.
- It seems unlikely that successful charter schools can be replicated on a large scale.
- Some evidence indicates that certain comprehensive charter schools, such as the 183 KIPP (Knowledge Is Power Program) charter schools, boost scores in poor cities. See: http://www. mathematica-mpr.com/newsroom/releases/2013/KIPP_2_13.asp.
- Charter schools in suburbs do not seem to make much difference. http://www.nytimes.com/2015/11/22/ upshot/a-suburban -urban-divide-in-charter-school-success-rates.html?_r=0.
- There is also some evidence that charter schools lead to more separation of students by race and income. See Bifulco and Ladd (*JPAM*, 2007).
- The best evidence (e.g. on KIPP) comes from comparing the winners with the losers of a lottery to get into an over-subscribed charter school.
- This lottery is a type of random assignment, so this approach gives a precise answer for the difference in performance between lottery winners and losers.
- But the answer may depend on what options are available for losers and whether the charter school induces changes in nearby public schools.

  ○ If public schools respond to the competition by improving, the study will understate the impact of charter schools.
  ○ If performance in public schools declines because many of the most motivated students have left, the study will overstate the impact of charter schools.

- Moreover, this evidence does not reveal either whether charter schools in general boost performance or whether placing more students in charter school would improve test scores:

  ○ Lottery-based studies only look at the impacts on students whose parents support their entrance into a charter school — not the impacts on any type of student.

○ Lottery-based studies cannot examine the impacts of charter schools that are not over-subscribed (and are therefore probably relatively low in quality).

○ Lottery-based studies cannot determine what would happen in the teacher labor market if the number of charter schools increased.

2.2. *School Vouchers*

- The constitutionality of vouchers, even if parents decide to use them for parochial schools, was upheld by the U.S. Supreme Court in 2002.

- The Florida accountability system gave vouchers to children in failing schools, but this provision was thrown out by the Florida courts.

- Recent random assignments studies in Indiana, Louisiana, and Ohio find that voucher recipients have lower performance than other students, especially in math. See: https://www.nytimes.com/2017/02/23/upshot/dismal-results-from-vouchers-surprise-researchers-as-devos-era-begins.html?rref=collection%2Fsectioncollection%2Fupshot.

- Even if one could design a voucher program that boosted student performance, a large-scale version still might not boost the performance of students in poor, urban school districts.

- Higher performance might indicate that voucher recipients are taken from the high-poverty environment of a public school to the low-poverty environment of a private school. This cannot be done on a large scale (without eliminating poverty!).

- Children in the Cleveland program primarily go to Catholic schools because subsidies to these schools from the Catholic Church keep tuition low enough that the voucher can cover it. Subsidies of this type would not be available in a large voucher program.

3. State Aid Reform and Capital Spending

- Most of the education finance court cases have focused on the equity of operating spending in the state, not of capital spending.

- Exceptions include the cases in New Jersey, Texas, and Arizona.
- The CFE case resulted in almost $10 billion in new capital spending in New York City.
- It seems odd to eliminate inequities in operating spending but to allow them in capital spending; after all, both types of spending are crucial for providing education.
- But capital spending is difficult to study and its link to student performance has not been established.
- Capital spending is lumpy, for example, so there is no link to performance in annual data.
- Moreover, state formulas for building and operating aid tend to be different from one another.
  - Building aid, unlike operating aid, often takes the form of a matching grant.
  - Building aid, unlike operating aid, is usually linked to projects.
  - Eleven states do not give any building aid.
  - Building aid does not have a strong equalizing tradition.
- The punchline is that building aid is obviously important.
- But scholars need to know a lot more before they can give meaningful advice on the subject.
- One key issue is whether matching grants can boost capital spending.
  - As discussed in an earlier class, a paper in the *National Tax Journal* by Wang, Duncombe and Yinger provides some evidence.
- The price elasticity in response to the matching rate in NY's building aid is −0.42 for most districts.
- But this elasticity drops to approximately zero (−0.023) for high-need urban districts; because their other needs are so great, they do not spend more on infrastructure even with a very strong price incentive.
- Extensive lump-sum aid or full state funding may be needed to ensure adequate school infrastructure in these districts.

References

Angrist, Joshua D., Susan M. Dynarski, Thomas J. Kane, Parag A. Pathak, and Christopher R. Walters. 2012. Who benefits from KIPP? *Journal of Policy Analysis and Management*, **31**(4): 837–860.

Bajari, Patrick and Matthew E. Kahn. 2005. Estimation housing demand with an application to explaining racial segregation in cities, *American Statistical Association, Journal of Business and Economic Statistics*, **23**(1): 1569–1591.

Bania, Neil and Joe A. Stone. 2008. Ranking state fiscal structures using theory and evidence, *Journal of Policy Analysis and Management*, **27**(4): 751–770.

Bayer, Patrick, Fernando Ferreira, and Robert McMillan. 2007. A unified framework for measuring preferences for schools and neighborhoods, *Journal of Political Economy*, **115**(4): 588–638.

Bergstrom, Theodore C. and Robert P. Goodman. 1973. Private demands for public goods, *The American Economic Review*, **63**(3): 280–296.

Besley, Timothy and Harvey S. Rosen. 1999. Sales taxes and prices: An empirical analysis, *National Tax Journal*, **52**(2): 157–178.

Bifulco, Robert and Helen F. Ladd. 2007. School choice, racial segregation, and test-score gaps: Evidence from North Carolina's charter school program, *Journal of Policy Analysis and Management*, **26**(1): 31–56.

Black, Sandra E. 1999. Do better schools matter? Parental valuation of elementary education, *The Quarterly Journal of Economics*, **114**(2): 577–599.

Bogin, Alexander Nicholas. 2012. Three Essays on the Property Value Impact of Neighborhood Disamenities, Ph.D. Dissertation, Syracuse University.

Bogin, Alexander Nicholas and Phuong Nguyen-Hoang. 2014. Property left behind: An unintended consequence of a no child left behind "failing" school designation, *Journal of Regional Science*, **54**(5): 788–805.

Boozer, Michael and Cecilia Rouse. 2001. Intraschool variation in class size: Patterns and implications, *Journal of Urban Economics*, **50**(1): 163–189.

Bradford, David F. and Wallace E. Oates. 1971. The analysis of revenue sharing in a new approach to collective fiscal decisions, *The Quarterly Journal of Economics*, **85**(3) (August): 416–439.

Bradford, David F., R. A. Malt, and Wallace E. Oates. 1969. The rising cost of local public services: Some evidence and reflections, *National Tax Journal*, **22**(2): 185–202.

Carroll, Robert J. and John Yinger. 1994. Is the property tax a benefit tax? The case of rental housing, *National Tax Journal*, **47**(2): 295–316.

Chay, Kenneth Y. and Michael Greenstone. Does air quality matter? Evidence from the Housing Market, *Journal of Political Economy*, **113**(2): 376–424.

Chetty, Raj, Adam Looney, and Kory Kroft. 2009. Salience and taxation: Theory and evidence, *American Economic Review*, **99**(4): 1145–1177.

Chingos, Matthew M. 2013. Class size and student outcomes: Research and policy implications, *Journal of Policy Analysis and Management*, **32**(2): 411–438.

Clapp, John M., Anupam Nanda, and Stephen L. Ross. 2008. Which school attributes matter? The influence of school district performance and demographic composition on property values, *Journal of Urban Economics*, **63**(2): 451–466.

Dee, Thomas S. 2004. Teachers, race, and student achievement in a randomized experiment, *The Review of Economics and Statistics*, **86**(1): 195–210.

Downes, Thomas and David Figlio. 2015. Tax and expenditure limits, school finance, and school quality, In Helen F. Ladd and Margaret E. Goertz (eds.), *Handbook of Research in Education Finance and Policy*, 2nd Edition (New York: Routledge), pp. 392–407.

Downes, Thomas A. and Thomas F. Pogue. 1994. Adjusting school aid formulas for the higher cost of educating disadvantaged students, *National Tax Journal*, **47**(1): 89–110.

Duncombe, William D. and John Yinger. 1993. An analysis of returns to scale in public production, with an application to fire protection, *Journal of Public Economics*, **52**(1): 49–72.

Duncombe, William D. and John Yinger. 1998. School finance reform: Aid formulas and equity objectives, *National Tax Journal*, **5**(2): 239–262.

Duncombe, William D. and John Yinger. 2005. How much more does a disadvantaged student cost? *Economics of Education Review*, **24**(5): 513–532.

Duncombe, William D. and John Yinger. 2011. Are education cost functions ready for prime time? An examination of their validity and reliability, *Peabody Journal of Education: Issues of Leadership, Policy and Organizations*, **86**(1): 28–57.

Duncombe, William D. and John Yinger. 2011. Making do: State constraints and local responses in California's education finance system, *International Tax and Public Finance*, **18**(3): 337–368.

Duncombe, William D., John Yinger, and Pengju Zhang. 2016. How does school district consolidation affect property values: A case study of New York, *Public Finance Review*, **44**(1): 52–79.

Eom, Tae Ho. 2008. A comprehensive model of determinants of property tax assessment quality: Evidence in New York State, *Public Budgeting and Finance*, **28**(1): 58–81.

Eom, Tae Ho, William Duncombe, Phuong Nguyen-Hoang, and John Yinger. 2014. The unintended consequences of property tax relief: New York's STAR program, *Education Finance and Policy*, **9**(4): 446–480.

Epple, Dennis, Michael Peress, and Holger Sieg. 2010. Identification and semi-parametric estimation of equilibrium models of local jurisdictions, *American Economic Journal: Microeconomics*, **2**(4): 195–220.

Epple, Dennis, Thomas Romer, and Holger Sieg. 2001. Interjurisdictional sorting and majority rule: An empirical analysis, *Econometrica*, **69**(6): 1437–1465.

Feldstein, Martin S. 1975. Neutrality and local choice in public education, *American Economic Review*, **65**(1): 75–89.

Figlio, David N. and Maurice E. Lucas. 2004. "What's in a grade? School report cards and the housing market, *American Economic Review*, **94**(3): 591–604.

Fisher, R. (2015). *State and Local Public Finance*, 4th Edition, Routledge.

Goldstein G. S. and Mark V. Pauly. 1981. Tiebout bias on the demand for local public goods, *Journal of Public Economics*, **16**(2): 131–143.

Golebiewski, Julie Anna. 2011. An overview of the literature measuring education cost differentials, *Peabody Journal of Education: Issues of Leadership, Policy, and Organizations*, **86**(1): 84–112.

Gravelle, Jane G. and Jennifer Gravelle. 2007. How federal policymakers account for the concerns of state and local governments in the formulation of federal tax policy, *National Tax Journal*, **60**(3): 631–648.

Gronberg, Timothy J., Dennis W. Jansen, and Lori L. Taylor. 2011. The adequacy of educational cost functions: Lessons from Texas, *Peabody Journal of Education: Issues of Leadership, Policy, and Organizations*, **86**(1): 3–27.

Hanson, Andrew. 2009. Local employment, poverty, and property value effects of geographically-targeted tax incentives: An instrumental variables approach, *Regional Science and Urban Economics*, **39**(6): 721–731.

Hanushek, Eric A. 1979. Conceptual and empirical issues in the estimation of educational production functions, *The Journal of Human Resources*, **14**(3): 351–388.

Hanushek, Eric A. 1986. The economics of schooling: Production and efficiency in public schools, *Journal of Economic Literature*, **49**(3): 1141–1177.

Hanushek, Eric A. (Robert Costrell, Eric A. Hanushek, Susanna Loeb). 2008. What do cost functions tell us about the cost of an adequate education? *Peabody Journal of Education*, **83**(2): 198–223.

Haughwout, Andrew F., Robert P. Inman, Steven Craig, and Thomas Luce. 2004. Local revenue hills: Evidence from four U.S. cities, *The Review of Economics and Statistics*, **86**(2): 570–585.

Hawkins, Richard R. 2002. Popular substitution effects: Excess burden estimates for general sales taxes, *National Tax Journal*, **55**(4): 755–770.

Heckman, James J., Rosa L. Matzkin, and Lars Nesheim. 2010. Nonparametric identification and estimation of nonadditive Hedonic models, *Econometrica*, **78**(5): 1569–1591.

Hines, Jr., James R. and Richard H. Thaler. 1995. The Flypaper effect, *Journal of Economic Perspectives*, **9**(4): 217–226.

Hu, Yue and John Yinger. 2008. The impact of school district consolidation on housing prices, *National Tax Journal*, **61**(4): 609–633.

Imazeki, Jennifer and Andrew Reschovsky. 2004. Is no child left behind an un (or under) funded federal mandate? Evidence from Texas, *The National Tax Journal*, **57**(3): 571–588.

Imazeki, Jennifer. 2008. Assessing the costs of adequacy in California public schools: A cost function approach, *Education Finance and Policy*, **3**: 90–108.

Jackson, C. Kirabo, Rucker C. Johnson, and Claudia Persico. 2016. The effects of school spending on educational and economic outcomes: Evidence from school finance reforms, *The Quarterly Journal of Economics*, **131**(1): 157–218.

Kane, Thomas, J., Stephanie K. Riegg, and Douglas O. Staiger. 2006. School quality, neighborhoods, and housing prices, *American Law and Economic Review*, **8**(2): 183–212.

Kang Hoon, Sung, Laura Reese, and Mark Skidmore. 2016. Do industrial tax abatements spur property value growth? *Journal of Policy Analysis and Management*, **35**(2): 388–414.

Kioko, Sharon N. 2011. Structure of state-level tax and expenditure limits, *Public Budgeting & Finance*, **31**(2): 43–78.

Krueger, Alan B. 1999. Experimental estimates of education production functions, *The Quarterly Journal of Economics*, **114**(2): 497–532.

Krueger, Alan B. and Diane M. Whitmore. 2001. The effect of attending a small class in the early grades on college-test taking and middle school test results: Evidence from Project Star, *The Economic Journal*, **111**(468): 1–28.

Ladd, Helen F. and John Yinger. 1991. *America's Ailing Cities: Fiscal Health and the Design of Urban Policy*, Updated Edition. Johns Hopkins University Press. (Reviewed in the *Journal of Economic Literature*, December 1990, pp. 1745–1747.)

Lafortune, Julien, Jesse Rothstein, and Diane Whitmore Schanzenbach. 2016. School finance reform and the distribution of student achievement, National Bureau of Economic Research, Working Paper 22011. http://www.nber.org/papers/w22011.

Lukemeyer, A., William D. Duncombe, and John Yinger. 2008. Dollars without sense: The mismatch between the no child left behind act accountability system and Title I funding, In R. D. Kahlenberg (ed.), *Improving on No Child Left Behind: Getting Education Reform Back on Track* (The Century Foundation), pp. 19–102.

McGuire, Therese J., Leslie E. Papke, and Andrew Reschovsky. 2015. Local funding of schools: The property tax and its alternatives, In Helen F. Ladd and Margaret E. Goertz (eds.), *Handbook of Research in Education Finance and Policy*. 2nd Edition (New York: Routledge), pp. 376–391.

Moretti, Enrico. 2010. Local multipliers, *American Economic Review*, **100**(2): 373–377.

Nguyen-Hoang, Phuong and John Yinger. 2011. The capitalization of school quality into house values: A review, *Journal of Housing Economics*, **20**(1): 30–48.

Nguyen-Hoang, Phuong and John Yinger. 2014. Education finance reform, local behavior, and student performance in Massachusetts, *Journal of Education Finance*, **39**(4): 297–322.

Nguyen-Hoang, Phuong and John Yinger. 2018a. The Flypaper effect: Methods, magnitudes, and mechanisms, Working Paper, Syracuse University, July.

Nguyen-Hoang, Phuong and John Yinger. 2018b. How salience and framing alter the behavioral impacts of property tax relief, Working Paper, Syracuse University, May.

Poterba, James M. 1996. Retail price reactions to changes in state and local sales taxes, *National Tax Journal*, **49**(2): 165–176.

Rork, Jonathan C. 2003. Coveting thy neighbors' taxation, *National Tax Journal*, **56**(4): 775–787.

Rosen, Sherwin 1974. Hedonic prices and implicit markets: Product differentiation in pure competition, *The Journal of Political Economy*, **82**(1): 34–55.

Rosenthal, Stuart S. and William C. Strange. 2003. Geography, industrial organization, and agglomeration, *The Review of Economics and Statistics*, **85**(2): 377–393.

Sexton, Terri A., Steven M. Sheffrin, and Arthur O'Sullivan, 1999. Proposition 13: Unintended effects and feasible reforms, *National Tax Journal*, **52**(1): 99–112.

Sheppard, Stephen. 1999. Hedonic analysis of housing markets, in P. Cheshire, and E.S. Mills, (eds.). *Handbook of Regional and Urban Economics* (Amsterdam: North-Holland), pp. 1595–1635.

Sjoquist, David L. and Mary Beth Walker. 1999. Economies of scale in property tax assessment, *National Tax Journal*, **52**(2): 207–220.

Srithongrung, Arwiphawee and Kenneth A. Kriz. 2014. The impact of subnational fiscal policies on economic growth: A dynamic analysis approach, *Journal of Policy Analysis and Management*, **33**(4): 912–928.

Stiefel, Leanna, Amy Ellen Schwartz and Ingrid Ellen. 2007. Disentangling the racial test score gap? Probing the evidence in a large urban school district, *Journal of Policy Analysis and Management*, **26**(1): 7–30.

Tiebout, Charles M. 1956. A pure theory of local expenditures, *The Journal of Political Economy*, **64**(5): 416–424.

Tosun, Mehmet and Mark Skidmore. 2004. Interstate competition and state lottery revenues, *National Tax Journal*, **57**(2): 163–178.

Verstegen, Deborah A. and Robert C. Knoeppel. 2012. From statehouse to schoolhouse: Education finance apportionment systems in the United States, *Journal of Education Finance*, **38**(2): 145–166.

Wang, Wen, William D. Duncombe, and John Yinger. 2011. School district responses to matching aid programs for capital facilities: A case study of New York's building aid program, *National Tax Journal*, **64**(3): 759–794. [Winner of the 2011 Richard Musgrave Prize for the most outstanding article published in the *NTJ*.]

Wassmer, Robert W. and John E. Anderson. 2001. Bidding for business: New evidence on the effect of locally offered economic development incentives in a metropolitan area, *Economic Development Quarterly*, **15**(2): 132–148.

Wilson, John D. 1999. Theories of tax competition, *National Tax Journal*, **52**(2): 269–304.

Wong, Wai-Ho Wilson 1998. Taxes and state and local economics development: The homestead tax option in New York, Dissertation, Syracuse University, Doctor of Philosophy (PhD), Public Administration.

Yinger, John. 2015a. Hedonic equilibria in housing markets: The case of one-to-one matching, *Journal of Housing Economics*, **29**: 1–11.

Yinger, John. 2015b. Hedonic markets and sorting equilibria: Bid-function envelopes for public services and neighborhood amenities, *Journal of Urban Economics*, **86**: 9–25.

Yinger, John. 2018. Bidding and sorting, Chapter 13 in John Yinger (ed.), *Housing and Commuting: The Theory of Urban Residential Structure* (Singapore: World Scientific Publishing Co. Pte. Ltd.), pp. 361–384.

Yinger, John and Phuong Nguyen-Hoang. 2016. Hedonic vices: Fixing inferences about willingness to pay in recent house-value studies, *Journal of Benefit-Cost Analysis*, **7**(2): 248–291.

Yinger, John, Howard S. Bloom, Axel Borsch-Supan, and Helen F. Ladd. 1988. *Property Taxes and House Values: The Theory and Estimation of Intrajurisdictional Property Tax Capitalization* (Boston: Academic Press).

Yinger, J. (2020). *Poverty and Proficiency: The Costs of and Demand for Local Public Education. A Textbook in Education Finance*, World Scientific Publishing Company.

Young, Douglas J. and Agnieszka Bielinska–Kwapisz. 2002. Alcohol taxes and beverage prices, *National Tax Journal*, **55**(1): 57–73.

Zhang, Pengju. 2018. The unintended impact of tax and expenditure limitations on the use of special districts: The politics of circumvention, *Economics of Governance*, **19**(1): 21–50.

Index

CPSIA information can be obtained
at www.ICGtesting.com
Printed in the USA
BVHW040453060220
571586BV00005B/15